# Darkling Plain

## other works by AIDAN HIGGINS

*Langrishe, Go Down*

*Images of Africa*

*Balcony of Europe*

*Scenes from a Receding Past*

*Asylum & Other Stories*

*Bornholm Night-Ferry*

*Helsingør Station & Other Departures*

*Ronda Gorge & Other Precipices*

*Lions of the Grunewald*

*Flotsam & Jetsam*

*As I was Riding Down Duval Boulevard with Pete La Salle*

*A Bestiary*

*Windy Arbours*

## about AIDAN HIGGINS

*Aidan Higgins: The Fragility of Form*

# Darkling Plain
## (texts for the air)

# AIDAN HIGGINS

edited and with an introduction by
DANIEL JERNIGAN

DALKEY ARCHIVE PRESS
CHAMPAIGN / LONDON

Library of Congress Cataloging-in-Publication Data

Higgins, Aidan, 1927-
Darkling plain : texts for the air / Aidan Higgins ; edited and with an introduction by
Daniel Jernigan. -- 1st ed.
p. cm.
ISBN 978-1-56478-537-4 (pbk. : alk. paper)
1. Radio plays, English. 2. English drama--20th century. I. Jernigan, Daniel. II. Title.
PR6058.I34D37 2010
822'.914--dc22
2009036220

Partially funded by the University of Illinois at Urbana-Champaign
and by a grant from the Illinois Arts Council, a state agency

www.dalkeyarchive.com

Cover: design and composition by Danielle Dutton, illustration by Nicholas Motte
Printed on permanent/durable acid-free paper
and bound in the United States of America

*For Zinnia, as always*

*A recapitulative rearrangement of exhumed material once frog-marched into line, since dispersed, pulped, gone out of print or consigned to the warehouse of remaindered stock, tidily arranged in alphabetical order on musty shelves and largely forgotten; gone to the dead stock of the book-morgue.*

—A.H.

*I speak about myself in diverse ways:
that is because I look at myself in diverse ways.*

—The *Essays* of Michel de Montaigne,
translated and edited by M. A. Screech

*The bars are closed, the hotel is empty, the nymphs have departed.*

—Cyril Connolly, *The Rock Pool*

*Time . . . attenuates memories.*

—Jorge Luis Borges, "The Zahir"

# CONTENTS

*Fabrication or truth? It little matters.*
*Authenticity is all that need concern us.*

# Editor's Introduction

Aidan Higgins's literary reputation has been largely founded on his fiction and travel narratives. Less well known is that beginning with *Assassinations: 4. Franz Ferdinand* (re-titled *Assassin* for this collection) in 1973, Higgins wrote ten radio plays for the BBC and RTÉ. The ten plays in this volume contain what Higgins himself has referred to as his last "unpublished work," making this collection both an invaluable resource for academics and an opportunity for his fans to read material that has not been widely available until now.

Fans of Aidan Higgins will find plenty to admire in this collection, as much for what is familiar—most notably, "Clouding Over," a thoroughly distinct early treatment of the material which eventually made up *Langrishe, Go Down*—as for what is unique to the radio plays (i.e., the intertextual experimentation of *Assassin*, *Uncontrollable Laughter* and *Discords of Good Humour*). Readers familiar with *Balcony of Europe* will also recognize something familiar in *Winter is Coming* (1983), which, like the novel *Balcony of Europe* before it, is set in Andalucía; while covering different narrative ground, it also includes characters and locations from the novel (including the Plaza Balcón de Europa—the very bar which is the namesake of the novel). And while *Winter is Coming* doesn't exactly rehash material found in the novel, it is a reasonable assumption given Higgins's tendency to "recycle" his material that the text might very well have been excised from an early draft of *Balcony*, especially since we know that "The original manuscript was over a thousand pages later reduced to 463" (Donnelly, 91). As we prepared *Winter is Coming* for publication, however, Higgins was vague about this possibility.

As for what else is familiar, it is also notable that the material for many of these plays—even when originally written for radio—eventually found its way into Higgins's larger works (*The Tomb of Dreams* was rewritten as Part IV of *Dog Days* (1998), *Texts for the Air* (1983) became *Flotsam and Jetsam* (1996), and *Zoo Station* (1985) was transformed into *Lions of the Grunewald* (1993)). With the exception of *Boomtown* (1990), however, none of the enclosed plays has been published in anything resembling their original forms.[1]

It is worth mentioning that Higgins's predisposition for intratextuality vis-à-vis the content of the radio plays fits with an oft-observed aesthetic in Higgins's work more generally. Neil Murphy explains:

> Higgins has reissued, relocated, and revised much of his writing in several ways, something that poses significant difficulties to serious readers of his work . . . *Ronda Gorge and Other Precipices* contains many autobiographical echoes of *Bornholm Night-Ferry* and also includes a reprint of *Images of Africa*, the early travel book. Many of the short fictions and prose pieces of *Helsingør* [*Helsingør Station and Other Departures*] and *Ronda Gorge* are reprinted in *Flotsam and Jetsam*, and the stories of *Felo de Se* again reappear, though they are renamed and revised. (50)

It is my contention that making these echoes as transparent as possible is essential, as Higgins's intratextuality will inevitably receive further consideration as critics begin the process of summing up Higgins's life's work; I would also contend that any such consideration

---

1 Even *Boomtown*, while retaining the original's narrative scope, was transfigured into prose for publication by Anam Press in 2002, when it was retitled *As I was Riding Down Duval Boulevard with Pete La Salle.*

of Higgins's intratextuality must also bear in mind that these echoes extend to the radio plays as well.

While the remainder of the radio plays—including *Assassin, Vanishing Heroes* (1983), *Imperfect Sympathies* (1977), and *Discords of Good Humour* (1982)—do not correspond with any material in the published Higgins canon, I would argue that these plays are of particular interest precisely because of the way they innovate intertextual techniques rather than simply relying on the intratextuality so familiar within Higgins's own body of work; and, moreover, that this unique use of intertextuality might very well serve to inform a deeper understanding of Higgins's past "recycling" of his own prose.

Sitting with Aidan Higgins while preparing this collection for publication, I was much impressed with how sharp his memory was as he recalled the various materials he had mined while writing the plays so many years ago: "That line is from Kafka—from his *Letters to Milena.*" "That one's from *Finnegans Wake.*" One morning—the day after a particularly long session working on *Uncontrollable Laughter*—I found Aidan eager to talk about a William Cobbett quote I had unceremoniously read right past without recognizing (indeed, why would I?). Needless to say, I could hardly keep up, even with Google Books at my disposal to help me try and track down lines which might deserve attribution. In this context it wasn't at all surprising to hear Higgins's wife, Alannah Hopkin, comment that Aidan could still remember lines of dialogue from movies he had seen only in his childhood. It all became increasingly clear. This, then, was the same man who had such a command of all these sources that he could carefully construct them into something little resembling their original contexts, and much greater now than the sum of their many parts.

To my knowledge, Higgins's sophisticated ability to remember the occasional stray quote from a wide range of authors—and then to co-opt that quote for his own uses within unrelated narratives—is, if not unique to these plays, then certainly employed here to unique effect. From this perspective, *Assassin* is perhaps the most notable play in the collection. Here, Higgins mines generously from the several volumes of collected letters of Franz Kafka, among other sources, in order to retell the story of the assassination of Franz Ferdinand by Gavrilo Princip (letters which themselves make no mention of the assassination). This co-option is both something more—and less—than the excessive intertextuality found in such masters of the form as his Irish compatriot, James Joyce. Where with Joyce, the intertextual referent is nearly always meant to resonate with the theme of the passage which contains it (at least when he's not simply pulling the critics' legs with a random red herring), with Higgins the source of the reference becomes immediately irrelevant, such that for all intents and purposes the line becomes entirely the author's own (i.e., in Higgins there is no intended resonance, and likewise nothing resembling a red herring). Such intertextuality is perhaps "something less than Joyce" because it lacks the intertextual sophistication of a master puzzle maker, of one who wanted "To keep the critics busy for three hundred years." I would argue, however, that Higgins transcends Joyce both in his unique approach to his sources (perhaps even mocking the inveterate puzzler) and in how the semantic distance from the original context is so bewildering that it forces us to wonder at the method Higgins employed in finding and utilizing the passages in question. In Joyce you see the method even as you are surprised by it; in Higgins, the seeming lack of method suggests an authorial ability to call up the esoteric and obscure to an extent that confounds critical assessment.

Indeed, I am increasingly convinced that there is an inimitable kind of genius at work in what Aidan Higgins has accomplished in *Assassin* (as well as in *Discords of Good Humour*, *Vanishing Heroes*, and *Uncontrollable Laughter*, if to a lesser degree). Consider, for instance, the following passage in a scene between the Archduke and his doctor, as they discuss Ferdinand's tuberculosis:

ARCHDUKE: (*Ruminates.*) Through all these years I have done everything demanded of me mechanically, and in reality only waited for the voice to call me.

*Distant hunting rifle, cries of beaters.*

(*Echo.*) Until finally the illness called me from the adjoining room and I ran towards it and gave myself to it more and more . . . (*Pause.*) But it's dark in that room and one isn't quite sure that it *is* the illness. (page 198)

What we find here is that the bulk of the Archduke's lines are taken, word for word, from Kafka's *Letters to Milena*; and, moreover, that while the lines function beautifully within their new context, they owe none of their impact to any intertextual resonance with the original source. As critics of the passage, we are forced to work out the possibilities ourselves. A man, alone and frightened with his illness, can be either an Archduke or a writer. Illness democratizes.

*Discords of Good Humour* presented some of the greatest editorial challenges. Subtitled *A Feature on the Life of Brian O'Nolan, alias Flann O'Brien, alias Myles na gCopaleen*, the play contains excerpts from numerous interviews with various people in O'Brien's life, including brothers Ciaran and Kevin and also Liam and Barbara Redmond. In comparing the most recent hard-copy text with the radio version, one finds notable discrepancies, including both omissions and additions. That the text does not match the radio version is rather odd, especially considering that the radio version contains excerpts of actual interviews. Except where the difference between the radio version and the text appears to be the result of an obvious mistake, I have chosen to leave the material as it is in Higgins's final draft, largely because some of the apparent additions by Higgins are really quite wonderful, as is the case with Kevin O'Nolan's description of he and his brothers dressing up a dog and taking it on a walk:

> And we were going out through the back of this place, and there were people called Armstrong owned the house, you know, three old ladies, and they used to go down to the end of the garden. And it was a small house and they saw us going along with this extraordinary creature dressed like some fella on all fours, you know (*laughing*) . . . with a bright jersey and coloured pants and the little legs coming down.
>
> And "oh!" they said. But not at all, maybe being Irish characters they just sort of took it as natural. "Oh," they said, "we'll get a flower for him," and they got a great big rhododendron and pinned it on the jersey, you know. (page 88)

As this goes well beyond what Kevin originally said in his interview, in lieu of cutting what would be best left in, I have chosen to err on the side of caution by trusting the text, even though there very well could be additions to the interviews that are quite simply "mistakes" or embroideries on Higgins's part.

In the final analysis there is a very rich and layered coherence to *Discords*. Bits of biography from interviews with family and friends are woven together with relevant passages from *The Poor Mouth*, *At Swim-Two-Birds*, *The Third Policeman*, and O'Brien's column "The Cruiskeen Lawn," in a way that might argue persuasively for the notion that O'Brien's work is itself quite autobiographical in nature—if not for the fact that biography is a rather difficult thing to pin down in an author with so many distinct identities: an aspect of O'Brien's persona of which the play is explicitly conscious (indeed, you need to look no further than the play's subtitle to see that Higgins himself is playing into O'Brien's legend). O'Brien is an enigma, and despite the play's finding coherence between the biographical and the fictional, Higgins's characterization of him never forgets his basic mystery.

The text for most of the plays came from editions archived with the University of Victoria Library Special Collections (UVIC). For *Uncontrollable Laughter* (UVIC Lot 12.2), *Vanishing Heroes* (UVIC Lot 19.1), and *Texts for the Air* (UVIC Lot 16.1), I worked exclusively with the manuscripts archived by UVIC library, as they are the only versions available, while with *Zoo Station, Boomtown, Tomb of Dreams* and "Clouding Over," I worked exclusively with the soft copy versions e-mailed to me by Alannah Hopkin,[2] as there were no versions available in the UVIC catalog. For *Assassin* (*Assassinations: 4. Franz Ferdinand*, Lot 12.1), *Winter is Coming* (Lot 18.1), and *Discords of Good Humour* (Lot 15.1), I had to negotiate differences between the UVIC cataloged versions, and the soft copy versions sent to me by Alannah. Moreover, this was complicated further by the fact that for *Boomtown, Discords of Good Humour*, and *The Tomb of Dreams* I also had the radio recordings available.

In the final analysis, numerous judgment calls were required, as it became clear that in some cases the typist for the soft copy version appears to have been working with earlier versions of the plays than the versions available from UVIC, while in other cases the typist appears to have been working with more recent versions, as indicated by the fact that many of the UVIC versions had considerable margin editing in Higgins's hand—some of which was duplicated in the soft copies, and some of which wasn't, with considerable inconsistency both within and across texts.

Consequently, the editing done herein may contain what appear to be inconsistencies in the various judgments made. Indeed, books designed to satisfy both casual readers and academics are unlikely to satisfy either. Why, for instance, did I rework *Zoo Station* to include some of the changes which came with the later *Lions of the Grunewald*—but then did not make all other similar changes for other texts? (*Texts for the Air*, for instance, received some nice revision before

---

2  According to Alannah these had been typed up "several years ago," when the possibility of publishing these plays was first being considered.

being published in *Flotsam and Jetsam*). The short answer is that Higgins himself was simply more concerned about *Zoo Station* than he was about *Texts for the Air*; in particular, he was quite distressed not to find that a scene from *Lions of the Grunewald* describing "two sad sodomites . . . copulat[ing] in the snow" (page 324) was missing from the play, and insisted that I add it. Still, I would note too that the looping structure of *Texts for the Air* would make the task of reediting it to include the changes of *Flotsam* far more prohibitive—and, as well, change *Texts for the Air* in a more deeply fundamental way than is true for the changes incorporated into *Zoo Station*. In any case, while much consideration was put into the choices that were made—and while I am pleased with the result—I also recognize that a different editor may well have made different choices, which would have been equally valid. Finally, some might also question how wise it is to include some of the less "politically correct" terminology apparent in these works, and to this I would only note that, for better or worse, the plays are products of their era, and should be judged accordingly.

With Higgins's blessing, I took the greatest editorial license with *Boomtown* and *Assassin*, focusing specifically on reworking them into plays for the stage, rather than the radio, not so much because we expect that they will ever be produced for the stage, but because this format is more familiar to readers. Indeed, it was Higgins's desire that all the enclosed works resemble stage plays on the page as much as possible, with the exception of "Clouding Over," which for all intents and purposes takes the form of a short story.[3] Accordingly, my work on *Boomtown* and *Assassin* involved numerous changes, which, while not exactly necessary for publication, would be essential to any

3 The inclusion of "Clouding Over" in this volume is something of an anomaly; having never been produced as a play, its provenance as such is questionable (i.e., at some unknown point in its history it was subtitled "A Monologue for Radio," and so was forwarded to me in soft copy by Alannah, along with the rest), but I think the quality of the piece, as well as its importance to Higgins's oeuvre, justifies this decision.

theater production. Most notably, while *Boomtown* originally had nearly fifty separate characters, in the version published here this has been scaled back to twenty by redistributing a large number of these roles to a "chorus" of students (e.g., in one scene the UVIC version asks that four marines trade dialogue, while in the *Darkling Plain* version, four students acting as marines trade dialogue instead).

In editing *Boomtown* as a stage play I realized that what Higgins had tapped into about academic life at universities is how it spills over so easily into the bars and restaurants that surround such large institutions as the University of Texas at Austin. Having grown up in nearby New Mexico—and having attended a large state school myself—I found that one of the more striking features of the play is how it looks with new eyes (those of a man out of his element) on scenes that are so familiar to me. This is Higgins the travel writer, although in this case he is not describing Texans so much as the residents of the University of Texas at Austin. And so with Higgins's blessing, I edited the play with this fact in mind, describing a stage where bar and classroom sit back to back, and suggesting that Higgins as Narrator continually walk back and forth between the two. And while this change did have Higgins's blessing, it ultimately required much greater manipulation of the material than I had expected, reworking a play composed of approximately seventy percent narration into dramatic form. Most of this was accomplished by reassigning narration as dialogue to the various characters.

In addition to format and structural changes, there was a substantial amount of dialogue in the UVIC cataloged version which was not included in the radio version, and which Higgins was continually surprised by as I provided the details to him; he decided it must have been the result of censorship, and we agreed to leave much of it in. Moreover, there are also numerous passages in the BBC version that are not in the UVIC version (notably, actual excerpts from Higgins' students at Austin); I have added these to the enclosed version. Finally, while the BBC radio version ended some six pages earlier than the UVIC cataloged version, I have maintained all the "extra" material.

As in *Boomtown*, I have also reduced the number of characters in *Assassin*, granting much of the dialogue to two characters who serve alternately as a pair of counts and a pair of bishops. Moreover, the play has also been reframed so that it isn't so much a play about the assassination of Franz Ferdinand as it is a play about a troupe of actors *putting on a play* about Franz Ferdinand. As Aidan himself had included hints along these lines already, I suggested that this be further explored and Aidan agreed. Moreover, as the play did receive a staged reading directed by Joe Dowling at the Cork Everyman Theatre while Dowling was touring with a production of *The Playboy of the Western World*, the meta-theatrical element of the play has taken this fact into account (albeit in a very muted way).

Finally, I would like to thank all those involved in bringing this collection to press: Aidan Higgins for agreeing to meet with me and putting up with my endless badgering during the four days that I visited with him in Kinsale; both he and Alannah for being so hospitable to me on that trip; Nanyang Technological University for granting me the research leave and funds to undertake the trip; the various editors at Dalkey Archive; Neil Murphy, for first suggesting this project to me and for always being available to sound out my thinking on Higgins; the Special Collections Department as the University of Victoria Library, for granting me access to the Higgins material in their archives; and of course my wife, Joy Wheeler, for her continual patience and support.

DANIEL JERNIGAN, 2009
Nanyang Technological University

# Works Cited

Donnely, Neil. "Aidan Higgins in Conversation with Neil Donnelly," *Aidan Higgins: The Fragility of Form*. Champaign, IL: Dalkey Archive Press, 2010.

Murphy, Neil. "Aidan Higgins." *Review of Contemporary Fiction*. 23:3 (2003): 49–84.

# Boomtown, Texas, USA

BAPTIST BROKEN HOMES. ALCOHOLISM. THE NEW LOST GENERATION.
THE MILITARY BASE AS CRIB. AMERICA, THE WARP IN HISTORY.

Broadcast on BBC Radio 3 on the 29th of March, 1973, directed by
Piers Plowright. Stage version prepared for this edition.

# CAST

### *The Faculty*

PROFESSOR HIGGINS

PROFESSOR SIVARAMAKRISHNAN (PROFESSOR S.)

PROFESSOR EMERITUS JONES

PROFESSOR PETE LA SALLE

PSYCH. PROFESSOR

### *The Students*

BONNY

BOB

STACEY

LEANNE

CYNTHIA ROSE

JIM

ROD

Extra students as available

*The Rest* (all of which can be played by The Students)

VOICES (from offstage)

ANNOUNCER (recorded for radio and television)

EXTERMINATOR

THE MARINES

BARMAN

WAITRESS

TINY E.

COACH AKERS

FEMALE MEXICAN

MALE MEXICAN

OLDSTER

MARJANA

WENDY

FELLOWS 1 AND 2

REPUBLICAN DEMONSTRATORS

FILIPINO GIRL

DAD

LYNN

CLARK BARNES

CAMPUS POLICE OFFICER

JIM APPLEGATE WOOD


*Recordings*

RONALD REAGAN

JFK


Sources: Billy Lee Brammer (*The Flea Circus*), Richard Brautigan (*Trout Fishing in America*).

*Stage right a classroom with desks facing centre stage: at least 8 students are always at the ready, throughout the entire play; these students make up the non-professorial contingent of the play as needed, frequently visiting the bar as either employees or patrons according to the needs of the script. The classroom has the U.S. and Texas State flags prominently displayed. Stage left a long Texas-style bar, with bartender (when there is one) facing centre stage. Between the two, a table which serves alternately as a teacher's desk, a table for the restaurant/bar, or, as in the first scene, as* PROFESSOR S.*'s living room.* HIGGINS *moves between the three locations fluidly, as if they are quite nearly a single setting. Occasionally he introduces a prop as he narrates, helping to set the scene. At other times, other actors serving as waiters might reset the table according to the needs of various scenes.*

PROF. HIGGINS: (*Urbane. Addressing the audience.*) Some years ago I encountered my first Americans in Spain. (*Pause.*) Grand People.

But to know a few Americans away from their own country is no preparation for meeting them *en masse* in their native habitat.

Particularly if they happen to be Texans, who may or may not even be representative Americans.

The University of Texas at Austin has a campus of nigh on fifty thousand students, with very few Negroes. I am scheduled to teach two weekly classes, comprising twenty-five students each, in the coming Fall Semester.

*Jet plane landing. Hold under.*

ANNOUNCER: "Boomtown, Texas, USA," by Aidan Higgins.

PROF. HIGGINS: Professor Sivaramakrishnan himself was waiting for me. (PROF. S. *enters, to shake* HIGGIN's *hand.*) A small neat cricket of a man in a wide-brimmed Brazilian sun hat.

PROF. S.: In Rio, I believe, the fruit in the market is rotten by midday.

PROF. HIGGINS: I, the Visiting Professor Higgins, was to teach "Creative Writing"—a trade recondite as falconry—through the Fall Semester. Class enrolment had already begun.

HIGGINS, PROF. S., *and* PROF. LA SALLE *gather around the table, which serves as the interior of the Sivaramakrishnans' home.*

PROF. S: (*Fastidious intonation, pipe smoker, patronising, slow delivery.*) I have a great sympathy for the eighteenth century novelists. Men like Fielding (*puff*) and Smollett. And people like that (*puff, puff*). I consider *Fanny Hill* a great novel. Do you?

*Silence. Offstage cry from Waldo the Cat.*

(*Complacently resumes, puffing at pipe.*) They are my boys. (*Pause, puff-puff.*) Why is that?

*Longer silence.*

PROF. LA SALLE: (*Bass; clearing throat.*) You look like Chekhov, Higgins.

PROF. HIGGINS: Maybe I am Chekhov.

PROF. LA SALLE: (*Rumbling laugh.*)

PROF. S.: (*Indulgently.*) An *Irish* Chekhov? (*Meditative puff.*) M'mm, maybe. Maybe. But certainly I am Professor Sivaramakrishnan . . . though regrettably no relative of the great Pakistani all-rounder!

*Polite laughter. Mrs. S.'s high screech. Cry of Waldo the Cat.*

Right, my Waldo?

*Music. Thelonius Monk, "Well You Needn't," hold under.*

VOICE: "America . . . often only a place in the mind." (*Louder, agitated.*) "No democracy in nightmares."

*Music.*

PROF. HIGGINS: On a midsummer morning not very long ago the sun advanced on the city and lit the topmost spines of the hill.

Then the light came closer, touching the tall buildings and the fresh-washed streets.

The nearly full-blown heat came with it, quick and palpitant. It was close to being desert heat: sudden, emphatic.

The sun's heat came through the cloud cover, steaming the streets, quivering upward through the . . .

The city was quiet; people stayed inside, sitting under fans, sipping iced drinks, barely stirring.

*Students stand and face the classroom flag, hands on hearts.*

The American flag is like a child's plaything. Vivid primary colours that would gladden a childish heart. Scarlet . . . no, crimson, and sailor blue on white. A joyful-looking thing, like a lacquered tin drum. Like a good day's work. Or a win on the turf. It flies free up there, seemingly.

A pretty girl, a very pretty girl, very free of brown leg and thigh in the briefest of white shorts, passes along Duval Boulevard on her modern bicycle, standing up on the pedals, hair flying. A gorgeous maroon helium balloon straining out behind her. Her infatuated boyfriend cycles alongside, pleased to be with her.

Where else would a smile be, but on a bonny face? (*Pause.*) . . . Ah America, my New-found land! (*Pause.*) . . . Land of Dreams.

HIGGINS *sits at the bar.*

BARMAN: (*Brisk.*) Did you say you wanted anything?

PROF. HIGGINS: Shiner.

BARMAN *turns to get* HIGGINS *his beer. Turns up the radio.*

ANNOUNCER: "Tiny" Edwards, Longhorn middle linebacker, was arrested and charged with aggravated assault on a police officer Wednesday after a fight in an Austin nightclub. Using profane language and with slurred speech and bloodshot eyes, the maddened Longhorn said:

TINY E.: Go ahead an' try an' arrest me!

ANNOUNCER: Four or five police officers got Edwards into a patrol car. He faces third-degree felony charges, punishable by up to ten years in prison and a $5,000 fine. Longhorn coach Fred Akers said he would not take any action until he received all the facts of the case.

COACH AKERS: Austin, Texas, is still part of America, and the last time I heard, you're innocent until proved guilty.

ANNOUNCER: Austin Police Officer Melecio Villaneve, who attempted to arrest the Longhorn linebacker outside the Rox-Z nightclub on Riverside Drive last night, was taken to Brackenridge Hospital for treatment of injuries, cuts and scratches, and a nose injury. The Longhorn had attempted to bite him on the chest.

*Football stadium, cheering.*

No charges were pressed by police. (*Pause.*)
Three murderers and a rapist have escaped from Leavenworth via an airshaft. Bloodhounds and helicopters patrol the rolling hills of northeast Kansas. The wanted men were serving life-sentences.

WAITRESS: (*Feminine, coaxingly.*) Did you say you wanted something?

*Music. 1960s Joan Baez recording.*
*Hold under: bar sounds. Two students leave their seats and approach the bar.*

PROF. HIGGINS: A Mexican couple sit near me. Middle-aged, close together, intimate but not touching. Whispering to each other in Spanish. She asks for a Jack Daniels.

FEMALE MEXICAN: Could we get two Jack Daniels?

MALE MEXICAN: (*Low, puzzled.*) *Whass' eet—whees*-kee?

*They continue to whisper to each other in Spanish.*

PROF. HIGGINS: Why do I feel more at home where Spanish is spoken? A World in a Word: the lingo of children, itself not childish. A protective language, until you encounter the hard menace of Spanish male abuse; but that's protective too.

*Bar sounds. Baez Sings.* HIGGINS *turns and faces his classroom. The two students at the bar shoot down their whiskey and return to their seats.*

(*In classroom.*) And then I'd like . . . Davis to read his paper, which is exceptionally good. And then Kurt, an extremely fine paper. (*Pause.*) All *A*s.

STUDENTS: (*Scramble. Each standing in turn.*) Adult means horny . . . coming on like B.O.
  Get *him*!
  Twenty-five years old for Chrissake and thrown out of college!
  My drinking problems only *increased.*
  Dropt it in there an' you've got it goin' . . .

HIGGINS *nearly retreats to the bar.*

BARMAN: (*Brisk.*) Would you like another?

*This chases* HIGGINS *back to his classroom. Tumult of bar abruptly cut.*

PROF. HIGGINS: Stacey . . . if you would be so kind.

STACEY: (*Standing.*) The month of September is like no other in America. The air is slightly spicy, but not heavy. And it makes the most beautiful, contented sound when it blows through the trees. And the sky is full of stars, more stars than I have ever seen in any other town.

*Whirr of phone ringing on* HIGGINS's *desk.*

PROF. HIGGINS: The phone rings. A tall, willowy girl bursts through the door and pounces on it, long braids flying behind.

STACEY *quits reading and bolts for the phone.*

STACEY: (*Breathless.*) I've got it!

PROF. HIGGINS: (*Bored.*) It's Ben. Ben Ryder. A swim in the pool in the evening before malts at the drugstore? Why not?

OLDSTER *has surreptitiously inserted himself at the bar.*

OLDSTER: (*Crotchety.*) I'm not as young as I used to be, Charles. It gets harder and harder to get the blood to my brain.

*Long puzzled silence.*

PROF. HIGGINS: The redmen and their frugal race are virtually extinct, confined to their Reservations, become drunkards. One of my female students who sends in interesting papers is Cherokee-Irish. She has widely spaced periwinkle eyes and the fixed stare of an owl.

No Negroes are seen in the campus. I was given directions by a Negro one night, having lost my way walking back from a production of *The Duchess of Malfi*; he was watering a lawn. I thought of Medgar Evers's last words. Turn me loose.

The Mississippi civil rights leader murdered in 1963 by a white supremacist who twice escaped conviction by all white juries. Thirty years later he was tried again.

There are no flies in Texas. No Indians either. An orange glow suffuses the Tower of the Union Building; like an extended penis, says La Salle. Signifying that Texas won the football game today. This Saturday at the beginning of October.

The stars over Austin are bigger than the stars over anywhere else, like the Texans themselves. Venus burns lopsided and below her to the southwest the Bull blinks a reddened eye. The topless bars, the Red Rose and the Yellow Rose, do a roaring trade. (*Pause.*)

You can drink and drive in Texas. Take in a ball game. Play golf. They drive about in large air-conditioned cars with windows closed, Budweiser in hand. There is no state tax; oil pays for it all. The All-You-Can-Eat nights are perhaps the most relaxing of all. The Hungry Horse Saloon, moving with the times, has become The Steel Penny. Don't ask me why. I guess I'm just a fool for the past . . .

BARMAN *turns off the radio and turns on the television.* JFK *speaking at Siemensstadt in Berlin.*

JFK: All free men, wherever they may live, are citizens of Berlin, and, therefore, as a free man, I take pride in the words (*in bad German*) *Ich . . . bin . . . ein Berliner!*

*German ovation, Siemensstadt workforce.*
BARMAN *switches channels.* RONALD REAGAN *speaks in* The Killers.

RONALD REAGAN: Sure I wanted North. He double-crossed me and made off with the whole bundle. And maybe I would have killed him if I could've laid my hands on him. But first I'd have gotten my money back.

BARMAN *switches channels. Elderly president* REAGAN *speaking in Ireland.*

RONALD REAGAN: Now I know some of us Irish-Americans tend to get carried away with our ancestral past, and want very much to impress our relatives here with how well we've done in the new world. Many of us aren't back in Ireland five minutes before, as the American song has it, we're looking to shake the hand of Uncle Mike and kiss the girl we used to swing down by the garden gate.

*Turns off television and turns to* HIGGINS.

BARMAN: Do you know what LBJ's dying words were? (*Deep Texas drawl.*)
    Boy, that was a good glass of milk!

HIGGINS *retreats to his students.*

PROF. HIGGINS: Next, please.

STUDENT: (*Standing to read.*) Dear Julian, so Manhattan life isn't quite what it's cracked up to be meaning you city folk want to hear how a Texan lives. (*Small female laughter.*) Everybody outside of Texas seems to think that all Texans have Cadillacs, oil wells and hundred-acre ranches. When you and your buddies come down to the world of the never-ending plain, you'll try and fit in as a cowboy.

PROF. HIGGINS: I feel more at home myself where Spanish is spoken, but not to the extent of going into Mexico to hear it.
    Leanne?

LEANNE: (*Rapid.*) Stayed with some friends in big old hotel at Port Isabel near the Mexican border. Faced the bay. Skinny-dipped in daytime. Up early. Walked half a block for biscuits and gravy with coffee. Ninety-nine cents. Stayed on beach. Met some crazies. Danced with a dwarf. (*Screech of laughter.*)

*Music and customers in bar have been escalating.* HIGGINS *finds himself drawn back in.*

PROF. LA SALLE: Austin is a great place to live. It is in what they call the Texas Hill Country. As you go west from here the climate gets continually drier, until you get to California, 1,500 miles away.

As you go east it gets greener with pine forests and lakes. Four hours to the south is Mexico, where the peso is still dropping.

*Babble of Spanish.*

PROF. HIGGINS: (LA SALLE *gossips and points as* HIGGINS *narrates.*) The place is patronised by young executives of the High Tech, known colloquially as Yuppies.

On Sunday afternoons, when church empties out, families come here for buffalo wings and French fries cooked in buttermilk.

Two annexes with long windows overlook Duval Boulevard. It's a place for assignations. The very talkative white-haired Professor of Psychology takes very passive girl students from his class to this romantic rendezvous.

A blonde Polish girl waits on tables. She comes from Warsaw; two years ago she could speak no English. Limps.

Marjana!

MARJANA: (*Low.*) Can I get you another, Professor?

PROF. HIGGINS: The winsome blonde divorcee behind the bar is Wendy. She looks pale and sad, knows her job, is good at it, comes from Boston, Mass., has a child. And smiles sweetly, wistfully, at the Professor.

WENDY: (*Efficiently.*) Everything okay here?

PROF. HIGGINS: It's unlucky, I know, to be in the presence of someone who's always sad. I know, only too well. Misery is contagious, it's catching. But Wendy isn't always sad, now smiling ever-so-wistfully in my direction.

HIGGINS *turns away from the bar, takes a stack of papers from his briefcase, and begins to read through them, as if marking.* BONNY *runs through, nearly tripping over him.*

BONNY: Sorry Professor.

PROF. HIGGINS: One hot Thursday before his second class, on the grassy area before Parlin Hall, erudite Professor Higgins met the longest brownest pair of legs in the shortest of briefs in the whole of Texas, en route to class, merry as usual. Bonny Bailiff!

*Taken aback by her beauty,* HIGGINS *begins to pack his briefcase.*

BONNY: (*Teasingly.*) You're *leaving*?

PROF. HIGGINS: I . . . have designs on thee, Bonny B.

BONNY: (*Laughingly.*) You're alarming me.

*Distant bell.*

PROF. HIGGINS: I'm sure I'm not.

*Distant bell.*

BONNY: (*Archly.*) Professor Higgins, I'm going to *cure* you!

*Distant bell.*

PROF. HIGGINS: It is your fault, Madame, and yours alone. I cannot go forward and I cannot go back. Why did you not come sooner into the world, or let me come later?

BONNY *ambles seductively away as* HIGGINS *narrates.*

PROF. HIGGINS: Bonny wears teeth-braces, to put it mildly. Her smile is like an opening gate. She smiles a lot, an odd, sweetly reasonable, lopsided smile. Her blue eyes sparkle. The Catholic family comes from Abilene. Dad would pull her ponytail when she was growing up, to make her do back-bends. Dad sure liked to shop for nails in hardware stores after Mass. She cut his hair. He called her Dollface. She thought of him as Handy Dan, her two hundred and sixty pound, six-foot-two-inch Daddy. By her senior year at High School she had saved up enough for a candy-apple red Ford Mustang.

*Mustang starting.*

When she was in her ninth-grade year, Dad had a heart attack. Her big strong Dad stricken down as the result of a clogged artery! Every Monday to Friday she'd had his kisses, on return from the office. "I love you," he said huskily, hugging her. The Bailiffs were a close-knit family.

DAD: (*Sour.*) Working my ass off for an honest dollar.

ANNOUNCER: Steven Gidden, twenty-seven-year-old student in the College of Liberal Arts, was today charged with first degree felony for possession of forty pounds of cannabis valued at $15,000. The arrest was made by (*police siren*) an Austin Police Department undercover narcotics agent posing as a student.

After viewing the box of marijuana, grown locally, stashed in Gidden's car, Officer Hamblin gave the go-ahead for the bust.

PROF. HIGGINS: Professor Warrilow, whose wife has left him, hears the cicadas shrilling in the pecan tree, like steel war-music by Hindemith. The armadillos pant and grunt as they dig in the leaves for roots. Dogs will turn them on their backs to eat them.

The Guggenheim Scholar tells me of the weedless fossil-water under Texas, pure water in the darkness under the Balcones Fault. Too much has been taken out of it, he says. He speaks of a time "when the heat will back off a bit." But the heat shows no sign of abating.

He admits that he "backed into teaching." I do not mention his absent wife. He played ice hockey in Toronto.

*A gesture from* HIGGINS *and* STUDENT *stands up and addresses the class.*

STUDENT: Uncle David is still working for one of the iron-rigging companies here in Austin. Last month he shaved his beard and moustache off. He now complains about the wind chilling his chin and cheeks and lips. You know he has had that beard for so long I can barely recognise him without it. Now that he looks just like Grandpa Jack minus twenty or so years, Uncle David finally finished his house up there in Sulphur Springs. Do you remember those castle stones we borrowed from Carthely Castle? Well one of them is now probably implanted in Uncle David's fireplace.

*The table becomes an office.* PROF. EMERITUS JONES *enters.*

PROF. HIGGINS: (*Urbane.*) My elderly colleague, Emeritus Jones, no doubt a good man in many ways, has drawn my attention to an original oil painting that hangs above my desk. Depicting, if my eyes do not altogether deceive me, a limp sort of tree in the act of collapsing into a pond of sorts, under a sort of a cloudy sky free of birds. Executed, the Fulbright man informs me with a hint of pride . . .

EMERITUS JONES: . . . by a South African lady painter, a friend of mine, with her fingertips.

PROF. HIGGINS: But I'll be damned if I ever saw such a tree or pond in South Africa, land of the mighty baobab, and the even mightier Apartheid.

Professor Emeritus Jones shows me a small wooden-handled awl, less the brass neck, which he procured in a Shoreditch flea market in London many years ago, for sixpence Old Currency:

EMERITUS JONES: (*Proudly.*) What do you think its trade value is today?

PROF. HIGGINS: A *borer*. We are speaking about borers. Awls!

EMERITUS JONES: (*Proudly.*) One pound!

PROF. HIGGINS: Emeritus Jones has returned to the academic fold after a sixteen-day sea voyage. He drones away about a pub lunch in London, at the Scarsdale Arms in Kensington, with *the* Wilson Harris.

EMERITUS JONES: . . . it was at the Scarsdale Arms in Kensington that I had lunch with Wilson Harris.

PROF. HIGGINS: I look down upon that speckled dome of his and marvel at such vanity contained in one old skully. Professor Jones, now retired, keeps fifty or sixty proof copies of a no doubt useless book, long remaindered, that carries his Introduction, stockpiled on a shelf over his head. It's like sharing an office with Sweeney the storyteller, or a dybbuk. Make sure the audience beholds you, not your gown.

Where is that faith which transfigures ignorance that Yeats spoke of? Not here. I think, not. (*His mind elsewhere.*) The Clementine Library, where Jaromir Hladík heard the voice of God, contains 400,000 volumes.

The Perry-Castañeda Library at Austin: (*pregnant pause*) three million.

EMERITUS JONES: In the eating of coarse rice and the drinking of water, the use of one's elbow for a pillow, joy is to be found. (*Pause, wheeze.*) . . . Wealth and rank attained have as much to do with me as passing clouds.

PROF. HIGGINS: Sometimes I feel like Steinbeck's mad preacher Casey. I see a fine title in the Jones Library, to raise the academic spirit.

*Pigs, from Cave to Corn Belt* (featuring such chapters as "Demigod or Demon?").

More irrigation ditches. Freedom's ferment! The Tattooed Lady in my early class admits to having been raped by a black brother at the age of sixteen. He comes in nightmares to rebuke her. His name: Hal.

EMERITUS JONES: Wealth and rank attained have as much to do with me as passing clouds.

HIGGINS *returns to the bar. The* BARMAN *turns on the radio.*

ANNOUNCER: A Moroccan immigrant, Abdel Krim Belacheb, was to-day sentenced to six life terms and fined $70,000 by a jury of eight women and four men, for slaying six patrons at a Dallas nightclub. Belacheb could be eligible for parole in twenty years . . .

*Fade.*

BOB: (*With* HIGGINS *still at the bar,* BOB *stands and reads.*) I met Sharon in the fall . . . I was dating Jocelyn at the time. A tall blonde girl with a gorgeous figure. She was feisty and a bit of a Nip, but lots of fun. Her father was a multi-millionaire surgeon. Banks, jets, hospitals, condominiums, apartments . . . yes, he owned them all. (*Pause.*)

I loved Sharon dearly, and I decided to sacrifice my summer for money. I got a job with the police department. I was determined that I would buy her a car and take her out to the best restaurants and buy her expensive gifts. Nothing was too good for Miss Sharon Cleveland. Nothing. (*Pause.*)

She was a flirt. She swatted my butt once when no one else was looking. That night at the hotel we took a quick dip in the pool. The water was too cold. It was still early spring. We went back to our room and watched TV for a while.

She sat on my bare back and rubbed my shoulders. Then the feeling came.

*Sound of a distant gong.*

VOICE: Now the dragons are coming down out of the sky. Those dragons are there for you to conquer, America! Truman had planned to drop fifty atomic bombs on Japan if two didn't do the trick.

MALE STUDENT: (*Bravely.*) Bonnie's into religion.

She's Catholic and always talks about it. (*Pause.*) . . . So, vacuum and wash pick-up truck. Order the flower, a rose of course. Pick up the shirts at the cleaners. Then breath-freshener and cologne. Then workout boots, khakis, button-down, sunglasses. Sharp. Small talk all the way to the Country Club. Lunch was okay. I didn't eat much. (*Pause.*) She did alright. (*Pause.*) Drove her home. Not much small talk. Invited in to watch old movie. H'mm, h'mm.

BONNIE: (*Close, hotly.*) I want you.

*The bar becomes a Mexican restaurant. Mariachi music.*

PROF. HIGGINS: In a Mexican restaurant run by a Bolivian on 24th Street opposite Les Amis, two fellows are finishing a meal. Possibly prison wardens on their off-duty. They are talking confidentially of prison breaks, security, the behaviour of inmates. The character of a certain Governor. That time, that place.

FELLOW 1: (*Man to man.*) You know where he is now?

FELLOW 2: No . . .

FELLOW 1: (*Whispers.*) In an Insanatorium.

FELLOW 2: (*Loud unbelief.*) In an Insanatorium! You don't say.

PROF. HIGGINS: Everyone works hard, gives smiling service. Feet thump the floor, nobody grouses. The girls laugh gustily, hair freshly washed. Inside backless dresses bare young brown backs cannot yet show the meat of middle age. Instant frump, Widow's Hump, that would never do. Not here. Youth lasts forever. The future is now. Hello, it's tomorrow! Today's the future. Never let up.

Has real life become a television commercial? Or vice versa? Pumped music never abates.

*Stevie Ray Vaughn, "A Flood Down in Texas."*

PROF. HIGGINS: (*Again in front of his class.*) All present and correct? Anybody missing? (*Pause.*) Anybody here not Texan?

(*Smoothly, aside.*) Could Professor Higgins tell the Methodists from the Presbyterians in fifty students of two E325 classes? Or the Fundamentalists from the Episcopalians? Or the Southern Baptists from Catholics? Were there Anglicans present?

Baptists, Methodists, bigots, Episcopalians, fish-fries, Catholics, Fundamentalists, Unitarians for all I know . . . All were much the same, as far as I could tell. Many came from broken homes, parents divorced, a father drinking, no religion practised.

They came from all over Texas, from Abilene, El Paso, Laredo, Fort Worth, the Golden Triangle, Somewhere . . . small towns out in Nowhere. They came to Austin, to the Great University . . . and found it good. Many of those sons and daughters of nonbelievers were for Reagan. They wanted good grades, a well-paid job in a secure future.

*Chattering and sound of TV.*

All think the same thoughts. All dread the future. Death and suicide are in the air. Family life disrupted. Father drinking. Mother ran away. They squat before a TV screen that is never turned off. Tranquilizers are taken. Herpes feared. Snort coke, drop acid, shoot pool, floss teeth, get laid. Those who have no past have a very limited future.

Let Bob Bragalone speak!

BOB: (*Standing.*) Apartment living is the life. It beats the hell out of dorms anyway. We're all set up with remote control colour television, a microwave. Plenty of wall decorations, lots of plants, cable TV and

HBO, a nice stereo system. Brand new carpeting, ceiling fans. Four telephones for convenience. A pool, racquetball courts, tennis courts. A weight room, and several other "necessities." I spend most of my time eating, sleeping and watching television . . .

LEANNE: . . . Stayed on the beach watching meteor showers. Had shrimp barbecue. Danced with a midget.

PROF. HIGGINS: The father of Leanne Hanna drank a lot and beat his wife. Her own father had been just the same, a drunkard and a wife-beater. He had been a gambler by profession. He left his family during the Depression. The wife was hungry. The day he left she had only a packet of peanuts to eat. They divorced. A year later he died. That was nine years ago. Now the daughter herself is going through a divorce. The mother says she doesn't give a shit.

LEANNE: (*Standing.*) My mother carries some great guilt with her. Her father was as bad as mine. The guilt prevents her sleeping at night, and she tries to give it to me. Anyway she doesn't go to bed alone . . . She takes her Baudelaire.

When she was going through her divorce, she often took something pretty to bed with her . . . a porcelain figure, a piece of tapestry. She drives a sports car, swears that she intends to dress in bright colours and go fast. She turned fifty this year.

HIGGINS *goes to the bar.* LEANNE *follows in time with the narration.*

PROF. HIGGINS: I invited her once for a drink at the Beach Cabaret. She worked around the corner at Zippy's Allnite Convenience Store. Leanne arrived punctually. Slouched in, gave me one of her dark, sultry looks. A "friend" was arriving. The "friend" turned out to be a randy young Moroccan in a red sports car. Jelloul Tenouri could speak French, German and Spanish, read the Koran. When you cut the light, where does the darkness go? His relationship with Leanne is . . . (*pause*) ambiguous.

Presently she left.

American girls shock Tenouri. They proposition him, touch his member. His record was five in one day. German girls were the best, but the prettiest were the Spanish.

BARMAN *turns on the television.*

ANNOUNCER: Thank you for joining us as the University of Texas Longhorns host the Texas A&M Aggies.

*Continued commentary, brass bands.*

PROF. HIGGINS: On the Saturdays when the Longhorns play at the stadium, middle-aged couples make their way there hand-in-hand, beset by fond memories. One cannot speak of victory or defeat. The bands are pumping up adrenalin. All opponents must go down before the Longhorns. Cheerleaders bump and grind. Girls in orange garters high-kick in the rain!

Orange umbrellas filled with helium lift vertically from passing cars. Longhorn emblems are sold outside the Co-op on Guadalupe Street. The fans arrive on foot from the packed carparks. They approach the stadium with an almost religious gravity. Cross-County Coaches are parked under the pecan trees. The voice of the Commentator drifts over Austin.

Even when the game is over, no matter the victor, the air of gravity persists. The long line of departing limousines, predominantly grey, file by Palm Springs Apartments. Conveying the impression of a church service ended, fans disperse silently, still full of the movement of the game. The feeling is almost . . . liturgical.

(*Poignantly.*) Football season is also the time of year that Large Mexican butterflies called Yellow Monarchs "overfly" Texas, coming from Mexico. This year they land in their thousands, exhausted, about Professor Sivaramakrishnan's pool. Alighting in the live oaks and chinaberry trees. To be set upon by Waldo the cat.

Meanwhile, an embarrassed, bearded father, with bawling babe in stroller, joins his class. Outside Dr. Sutherland's office a girl appears to be reading *Crime and Punishment*, and Professor Higgins prepares to dumbfound his second class with a paper entitled "The Forest as Metaphor and Place in the Work of Hamsun, Malaparte and Beckett."

*Reading to the audience from his book* As I Was Riding Down Duval Boulevard with Pete La Salle.

Riding down Duval Boulevard at night with La Salle behind the wheel of his brown Ford convertible. Along Martin Luther King Boulevard, named after the murdered pacifist, the dreamer, past the fake Tudor bar with its beams and leaded windows.

*Affable* LA SALLE *collects* HIGGINS *from his position in front of the audience and delivers him to the bar.*

Bound for a small quiet bar below street level near the State Capital. (*Pause.*)

La Salle, somewhat given to repeating himself, the way with rising pedagogues, recommends again that I read de Tocqueville's *On Democracy.*

PROF. LA SALLE: (*Standing for* HIGGINS, *in the same manner as the students.*) Nothing has changed in America since the canny Frenchman saw it all in 1840. The people believe, or suspect and fear, that in the very inner processes of governing, decay has set in. When the unthinkable is accepted as a "concept" for debate—the ethical "point" of nuclear warfare—nothing is clear anymore. Armageddon is just around the corner. We are on our way down, some would hold. Too much power in too few hands. When security is breached, the FBI man himself passes over military secrets to the enemy.

PROF. HIGGINS: So says La Salle.

Above the great door of the Union Building is cut in granite the grandiose axiom:

"YE SHALL KNOW THE TRUTH AND THE TRUTH SHALL MAKE YOU FREE."

From the tower, since closed, a crazed gunman shot 15 U.T. students dead in '64, in the cause of some kind of freedom. And had been shot dead himself by the Austin police, in the cause of civic order.

PROF. LA SALLE: Don't stare too long at certain characters in Texas bars. Tough Texans don't like being eyed too long and can get touchy.

PROF. HIGGINS: But it's hard not to stare as much stuffing of gut goes on. Hairy male chests erupt from bushranger shirts unbuttoned to the navel. The banter and chatter never abates.

In all the great space and rush of America there's no room for silence. American expansiveness won't allow it.

Everybody at the Cactus Bar on campus loves to be looked at, of course. The Cornish Cod had just arrived, a rare visitation. He gives a poetry reading tonight. An Arab sits cross-eyed with lechery. A voluptuous, glistery-lipped brunette, leaning dangerously forward, gives him the eye.

Young couples shout into each other's faces. Everybody explains everything at great length. The conceited barman is studying his bearded face in the mirror behind the bar, arranging his hair. The small neat Filipino girl smiles. Her name is Mary.

PROF. HIGGINS: (*Avuncular.*) How's my favourite Filipino girl?

FILIPINO GIRL: How's my favourite Irishman?

*Din of Cactus Bar fades out as* HIGGINS *again approaches his audience.*

PROF. HIGGINS: Dozed this afternoon at Palm Springs Apartments. Summer Time ends today. The rain in the live oaks again, squirrels racing along the branches, the fat caretaker laughs below. Mr. Lu, my late neighbour, has been thrown out of his apartment along with a covey of drug-pushers and skateboarders. (*Pause.*)

Broad-beamed female students with empty backpacks cycle home to Jester Dorm. A storm is brewing in the hills. Tumblers come frozen from the icebox. The food stores at night are cold as refrigeration plants. The air-conditioning unit out back thunders like a waterfall all night.

A brown-faced lean man, intent on his own business, with a briefcase containing notes on Ezra Pound, passes down the steps, en route to Parlin Hall: Professor Sivaramakrishnan! Who is no longer inviting Professor Higgins up to his mansion on the High Road.

A bronze President leans forward into the fountain as if taking a shower with his robes on. Honest, Innovative, Caring (the triple-pronged, vote-seeking lie) Lloyd Doggett is putting his name forward, dogged Doggett, as Austin's sole Democrat for the U.S. Senate. His supporters hold a rally next Wednesday on the West Mall. He has as much chance of office as hand-wringing Senator Mondale or Geraldine Ferraro, which is not saying much.

STUDENTS *as* REPUBLICAN DEMONSTRATORS *march across stage holding signs for Reagan.*

REP. DEMONSTRATORS: Geraldine is too extreme.

PROF. HIGGINS: I hear the bulky, beefy breathing of the herds.

REP. DEMONSTRATORS: Go home to New York—this is Reagan Country!

ANNOUNCER: (*Fulsome.*) Thomas Andy Barefoot, convicted of killing a policeman, was executed Tuesday night by lethal injection at the unholy hour of 12:24 A.M., at Huntsville, Texas.

*Sound of gong.*

PROF. HIGGINS: Austin is developing in a westerly direction. Bagmen and fixers. Bump-and-grinders. Horn-man Iagos. Drug-peddlers. Property developers. Slush piles, the fix. What are we looking at here—the Higher Animals, or the crazies?

HIGGINS *finds himself in front of his class again. Not knowing what to do next, he calls on another student.*

STUDENT: (*Standing.*) Hello it's tomorrow! (*Laughter.*) Monday the 19th of November the year by law 1984. Dramatic intro huh. I said that I'll tell you about my life in Austin well here it comes. (*Softer.*) When I moved here for the first time I lived . . .

PSYCH. PROFESSOR *enters, causing* STUDENT *to trail off. Courteous and curious,* HIGGINS *finds himself shuffled to a seat himself.*

PSYCH. PROFESSOR: (*Evenly.*) How do personality disorders develop? (*On the blackboard, he writes:*)
> Oral
> Anal
> Phallic

PROF. HIGGINS: The class is packed. They're all taking notes like mad.

PSYCH. PROFESSOR: After this stage of turmoil comes the fear of castration!

PROF. HIGGINS: The pencils fly. Towards the end of the fall semester I watched him in the Hyde Park grill, being very thick with a stunned female student. The Professor's head is crammed with Freudian filth.

PSYCH. PROFESSOR *leaves.*

There were mornings on the campus when all seemed insane. A placard hung on a pecan tree full of grackles:

*Two students walk through with a sign which reads:* Why Do Jews Not Accept Jesus?

A coloured insano in a Frank Sinatra trilby walks about the grass area with a fistful of arrows, fixes on a girl on a bench. The Professor never stops talking, eagerly, as if offering veritable manna. On the board he chalks up "nuts," "sens," spelled s.e.n.s, "desire."

*Bob Dylan, "I Believe in You."*

Austin is deserted. Texans play elsewhere. A grey overcast almost Irish day. Where would it be elsewhere? Lovely jogging weather!

BONNY *and* JIM *enter. Sit at table. Drink Coke. Kiss.*

Bonny is a busty blonde with teeth-braces, the set smirk of a sexual tease. To her doting father she was "Dollface," the night-shift nurse, the ward sister, floating through the wards.

She works eight hours a day with terminally ill cancer patients, hears the groans of those who have little hope, remains cheerful. Dates different boyfriends, looks forward to the time when her teeth-braces can be removed. Aged nineteen, she drinks Coke, likes brownies, likes Jim. Likes Jim *too much*, becomes pregnant.

JIM *leaves.* BONNY's DAD *shuffles in, slowly. Sees her. Stops.*

BONNY: (*Coaxing.*) "Please don't be sad, Dad."

DAD: (*Whispers.*) "Git outta ma house, ya whore."

BONNY: "Don't say that, Dad."

DAD *leaves.* BONNY *sits with her head on the table.*

PROF. HIGGINS: A Valium, a gown for Bonny, nineteen years old, with teeth-braces, three weeks pregnant. The abortion costs $225, gas $20 extra. She bleeds for thirty minutes after the operation. Lies on her bed all day and doesn't speak. Won't speak.

BONNY *leaves.*

Jim cruised by last night on his way to Nashville, a Budweiser in one hand.
*Immer denken, immer denken.*
America, often only a place in the mind.

*The bar has become a fancy restaurant.* HIGGINS *sits for dinner.*

Indoors the candles are lit, one to each table, lending a festive light to the proceedings, the daylight dying outside.

LYNN *approaches.*

Waiting on his table, the lovely Lynn. See the fresh old Professor who stared at you, Lynn, embarrassed you by an invitation out to dinner. You understood my intent at once, your amatory perception's matchless.

LYNN: (*Unemotional.*) But I have two boyfriends already.

PROF. HIGGINS: (*Logical.*) Then a third won't matter.

*Campus bell strikes quarter.*

LYNN: (*Low.*) I don't operate that way.

PROF. HIGGINS: (*Equable.*) Nothing disagreeable should ever be looked at long. (*Pause.*) Don't be a sheep.
(*Pause.*) In the dark bars they drink to forget. A fellow seated on a barstool, not moving for twenty years. The lovely Lynn passes.

LYNN: (*All business, with her notepad.*) So . . . what can I get you . . . the usual?

PROF. HIGGINS: (*Sigh.*) The usual.

LYNN *leaves.*

The fleshly presence. All the great arses, and yours like a peach by Donatello. (*Pause.*)
This isn't the real world. It's toy land, the high silliness. Strolling archetypes. Inane figurines.

CLARK BARNES *strolls into the bar. Asks the* BARMAN *if he can borrow the phone. Takes the phone and dials. The phone on the table rings.* STACEY *comes running to answer it.*

CLARK BARNES: (*Vibrant.*) Hi, Stacey! This is Clark Barnes. Remember from high school? I'm just in town for the day. Wouldja . . .

*Abruptly cut off.*

STACEY: (STACEY *opens her journal and writes.*) He took me jogging. Then on country hikes into the hills. We expressed our love in terms of deep friendship. Latterly, boyfriends had been so rough, so calculating, so cold, so unsupportive, so unfaithful, so uncaring, so distant, so Damn Cold! (*Pause, triumphant.*) Not this one! Love seemed a radical term. One day in late September we went tubing together. It was one of those days when . . .

*Abrupt fade.* STACEY *returns to the classroom. Stands and reads from her journal to the class.*

(*Lyrical.*) It was one of those days when the sky seemed to blaze with the sheer absence of clouds. Not even a fluff was visible. The sun hung like a golden fruit. It looked succulent, almost. So round. Bursting with warmth. The flowers along the riverbank were in profusion.

> She felt extremely blissful . . .
> They floated on it like swans.
> They went over the rapids laughing.
> Clark's tube was next to hers.
> She held onto it because she did not want to float away.

*Receding laughter, cries.*

(*Close.*) Then she looked into his verdant eyes as verdant as the grass. They seemed to embody all that was lovely in their flagrant greenness. She drank him in.

PROF. HIGGINS: First love, then la pharmacia. So says the cynic Cioran.

HIGGINS *at the table, marking papers.*

Sunday, 18th November. 22nd after Trinity. An unexpected visitor. The manageress of Zippy's Convenience Store around the corner: Cynthia Rose herself.
Scent of Cynthia Rose, the Acid Queen, her neck bent over the papers. Heart-shaped plastic earrings depend from her earlobes. (*Pause.*)
The dark hair and scent of her Polish-Mexican blood: Cynthia Kurkowski.
Her fresh old lecherous Professor buys her a cappuccino at Captain Quackenbush's off campus between classes.

CYNTHIA ROSE *and* HIGGINS *move to the bar.*

(*Equable.*) She was born in San Antonio, speaks Spanish, lives out of Austin with Tim and his two children, some Doberman Pinschers.
She tells the Professor of the cats in the San Antonio Zoo.

CYNTHIA ROSE: There are jaguars and cheetahs. And some other big cats.

PROF. HIGGINS: She tells hunting stories.

CYNTHIA ROSE: Brown owls roost in the hides, make their messes, leave droppings and feathers. The hunters arrive, see the mess, and blast away at the brown owls, wiping out entire families.

PROF. HIGGINS: Cynthia Rose removes her spectacles, as if removing her clothes, to stare more pointedly, nakedly at her interested Professor.

HIGGINS *exits the bar for the classroom.* CYNTHIA *finds herself alone in the bar. A man approaches. Money is exchanged for goods.*

(*Low.*) She seems permanently depressed, drops acid. The past eats at her like a big fish eating a smaller fish. (*Pause.*) She's oversold on love.

*Looking for* CYNTHIA ROSE.

Comes late to my early class when she comes at all, her black hair still damp from showering. (*Pause.*) Hollywood has much to answer for. The young are deeply confused. (*Pause.*)
My students fear to say the wrong thing. They feel threatened. They are afraid, but especially afraid of the girls' strong feelings; so loving of nature, yet so paranoid with it.

*Shuffle of feet, class assembly.*

JIM: (*Reads his paper.*) I was at Port Neches one morning, and a ship was coming up the river which flows by the park. And as the ship passed a man leaned over the rail and screamed "I love you!" to a woman who ran along the shore.

A VOICE: I Love You!

PROF. HIGGINS: (*To an attentive class.*) Richard Brautigan the Hipster Writer is dead. Shot himself in the woods in Montana.
Associated with gunslingers, Cosmic Cowboys who liked to pretend they were back in the Wild West, who shot the ranch-house

lanterns out every night, laid all in sight, were seldom sober, hardly knew themselves. High as kites on angel dust.

Brautigan, like Lucifer himself, was forced to exercise his talents in infernal regions among fallen spirits, a long way from Walden Pond. (*Pause.*) A long way from home.

*Class responds with excited chatter.* HIGGINS *approaches the audience.*

Austin population today: 436,188. The loose sun-drunk city may be the archetypal metrollops of the future.

A city geared for the young. The daylong din of Dobie Mall. Porn movies on Guadalupe. Alarms and police sirens at night. Taped music plays full blast until two A.M. in the loud bars.

Kurt Weill in Garner & Smith's bookstore. The air-conditioning may sometimes fail, but piped Muzak? Never.

Noise, racket, din, is a modern sign of Original Sin, argues Cioran. But who today believes in Original Sin? Southern Baptists believe in redemption, sure . . . (*Pause.*) For Southern Baptists. Fundamentalists believe, fundamentally, in salvation . . . (*Pause.*) For Fundamentalists. Hell-fire for the rest of us.

(*Evenly.*) The clock on the Union Building has not been functioning since Thanksgiving.

*Students speak in turn.*

STUDENTS: The Lord deliver me from assholes!

(*Deep.*) Lickin' ass from here to Santa Fe!

A fine pair of pecs!

Tight jeans can work miracles!

Keeping in shape is a full-time occupation. Some girls swim a mile a day.

(*Persistent.*) All the great arses . . . and hers like a peach by Donatello!

When the weather's hot an' sticky,
That's no time for dunkin' dickey;
But when the frost is on the pumpkin,
That's the time for dickey dumpin'.

PROF. HIGGINS: The dried-up nuts in the hackberry bush tremble. A sudden sharp love-cry comes from the girl caller in the room next to mine being ravaged in 303 Palm Springs Apartments on East 30th. It's Sunday in the Austin fall. The tremulous female cry—curlew or cat—goes straight up and hangs in the air so that you could eat your boots in mortification. In Austin, says La Salle, "the fall lasts forever."

*At his table marking papers.*

This morning I had a rare visitant at 303 Palm Springs Apartments. A strapping Amazonian belted about with equipment for dispatching rodents and roaches. The Exterminator!

The late great Borges said that he dreamed well in Austin. But I am haunted by nightmares, strange even by nightmare standards. The air-conditioning unit behind these apartments goes like a great waterfall all night. At dusk, the din of grackles.

EXTERMINATOR: (*Voice of Lauren Bacall.*) Hi, I'm the Exterminator!

*Sound of wind and grackles.*

PROF. HIGGINS: (*Resigned.*) *Immer denken, immer denken.*

A VOICE: America . . . often only a place in the mind.

*Sound of wind continues. Grackles louder.*
*Sudden silence.*

STUDENTS *standing in turn, emulating the voice of the* ANNOUNCER.

STUDENTS: (*In turn.*) Thomas Andy Barefoot, convicted of killing a policeman, was executed Tuesday night by lethal injection at the unholy hour of 12:24 A.M., at Huntsville, Louisiana.

Minutes earlier, Knighton, the killer of a service station owner, was executed in the electric chair of the State Pen at Ayolao.

Meanwhile, in Texas, convicted mass murderer Abdel Krim Belacheb is filing an appeal for a retrial.

Jinkeum Kim, 38, a native of Korea, died at Brackenbridge Hospital at 6:45 P.M. Tuesday, of a fractured skull and brain contusions. He had been mugged on Morris Williams Golf Course by a fifteen-year-old male. Kim, an engineering graduate student, was planning to return to Korea with his wife and two small sons.

In Houston a thirty-year-old man and a pregnant girl were shot to death, with robbery ruled out as motive. In Dallas, a nineteen-year-old teenager died of acute alcoholic poisoning after swallowing a half gallon of eighty-proof whiskey and several beers, in a drinking contest for a car.

(*Windily.*) In Palmdale, California, the first operational B-1 bomber was unveiled Tuesday, less than a week after the crash of the prototype strategic jet, the $220 million aircraft replacing the nation's ageing B-52 force.

*Lockheed plant, testing, under following.*

(*Warming to theme.*) Thomas Douglas Benefield, fifty-five, Rockwell International's chief test pilot, died tragically in the crash.

General Lawrence Skantze, head of Air Force Systems Command, said that the bomber rolled out on the tarmac was the dead pilot's legacy.

(*Bombastically, in echoing hanger.*) Doug, wherever you are, we are going to follow through! (*Pause.*) And we are going to do it damn well!

*Handclapping, grunts of approval.*

Air Force Secretary Vern Orr said it was a "benchmark in the defense of our nation."

(*Interrupts.*) And expressed a pious wish that it would "never fly in anger."

(*Voice of God.*) May it never fly in anger!

The nuclear bomber, worth $220 million, leveller of cities, was being lauded like a Bride. (*Pause.*)

(*Proudly.*) Four B-1s were commissioned for the Strategic Air Command in '85, thirty-two in '86, forty-eight in '87, and fourteen in '88.

(*Aside.*) The Federal Eagle, bearing an olive branch, was armed with hunting arrows.

*Mix to brass band. Marine song.*

ALL STUDENTS: (*Fullthroatedly.*)
    Like a lion in the jungle,
    Like an eagle in the sky,
    Like a shark in the ocean—
    2041, do or die!

STUDENT: (*Truculent.*) Do the Reds want war? (*Pregnant pause.*) Then we'll give it to them. (*Pause, spits.*) Get it up from the lower gut! Study your enemy. Unless you know your enemy, *you're dead!* (*Long pause, emphatic.*) Once more! There are no second chances in combat. (*Pause, pleased.*) Clean up when you finish!

PROF. HIGGINS: Texas gigantism has to be seen to be believed. The new houses are built for giants. No Texan is too big for his goddamn boots; they all have big feet, big ids, big aspirations. They eat space.

ALL STUDENTS: (*Resume.*)
> . . . The roughest, the toughest,
> The leanest and the meanest,
> The baddest motherfuckers in the whole damn valley!
> Rain makes the grass grow,
> Marines make the blood flow!
> Platton 2041, ooorah! Ooorah! oooRAH!

STUDENT: Semper Fi, do or die!

STUDENTS *take the role of the* MARINES.

MARINES: (*In turn. At attention.*) Password: Bold Reagan!
(*At attention.*) Counter Password: Nancy's hole!
(*Proudly.*) A tough, ready Marine. A *United States* Marine. Platoon 2041, U.S. Marine Corps!

*Armsdrill, distant bawling of drill sergeants.* MARINES *relax.*

(*In turn.*) Scorin' any butt. Funhauser?
Not enough, Twinkie.
Hey hotshot, I hear yare goin' to the coast with Anney! How ya makin' out? Feelin' yore oats?
Hey, Twinkie, you sure stink of score!

*Armsdrill, distant bawling of instructors. Sudden silence.*

PROF. HIGGINS: Truman intended to drop fifty atomic bombs on Japan to destroy Koyoto because the entire city was a religious shrine.

Fermi held out for moderation (only two atomic bombs) against Nobel Prizemen Lawrence and Compton, through the last desperate all-night argument.

Oppenheimer had deliberately misinformed Washington. It took twenty years for the true statistics of the Hiroshima dead to be revised from the figure given—70,000 to 130,000, and others still dying today from long-term radiation effects.

*Addressing the audience.*

The kids on the Drag and on campus here feel that they are playing parts, maybe dangerous parts. Prince Myshkin or Che Guevara or the Last Redskin: the last parts in a discontinued series; regressing to earlier states of living and being. Back to the prairies. Or, "streetwise": meaning—ignorant as dirt, the imagination of savage practices!

As long as you know where the soul is, wrote Saul Bellow, there is no harm in being Socrates. It is when the soul can't be located that the play of being someone turns desperate. At Wallace's on Guadalupe a Texan shopgirl is offering free handouts.

HIGGINS *sits for dinner at the table.*

There is probably no way for human beings to avoid playacting . . . least of all adolescents.

JIM APPLEGATE WOOD *enters.*

Jim Applegate Wood, the eccentric chef at Les Amis on 24th Street, does impersonations of Marlon Brando; contorting his features, he *becomes* Brando. Recites a line from *The Men.*

JIM APPLEGATE WOOD: What do you think I am—some sort of bug? (*Demented guffaw.*)

PROF. HIGGINS: The tall kitchen-help, a meat-chopper and fish-gutter, is got up as one of the Pirates of Penzance, and also looks crazy. Are all the cooks of Austin mad?
    I take a beer with Jim Applegate Wood. Gregorian chanting issues from the speakers. The bell on the Union Building just struck two. A fall day. On the swing in the deserted playground behind the Presbyterian Seminary and the Animal Resources Center, a giddy girl is moodily swinging her legs up. Three ambulance men with their uniform jackets off are engaged in clock-golf on a weedy green. A line of unsober merrymakers are being photographed against the side wall of the Beach Cabaret, fresco of a large turtle in a breaking wave, wading pink flamingos, under the sign: "Life's a Beach," which I'd already read as "Life's a Bitch!"
    In Miami shirts and baseball caps, unsober, themselves figures out of a frieze, they disperse. (*Pause.*) Ain't life the giddy whirl?

*A* CAMPUS POLICE OFFICER *enters.*

CAMPUS POLICE OFFICER: You got someone called Dillon workin' here?

BARMAN: (*In derision.*) I am he.

MEXICAN DISHWASHER: (*Poking his head in from backstage.*) About time they came to take you away.

CAMPUS POLICE OFFICER: (*To* BARMAN.) Can I have a quick word with you outside?

BARMAN *leaves with* CAMPUS POLICE OFFICER. *A* STUDENT *leaves the classroom to take his place. Campus bell strikes one.*

PROF. HIGGINS: Openness to experience may be something animals and birds know of. Such irrational creatures are caught in traps, in nets. Assailed by all manner of aches and pains, I am *infested* with sadness. The new, the unfamiliar, is always sad, and grows sadder. Why is that? An air of unutterable melancholy clings to Guadalupe Street, clings to the campus, infested by nearly 50,000 students. It clings to me. (*Pause.*) Comport yourself! (*Pause.*)

Compose yourself.

*Sad campus bell strikes quarter.*

That's all very well and good if you can do it.

(*Resigned.*) I cannot go forward and I cannot go backward. Austin in August was the hottest on record. 110 degrees at sundown was common. A narcotics informant was shot dead by an undercover Travis County DA investigator for bothering a woman, at a nightclub. Texas Rangers investigated this, in Burnet County adjacent to Llano County, approximately seventy miles southwest of Austin. Tempers frayed. The great heat takes its toll.

Borges claimed that he had slept well in Austin; I have nightmares, extreme even by nightmare standards.

*The* BARMAN *turns on the radio.*

ANNOUNCER: Before, there used to be an export of industry from the North to the South, and now there's an export of industry into the Third World. The reason being in both cases cheap labour and cheap operating costs. And there's nobody watching how they do it. Right?

VOICE: (*Sarcastic.*) This guy is runnin' deep.

ANNOUNCER: If you want a message from the High Technologists, it's the exact equivalent of what the Ecologists are saying. Right? If you look at Ecology and you look at Computers, it's the same Rules, the same Message. Right? We're in a direct feedback loop.

We're in a warp in history. The world is being recreated, and we're right in the middle of it. People have a lot of power right now. That's why it's important for us to spread the possibilities on the higher side of Force. Or should I say Farce? Right?

VOICE: Wrong. More suicides here than you can shake a stick at . . .

STUDENT: (*Crazy.*) I recently saw the results of a Body Image Study, revealing that a whopping sixty-one percent of women surveyed were unhappy with their Buttocks.

VOICE: (*Derisive.*) Hold your horses. Cool your jets.

STUDENT: (*Running in place and breathing hard.*) Walking, jogging, climbing stairs, skipping rope or just plain vertical jumping—that is, jumping up and down on the one spot—are great activities for shaping up your Buttocks. Try to incorporate these activities into your Lifestyle.

ANNOUNCER: Body-building! Hoopla! Hoopla! You gotta problem? Rosemary Cambell's home workouts help maintain the fit body she needs for a dual career as Trainer for the U.S. Secret Service and Model for Hawaiian Tropics and American Physical Fitness.

President Ronald Reagan was enthusiastic about Rosemary's fitness message. She designed a weight-training programme for his son.

STUDENTS (*In turn.*): When in doubt, punt! A movement has started advocating all-female graveyards.

*Bimbo-Fu* is showin' at the drive-in, with Lucinda Dickey. (*Pause.*) She sure has a great pair of pecs on her.

Medically approved electrolysis will permanently remove any unwanted hair you have. Men and Women Treated. Take it off!

Suicide on the rise among students!

Hysterical statistics.

PROF. HIGGINS: This, as sure as hell, is no country for old men. Nor old women, either. One sees very few such around the streets or suburbs of Austin. A few desperate septuagenarian joggers or other health freaks with dumbbells totter around Cherry Lane, sure, but nothing else.

To know a few Americans may be no bad preparation for meeting them in bulk; by and large they seem a kindly people. Is the courtesy genuine? Service in hotels, airports, restaurants and such places is lightning-fast, the ordering specific; the customers know what they want and like to get it.

*Beach Cabaret* BARMAN.

BARMAN: Everything okay? You want another?

*Hyde Park Bar and Grill* WAITRESS.

WAITRESS: Everything okay?

*Les Amis* WAITRESS.

WAITRESS: Enjoy your meal!

PROF. HIGGINS: Many of these already have degrees or are working their way through the College; waiting on tables or serving at bars by no means demeans them—they are pleased to be efficient, and ask so winningly: "You okay? Everything okay?"

Some male Texans like to dine and drink in high white Stetsons, perhaps go to bed in them. The rude sand-blasted face under the broad dome, brown as saddle-leather—the Marlboro Man incarnate.

They have so folded into themselves that the real world has disappeared, for them; just supposing it was ever there in the first place. Unreality is very real to them; just listen to how they speak.

*Union bell rings one o'clock. Voices.*

FIRST VOICE: Hey, asshole!

SECOND: Sucker!

THIRD: Whar' ya'll at now?

PROF. HIGGINS: They have this brawly way of speaking among themselves. Maybe it's to do with space, what-was-once. They believe it's stylish to have loud music on all the time.

EMERITUS JONES: (*Old.*) Kind Words Can Never Die.

HIGGINS *joins* LA SALLE *at the Hole in the Wall bar.*

PROF. HIGGINS: The new bar-girl at the Hole in the Wall is a good-looker, a smiler. Asked by La Salle where the other girl was, she said:

BAR-GIRL: On vacation.

PROF. LA SALLE: Where?

BAR-GIRL: (*After pause, setting table.*) In hospital.

PROF. HIGGINS: Odd place for a vacation. What was she in for?

BAR-GIRL: (*Going.*) Rectal warts.

*Walking down Sixth Street at night with* LA SALLE.

PROF. HIGGINS: "Screw Armigdoon (sic) this is hell," the graffiti reads. "Skate Tough, or Rot in hell!" On Sixth Street the topless bars are doing a roaring trade, the Happy Hour (with drinks half price) extending from four to seven. The Red Rose and the Yellow Rose are serving Double Margaritas.

WAITRESS: (*Seductively, as* HIGGINS *and* LA SALLE *pass an open door.*) Did you say you wanted sprouts?

*Din of evening assembly of grackels.*

PROF. HIGGINS: I look forward to something that hasn't happened, running away from something I've just seen. Celibate as the dodo, that farsighted loner who mates every three years, I live anywhere I am.

*Music. Harmonia, Bob Dylan.*

Out there lies the Hill Country, the rapists of Travis County, the black gumbo soil of central Texas. All of that. The panhandle. Horses. Lords of the Plains—the Comanches, told by Texan rubes to shove off. Somewhere out there too lie the prairies, land-space: the very heart of the inarticulate.

Every Saturday night, bedlam breaks loose. The Wilderness becomes all too soon Goontown. Mardi Gras, Sixth Street and Guadalupe. Even new life is fuel.

*Traffic.*

PROF. LA SALLE: (*Calling above it.*) . . . Living a life filled to the brim with Experience and Time!

*Car horn, shouting drunks.*

ROD: (*Lecher.*) I mean, she's a real sex fiend. She's, like, *shaved.* She keeps an electric friend in her room. It's "Do me like a dog." The evenings spent with her on the sand were Warm and Alive with Passion. I mean, she sounds like a real flip-tripper.

*Sixth St. Bar, loud Negro vocal, full amplification above din of bar.*

PROF. HIGGINS: The old are seen as Distinguished Momentos, and somehow superfluous, like oldstyle stoves and skillets. Or Prudence and Honesty. Or Darby and Joan. Probity!

BONNY: (*Sexual tease.*) I'm the hot girl on the sand!

PROF. HIGGINS: That's Texas.

# Discords of Good Humour

A FEATURE ON THE LIFE OF BRIAN O'NOLAN, ALIAS FLANN O'BRIEN, ALIAS MYLES NA GCOPALEEN.

Broadcast on BBC Radio 3 on the 13th of October, 1981, directed by Maurice Leitch.

# CAST

NARRATOR

NARRATOR (GERMAN)

NARRATOR (ITALIAN)

NARRATOR (FRENCH)

NARRATOR (IRISH/GAELIC)

BRIAN O'NOLAN (BOWMAN TAPE)

AMERICAN ACADEMIC

GERMAN

OLD GREY FELLOW

MISS O'FLAHERTY

DUBLINER

GEORGE GORMLEY

CIARAN O'NOLAN

KEVIN O'NOLAN

LIAM REDMOND

BARBARA REDMOND

INTERVIEWER

MYLES

TIM O'KEEFE

JOHN RYAN

LAMONT

FURRISKY

SHANAHAN

CRONIN

ARTHUR POWER

BEN KIELY

MAGEE

SIDE-KICK

# SCENES

"Into the Ditch with Me!"
*Interpolation (from "Cruiskeen Lawn")*
*Eggs (from "Cruiskeen Lawn")*

"Fit to be Rolled in the Aisles"
*Dancing in the Dark*
*"Breaking Down the Images"*
*"Was It, I Wonder, a Real Story or Was It One of Those Fantasies."*

The Background
*Steam Trains*
*Boglands*
*The Brother*

A Plethora of Pseudonyms
At Swim-Two-Birds
*"That Refurbisher of Skivvies' Stories!"*
*Dublin Conversation Overheard, from "Cruiskeen Lawn"*

The Brother
*The Flies and Liam*
*Craddock and Co.*
*In the Guise of an Uncle*

I DOUBT IF IT'S A PHOTOGRAPH OF ME AT ALL

*From* The Third Policeman

*The Chiners (Incident)*

*The Three Brothers*


RATE-PAYER'S OPINIONS

*The Rate-payer's Friend*


THE DALKEY ARCHIVE

Sources: Flann O'Brien (*At Swim-Two-Birds, The Third Policeman, The Poor Mouth, The Hard Life, The Dalkey Archive, The Best of Myles, At War, The Hair of the Dogma*); *Alive Alive O!: Flann O'Brien's At Swim-Two-Birds*, edited by Rüdiger Imhof; Anne Clune and Anne Clissman (*Flann O'Brien: A Critical Introduction to his Writings*), various BBC and RTÉ interviews.

## "INTO THE DITCH WITH ME!"

NARRATOR: As pundit and pedagogue, Myles na gCopaleen always felt free to attack not only the established living, but even question the reputations and abilities of the Established Dead. Shaw was a mountebank, O'Casey's last plays were poor things, and John Millington Synge was "a moneyed dilettante coming straight from Paris to study the peasants of Aran" . . . and "to pour forth a deluge of homemade jargon all over the Abbey stage."

Of these, some were born into poverty, others came to it in their early careers—Shaw, Yeats, O'Casey, Synge, Joyce, and Beckett in Paris until he was plucked from obscurity by the success of *Waiting for Godot*, all had been in very needy circumstances and often gone hungry.

Ellmann, Joyce's biographer, describes the fortuitous meeting of the established Yeats and the young Joyce just out of University, meeting by chance in O'Connell Street, and retiring to the "smoking section" of a restaurant, in order to disagree. "The defected Protestant confronted the defected Catholic, the landless landlord met the shiftless tenant."

All had for their only theme "the poor little brittle magic nation, dim of mind," called Ireland for short.

O'Nolan-O'Brien-na gCopaleen, who liked to invert things, himself went through a career of prime inversion. Born into comfortable means, sent to a good enough school and University, followed by a career in the Civil Service, pensioned off early (he had just turned forty, or about the age when Joyce's father was made redundant); from that point to his early death his career had gone downhill. In the last fourteen years of his life he was reduced to writing advertising copy for Guinness's brewery and the Irish Sweep. His first two books were lost, out of print, the third in a language that few could read.

Samuel Beckett had described the alternatives facing the Irish writer in the '30s as a "choice between the antiquarians and the others, the former in the majority." That was O'Nolan's time: the nervous decade that ended with the death of Yeats aged seventy-four in the South of France in 1939, the publication of *Finnegans Wake* on May 4th, less than two months after *At Swim-Two-Birds*, the outbreak of World War Two in September.

O'Nolan had been born just eleven years after the Dublin Visitation of Her Serene Royal Highness and Empress of India, the Queen, to whom Joyce kindly referred to as "the flatulent old bitch"; in her eighty-first year, with a whine in the left ventricle; she to whom all labours must be a weariness "wearing horn-rimmed glasses on a livid and empty face," had come to do the work her recruiting sergeants had signally failed to do—recruit wild Irish for the Boer War then in progress in South Africa. George Moore, the genuine Irish gent, was moving into 15 Ely Place, off Stephen's Green.

*Interpolation (from "Cruiskeen Lawn")*

. . . The landlady was telling me that he's thinkin of openin himself some night.

*What?*

You'll find he'll take the razor to the nose before you're much older. He's a man that would understand valves, you know. He wouldn't be long puttin it right if he could get his hands at it. Begob there'll be blood in the bathroom anny night now.

*He will probably kill himself.*

The brother? . . . Shure he opened Charley in 1934.

*He did?*

He gave Charley's kidneys a thorough overhaul, and that's a game none of your doctors would try their hand at. He had Charley in the bathroom for five hours. Nobody was let in, of course, but the water was goin all the time and all classes of cutthroats been sharpened, you could hear your man workin at the strap. O a great night's work. Begob here's me 'bus! (*Fade last line.*)

NARRATOR: For O'Nolan himself, or Ua Nualainn, or Flann O'Brien or Myles na gCopaleen ("Myles of the Ponies" in racing parlance) or whatever you prefer to call him, the broken lights of Irish myth, the gems of storytelling and next-door folklore, were still visible in the 1930s when he began writing a book with three openings and three endings, or was it three versions of the same beginning?

BRIAN O'NOLAN (Bowman tape): Irish properly managed is a far, far more exact language than English. The Irish mind, when there was such a thing, an uncontaminated simple one, was very much more subtle, I think, than the Saxon mind.

### Eggs (from "Cruiskeen Lawn")

The brother can't look at an egg.

*Is that so?*

Can't stand the sight of an egg at all. Rashers, ham, fish, anything you like to mention—he'll eat them all and ask for more. But he can't go the egg. Thanks very much all the same but no eggs. The egg is barred.

*I see.*

I do often hear him talking about the danger of eggs. You can get all classes of disease from eggs, so the brother says.

*That is disturbing news.*

The trouble is that the egg never dies. It is full of all classes of microbes and once the egg is down below in your bag, they do start moving around and eating things, delighted with themselves. No trouble to them to start some class of an ulcer on the sides of the bag.

*I see.*

Just imagine all your men down there walking up and down your stomach and maybe breeding families, chawing and drinking and feeding away there, it's a wonder we're not all in our graves man, with all them hens in the country.

*I must remember to avoid eggs.*

I chance an odd one meself but one of these days I'll be a sorry man. Here's me Drimnagh 'bus, I'll have to lave yeh, don't do anything when your uncle's with you, as the man said.

*Good-bye.*

NARRATOR: The dim light shone into the depth of the past, where Lady Augusta had gone to join Mary Battle, of all people.

Folk imagination, Yeats wrote, "creates endless images of which there are no ideas. Its stories ignore the moral law and every other law; they are successions of pictures like those seen by children in the fire."

Well, O'Nolan's peers had scattered before him—Shaw and O'Casey to die famous in England, Yeats buried for the time being in the South of France, Joyce buried permanently in Zurich. O'Nolan remained behind in Dublin, that most rancorous of small cities, as his talent diminished and he himself became cantankerous, to die at the age of fifty-four. Gibbon had a theory that men of imagination were dogmatic. Sorrow follows Jollity.

AMERICAN ACADEMIC: (*Boisterous.*) Flann O'Brien was an eccentric Irishman caught up in the confusion of three identities. Under his real name, Brian O'Nolan, he was an Irish Civil Servant. As Myles na gCopaleen, he was a columnist for the *Irish Times* and wrote the contemporary Gaelic classic, *An Béal Bocht*. But it was as the pseudonymous Flann O'Brien, the author of *At Swim-Two-Birds*, that he was best known. That brilliant comic curio—a novel about a student who was writing a novel—attracted praise from James Joyce and Dylan Thomas.

The latter said: "This is just the book to give your sister if she's a loud, dirty, boozy girl!"

Flann O'Brien was to be the victim of his own creation, generally acknowledged in Ireland as the pretender to the Joyce mantle, he was pursued by the ever-lengthening shadow of his own early genius.

NARRATOR: But he did not, as *TIME* magazine reported, marry a Cologne basket-weaver's daughter who died soon after, never again to be referred to by Brian O'Nolan. His books were translated into the major European languages, as his posthumous reputation began.

NARRATOR (FRENCH): In what manner was he born?

NARRATOR (GERMAN): He awoke as if from sleep.

NARRATOR (ITALIAN): His sensations?

NARRATOR (FRENCH): Bewilderment, perplexity.

NARRATOR: He was consumed by doubts as to his own identity, as to the nature of his body and the cast of his countenance. In what manner did he resolve these doubts? By writing.

NARRATOR (IRISH/GAELIC): I was coming home today from Ventry . . . and I noticed a strange, elegant, well-dressed gentleman coming towards me along the road. Since I'm a well-mannered Gael . . .

OLD GREY FELLOW: (*Hoarse whisper.*) I was coming home today from Ventry . . . and I noticed a strange, elegant, well-dressed gentleman coming towards me along the road. Since I'm a well-mannered Gael, into the ditch with me so as to leave all the road to the gentleman and not have me there before him, putrifying the public road. But alas! There's no explaining the world's wonders! When he came as far as me and I standing there in the dung and filth of the bottom of the ditch, what would you say but didn't he stop and, looking fondly at me, *didn't he speak to me*! . . .

But . . . wait! *He spoke to me in Gaelic*!

NARRATOR (IRISH/GAELIC): . . . and I standing there humbly in the dung and filth of the bottom of the ditch, what would you say but didn't he stop and, looking fondly . . .

MISS O'FLAHERTY: Everyone was anxious to talk to Myles. He would be perfectly satisfied to talk to Patrick (Kavanagh) or even to be in Patrick's company and not talk to him. One afternoon when I was in the shop . . .

NARRATOR: Who arrives in but the seldom-seen legendary Flann O'Brien, the ill-humourous Patrick Kavanagh and a third who might have been the good-hearted Ben Kiely or the toss-pot Brendan Behan.

Miss O'Flaherty's bookshop was situated just over Baggot Street Bridge and conveniently adjacent to Mooney's Pub across the road. The three roisterers had accidentally convened in the bookshop. Miss O'Flaherty had high hopes of overhearing some "gems of conversation." Little did she know this trio. Myles tended to be silent or sour depending on the time or day. Behan was a most unremittingly foulmouthed man. Kavanagh was a bowsy. Their conversation was neither illuminating nor uplifting—so much far from the gems of conversation.

## "Fit to be Rolled in the Aisles"

NARRATOR: Brian O'Nolan was born on October 5th, 1911 at number 15 the Bowling Green, Strabane in County Tyrone, under the tricky astrological sign of Libra, also called the Scales or Balance, lying between Virgo and Scorpius on the Eclipse; a nature ruled by good common sense but difficult to deal with, a loner. He was the third son in a family of twelve children, seven sons and five daughters.

His father Michael Victor Nolan—the prefixed "O'Nolan" came from the Gaelic form of the name Ua Nuallain adopted by the sons in college—was the son of a music teacher. Four brothers, two of them ordained priests, one a Carmelite nun and the other a Professor of Irish at Maynooth College, had Latin and Greek; also an abiding interest in the Irish language when it was "neither popular nor profitable." Brothers Gerald and Fergus jointly published a book in Gaelic later translated as *Intrusions*; Fergus O'Nolan wrote a one-act play which was produced by the Abbey Theatre; and Michael Nolan wrote a detective novel in English which was highly praised by the reader for Collins, who made an offer for publication, but his agent Curtis Brown advised against the small advance offered. This would be just prior to or during the Great War.

Michael Victor Nolan married Agnes Gormley in 1906 in the same parish church of Murlough near Strabane. Both parents came from Omagh where the Gormley's owned two shops, and where Michael Nolan was stationed as an officer in the Customs & Excise.

Michael Nolan taught Irish before his marriage, spoke Donegal Gaelic and was a close friend of Seamus Mac a' Bhaird, King of Tory Island. Shortly after Brian's birth the family moved to Dublin and were living in Inchicore at the time of the 1916 Rising. Receiving promotion, the father moved his family about; they were in Uddington outside Glasgow for a few years; from Inchicore to Tullamore, Strabane again, then to Herbert Place in Dublin, settling finally in Blackrock.

The War of Independence was a plume of smoke over Tullamore and grim-faced irregulars—Black & Tans—removing stones from their garden wall. Their father was then appointed Revenue Commissioner with an office in Dublin Castle; a chess-player and keen theatergoer, somewhat casual with his childrens' education—but then he had so many.

The Gormley's—the mother's family—were well-schooled, although lacking the advantages of an university education, but sufficiently close to a rich unlettered tradition to give them a command of a vocabulary and modes of speech not to be found in ordinary dictionaries. Kevin O'Nolan tells a story of two of the Gormley uncles at the Leopardstown races, and how George the racing journalist downfaced a Dubliner on the train returning to Harcourt Street Station.

DUBLINER: Is this the first time you gentlemen were at the races?

*Murmuring in the carriage, sound of the steam-train.*

(*Louder.*) Is this the first time you gentlemen were at the races?

GEORGE GORMLEY: (*Resonant Tyrone accent.*) It's the first time we were at today's races!

NARRATOR: His brother Ciaran recalls those days.

CIARAN: We are native speakers in the sense that our first language was Irish and my father was born in, both my father and mother were born in Omagh, funny enough, but they didn't meet until my mother's people had transferred from Omagh to Strabane where they had two shops actually. And what was I saying now? Yes, Strabane . . . my elder brother and Brian were born in Strabane, I think we were the only ones born there. And after he was born my father was in the Customs & Excise and he started off of course like everybody else as Customs Officer and was transferred to Glasgow, and we were there for a couple of years in this place Uddington. And then we came back to Dublin to Inchicore and we were living in Sarsfield Road there, for instance, in 1916, and I remember 1916 . . .

KEVIN: There was no sign that he was interested in writing. But he was interested in slapstick . . . monkeys driving aeroplanes.

CIARAN: He was no different in any way from the rest of us, and he did what all the rest of us did, you know. When we were living in Tullamore we used to walk in two miles to buy jotters, you see, to write rubbish in. But he never did that, you see. He never wrote, as far as I know he never wrote. He and I used to go around together and most . . . there were ten in our family you see. And most Irish families might have a big group like that. And we used to sleep together in the same bed . . . up to our University days and . . . er . . . not necessarily everywhere. But when we were living in Herbert Place . . . but I have no recollection of his writing anything up to the time he went to University, and if he had been writing anything I would have known about it.

KEVIN: In a big family . . . too big for everyone to be together . . . and what happened in our family is that the senior brothers of which he was the third, stuck around together, you know, while they were growing up, and we would become attached at various times. For example, when we were on holiday we used to go to Skerries for a couple of months in the year, in the summer. For a number of years, two years certainly, and in that time we would all tend to be together. Five of us, that is my brother Fergus immediately above me, and some of the girls might be there, or they might not. But the five of us would be out with the dog, you know.

There was a marvellous thing that happened in Skerries . . . to interrupt myself . . . one time. We had a dog called Bran, he was a Collie dog, and of course like dogs and boys you know the dog is one of them. He's out, you know, and says, "Marvellous. Where are we going next." You know, and the dog always came up with the same kind of comic thing. I don't know whether it was Brian or somebody else, but we decided to dress up the dog at one time, and we put a jersey on it, you know, front paws into the jersey, small short trousers on the back, you know, and everything. And we were going out through the back of this place, and there were people called Armstrong owned the house, you know, three old ladies, and they used to go down to the end of the garden. And it was a small house and they saw us going along with this extraordinary creature dressed like some fella on all fours, you know (*laughing*) . . . with a bright jersey and coloured pants and the little legs coming down.

And "oh!" they said. But not at all, maybe being Irish characters they just sort of took it as natural. "Oh," they said, "we'll get a flower for him," and they got a great big rhododendron and pinned it on the jersey, you know.

And anyway we went out into the fields and we were walking along. And we're walking along the road at one stage, and here were the five of us, you know, maybe six. And apparently another member walking along the gutter, you know. And there were people coming up the road. What they must have thought of this! And when they came up they began, oh, they stopped, you know, and said, scandalous, you know, a way to treat a dog, you know, and they were, you know, audibly disapproving of the whole thing. And the dog with great loyalty began to bark very fiercely at them, you know, just sort of sensed the criticism. Of course he was enjoying himself marvellously, you know. But that sort of . . . that's the sort of experience that I remember best.

## Dancing in the Dark

NARRATOR: In common with Joyce he had a strong feeling for the mythical and remote past, which presumably had once been more real than now supposed; at all events the company of "Ivy Day in the Committee Room" with their Parnell relics were to be joined by Finn MacCool and mad King Sweeny. In common with Beckett, he had an obsession with bicycles and ditches, not quite *Monsewer* Beckett's Last Ditches but recognisably Irish ditches for all that, probably found in the Co. Tyrone.

His mannered style was always as old-fashioned as Chaplin's in film, he had not found it necessary to extend his technique in the way Joyce had in the *Wake* or Beckett with *The Unnamable* and *How It Is*. What might have forced a change had not yet happened. Four years after his death the Catholic-Protestant-Presbyterian minefield went up; but he was not there anymore.

A strong vein of misogyny referred to as "the opprobrious bondage of the flesh" was always present.

A Dublin wit had once said—dispensing with the known in the interests of the alliterative—"Woman is an animal that micturates once a day, defecates once a week, menstruates once a month, and parturates once a year"—and Joyce had shocked his brother by repeating it. The "soft-skinned" animal did not feature much in O'Nolan's work. "If you are ever troubled, send for me and I will save you from the woman," the wooden-legged robber Martin Finnucane tells the wooden-legged narrator of *The Third Policeman*, who replies as woodenly: "Women I have no interest in at all . . . A fiddle is a better thing for diversion."

A phrase from *At Swim*, "You can get too much of them the same women," is a gnomic parody of a phrase from *Ulysses*, referring to horses, dropped comma and all. The man at the races is accompanied by "the big heifer of a wife standing about in the fur coat." He defended Edna O'Brien his namesake in "Cruiskeen Lawn," when the Censorship of Publications Board banned *August is a Wicked Month*. He dearly wanted his own work to be banned.

Accused of misogyny by Peter Duval Smith in a television interview he defended himself with a sour touch of the paternalistic: "We in Ireland have a different attitude to women from you over there in England." A vein of prudery not found in Joyce is there in common with Beckett. "And where is that fellow this night? In some dirty dance hall across, full of fallen women and *sheep-shucks* with less than nothing on them." It sounds like the bachelor at the door afraid to go in. *Dancing* was "a dark rite." Ireland of the '40s was obsessed with it. Women as such do not appear much in the column and are notably absent from his fiction, and when they do appear are given menial chores. Parturition in *The Hard Life* is associated with a "tidal surge of vomit" that ends it not very convincingly. It was no accident that St. Augustine was one of the heroes. The one-legged men would remain one-legged men to the bitter end. The young Joyce was not lice-ridden because lice could not live on his body; not so the narrator of *At Swim*. No symbols where none intended.

### "Breaking Down the Images"

NARRATOR: A not-generally-known side of him was the orator of University days, the leader of the opposition (he had adopted that position early on), as recalled by the actor Liam Redmond.

LIAM REDMOND: So I'll start by talking about the way he used to talk in the College. Well, Brian and Barbara and Niall Sheridan and Niall Montgomery were all graduates in the National University, UCD, University College Dublin. And Brian among his other activities liked speaking at the L&H—the Literary and Historical Society, and it was here his iconoclastic quality came out. Barbara was saying yesterday that some lady got up and said, "I'm going to talk to you about my education in France." (*Laughing.*)

Then Brian got up afterwards and said, "I'm going to talk to you about my education in Moscow." (*Laughs.*) But he was like that.

NARRATOR: When James Joyce arrived in the fall of '98 his Professor was Thomas Arnold, the brother of Matthew Arnold. Joyce was to distinguish himself as an orator in the old style of Taylor and such lofty and hostile eminences. O'Nolan, some thirty years later, was to be described as "venomous, a man in love with publicity, vain, lopsided and foolish." He admired J. C. Flood for his wit and scorching tongue, and Tim O'Hanrahan who was "a first-class debater on any subject under the sun."

CIARAN: There was always a mob standing on the landing outside the door. There were people sitting inside but most didn't . . . Well, a lot of people did go and sit inside, but he wouldn't have done that, and we were always in the mob. But he was in the mob-force and started to interrupt speeches, you see, that were being made inside or make some comment, you see, and this used to evoke great laughter, you see. But after a while he was expected, you see, and this voice right in the middle of the mob. After a time of course he was recognised, but in the beginning he wasn't known at all.

LIAM REDMOND: He was very, er . . . cat among the pigeons as a speaker. Vivian de Valera, the son of de Valera, was one of the principle speakers, but he was always terribly serious, and Brian used to take command, you know. And it was all . . . (*Laughing.*) He was over-harsh in his denigration, as it were. The people in the L&H were all . . . there was a wild element. He was writing for the College magazine, *Cromthrom Feinne* as it was first and the *National Student* as it was later. I think he wrote under the name of Brother Barnabas. And then as I told you he founded the *Blather* magazine when he was some time out of College.

NARRATOR: The standard of debate was high. Robin Dudley Edwards was Auditor at the time of O'Nolan's admission. In 1931–32, Cearbhall O'Dalaigh, future President of Ireland, was elected. O'Nolan approved of his attitude to the mob but deplored his obsessive interest in Fianna Fáil politics. "Do not," he said, "address dock labourers on Canon Law. And, if you must, speak to them in their own language. Silence them and compel their attention. Having compelled it, hold it. If you once flag, they will swamp you."

BARBARA REDMOND: He was a very good sniper. He didn't actually make speeches himself at all that I can recall. But he was very good at sniping other people.

LIAM REDMOND: He was a negative person in ordinary life, really. I suppose that was part of his iconoclasm, as it were; that he was an iconoclast really and so was rather inclined to say no rather than yes to things—because he was breaking down the images as it were.

In the latter part of his life I think he must have become quarrelsome, but at the stage when I knew him he wasn't at all quarrelsome. He was sharp in his criticism of things, but never quarrelsome.

There was a shyness in the man. I don't think he was a very public man. He was a very private person, and I think that would explain the pseudonyms; that probably with each one he felt a certain reluctance to appear before the public, as it were. And this was a kind of barrier between him and the public. And yet there was a great shyness about Yeats as well. Behind the public image there was a great shyness there too.

### *"Was It, I Wonder, a Real Story or Was It One of Those Fantasies."*

KEVIN: Yes, and I think that the sort of looking at the whole history of Ireland was really getting a bit thin. I mean Finn and all those people were revered figures. And there's another way of looking at them. These people existed, you know. Sweeny and so on. It's really funny if a man is crucified to such an extent, you know, and he used to say when he was nearly dying: "You know," he says, "being ill is no joke, you know." But he'd make a joke of things, you know.

BEN KIELY: He could pick on a name and make a fantasy out of it. Like Ardstraw near Newtownstewart, you know, which to him was always a fantasy-name. Then I remember telling him there's a local ballad up there in Drumquin about the River Derg which flows down from Loch Derg and actually flows into the Mourne at Ardstraw—which is an old diocesan name oddly enough. But the line goes when it reaches the town it gives a ha ha for the joy of flowing through to bonny Ardstraw. And he would pick on names like that and make fantasies out of them.

KEVIN: He'd make a joke of things . . . I remember we were a number of us, a number of the family on this occasion, we were in a pub in Booterstown—Gleeson's—and he was there, and we were just sitting on our own and a whole lot of people round about were just listening in to what he was saying. And it had no importance in itself, in fact he was describing—he said—he had a cat there at the time and he said, this cat had a kitten, you know. And he said, there's obviously going to be a birth. And finally the kitten arrived and it was, he said, *a ball of fire*, it was all . . . came into the world scratching and clawing its way, you know, and a fierce little thing. And then he talked about the mother cat sitting on the roof and saying, "God, what have I brought into the world!"

BEN KIELY: Just as Santry Court, you know where the place is, his great house at Santry, that ran all through the column and which was a long-continuing fantasy with him. The horsey women who came to see him and before he could intervene had been yoked into his carriage by his footmen, because they looked like horses. And then he had a showroom, a jumping-ground in either his dining room or drawing room at Santry, and he would do a faultless round regularly at intervals to show that he was no clodhopper. Ridiculous things like that.

KEVIN: And yet all these people were just listening to this totally, you know. No, not funny, but it was the sort of thing that you made the thing fascinating by describing and ascribing a certain, you know, attitude to the mother cat and all that sort of thing. That's the sort of thing he did very easily in conversation. He was always trying to reproduce what he enjoyed himself, you know, a kind of slapstick sort of thing. But just something that seemed to be leading somewhere and was interesting on the way, but not coming to any great conclusion.

# The Background

NARRATOR: We spoke to his brother Ciaran, editor of the Irish magazine INU in Dublin.

CIARAN: My elder brother and myself and Brian were born in Strabane. I think we were the only ones born in Strabane. And after he was born my father was in the Customs & Excise and he started off of course like everybody else as a Customs Officer, and he was transferred to Glasgow. We were there a couple of years living in this place Uddington, and then we came back to Inchicore and we were living in Sarsfield Road there, for instance, in 1916. And I remember 1916. In 1917 he was promoted to Surveyer Unattached, which meant he would be moved around from one town to another. So he decided that the best thing he could do would be to go and take a house in Strabane where my mother would be near her relatives, you see. Which he did, and that was Ballycolman Lane as it was then called and now it's Ballycolman Avenue . . . You see as I say, when we were young we all did the same thing and for instance we produced our own films when we were in Tullamore . . . Well, we used to . . . and walk, and we were living in the big house outside Tullamore two miles out, and we used to go into the films there. And of course that was the big thing at the time. So we decided to make our own, show our own films—was that in Tullamore? Yes it must have, it must have been, yes at Tullamore.

And we had discovered a large lens in the house and we mounted it, you see, on a sort of frame. And of course the only source of light we had was the oil lamp, but if you put an oil lamp behind a lens like that and station it at a proper place . . . And we used to draw whole stories, you see, with ink on strips of paper, and we would then just put a drop of oil on the paper, it would spread out and make it transparent, sufficiently transparent to be shown on the screen you see. Well, that was all, nothing to it.

You must remember that we were not at school until we returned to Dublin in 1923. He was twelve years of age before he went to school. I was thirteen. My older brother was old enough to be leaving school when he went there first . . . My father got out an Irish paper that existed at that time, *Fáinne an Lae*, which could be translated as "The Dawn." "The Dawn Weekly." There were manuscripts by my father in the house, I don't know if they're extant now. There was a novel and a letter from an agent in London, Curtis Brown I think is the name, who advised him against accepting some offer that was made for it. Then he used to collaborate with another uncle of mine, his brother Fergus O'Nuallain, who actually had a one-night play produced at the Abbey in 1920, on that date here. And these were the actors: F. J. McCormack, Barry Fitzgerald, Maureen Delaney, Katherine Fortune. But he used to be a regular theatergoer, he used to go to the Abbey Theatre.

NARRATOR: That's the background. A big family moved about, schooling delayed, the father's attempt at educating them, their free time in the fields around Tullamore in the Midlands. The father wrote in English a detective novel for which an offer was made, title forgotten and manuscript lost in the moving about. Brian was five at the time of the 1916 Rising when the family lived in Inchicore, which may go to explain a later obsession with steam-men and steam-trains. His alter ego Myles writing an open letter to Lord Glenavy, one of the Directors of the Great Southern Railway:

"Dear Glenavy—From letters appearing over your name in the newspapers I infer that you are a steam fan. Accept my oath that I make no jocose distinction as between steam and electric fans but rather that I credit you with the wish that the Irish railway world should yet enter upon a golden era, playing a noble part in the transportation problems that await us in the new Ireland when once more the sword is sheathed and happier counsels are permitted to prevail. If in this belief I do you no injustice, will you kindly let me know why my proposal for fitting Irish locomotives with thermic siphons was scotched by a boardroom ukase in 1919? Is it because those siphons are made of copper that my proposal was not acceptable to the vested tin-trusts? Je suis, dear Glenavy, bien cordialement, à vous,

gCOPALEEN
Cabman's Shelter,
Broadstone.

*Steam Trains*

NARRATOR: (*Reading two parts.*) Your man is here.

The boss says your man is to be watched.

Don't let your man near the engine.

Your man'll do something to this train if we aren't careful.

There'll be a desperate row if your man is let up in the engine.

Your man ought to be heaved out of here, he'll do something before he goes and gets somebody sacked over it.

Don't let your man near the sheds.

NARRATOR: The Myles na gCopaleen Central Research Bureau, having already distinguished itself by inventing an intoxicating ice-cream called "Trink" and a new Dublin street-lighting system manufactured cheaply from sewer gas, now turning its energies to the problem of maintaining efficient railway services in those days of inferior fuel, duly came up with an ingenious solution. All the lines were to be re-laid to traverse bogland only, and the locomotives fitted out with a patent scoop apparatus which would dig into the bog underneath the moving train and supply an endless stream of turf to the furnace, to be dried in the furnace before being consumed. But there were difficulties.

### Boglands

NARRATOR: (*Reading.*) . . . an express careening across a bog at full tilt might encounter a quagmire and disappear into the bowels of the earth, passengers and all. To prevent this, it would be necessary to precede every heavy train by a light engine fitted with a prodding apparatus. This would consist of a battery of steel poles, which would be fitted to the front of the engine. The poles would rise and fall as the engine proceeded, probing carefully into the nature of the bog strata and ringing bells in the driver's cabin where the resistance encountered was less that a given limit. When the bells are heard, the driver would press a button and set in motion another machine at the engine's rear. This rear machine would consist of mammoth pounders, which would descend on the bog, feed builder's rubble into it and pulverise it to a suitable firmness . . .

Another snag is the difficulty of finding continued bogland between, say, Dublin and Galway . . . Our plan will be to follow the bog wherever we find it and get to Galway one way or another, even if we have to spend weeks in the train and wander through every county in Ireland. The unrelieved bogland scenery on such a journey would be a bit tedious on the eye, but telescopes could be supplied for viewing the more distant vistas.

Then there is another snag: After the train has been scooping along for a week or so, the trench between the rails will become gradually deeper, and there will be a tendency for water to drain into it, Nature being what she is. If the engine encounters a damp patch the scoop will deliver gallons of water to the firebox and put the fire out. Our obvious remedy here is an army of men equipped with giant sponges. Night and day these sponges must be used to drain the scoop-trench . . .

Then, supposing the train ploughs into some of our bogland poteen deposits. A keg of the drastic brew is scooped into the fire and a blinding blue flash is seen to envelop the engine. The train pulls up and the passengers dismount to root madly in the bog with their nails, like the beasts of the field. When they have found any other kegs that may be buried in the vicinity and duly refreshed themselves they resume their journey. . .

The Great Northern Railway Company have courteously informed me that they are unlikely to operate my scheme, owing to the scarcity of bogland in their territory. The Great Southern Company, however, are experimenting somewhere in Kildare.

BARBARA REDMOND: Well, I met him in Donegal and I must say the only thing he had to say about the place was to tip us off about a particular kind of whiskey. It was a roundish bottle plastered with shamrocks and said Fine Old Irish Whiskey, and it really was very good whiskey. And they were very evasive when they asked where to get more of it, really get you a drop. I think it's fairly obvious what it must have been.

Brian had some pal in the Customs & Excise department where they had to take a glass out of every bottle. Maybe a glass out of one bottle in the case. And this friend of his was known as The Man With a Load of Mischief, and he arrived with a suitcase full of, almost full of, all kinds of things. Port, Chartreuse, you name it, it was there.

He was always very kind to me, very nice to me. He was fond of me, I don't know why, but he just was. He kept visiting me, went right out of his way in Donegal when he heard that I was staying with some people there. That's when he told me about the Fine Old Irish Whiskey.

He was quite small really, not much taller than I am. I'm five foot two. He was slightly podgy but not fat. I can't explain it, if you caught him by the cheeks your fingers would go in a little. Er, very pallid, I'm not sure even what colour his eyes were. I think they were grey. He had a kind of grey appearance. He usually wore an overcoat, which wasn't all that common, and this hat, but I don't think it was any special kind of hat. It was just hardly anybody wore one. He did. Smyllie did, um, O'Connor did, Austin Clark did. But mostly people didn't wear hats at all, which was why it was noticeable.

He really wasn't a heavy drinker when I knew him. He was barred from the Scotch House eventually, but that wasn't because of losing his temper and drinking too much. You see the Palace now was different. There was Men Only and a particular time they drank through the Holy Hour. Oh no it was on Christmas Day you drank through the Holy Hour, but I don't know really. I can't recall him drinking. I honestly never saw him drunk. I'm sure he was, but I never saw him.

### The Brother

NARRATOR: (*Reading two parts.*) The brother was makin inquiries about the pubs. Peepin in here and there, askin an odd question, chattin the curates, maybe takin an odd sip for himself on the Q.T. Do you know what the brother says?

*I do not.*

The brother says there's stuff been got ready.

*Indeed?*

The brother says there's special stuff been got ready for the Christmas.

*You mean inferior and poisonous potions?*

The brother says there's lads below in the cellars at the present time getting stuff ready be the bucketful. They do be below in the daytime mixin stuff in firkins. Whiskey by yer lave. For the Christmas. Two bob a glass.

*Surely the police should be informed?*

There's mixtures been made up that was never made up before. This year it's goin to be the works altogether.

*Surely the reputable houses in their own interest should communicate with the police?*

I'll tell you another thing. The brother says there's a black market in turps.

*Indeed?*

Yer men use a lot of turps for the mixtures, you know. Turps, sherry-wine and a drop of the Portuguese brandy that was brought in early in the war. That's yer glass of malt. And I'll tell you a funny wan. Do you know what a fine old glass of brandy is, three and six a knock?

*I do not.*

Turps and sherry-wine.

*You astound me.*

The brother says the North of Ireland crowd is goin to be sorry men.

*You mean the undiscerning stranger will be poisoned?*

And there's wan particular crowd getting their own cigars and cigarettes ready, the brother says. Word'll be sent round that so-and-so has bags of cigarettes and your men will march in and do their drinkin there. First they'll get the sherry-wine and the turps. Then on top of that the special fags got ready downstairs be the boss himself. And goin out, a half-naggin of turps for the morning.

*I sincerely hope you exaggerate.*

NARRATOR: Dr. Moorehead wrote to Oliver St. John Gogarty in America: "We carry on quietly, rather depetrolised and daily more or less petrified by censorship and rumour." Standing at the front window of his house in Morehampton Road, Seamus O'Sullivan watched a man passing with a load of manure. "I see Paddy Kavanagh's moving," he reported. "There go his furniture and effects."

While England was bending to the blast, Ireland was sleeping. Cecil ffrench Salkeld, Brendan Behan's father-in-law to be, was receiving guests in his bedroom, discussing ballistics. In the noisy company of Behan himself, Myles was retrieving his watch from a pawnshop in Cuffe Street, en route by taxi to the Brazen Head.

It was the Dublin of Clann na Poblachta, Clann na Gael, the Catholic Truth Society, the Knights of St. Columbanus, Alcoholics Anonymous, Edwards and MacLiammoir at the Gaiety, Lord and Lady Longford at the Gate. Alton at Trinity and Tierney at UCD. Maritana and the Yeoman of the Guard, Messengers of the Sacred Heart, Pimms and Arnotts, Switzers and Brown Thomas, the Bailey and the Bodega, Jammet's and Davy Byrne's, the Metropole and Savoy, the Carlton and the Capital.

The imagination going back. Elvery's and Findlater's, Grangegorman Asylum and St. John of Gods, Sinn Féin in office.

It was that Dublin then and I remember it well.

The Walls of Limerick, Rodney's Glory, the Star of Munster and the Rights of Man! Huge Civic Guards armed with truncheons walked the streets. Myles wrote in the *Irish Times*: "Your men of the *United Irishmen* interpret freedom as a system whereby the fancies of clods are to be imposed by force on everybody." And Andy Clarkin's clock was still stopped. Would it ever go again?

Myles wrote in "Cruiskeen Lawn," "We in this country had a bad time through the centuries when England did not like us." Now it was England's turn again.

A Paul Vincent Carroll play was running at the Abbey. Myles suggested an inverted Abbey-plot: "[T]hree bangs of the gong up with the curtain and on the stage twelve characters sunk in a frightfully Celtic condition of rural lunacy. *Then one by one they all get better.*"

No one knew of De Selby the eccentric savant found not in the text but in the voluminous footnotes of a novel set in an Irish revolving hell, as the typescript had been (a) lost in the Dolphin Hotel, (b) left in a tram, (c) chapter by chapter blown from the boot of a car and lost over Bloody Foreland (the novel had in sorry fact been rejected by Longmans at a time when hell itself was drawing closer)—De Selby with his Thoreauesque notion of contaminated human dwelling places. His creator, in the public persona of Myles na gCopaleen, considered a belowground dwelling place, the downward house. Six cogent reasons were advanced; four drawbacks given:

1. No back door.

2. Danger of flooding.

3. Danger of astronomy becoming an obsession with all householders.

4. Danger to inebriates in manipulating a horizontal hall-door.

And add to those, if you want to be funny, the danger of people dropping in on you at all hours.

If you reflect, however, you will see that most of the disadvantages of the underground house are bound up with the householder's persistence in the old habit of going 'out'—that is, up, and out along the crust of the earth . . . Consider a clerk living in a small basement flat on the outskirts of London. He gets up so early that he does so in darkness nearly all the year round. He rushes up and out and after a few seconds on the surface, he has disappeared into the bowels of the earth to get a train to town. His office, even if not a basement, will be dark and sepulchral. He goes home by tube and is soon asleep in his underground bed. He has never really been up or out at all, and if private subterranean accommodation roads could be built from underground houses to tubes and underground traffic arteries of one kind and another, an entire city could be permanently submerged, with no worse effects than an owl-eyed and untanned citizenry.

A lot of nonsense is talked about the sun . . . Better the genial battery that has ever digested and stored the sunlight—the earth. Go into the earth, burrow into your progenitrix, live among your travelled and returned predecessors, lie on top of your descendants.

We who are Irish come from the earth of Ireland and to it we will one day return. I am not sure that we have not taken a grave risk by coming up at all." (*Pause.*)

"The room where I found myself was thick with dust, musty and deserted of all furniture. Spiders had erected great stretchings of their web about the fireplace. I made my way quickly to the hall, threw open the door of the room where the box was and paused on the threshold. It was a dark morning and the weather had stained the windows with blears of grey wash which kept the brightest parts of the weak light from coming in. The far corner of the room was a blur of shadow. I had a sudden urge to have done with my task and be out of this house forever."

This from the beginning of *The Third Policeman*. He is about to remove the black box which unknown to him has been booby-trapped by his companion and co-murderer Divney. The murdered man sees his murderer and off they go together, *shackled by a common guilt.*

Yeats had written elsewhere: "There are two living countries, one visible and one invisible, and when it is summer there, it is winter here, and when it is November with us, it is lambing-time there."

And again: "There is a war between the living and the dead and the old Irish stories keep harping on it."

## A Plethora of Pseudonyms

LIAM REDMOND: Well, actually he first wrote in Irish. It was in the Palace Bar that controversy between O'Connor, O'Faolain and himself started.

NARRATOR: The Palace Bar! Cyril Connolly who had been on the fringes of the Spanish Civil War, retreated appalled from this hostile hostelry—"an alligator tank!" When Frank O'Connor's Abbey play *Time's Pocket* was lambasted by the Dublin critics and defended by fellow Corkman Sean O'Faolain, Brian O'Nolan attacked both under a smokescreen of pseudonyms. This row was carried on in a most public fashion in the correspondence columns of the *Irish Times*. Some time later O'Nolan and his UCD friend Niall Sheridan attacked Edwards and MacLiammoir under a plethora of pseudonyms known only to the instigators themselves. One of the names used was Hazel Ellis. The real Hazel Ellis, who had had a play put on at the Gate, went to their defence; whereupon she was attacked by the false "Hazel" (Brian O'Nolan himself) who denounced her as an obvious imposter. So much fur and feather flew it was impossible to say who was real and who was not.

LIAM REDMOND: It was in the Palace Bar . . . and Brian was writing letters to the *Irish Times*, and I remember I spoke to Smyllie about it.

I said, "Why don't you get Brian to write a column for you?" And he said it was a jolly good idea. And then I went to Brian and said "Well, why don't you instead of writing all these letters, why don't you write a column for the *Irish Times*?" And he said "I think that's a marvellous thought." And so they got together but you know (*laughing*) the astonishing thing was he didn't write a column in English, *he wrote a column in Irish*! That was the first thing that ever appeared.

NARRATOR: Barbara Redmond recalls that his first column in English was on St. Patrick's Day, but of course St. Patrick was really an Englishman.

The column began in late 1940 and was to run for a quarter of a century, with illustrations from a Victorian encyclopedia claimed as the columnist's own woodcuts. Five articles appeared before the hornets' nest stirred, composed of West Britains and Gaelic revivalists.

The man who was more inclined to say: "No" than "Yes" had found his metier, his platform and his public, or they had found him, and they would not let him go until the day he died. Indeed the column ran on the day he died, April Fool's Day '66, and would continue to run after his death, as if his passing hardly mattered, some proof of immortality perhaps.

The more rigid, old-fashioned Gaelic revivalists were driven up the walls by his mockery—so Ben Kiely said. The Hon. Patrick Cambell wrote the "Quidnunc" column and editor Smyllie was the avuncular Nichevo on Saturdays. Hiring staff was done on a hit-or-miss basis. The Irish Times circulation of 30,000 began to rise almost at once.

All Ireland read Myles: I have seen old Martin O'Donnell, a bilingual islandman, studying back numbers in his inglenook on Inishere.

Myles na gCopaleen—as his late Features Editor expressed it—sprang fully grown from the brain of Brian O'Nolan in the autumn of the year 1940. Ireland of the 1940s had need of a satirist, and now Ireland had found one.

It began in Irish and in Gaelic script, so that neither the editor nor ninety percent of the readership could understand it; six articles a week, three in Irish and three in English, but by 1945 an article in Irish was a rarity. Editor Smyllie liked to tease and provoke the prejudices of the Gaelic-Leaguers.

## At Swim-Two-Birds

NARRATOR: Our author argues that "a satisfactory novel should be a self-evident sham to which the reader could regulate at will the degree of his credulity." Characters are to be allowed "a private life, self-determination and a decent standard of living" and should be "interchangeable as between one book and another." "Characters possess not only an independent existence which can be carried over from one book to another, but they move from one to another of the three plots of the same book."

It was five years in the writing, taking the author from the age of twenty-two to twenty-seven, reduced by his friend Niall Sheridan (the fictional "Brinsley") by one-fifth from eight hundred pages to three-hundred odd, and odd they certainly were. What remains are the three main plots.

Mr. Mays of University College describes it: "First there is the story of the narrator himself, his life at home with his uncle and as a student in University College; second, there are his occasional ventures into the legendary world of Finn McCool and the Frenzy of Sweeny; and last there are his incursions into the fictional world of Dermot Trellis."

All three plots move at speeds appropriate to the worlds they inhabit. The frame story moves carefully through the seasons of the narrator's final undergraduate year; by contrast the Finn story is timeless, recurring through the book as if at random and with minimal progression; the Trellis story moves between the two . . .

The effect of three narratives moving forward at an unsynchronized pace and at different removes of sympathy from the author who stands behind them, the movement from one world to another unprepared, the insertion of extracts drawn from such random sources as Falconer's *Shipwreck* and a forty-volume *Conspectus of the Arts and Natural Sciences*, in particular the complications and inversions of the Trellis plot, is of a swirling phantasmagoria in which a great deal of movement is accompanied by less advance."

Commentaries on this flush oddity of modern Anglo-Irish fiction, praised by Joyce but dismissed by its author as a "painfully bad book," produce a sub-species.

Witness Mr. Graham Greene's 1939 Pantheon blurb for the American edition, with reference to "the absurd Harry Casey"; when those who know the book know only of Jem Casey, Poet of the Pick and Bard of Booterstown, who was probably related to "John Casey" in Joyce's *Portrait of the Artist*, who was in life John Kelly of Tralee, imprisoned several times for Land League agitation and taken in by Joyce's father. Mr. Mays himself refers to "Cashel" Byrne. Now no such character exists in the book. I once had the pleasure of meeting the voluntarily bedridden "real" character on which the fictitious "Michael Byrne" (painter, poet, composer, pianist, master-printer, tactician and authority on ballistics) was based: Cecil ffrench Salkeld, father-in-law to Brendan Behan. I spoke to him of *At Swim-Two-Birds*, not knowing then that he was supposed to be a character in the book. It was more complicated than that; he had a fixed notion that he himself had written it. It was his habit to rise about six in the evening and stay up all night. When I met him he wasn't rising at all. Guests were received in the bedroom.

Of course everybody was somebody once, no matter how insignificant now. Pisser Burke was really Pisser Duff, the violent ostler and friend of Citizen Cusack founder of the Gaelic League a couple of years after the birth of James Joyce; and Pisser Duff had really been beaten to death by the police in Gardiner Street in or around 1892, a short time after Gerard Manley Hopkins had held the chair of Classics at UCD "in a state of exalted misery" just before Joyce arrived there.

Earlier in the century a certain lover called Bloom, namesake of Mr. Joyce's man of many devices, had done-in his girl, botched his own suicide, and scrawled once, not thrice, LOVE on the wall.

In *At Swim-Two-Birds* there was a suggestion that both Sergeant Craddock and Bagenal of Cork, Champion of All Ireland at the long jump, were somehow related to Joyce's grandfather, who had held the record for the hop, skip and jump in Queen's University, Cork, a generation earlier; and all were related to mad King Sweeny who could get from Dublin to Carlow in one leap.

At the turn of the century a man called Myles Joyce had swung for a crime he had not committed, after a trial not one word of which he had understood.

"The traits featuring the *chiaroscuro* coalesce, their contrarieties eliminated, in one stable somebody"—wrote Mr. Joyce in the convoluted lingo of the *Wake*.

And: "A brother," said he, "is as easily forgotten as an umbrella."

INTERVIEWER: Were you a close friend of your brother?

KEVIN: Not outside the family sense, I wasn't you know. I wasn't literary except more or less . . .

INTERVIEWER: Was there anybody in the family that he would be an intimate of?

KEVIN: He would be intimate enough with Ciaran during his College time. But Ciaran wasn't particularly interested in English writing at the time, although he did some of it himself. But they would be together with people like McManus and there was a chap called Quigley.

INTERVIEWER: These are two of the seven brothers of Brian O'Nolan: Kevin and Ciaran—the Gaelic scholar who didn't care for the rash exuberances of *At Swim-Two-Birds.*

CIARAN: Well, I never liked it. And I put it as the last of us. But I don't think . . . I'm not sure that the views of the family about . . .

INTERVIEWER: No better than the author himself liked it, twenty-two years after the publication when he was interviewed by John Bowman in Dublin.

MYLES: I cannot express my detestation for that damn book. There must be some diabolical code, some anagram buried in it . . . a painfully bad book.

CIARAN: He was no different in any way from the rest of us and he did what the rest of us did, you know. He showed no signs of . . . of being different from us in any way.

KEVIN: I think it's extraordinary in a way. But I mean I can't . . . there's nothing I can say that can explain it in any way. Because it just suddenly happened without any great interest on his part . . . It was very comic to him when he was doing it, he must have worked quite hard on it in the sense that it took a lot of time. But he didn't really spend a lot of time writing even, at any time, you know.

I remember Paddy O'Leary saying that he came up one day and said "I'll have to have an article in this evening." You know. And he sat down and typed it up. He typed all his work latterly, directly you know. But he had it done in a very short time, you know.

NARRATOR: Does anyone know anything about the genesis of *At Swim-Two-Birds*? Was it done in great secrecy?

KEVIN: Not at all, no. It was just a manuscript which was in the house. And he was typing away, and he was working on it and working very extensively at the typewriter. But it just suddenly came out. I mean you could say it started well after he went to College, which was 1935. Say from 1936 to the time it was published, which was 1939 I suppose. It would have been done in two years, along with a lot of other work.

He wanted to have another academic year, you see. He was finished with his degree and he wanted to do something and he picked what I think was an easy supervisor, who was Agnes O'Farrelly who was in charge of poetic studies and that sort of thing, to do the degree under, rather than somebody like Bergin.

NARRATOR: Is she alive?

KEVIN: No. She's dead a long time. She was a very easygoing kind of person. And a very serious man would have been Osborn Bergin. If he wanted to do a degree of Irish study of some kind, and got him, it would really be a whole-time job. You know, to satisfy him. And he picked this thing and was given . . . "Nature Poetry in Irish." He really liked it, I think, and got a lot out of doing the thing. But the actual thesis was a very straightforward sort of thing, you know, cataloguing different poems, and all that sort of thing, and talking about them in a critical way.

. . . I think, as I was saying, that a terrible lot of his own life is in the thing. But in a distinguished way, you know. Like experiences of, funnily enough, in . . . *At Swim* was written in Blackrock in maybe 1937 and a terrible lot of it goes back to pre-1927.

Like the scene of the . . . is really Herbert Place, you know. Not where we were living in Blackrock. And things like that. So that I think the father . . . that would be his father when he did his degree.

And talking about coming in and being given a watch and all that. All this is fiction, but slightly . . . but no, reproducing his own experience that he was engaged on while he was in the College and doing . . . oh you know things, there's stories told about him by all sorts of people, mainly in the L&H and places like that. Really being a student and not apparently being very serious about his academic work. And then he does well when the thing comes, and he describes the author coming home and being given a watch by the uncle, you see. Well, there is no uncle in the house, you see . . . there's no father either, you see. The family really is . . . it's made out of all his experience, and the physics and so on that comes into it, it's really part of his school work really. And even the chap that's writing . . . the character writing about the author and closing the copy-book, and there's a whole row of DON'T CROSS THE STREET WITHOUT LOOKING BOTH WAYS. Now it's just absolutely history, if you go back you can get it, if you go back and find these copy-books, you see. And you'll find all that to the letter, written out in them, you know. So that in a way he was really pushing into service the slightest element. That's why I find it a bit strange that this should fascinate people.

Maybe it's how it's done.

If you know, your ordinary experience seems to be . . . well, it's mundane, it's everyday.

Who would ever bring the back of a copy-book, what somebody wrote for children, into a serious work, you see. But everything was brought into this, you know. Personal experiences, remarks of people and everything like that, it's all sort of . . . And the art or impressiveness I suppose is in making this material all work together.

. . . There's a terrible lot of his own life in it. Trellis's house was really 25 Herbert Place . . . the top rooms had to have curtains put on them to give the impression the house was occupied.

## "*That Refurbisher of Skivvies' Stories!*"

NARRATOR: On his honeymoon in Paris in May 1939, Niall Sheridan conveyed a presentation copy of *At Swim-Two-Birds* to Joyce at 34 rue des Vignes. A large woven rug covered the floor with a design showing the course of the River Liffey from source to mouth. The Master thought well of it; what he said to Beckett and what Beckett said to O'Nolan back in Dublin, and the young O'Nolan's impudent reply, Beckett told Anne Clissman, author of a critical study of O'Nolan, is "best forgotten."

Beckett himself repeated the rebuff to me twice, the second time in Berlin with emphatic distaste. "His reply was the following," Beckett said—"Joyce, that refurbisher of skivvies' stories!"

*At Swim-Two-Birds* did rather less well than Joyce's first published work: 244 copies sold in the first six months as opposed to 499 of *Dubliners* in the same period, twenty-five years before. Sales of the latter then sank very low and the entire stock of the former went up in the Blitz in the company of Beckett's *Murphy*.

Joyce's father had urged his gifted son, on graduation from UCD, to try for a clerkship in Guinness's brewery. The fates of second books from both these writers were curious—*Stephen Hero* thrown into the fire, recovered, amalgamated into *A Portrait of the Artist as a Young Man*; O'Nolan's *The Third Policeman*, set in hell, refused by Longmans, and not appearing until twenty-seven years later in 1967, a year after the author's death.

*Dublin Conversation Overheard, from "Cruiskeen Lawn"*

I tried to get it many a time. O many a time.

Well I could never see any harm in it.

I seen it once in a shop on the quays, hadn't any money on me at the time and when I came back to look for it a week later bedamn but it was gone. And I never seen it in a shop since.

Well, I can't see what all the fuss was about.

You read it, did you?

I couldn't see any harm at all in it there was nothing in it.

I tried to get it many a time meself . . .

There's no harm in it at all.

Many's a time I promised meself I'd look that up and get it.

Nothing at all that anybody could object to, not a thing in it from the first page to the last.

It's banned o'course.

Not a thing in it that anybody could object to . . .

NARRATOR: It was the Dublin of Eire Abu, the Knights of Columbanus, St. Vincent de Paul, Maritana and the Yeoman of the Guard, *The Rugged Path* at the Abbey, hand-cranked gramophones, "In Cellar Cool," horse dung on the streets, high unemployment and a low standard of living. Strong basement smells assailed all nostrils. Old Dublin was so picturesque, Myles wrote in "Cruiskeen Lawn," that you "can smell its nostalgic charm when the mail boat is ten miles out coming in by Lambay."

# THE BROTHER

NARRATOR: (*In two voices.*) I was out in a boat with the brother down in Skerries, where he's stopping with the married sister. On his holliers, you know. A great man for the sea, the brother.

*Indeed?*

Ah yes. If the brother had his way, of course, it's not here he'd be but off out with the real seafarin men, dressed up in oil-skins, running up and down ropes and all the rest of it.

*I see.*

The brother was givin out about the seals. "Tumblers," he called them. The brother says all them lads should be destroyed.

*That would be a considerable task.*

They do spend the day divin and eatin mackerel. If them lads had their way, they wouldn't leave a mackerel in the sea for you and me or the man in the next street. They do swally them be the hundred, head an' all. And the brother says they do more than that—they do come out of the water in the middle of the nighttime and rob gardens. You wouldn't want to leave any fancy tomato plants around. And you wouldn't want to leave one of your youngsters out after dark, either, because your men would carry it off with them. The brother says they do take a great interest in the chisels. They do the barkin out of them during the day-time at the chisels on the beach.

*That is most interesting.*

The brother says the seals near Dublin do often come up out of the water at nighttime and do be sittin above in the trams when they're standin in the stables. And they do be upstairs too. Begob the brother says it's a great sight of a moonlight night to see your men with the big moustaches on them sittin upstairs in the trams lookin out. And they do have the wives and the young wans along with them, of course.

*Is that a fact?*

Certainly, man. The seals are great family people, always were. Well then the brother was showin me two queer lookin men with black and white feathers on them and black beaks, out sittin there in the water.

*Two birds?*

Two of the coolest customers I ever seen, didn't give a damn about us, although we went near enough to brain them with the oars. Do you know the funny thing about them lads?

*I do not.*

Them lads takes a very poor view of dry land. Never ask to go near the land at all. They do spend their lives sittin on the sea, bar an odd lep into the air to fly to another part of it. Well do you know what I'm going to tell you, I wouldn't fancy that class of life at all.


### The Flies and Liam

LIAM REDMOND: I don't know whether it was—Barbara brought back the two volumes of *Ulysses* from Paris. And I loaned him the first volume of it, of *Ulysses*, and he kept it for a long time; and then he came back to me and said, "Can I have the second volume—I'm only half-educated." (*Laugh.*)

The first one, *At Swim-Two-Birds*, the reception may have disappointed him; though we were all very enthusiastic about it, his friends were all very enthusiastic. It was a little bit in advance of its time; though Joyce had been there a long time before that.

KEVIN: It's only a small paragraph . . .

LIAM REDMOND: Now one of the interesting things was that in the *Irish Times*, around the 1940s, there was a spate of letters . . . there was this kind of thing against the established writers. Brian started needling them, and there was a kind of literary controversy at that time in the *Irish Times*.

KEVIN: It's this paragraph that Orlick keeps repeating because their companions aren't satisfied that he's doing the thing properly. And he has to begin again because the punishment isn't strong enough. So he says okay we'll try and give him a rougher time. So he repeats this paragraph every time. He says, "Tuesday had come down through Dundrum and Foster Avenue, brine-fresh from sea-travel, a corn-yellow sun-drench that called forth the bees at an uncustomary hour to their day of bumbling. Small house-flies performed brightly in the embrasures of the windows, whirling without fear on imaginary trapezes in the limelight of the sun-slams." Well, this is the sort of paragraph which is sort of fine writing, but to me when I read that originally, I felt this recalled to me, this fly not the bumbling . . . that's a joking way, not the sea-travel and all that sort of thing, not as though Foster Avenue and so on was new to us. But what really came home to me in that is the really marvellous description of small house-flies performing brightly. Because I mean you don't see that now, it's passed. There's a fly there but an odd fly, but at that time the flies were equal to the human population and if you were in a sunny room in a house there would be this incredible accumulation in every window. And that describes it perfectly—*on imaginary trapezes*, you know.

It kind of . . . recreates a sort of experience; it's minute. Everything you go to in this is something, of course, that recalls exactly to me what it was, and yet it's just a bit of a paragraph with something else in it, you know . . . This would sound to people, well this is high-falutin stuff, that is; but in fact it's built up, you know, a kind of clarification of experience . . . But the real climax of the paragraph is the end, from my point of view; because it's something that, you know, nobody would understand unless they have lived through that.

If you put down a piece of bread, two flies landed on it. And flypaper hanging from the ceiling in every room.

They were covered, and how any fly could find a footing on it in the end, you know, was incredible. (*Pause.*) I will definitely read this book again. (*Laughing.*)

NARRATOR: His publisher Tim O'Keefe had this to say:

TIM O'KEEFE: In the middle '50s I think it was I offered it to a distinguished firm I then worked for, but being a junior editor at that time I'm afraid my recommendation was turned down. Later on, back in '59, I went to work for a smaller publisher that was more editorial independent, which is very important in terms of writers, and among the first books I introduced there was the idea of reprinting *At Swim-Two-Birds.* And on the 7th of May, 1959, I wrote to Brian O'Nolan saying that along with a number of other people I had been a great admirer of *At Swim-Two-Birds* and some time ago began making the preliminary moves to try to get the book reissued here. Well, the book eventually did appear, 1960, and got . . . for a reissue . . . an extraordinary amount of attention. Some of that attention I think was partly arranged by the author, mind you, but, nonetheless there was a genuine response, and a genuine feeling that a fine book was re-establishing itself.

NARRATOR: John Ryan, founder-editor of the magazine *Envoy*, to which for a time Patrick Kavanagh contributed a diary, had this to say:

JOHN RYAN: He greatly admired Joyce but he wouldn't say it. He thought him a bit of a fraud in some respects. Not as a writer.

I told him once, "Dublin has been well served by Northern writers. And your good self." (*Refers to line in Ulysses.*) Bloom coming out of a brothel. "Hey, mister! Your fly is open, mister!" Though my ear is keen for the Dublin dialect, I wouldn't have got the second mister.

There's never been a mark, to . . . Myles na gCopaleen. He was the most wonderful person to us because he killed all our pretensions and he made us think again, he made us aware.

Myles, in a way, and Paddy Kavanagh, by the way, another Ulster Man, were my Universities. Those two people . . . they made us think right from the beginning of the game . . . they made us doubt everything we ever believed in . . .

NARRATOR: Good-hearted Ben Kiely, late of Omagh, who had settled in Dublin in 1940, himself incapable of malice in a city given over to backbiting, calumny and detraction, made this point:

BEN KIELY: Considering how much sharpness there was in the column you know too it is amazing that it in the long run compelled a fiction. Of course if people they think identify in that, well, they say "he doesn't mean me." And that's to say the people he attacked, you know they were people they say in official positions and all that and professors and that sort of thing and while he did concentrate on some people he didn't carry on spites. And the identities are different, there's no doubt about it. Brian O'Nolan and Flann O'Brien and Myles were three different people.

TIM O'KEEFE: Well that's a fascinating subject in itself, *the need for the writer to take pseudonyms* but I can't think of many who have been so greedy as he has. In later life a lot of them were simply when he was trying to do this sort of fairly reach-me-down journalism. I think they were simply disguises and also partly to do with his conflict with the *Irish Times*, that he had to appear under a different name. But nonetheless, all that aside, the fact that a man should feel the need so strongly to banish himself, or his name, which is the key thing to most people I suppose, and detach himself from it so determinedly, is of considerable psychological interest I think, and I cannot explain why.

I think *At Swim-Two-Birds* is such a complex tissue of so much very, very precocious learning really, he was only in his twenties when he wrote it. He was out to show a very brilliant group of his fellow students at University College in Dublin that he was as good as . . . and probably better than . . . I think there was a certain competitiveness in the making of *At Swim-Two-Birds* which Sheridan brings out. They were all going to write the great American or English novel or Irish novel. And I think the complexity of *At Swim-Two-Birds* is part of the determination I think to show everybody he had the keenest pair of heels in the business. There is a certain amount of young man's arrogance I imagine and deservedly so, and justifiably so. And he did it.

Given the fact that there was far more magazines and space given to books in 1939 then there is now, there was an extraordinarily good reception to it, with one exception, and a very important one so far as Brian O'Nolan was concerned, because *The Observer* at that time was sort of the key literary newspaper and its major reviewer at that time was Frank Swinnerton, and Frank Swinnerton unfortunately, a most unpleasant man, saw no virtue in *At Swim-Two-Birds* . . . saw no virtue in its linguistic virtuosity or its comedy, and its intricacy. I am afraid he took a very Southern English view of it, and panned it at some length. And a friend of Brian O'Nolan's went to one of the railway stations to one of those old machines where you could cut your own letters with a handle . . . you pull the handle and you cut

out letters . . . and somebody kindly sent the slogan "FUCK SWIN-
NERTON" which he put beside the review.

*Craddock and Co.*

LAMONT: The hard Furrisky!

FURRISKY: Is your man asleep or what?

SHANAHAN: Maybe he is, but by God he didn't sound like it five minutes ago. Mr. Storybook was wide awake.

LAMONT: (*Soberly.*) He was wide awake.

SHANAHAN: Five minutes ago he was giving out a yarn the length of my
arm. Right enough he is a terrible man for talk. Aren't you now? He'd
talk the lot of us into the one grave if you gave him his head, don't ask
me how I know, look at my grey hairs. Isn't that a fact Mr. Lamont?

LAMONT: (*Slowly and authoritatively.*) For a man of his years, he can
do the talking. By God he can do the talking. He has seen more of the
world than you or me, of course, that's the secret of it.

FURRISKY: That's true. Yes, he's an old man, of course.

LAMONT: His stories are not the worst, though, I'll say that. There's
always a head and a tail to his yarns, a beginning and an end, give him
his due . . . I mean to say, whether a yarn is tall or small I like to hear
it well told . . . I like to know where I am, do you know. Everything
has a beginning and an end.

SHANAHAN: The story is about this fellow Sweeny that argued the toss with the clergy and came off second-best at the wind-up. There was a curse—a malediction—put down in the book against him. The up-shot is that your man becomes a bloody bird.

LAMONT: I see.

SHANAHAN: Do you see it, Mr. Furrisky? What happens? He is changed into a bird for his pains and could go from here to Carlow in one hop. Do you see it, Mr. Lamont?

LAMONT: Oh I see that much alright, but the man that I'm thinking of is a man by the name of Sergeant Craddock, the first man in Ireland at the long jump in the time that's gone.

FURRISKY: Craddock?

SHANAHAN: (*Urbane.*) That was always one thing that the Irish race was always noted for, one place where the world had to give us best. With all his faults and by God he has plenty, the Irishman can jump. By God he can jump. That's one thing the Irish race is honoured for no matter where it goes or where you find it—jumping. The world looks up to us there.

FURRISKY: (*Wisely.*) We were good jumpers from the start right enough, the name of Ireland is honoured for that.

SHANAHAN: Go to Russia, go to China, go to France. Everywhere and all the time it's hats off and a gra-ma-cree to the Jumping Irishman. Ask who you like they'll all tell you that. The Jumping Irishman.

FURRISKY: It's a thing that will always stand to us—jumping.

LAMONT: When everything's said, the Irishman has his points. He's not the last man that was made now.

FURRISKY: (*Adamant.*) He is not.

## In the Guise of an Uncle

NARRATOR: In 1935 he became a state employee in the Department of Local Government under John Garvin whose responsibility it was to supervise the undertakings by local authorities of waterworks and sewage schemes by ways of grants from government sources.

He was to remain there eighteen years, working his way up the Civil Service ladder, writing over 1,000 columns of "Cruiskeen Lawn" for the *Irish Times* at the rate of two guineas an article of five hundred words. He was in turn Sean T. O'Kelly's Private Secretary and speech-writer for the suave Sean McEntee.

By then he had started work on *At Swim-Two-Birds*, aged twenty-four, smallish, slight, pale-faced, with two prominent front teeth. Never show your teeth unless you mean to bite.

In 1937 his father dropped dead when playing with his youngest child. Brian asked for his pen, a very old Watermen which he had used all his life; with this he had probably written a detective novel, never published, title unknown, and now lost.

No father appears in his fiction; the narrator would always be an orphan. In *At Swim-Two-Birds* the father appeared in the guise of an uncle, a lowly clerk in Guinness's brewery:

"I recall that I went into my uncle's house about nine P.M. one evening in the early spring, the sharp edge of my perception dulled somewhat by indulgence in spirituous liquors. I was standing in the middle of the dining-room floor before I had properly adverted to my surroundings. The faces I found there were strange and questioning. Searching among them, I found at last the features of my uncle."

*Nature of features*: Red, irregular, coarse, fat.

He was situated in a central position in the midst of four others and looked out from them in my direction in a penetrating attentive manner."

"Description of my uncle: red-faced, bead-eyed, ball-bellied. Fleshy about the shoulders with long swinging arms giving ape-like effect to gait. Large mustache. Holder of Guinness clerkship the third class."

His second novel in English, *The Third Policeman*, was begun sometime in 1939 and completed by January of 1940, when O'Nolan posted it to his agents in London, Heath & Co. According to Donagh McDonagh, later a Justice of the Peace, it was lost in transit.

William Saroyan, who had met O'Nolan through McDonagh in June 1939, tried to place it with his American agents. They had no success in placing it with American publishers who had found the first novel fairly baffling, and lost the typescript of the second. For America it was titled *Hell Goes Round and Round*. After the success of the reissued *At Swim-Two-Birds*, Brian O'Nolan rewrote it as *The Dalkey Archive* and it appeared under that title in 1964. The typescript of *The Third Policeman* was put away, its author saying he had lost it, and remained unpublished for twenty-seven years, appearing the year after his death. A year later *The Best of Myles* appeared, a selection from "Cruiskeen Lawn" edited by his brother Kevin. In 1973 a translation of *An Béal Bocht* appeared under the title of *The Poor Mouth*. In Gaelic and in Anglo-Irish dialect, "putting on the poor mouth" means making a pretence of being poor or in needy circumstances, or it may simply mean grumbling.

His friends knew of the existence of a novel but none of them actually saw it, although Liam Redmond did try to place it with a filmman in London.

LIAM REDMOND: Yes, in London I knew David Rawlings. He was working over there and he was particularly interested in doing experimental films, and I had got the typescript of Brian's book *The Third Policeman* and I thought this would fit very well into the Rawlings world. I got in touch with Brian but he wouldn't have it at all. He said that the manuscript had . . . the typescript had been lost in a train. But I just think that he must have felt it to be seen by the public at that time.

KEVIN: But I think at that stage the second book, *The Third Policeman*, that he wanted to say, "Well, this could be reality. I mean what are we to think about eternity, you have to begin thinking about that, and so on, nobody knows what's in store."

He wanted Joe, the conscience, out of it. He never meant—he could have published that in the latter part of his life by simply offering it, but said no. In fact he told me when he was describing, I remember he came in describing *The Dalkey Archive* at one stage, and he said that he thought that *The Dalkey Archive* was going to be a great moneymaker and, you know, original and so on. But he said, at some stage, you know, the other thing, that's going to need a lot of revision, and I don't know at what stage it would appear. It just appears now as it more or less was, with his own comment at the back, you know, that Joe soap would have to be got out of it. That in other words he wasn't happy about it, as it presently appears, but it's been a great success, as it appears.

NARRATOR: As with all O'Nolan's characters, the nameless narrator of *The Third Policeman* is early orphaned. He is sent away to boarding school—the Expulsion from Paradise, from the freedom of the fields around Tullamore.

"My father I do not remember well but he was a strong man and did not talk much except on Saturdays when he would mention Parnell with the customers and say that Ireland was a queer country.

"My mother I can recall perfectly. Her face was always red and sore-looking from bending at the fire; she spent her life making tea to pass the time and singing snatches of old songs to pass the meantime. I knew her well but my father and I were strangers and did not converse much; often indeed when I would be studying in the kitchen at night I could hear him through the thin door to the shop talking there from his seat under the oil lamp for hours on end to Mick the sheepdog.

"Always it was only the drone of his voice I heard, never the separate words. He was a man who understood all dogs thoroughly and treated them like human beings. My mother owned a cat but it was a foreign outdoor animal and was rarely seen and my mother never took any notice of it. We were all happy enough in a queer separate way."

Upon beginning his search for the works of the mad philosopher De Selby, he suffers an accident:

"In one of the places where I was broadening my mind I met one night with a bad accident. I broke my leg (or, if you like, it was broken for me) in six places and when I was well enough again to go on my way I had one leg made of wood, the left one."

At the age of twenty he returns home with a travelling bag in each hand to the bar run by the tricky Divney to claim his inheritance—rather in the manner of Watt arriving at the house of Mr. Knott at Foxrock in Mr. Beckett's novel.

Irish heroes setting out on their travels "in a commodious vicus of recirculation" arrive back home, to an unrecognisable place. "It was an evening in a happy yellow summer and the door of the public house was open." It was to stay invitingly open, as open as the jaws of hell.

Analysis reveals it to be hell for all eternity where the damned soul goes round in circles which repeat themselves ad nauseam without any recollection on the victim's part of his having already made the same circuit.

The hell is recognisably an Irish hell, situated somewhere near Tullamore, and more or less unpeopled save for the elementals who staff it—three policemen, two of whom are also attending a mechanized purgatory devised by a third, Constable Fox.

The Peelers, Civic Guards, or police were a force to whom O'Nolan was allergic and here is at it again, presiding over an inferno run by his dearest enemies, "the Rozzers." The landscape in which the prisoner finds himself pending his hanging is finely portrayed, as is the condemned man's ideas of his life after death, a death which has already taken place and will continue to be repeated. Some of this is reminiscent of the hanging of the Croppy Boy in *Ulysses*, less Mrs. Bellingham and Mrs. Tellboys, for the proceedings are remarkably free from elements of smut. As with most of his fiction, women—"the same women"—being conspicuous by their absence, except in very menial roles, as mothers or servants.

The flowing and existing world is given its due, that Nature which was to disappear from his last three works.

"The sky was grey and stormy and out of it I heard the harsh shouts of wild geese and ducks labouring across the wind on their coarse pinions. Black quails called sharply from their hidings and a swollen stream was babbling dementedly. Trees, I knew, would be angular and ill-tempered in the rain and boulders would gleam coldly at the eye."

The pathetic fallacies are not fallacies but animisms with their own intent. There is a profusion of wooden-legged men: Martin Finnucane and O'Feersa, "the middle brother," and their seven one-legged friends, or was it fourteen roped together?

Preparing to hang the condemned man after a breakfast of porridge and milk, the Sergeant attempts to distract him by telling of a man who had himself "let up into the sky in a balloon to make observations," who never came down to earth again.

"When the boys reached the home of the balloon-man the next morning, lo and behold the bed was empty and no trace of him was ever found afterwards dead or alive, naked or with an overcoat. And when they got back to where the balloon was, they found the wind had torn it up out of the ground with the rope spinning loosely in the windlass and it invisible to the naked eye in the middle of the clouds. They pulled in eight miles of rope before they got it down but lo and behold the basket was empty again. They all said that the man had gone up in it and stayed up but it was an insoluble conundrum, his name was Quigley and he was by all accounts a Fermanagh man."

If hell lies below, what then lies above?

(*In two voices.*) The brother is thinkin of goin up.

*Going up what?*

The brother is thinkin of standin.

*Standing what? Drinks?*

The brother is thinking of having a go at the big parties.

*Do you mean that your relative is considering offering himself as a candidate when the general election becomes due by reason of constitutional requirement?*

The brother is thinking of goin up at the elections.

*I see.*

Of course it's not the brother himself that is all mad for this game. He's bein pushed do you understand me. Certain influential parties is behind him. They're night and mornin callin to the digs and colloguin with the brother inside in the back-room with the brother givin orders for tea to be made at wan in the mornin. Any amount of fat oul' fellas with the belly well out in front, substantial cattlemen be the look of them. No shortage of the ready there. And do you know what I'm going to tell you?

# I Doubt if it's a Photograph of Me at All

NARRATOR: "I write for my own race," the novelist and critic John Wain quoted him as saying, although I cannot find the quotation. Those who wrote for their own race had a way of disappearing in their own lifetime: T. S. Eliot into another country and then into a bank and a publishing house. Joyce into Pola and Trieste, into a bank in Rome. Pound into St. Elizabeth's asylum and then into silence. Brian O'Nolan disappeared for eighteen years into the Irish Civil Service; became a public man, whom relatively few knew to see, behind an Irish pseudonym, wrote fiction under another. His brother Kevin admits that the period in his life from 1927 to 1937 "I cannot adequately describe." Arthur Power, who knew him to see and speak to, refers to evasiveness, furtiveness; he objected to being introduced to Power's wife and the painter George Campbell upstairs in a double-decker Dublin bus. Both Mr. Cronin and Miss O'Flaherty speak of his secretiveness, his hidden quality. For his second published novel, *The Hard Life,* he instructed Tim O'Keefe his publisher that "absolutely no biographical details" were to be given, and "I doubt if it's a photograph of me at all," he said of the image supplied.

The early pencil sketch by Seamus O'Sullivan is certainly not of O'Brien. The hat seemed to overshadow and almost extinguish his small, rather secretive face.

Myles wrote: "If a man stands before a mirror ... what he sees is not a true reproduction of himself but a picture of himself when he was a young man ... There is therefore an appreciable and calculable interval of time between the throwing by the man of a glance at his own face in the mirror and the registration of the reflected image in his eye." (An Irish construction is here hidden, in an English sentence.)

"If a line were drawn vertically down the centre of the face one half is by no means a replica of the other. There is, in fact, a startling difference. This can be demonstrated by the camera. A full-face picture is taken and bisected. One half is duplicated by a reversal process and reintegrated with the other half of itself: the result is an entirely different face, with a different expression from the original whole. And if the process is repeated with the other half of the bisected face, we get still a different second face ... an original face and the two faces of which it is composed."

TIM O'KEEFE: One noticed the small face, the fairly small physique, the sharp teeth, the thinning hair. But one tended mostly to notice merely a large black hat ... which is part of the writer's costume of the '40s and '50s ... which he kept up. Brendan Behan said you had to look twice at him to be sure he was there at all. Which is a fairly accurate description ... a fairly perceptive description I think of him.

Because he did not command physically and did not impress himself physically ... and he made nothing of gestures or the usual tricks of personality ... *Elusiveness* I think was one of the keys.

NARRATOR: Gogarty once said to Lennox Robinson, "James Joyce got the King's bounty from Asquith when he hadn't written a line." Robinson, not known for his ready wit, replied: "What line hadn't he written?"

Brian O'Nolan was a multiplicity of characters. When Yeats, abstemious and not often in good health, was building up his strength with hot Bovril and Lady Gregory's gift of a crate of port, O'Nolan was subdividing himself, hiding himself away, as Brother Barnabas, as Flann, as Myles.

The first President of Ireland, Douglas Hyde, who was O'Nolan's Irish Professor at UCD, was taken aback when his most brilliant student by accident attended a lecture, saying "*Ni feider, ni feider!*" (Impossible, impossible!). He wrote a parody-novel which has claims to be greater than the original; his claim, "My field of study will be the whole of Europe, but on the understanding that Ireland is the centre of it," when setting out to write a column for *The Southern Star* of Skibereen, was not entirely ironic.

He was known affectionately throughout Ireland as "Myles," though few knew him to see in a time before television made nonentities famous.

He created in a curious and charming English the "last glint of colour in any Irish word."

Shy himself, a greatly gifted writer of address, he created "invisible" characters: "hidden" Conán and the Good Fairy in *At Swim-Two-Birds*, Joe the soul of the narrator in *The Third Policeman*; and relegated others like Hatchjaw and De Selby to a miserable existence in the footnotes, where Hatchjaw wrote a book on the work of De Selby. Mann and Laurence Sterne had done this before, but none quite like the First Year Gaelic scholar with rodent teeth, the cross little fox-terrier face.

Myles wrote, not in derision now, of a ravenous peasantry reduced to devouring their own land. In his *Compthrom Feinne* and *Blather* days he had made a modest proposal for shifting Ireland itself into a more comfortable geographical site. The country was to be sawn in twain and sailed by England, causing ruinous tidal waves.

MISS O'FLAHERTY: Himself? He had a quiet gentle manner. He wasn't very interested in clothes—just the blue Burberry, his hands in his pockets.

CRONIN: All in all the hat was worn and used to good effect. He's wearing it in that photograph you're talking about. And he had it slightly pushed back towards the back of the head, which would have a high significance about his mood at the time. You know, he is being slightly belligerent. He was slightly belligerent throughout most of the proceedings that day. And the hat pushed to the back of the head was probably evidence of coming out fighting, you know. Shaking hands now and coming out fighting.

BARBARA REDMOND: Someone trying to describe the state of somebody completely different from Brian referred to her as "indrawn." I think that was Brian too. A bit different from "withdrawn," you know. Drawn into himself.

On the whole he actively disliked most women, and he was quite old when he got married.

He was always very kind to me, very nice to me. He'd go out of his way, if he was standing at a bus stop to come over and chat. He'd be going one way and I'd be going the other. Over he'd come.

BEN KIELY: What I remember most about him was the sort of fantastic stories he would tell. I once said to him that the Tory Islanders once had been in schism from the Church of Rome. And it was known up where I came from as the Second Great Western Schism. Because they wouldn't let the old curate so to speak off the island and they wouldn't let the new fellow on, which was very easy for them to do. And then he went into a tremendous story about, *did I know about what happened in the British days when the Tory Islanders wouldn't pay the rates?* He had a great sense of timing in telling a story, as if he was a stage man.

The Tory Islanders, anyway they wouldn't pay the rates. And then he would say to me: "And the British sent a gunboat out from Galway, but you don't know, Ben, what happened to the gunboat!" And then there'd be a significant pause, until I would have to admit that I didn't know what happened to the gunboat. And he would say: "The Tory Islanders knelt down and prayed. God only knows who they prayed to, but that gunboat sank, all hands on board." Which apparently is historical truth. I don't know about the praying, but the gunboat sank anyway. And the Tory Islanders went on not paying their rates.

CRONIN: There were very few people who were intimate with him in his domestic circumstances, that's the thing first of all about him. He was a person, not exactly an outdoor person, but a person one saw and conversed with *after* he had left his house for the pub and/or the office, and the streets. Therefore one remembers him with the hat. Of course there was an Irish literary hat in his youth; it was a black hat which the versifiers used to wear . . . They used to buy it in a clerical outfitters down in Talbot Street where I believe the clerical outfitters was. It was the only place where you could get these wide-brimmed black hats. And the wide-brimmed black hat was almost de rigueur for the Man of Letters. Even when I was growing up, but much more so when Myles was of course.

LIAM REDMOND: We were sitting up at the counter in the Club. Charlie the barman was behind; he was a rather dour but very charming man. And Brian was talking about literature. Now he had an extraordinary wide knowledge of German literature, and he was talking for hours and hours and hours and I was listening to him, fascinated. And the lucidity of his thought was what was absolutely astonishing. And then he got off the stool and collapsed on the floor. (*Laughs.*) Well, the extraordinary thing was to maintain such clarity of thought and such brilliance of speech, and then at the same time his mind was working, but his body failed him.

INTERVIEWER: Smyllie had one of these hats?

CRONIN: Er no, Smyllie didn't have one. Austin Clarke had one, Brinsley MacNamara had one, Donagh MacDonagh had one. Oh you name them, they had them you know.

INTERVIEWER: But Myles's was slightly different?

CRONIN: Now his hat was somewhat different. And the brim was pulled down in front in a way this was probably very modern in 1935 or '36, a bit reminiscent of the gangster films of the year, and the hat was tilted about on his head according to his mood and the time of day.

INTERVIEWER: Was he an easily dominated man?

CRONIN: Oh no. Oh no. He took charge. Whatever company he was in he took charge.

INTERVIEWER: Was he in charge of Kavanagh? Did he dominate Kavanagh?

CRONIN: Er, no, no.

INTERVIEWER: Did Kavanagh try to dominate him?

CRONIN: Whatever little company Myles was in he decided what the topics of conversation were going to be. And he told his stories and went on about his obsessions of the moment, frequently in a very humorous fashion. I mean . . . he could be sometimes as amusing in life as he was in print, but often in a sort of obsessive and repetitive sort of way, according to . . . the amount of drink he had taken, which wasn't so amusing.

BARBARA REDMOND: Er, it's funny: I can think of him as playing poker. Remember those poker sessions we used to have?

INTERVIEWER: What sort of poker player was he?

BARBARA REDMOND: He wasn't outstanding, but he didn't lose his shirt either.

INTERVIEWER: What sort of stakes did you play for?

BARBARA REDMOND: Oh very tiny. We . . . none of us could afford big stakes.

INTERVIEWER: He liked gambling?

BARBARA REDMOND: Not really.

BEN KIELY: Yeah. I remember being told once by . . . that one of the most significant scenes she ever saw was, a lady told me once, in Westmoreland Street was Smyllie . . . R. M. Smyllie, enormous and impassive, puffing on his pipe. And Myles, small and intense, talking continuously and pointing at Smyllie. And she said, "I wonder what they were talking about?" It's quite obvious what they were talking about—money. And what Smyllie was paying him for the column, which was always a very sore topic in those days.

LIAM REDMOND: I think he belonged to this country, very much so. And I think he would be rather lost in another country. Joyce discovered himself, I think, by going abroad, but Brian was so much a Dubliner. Of course Joyce was also very much of a Dubliner. But I don't think he'd have been able to rest in exile, as it were. Or flourish as Joyce flourished in exile.

## From The Third Policeman

NARRATOR: There was another thing. My surroundings had a strangeness of a country of a peculiar kind, entirely separate from the mere strangeness of a country where one has never been before . . . I was clearly in a strange country but all the doubts and perplexities which strewed my mind could not stop me from feeling happy and heart-light and full of appetite for going about my business and finding the hiding-place of the black box. The valuable contents of it, I felt, would secure me for life in my own house and afterwards I could revisit this mysterious townland upon my bicycle and probe at my leisure the reasons for all its strangeness . . .

### The Chiners (Incident)

KEVIN O'NOLAN: (*Laughing.*) . . . Going in cart around Ireland at one time, and at one time, and that would have been hilarious if anybody was there to describe it, you know. Even my sister—I've one sister who's dead now, the rest of the family are alive—there are two members who are dead and my sister Nessa at one time went off with his wife Evelyn and Brian on a holiday that became a kind of a modified pub crawl. They'd come into a town . . . (*Laughing.*) He came around anyway, and at the time, it's funny the way this sort of thing—several people have remarked this to me later: that he was always up-to-date in his language. I mean style is a peculiar thing, and yet you can take words that become current and use them and maybe you drop them again. But at the particular time the word . . . he used the word "chiner." I suppose it's an English word really: chiner is slang for Chinaman. It was a Dublin word for a long time but I never hear it now.

He said "Let's ask the chiner." And he used it a lot of the time, and anyway he said—Nessa described this—we came to this town, she said, we went into a pub and it was absolutely jammed to the walls, you see. And you couldn't hear yourself speak and everything and he said, and Evelyn said, let's get out of here. "Oh," he says, "not at all," he says. "I'll have all these chiners silent in a few minutes. I'll have these fellas as quiet as anything in a few minutes." He got a table and he put down matches on the table—he was a great man for match tricks you see—take away a match and leave four squares, you see, and he got some fellow over and he said, "Look here you," he says, it's true he said . . . it was like a church she says. In no time at all the table with matches out on them, you know. (*Laughing.*)

And he said, "I'll have all these chiners quiet in no time," and he had you know.

BEN KIELY: Oh I suspect just as he knew he was very, very good and er . . . You know the kudos would be going somewhere else and perhaps even the money and that sort of thing, and that always annoys. Annoys a man very much, and that might have made him sensitive too. And then he had a supreme contempt, I think, for any sort of inferior mind, having a very sharp and well-stocked mind himself, and I suppose he could see all sorts of fools all around him and he didn't suffer fools gladly at all.

## The Three Brothers

CIARAN: Yews, he learnt his Irish—I don't know when he started learning—but he went to the Donegal Gaeltacht and learnt his Irish there, and he was a very good speaker and so of course the rest of the family—you see, an uncle of mine was Professor of Irish in Maynooth—but we were all brought up speaking Irish and of course learnt English later on—but so strong was this tradition of Irish that it was impossible—this is a funny psychological business—it would have been impossible for me until the family broke up you know and went off and got married and that sort of thing—it would have been impossible for me speak to Brian in English, actually impossible—it's a psychological barrier and the only way we would speak English would be if somebody came in and didn't know Irish, or wasn't used to speaking it and spoke in English to him—then the barrier was broken and I could speak you know—now that's a fact.

KEVIN: People said, "Oh you know he made a laugh of the Irish language." But one of his great abiding interests you know was the Irish language and the quality of the Irish language and so on and he never had any—I mean that would just amaze me that anyone would think that. But because he makes fun of people who regard the language as something you know, a badge, you know, everything and that. People say "Oh he's against the language." There's no such thing. You couldn't find a word anywhere about it.

BRIAN: "The Irish mind, when there was such a thing, an uncontaminated simple one, was very much more subtle, I think, than the Anglo-Saxon mind."

## Rate-payer's Opinions

INTERVIEWER: Did he hold political opinions?

CRONIN: No. (*Decisive.*) What he had was *rate-payer's* opinions. He had adopted the point of view of the citizen, the respectable citizen, who paid his rates and taxes and expected service and good government and honesty and probity and efficiency as a result, *and did not get it!*

And this was a constant point of reference for him. He judged government and authority from the point of view of the respectable citizen who paid his rates and taxes; and indeed he did pay his rates and taxes. John Ryan once told me that he had met Myles one day and Myles was actually . . . he had actually written off that day for a tax-return form, and he was bitterly abusing the authorities for their remissness in not having sent him one, since he should have made a return at least six months ago. And why hadn't they sent him one, and what did they think they were doing up there in Dublin Castle?

JOHN RYAN: He was very much a civic person . . . etc. He was global. He was concerned with it—he had a civic concern. I think that we have lost in the last ten years . . . two great voices, Kavanagh, who was also an Ulster Man, and Myles. Because what they would have said about the Northern situation could have been extremely important. And you can be sure of one thing, it would have been trenchant and it would have been mannerable. Probably witty as well, too.

INTERVIEWER: About this time Myles was harrying the Dublin Corporation and in particular the Lord Mayor, Andy Clarkin, a kindly coal-merchant in private life. The clock over his office had stopped and Myles mounted an all-out campaign for its repair. He ran a series of columns under the heading ACCISS—ANDY CLARKIN'S CLOCK IS STILL STOPPED—and tried to mobilise readers to give the ACCISS salute, holding one arm up and the other out horizontally.

ARTHUR POWER: There wasn't the rage there is in Swift or the elegance and the rapier-thrust that there is in Voltaire.

INTERVIEWER: Still, he didn't do a bad job with the weapon he had.

ARTHUR POWER: Well, it was a shilliegh. (*Laughs.*)

INTERVIEWER: Still, he split some heads with it.

ARTHUR POWER: (*Resumes.*) Myles didn't like the Anglo-Irish. Country-gentlemen type. He objected to them. And though he was never friendly with me, down in this country house the man who was really pleased to see him was the gardener. I remember sometime back I was in the Pearl bar, The Yellow Pearl as it was called. And the man began attacking me, and I said, "Myles, the gardeners won't listen to you." He got up and walked straight out. He was furious.

## The Rate-payer's Friend

CRONIN: (*Resumes.*) Now, he fancied himself as the Rate-payer's Friend. Now we have to take this on its various levels. First of all there was the comic-persona level, which he would have known very well. Deep down he was an anarchist or something, but he had adopted the persona. (*Cough.*) Now this suited him originally for comic purposes in the column. Because it's a good comic stance now—to be the respectable citizen that pays his rates and taxes. And it is I think a good comic stance. But it grew on him a bit and in the later years when he did really take himself seriously as a critic of society—in the later days. I think not in the earlier days but in the later days, yes, and as somebody who kept the politicians and the Corporation people in order. He began to fancy himself as that; so this grew on him and became serious and unfortunately it tended to lose its comic aspects then. And that applied to him conversationally as well as in the column. You will notice if you look at the column over the years that there is a growth of this—there's a loss of humour and this is part of . . . Well, people use big words, "paranoic" and all that kind of thing. Of course these words don't fit, but you know what I mean. It's a growth of something. Taking yourself too seriously like in the way of persecution mania.

KEVIN: Yes, but the derisive element has a great deal of . . . I mean like the Plain People of Ireland were the people that he would, you know defend. He said some terrible things about Frank O'Connor, because Frank O'Connor went to America and wrote in an American magazine, and this came back to him. He says, what is Frank O'Connor saying about the Irish people? Yes, I knew, but I mean he really took him apart with this particular thing, you see. And made a reference saying to the Plain People of Ireland, Oh well, you have me to defend you, more or less. And he really meant that, you know. He was not going to let those people get away with it, you see.

But he wasn't really deriding, you know. He got on very well with all kinds of people . . . He could be very hard on cant and that sort of thing. You know, you look very critically at your own people . . . But you don't overlook the really good things.

BEN KIELY: I must say, though, I had the good luck never to have fallen foul of him, which I personally would not like to do at all. Because if he wanted to make you ridiculous he certainly could do it. You know. There was . . . Cormac . . . the Gaelic Professor of Irish in College. He took some sort of special spite against Cormac because he'd been a student in College, and Cormac's early days I think as a Professor . . . So that he regularly came up for a pasting. And there were other victims. Well Alfred was easy to draw out . . . Myles was not the only one who played on him. There were references to a "certain learned economist to whom I was talking the other day."

There's the case of the great Professor George O'Brien. And George's great dread was always that he'd be pilloried in the column. He had no reason to think so because Myles had nothing against him at all. But there were three Kevin Nolans in the College at the time. There was Ciaran, Brian's brother. There was another Kevin Nolan who was an Army Officer at the time; I don't know where he went to. And there was a third Kevin Nolan, still well known, who's a close friend of mine.

But George O'Brien thought that the last Kevin Nolan that I mentioned was actually the brother, and spent a great deal of his time—at least this was our College joke—being charming to this Kevin Nolan, so that to keep himself out of the Myles na gCopaleen column. The joke was made about this Kevin Nolan was that while he didn't say he was, he never said that he wasn't, because he was doing Economics as well as Law and History.

CRONIN: Towards the end there was a strong element (of persecution mania), and a strong element also was the feeling that his masters in the Civil Service had been stupid and unworthy people. Of course the man who was not actively engaged in anything always fancies himself as being more efficient at it than he would if he was actually doing it, you know. It relates to what Yeats called "the exorbitant dreams of beggary." So that once he was safely out of the Civil Service, and I suppose when he was in it too, he could safely criticise everybody in it from the standpoint of total inefficiency.

TIM O'KEEFE: There were tremors of libel actions all over the place. He had a certain amount of brutality in his nature. The way he was part of a journalistic business, where you run after the hair. And I think he had that, which is a pity. He did pursue . . . as he pursued things in his own writing, as he pursued for example in *The Third Policeman*, which are pursued with a kind of demoniacal singlemindedness. Well, if you coarsen that into journalism, it becomes a wee bit unpleasant.

BEN KIELY: He never went, so to speak, for the ordinary Plain People of Ireland really in any way at all. It was generally for people in public position or for people that he thought were guilty of rather ridiculous poses in the world of literature and art, to coin a phrase. He was inclined to do that sort of thing. (*Pause.*) Sometimes it's all cases like that there—attacks and abuse could get a little repetitive and a little bit weary. But he did say many funny things about the sort of phoneyness that went on around, or goes on around any large city.

But the column did an enormous amount of good too. It wasn't just that you laughed at it; but there was a good deal of sound common sense in it too. And it did incline people from ridiculous poses.

TIM O'KEEFE: I think from the '60s onward he was probably tired, and I felt that if I had known him in 1939 or whenever, what an amazing man he would have been, but there was a certain amount of drudgery there's no doubt about that in the '60s. He's got to cap himself each day, this is the dreadful thing. O'Brien would have had the same kind of pangs as any contemporary columnist would have. And given the fact that he was operating in a smaller city, in Dublin, the pressures I think on him through that I think would be enormous.

CRONIN: I never found him disappointing, because I was fascinated by him. Not only, I mean, did I have a great admiration for him as a writer, both on the grounds of the column and on the grounds of *At Swim-Two-Birds*, but he was a fascinating person. I mean you don't actually separate one from the other do you. You don't say, here's this fellow in the pub, and the work's a sort of backdrop to the man you're talking to always . . . So, you know, in combination with the work, he was a fascinating person. He thought he was the invisible man, now that's accurate enough, that he thought he was. You see he was garbed as a certain kind of respectable, rather lower-grade, I would think, civil-servant person, who perhaps didn't work in a government department so much as in Dublin Castle or something like that, was garbed in at a certain point in Dublin history, say rugged by 1938 to 1944 or thereabouts. And he was garbed like that. And so he probably fancied the thought of being an invisible man who was the same as everybody else in the kind of pub or milieu that he chose to frequent. But of course he wasn't at all like that. First of all he tended like many annecdotalists to take in the whole shop in his converse. Not only would he want your attention, but frequently the bystanders also would be the recipients of this story. So he wasn't as invisible as he thought he was.

ARTHUR POWER: Ferguson the industrialist treated Myles in an off-hand way. He treated Myles in a very offhand manner . . . But Myles got it all back in the car coming home. I couldn't hear what they were saying. He wasn't a great talker . . . *furtive* almost. He objected to being shown around.

Myles was deadly sober the whole time.

INTERVIEWER: That would make him waspish.

ARTHUR POWER: He didn't open his mouth at all. Very silent. He wasn't much of a talker. He was friends I think with Paddy Kavanagh.

Paddy Kavanagh and Myles sitting in the Palace Bar together . . . I don't know I saw it. The Dubliner and the countryman, the semi-tinker.

INTERVIEWER: He was from the North. Strabane.

ARTHUR POWER: A Northern man, I never knew that.

INTERVIEWER: Did he have a Northern accent?

CRONIN: No. No trace of a Northern accent at all. You wouldn't know he was from the North . . . Nothing in his accent or general disposition. I'm not sure whether you would know a Northern person by their general demeanour, but I think there are Northern traits and he didn't have them. I didn't think he had them anyway.

INTERVIEWER: Was it a thin voice?

CRONIN: (*Cough, pause.*) No. It wasn't deep or thin.

INTERVIEWER: Dublin?

CRONIN: Dulcet. He had lost a country accent—I presume he had one to begin with—and had replaced it with an accent which was partly his own invention and was used for anecdotal effect. Like many people, he didn't exactly put on a Dublin accent at a certain point in the story. But what he did was he broadened the accent he had so that it would fit, it was flexible in that way, the accent he had.

INTERVIEWER: Brian himself, defender of the Plain People of Ireland, implacable foe to Bores, Buffs & Bowsies of all degrees, was interviewed on RTE Radio by John Bowman in Dublin. Questioned in a very deferential manner as to whether or not he thought any of his work would survive, Brian had this to say, modestly:

BRIAN O'NOLAN: I doubt if anything at all will survive. I think *An Béal Bocht* should survive as a little piece of our innocent fun in the 1940s. Now I realize that that book was written twenty-four years ago. It will suruve as long as I say the great book which provoked it, that is *An t-Oileánach*, the Blasket book, which I believe is one of the most important books published in this century in Europe. The Irish of the author is so magnificent, and my attempts to deride and parody it, as everyone knows you cannot parody anything but a great big thing. I still think the book in part anyhow is funny. The Irish canon that is so preoccupied with hunger and poverty and bogs and all that stuff.

NARRATOR: *An Béal Bocht*—the book referred to and published in English as *The Poor Mouth*—is "a ferocious and highly technical assault on the Gaels," O'Brien wrote to O'Keefe his publisher—"an enormous jeer at the Gaelic morons here with their bicycle clips and handball medals, but in language and style . . . an ironical copy of a really fine autobiographical book."

CRONIN: But really what I thought about Myles na gCopaleen was the interrelationship between the journalist and the writer and the journalist and the man. Now particularly the comic journalist and the writer and the comic journalist and the man, and of Myles na gCopaleen as the delight and darling of intellectual Dublin. And I think that was rather sad in the end. You see there was a sense in which he became Myles na gCopaleen. Myles na gCopaleen ate up Brian O'Nolan. It nearly destroyed Flann O'Brien.

Myles na gCopaleen, in this three-cornered battle or three-cornered tug-of-war between Brian O'Nolan, Flann O'Brien and Myles na gCopaleen, Myles na gCopaleen was unfortunately the winner.

Now part of this was circumstantial, you know. He had to write the column. But also it was the audience temptation. Dublin loved it, Dublin grew to be like it, it grew to be like Dublin, unfortunately. Its jokes became their jokes. Its style of humour, its points of reference, became their style of humour, their points of reference. But of course it was a two-way traffic, because he was giving them what they wanted.

I mean the kind of University or Civil Service intellectual who was its real audience. It was a two-way traffic between Myles and them, and he all too much lived up to their expectations. Also it was too heavy a thing to take on . . .

It was far too much to do over that period of time and to keep up the standard that he kept up, you know.

BEN KIELY: Well, you know how difficult this town is, to live in it or to work in.

I mean that's just the basic fact. It's not so much an economic matter nowadays. Padraic Colum said that he would have stayed in Ireland at that time if he could have got a job at a pound a week. Of course that's a long time ago. But he couldn't. So, having some sort of patron, he headed off for the States. But the economic thing is not so crushing nowadays; it's just that Dublin was a difficult town to work in, if you had any gregarious tastes or inclinations at all. And Brian certainly had them to excess.

Then I suspect there was always the problem if you were in the Civil Service, you're in town but you're only in at work, you might stay a few hours of the day, and the temptation for a talk and company is practically overpowering there.

NARRATOR: The late lamented Jack White, then Features Editor of the *Irish Times*, recalled that the remuneration was at the rate of two guineas an article of about five hundred words, but this was per article printed, and the rate of rejection was high. Copy usually arrived in batches of two or three articles typed on foolscap paper, Government issue.

Fearful outbursts of invective against the "corner-boys," who had meddled with copy or allowed misprints to creep in, came in a covering letter. White claimed never to have encountered their equal "for sheer scurrilous abuse." The *Irish Times* office faced the Palace Bar across D'Olier Street; the Pearl Bar being conveniently situated midway around the block.

CRONIN: I think this relationship between the comic persona and the real man is one of the most important and interesting things about him . . . The dividing line in his case was not as clear as it was in most. He had made of himself in a sense a Mylesean character . . . and it was very difficult to know where one stopped and the other started.

Particularly since he belonged to an era when there were people who had developed the art of being People in a Pub and presenting themselves through a sort of persona to a high degree . . . I don't know what induced certain . . . some of them considerable people, like Kavanagh and Myles, to develop this art of the persona in the pub. I think it was partly the way of life of the time. But of course it had its economic reasons. They did live their lives in the pub to a considerable extent, and in the pub they didn't wish to present themselves as the private people that they otherwise were. They wanted to present themselves with a carapace and they did this with enormous consistency and with a great development of technique. And Kavanagh, I mean in the same way as Myles. It was a life necessity. I did have conversations with Myles in which he was being more the real man . . . more than the one he presented publicly in the pub like sort of thing. Even though when you were alone with Myles in the pub he tended to keep this up. I mean most of the time he was the man you expected on that level, but there were one or two occasions when one had another kind of conversation with him and . . . But I think I mean there were . . . rare enough in my case, but I think they were rare absolutely. I wouldn't think that many people ever had a conversation with him in which he had ceased to be either Myles na gCopaleen nor Brian O'Nolan with his hat and his way of looking at the world.

MAGEE: Do you know what I am going to tell you, there was a rare life in Dublin in old days.

SIDE-KICK: There was certainly.

MAGEE: (*Forcefully.*) That was the day of the great O'Callaghan, the day of Baskin, the day of Tracey that brought cowboys to Ringsend. I knew them all, man.

NARRATOR: It was the day of the eight penny pint, pawnshops, trams and glimmer-men, gas brackets in Grogan's and Toner's, seven days hard without option for minor offences, Seventh Day Adventists everywhere, language revivalists bawling in Abbey Street, Nelson aloft on his Pillar—a solemn Dev-dominated epoch. A stall seat in the Abbey cost three and six, a back seat in the Gate costs two, a two-pound loaf costs six and a half, cigarettes ten for six pence, fine old brandy three and six a glass, the *Irish Times* (four pages) three pence. Working men shared digs for 14/6 a week and holidays with full pay was a dream of the future. Half the adult population or more than half had been born in the nineteenth century: wisps of the virgin idealism of 1898 still hung in the air.

BARBARA REDMOND: He was barred from every pub in Dublin!

LIAM REDMOND: Well I think that was . . . in the latter part of his life I think he must have become quarrelsome. But at the stage when I knew him well, I never saw anything like that. I never knew him to be at all quarrelsome. He was . . . sharp in his criticism of things, but never quarrelsome.

INTERVIEWER: What about his drinking habits?

BEN KIELY: Well, I suppose they were fairly excessive, like a lot of people in this town. He drank I think generally rather early in the day, you know, and quit—that's if he was drinking. But in this you know, when you talk about people drinking you only see them when they are drinking. You never see them when they're sober at all. So that people get a reputation for wild drinking, but he wasn't a wild drinker. He drank I would say rather steadily and he could get quite sharp, I never found him nasty in argument. But I think people say that he could get quite nasty in argument when he was intoxicated. I must say that I never found that so. I always found him very gracious, but he was inclined to insist on making his point, but his points were always well made.

ARTHUR POWER: He was very often completely stocious. I suppose he was stocious. Wobbling in queues. He came up to me one day . . . I've written the funniest book . . . not a great ambition: wit, yes, not just funny.

He was a very good art critic. First class. He really was a good art critic—he knew about the painters. Kernoff and O'Sullivan at the Pearl. They say he used to drink a lot but I don't think he did. I never saw him under the influence. Yeats has a line:
> . . . the 'lad man with a fine fly-fisher's wrist
> Turned to a drunken journalist

It was supposed to be Smyllie. He took this very much to heart. He came from Sligo, so he would have known him.

INTERVIEWER: Hard to imagine Smyllie as a young man; but I suppose he must have been young once.

BARBARA REDMOND: One of the reasons he was banned from the—I beg your pardon, barred is the word—I discovered by accident when

I was coming out of the Palace with my brother and his wife. Don looked down at the mat inside the front door, and it was about two inches too small, and my brother being a lawyer looked with great interest and said, "I wonder what the situation now would be if Brian came in here, was put out, and fell over on the way out. Because he isn't allowed here—but would he still have a legal right to be here?"

LIAM REDMOND: Wouldn't it be a WELCOME mat, Barbara? (*Laughter.*)

NARRATOR: I recall, this would be in the early 1950s, two grimly over-weight weekend golfers, similar as to rotundity and shabbiness of apparel, the more florid one a pipe-smoker, who at weekends were to be seen toiling up the steeply angled fairways onto plateaued greens at Delgany Golf Club in Co. Wicklow. They would sometimes play together, parting company immediately as their drives diverged, toting shabby canvas bags, some mismatched old hickory-shafted clubs. This pair would be R. M. Smyllie, editor of the *Irish Times*, and his obituary writer Eamonn Lynch. The latter offered to place anything I had in Irish writing, as he "had something" on the editor Peadar O'Donnell.

Myles na gCopaleen himself, it was said, sometimes used the clubhouse for after-hours drinking on *Irish Times* golf club outings. In the background of a group of weekend golfers in a sepia photograph that hung in the bar a round Oriental face was pointed out to me as the legendary Myles na gCopaleen alias Flann O'Brien, whose real name was thought to be Brian O'Nolan. I only half-believed this. Since he adopted pseudonyms at will, could he not also adopt other disguises? The round, crafty, clean-shaven, half-averted face gave nothing away.

Some years later I found myself on a television "panel" in the Donnybrook studios with Anthony Cronin, Ben Kiely, the bookseller Allen Figgis, and Myles himself. The programme was going out "live" in the afternoon. Kiely, the many-storied man from Omagh, ever strong on genealogies, as the Pope O'Mahony before him, intent on proving that all the families of Ireland were interrelated, arrived with Myles, both men of old Tyrone, having just proved that he was his 42nd cousin.

BEN KIELY: The days of the *Irish Times*, Smyllie's time.

INTERVIEWER: How would you describe the appearance of the man?

BEN KIELY: He had a sort of family appearance. All the O'Nolan family seemed to be small, dark rather intense men. Ciaran the elder brother was sort of more relaxed in appearance; but they had a sort of family appearance—black of eyes men and intense and very exact in their way of speaking to you, as he was nearly all the time.

INTERVIEWER: Did he have a Northern accent?

CRONIN: No. No trace of a Northern accent at all. You wouldn't think he was from the North you know, nothing in his accent or general. I'm not sure if you would know a Northern person by their general demeanour but um. I think there are Northern traits and he didn't have them. I didn't think he had them anyway.

NARRATOR: The plan was to get Myles into the studio to soberly address the Plain People of Ireland on whatever subject he cared to talk about. This didn't work out too well. For presently he began rounding on his favourite targets—Them—the City Fathers, the gobshites in high places, Kerry peasants in Treasury pants—and seemed on the point of naming names when the programme was cut short. The late Jack White was the producer.

Myles turned to me and inquired how it went, under the impression that I was one of the technicians. Fine, I said, just fine. I recall him being rather rude to a Miss O'Farrell who had arranged the programme.

Later in McDaid's I brought Myles a double whisky and made the mistake of praising *At Swim-Two-Birds*, which I had discovered in Delgany County Council lending library.

"You ought to know better than that," he rebuked me, clearing the throat with small coughs and voiceless fricatives, a lizard tongue darting in and out—"a Christian Brothers boy like yourself." Confusing me with somebody else. I could see he was a difficult man to talk to, sitting alone and not meeting your eye, both feared and loved, part mad Sweeny, part devil Pooka, part Good Fairy, part Trellis, part nameless Narrator, a chameleon figure sitting there in the shadowy interior of McDaid's Bar. And if it came to abuse, and McDaid's was like that, this Sepia Man would surely get the jump on you. They all called him Myles. He was Myles na gCopaleen, the Town Crier. It is not easy to be famous in a small city. I never saw him again.

# THE DALKEY ARCHIVE

NARRATOR: He was fond of puzzles and dined out on matchtricks. Those who were near him agreed that he was shy, put on an act in public, made himself invisible, liked company as long as he could dominate it, liked a drop, and this dominated him.

If he wished to repel he could, he had a wicked tongue. He discovered himself in his early writing, his first three novels, one in Irish, one unpublished in his own lifetime; lost himself again in the last three, after a lapse of twenty years during which he was writing "Cruiskeen Lawn," got out of touch with his talent, his "powers of sensual perception" lagged.

Possibly he had willed his imagination too much, forced the vision. The doctrinal disputations of *The Dalkey Archive* would hardly interest even a theologian, much less that apocryphal judicial personality, the reasonable and prudent man; but the fancy stuff in this case could not be kept down. Blank anonymity coming suddenly in the middle of life should be at least alarming, a sharp symptom that the mind is in decay.

"I know some of the writing is deplorable for a man of my pretences," he wrote to his publisher O'Keefe in a rare moment of self-criticism. "Your jokes against religiosity are not quite as good as you think they are," O'Keefe wrote. "You ought to re-think the set dialogues." The material itself was not intrinsically funny, but no material is. The pliancy

and fun had vanished into some dark place; he had developed an unpleasant habit of disparaging others, in life and in his fiction. Joyce
came in for much abuse. You can perhaps make good jokes about St.
Augustine, but not about Joyce; his own life after all had been a sort of
joke; his work stood above it, in a way beyond criticism. The pious curate of *The Dalkey Archive* who disclaims authorship of *Ulysses* could
never had been Joyce, "screwing up his courage" to enter the Jesuit
Order. These are jokes in poor taste, damp squibs, humour in vacuo.
Sylvia Beach, as here suggested, could never have conceived *Ulysses*,
much less written it; nor would Gogarty have wished to collaborate
on *Dubliners*.

Brian O'Nolan had learnt much of what he knew as a writer from
Joyce, who had it from source, and recorded it in a way impossible
to emulate again. The disciple grew to detest the Master, you have
to murder your mentor. Against the eighteen hours in the life of a
contemporary man that is *Ulysses*, he set the forty-two extracts written in thirty-six different styles that is *At Swim-Two-Birds*, the comic
masterpiece praised by Joyce. Compressing the mythic into the commonplace was a trick few could emulate, not Gilbert Sorrentino in
*Mulligan Stew* for one. Joyce's own imagination had no will of its own;
he never knew what his characters would say next. And what did not
come from *Ulysses* came from *Dubliners*: Jem Casey's "A Pint of Plain
is Your Only Man" comes from Joe Hyne's doggerel, "The Death of
Parnell," in "Ivy Day in the Committee Room"; as well as much of the
banality of Dublin common speech from "Grace"—the conversation
of the men in the bedroom, from the Gardiner Street Mission.

Stanislaus Joyce laid insistent claims to some of the ideas in *Ulysses*,
and moreover "gave" his brother the plot of "Ivy Day." Cecil ffrench
Salkeld (who is Byrne in *At Swim*) believed that he had written (perhaps in his sleep) *At Swim*, or at least put the idea into the author's
brain by lending him *The Conspectus of Arts and Natural Sciences*,
which is freely quoted from when other inventions fail.

I sometimes think that, given another set of circumstance, a greater writer might have evolved; but then Myles would not have existed, and there would have been no "Cruiskeen Lawn" with the morning eggs and bacon.

Anthony Cronin has compared O'Nolan's work to James Stephens; but a closer comparison might be Ettore Schmitz, the Triestine paint manufacturer who wrote two novels ignored by Italian critics because of their "bad" Italian: Triestine argot. Encouraged by Joyce he wrote the book by which he will be remembered, *Confessions of Zeno*, under the pseudonym Italo Svevo.

As the Good Fairy in *At Swim* proclaims, "It is a great art that can evolve a fifth Excellence from four Futilities." It is indeed. Truth is an odd number. Joyce constructed *Ulysses* on the pyramid of *Stephen Hero* and *A Portrait of the Artist as a Young Man*; Beckett the great French trilogy on *More Pricks than Kicks* and *Murphy*. The reader in Longmans who turned down *The Third Policeman* has much to answer for. (*Pause.*)

He may have known he had cancer. At all events he had to take a large quantity of drugs to relieve the pain, and several times had recourse to the last rites. His last years were not easy. But then his life had been, as the Irish say, crossed. He was difficult company in those later years; his "scorpiousness" finding expression in outbursts of scorn that no longer distinguished between humbug and genuine. The late Jack White wrote of the "drab little figure in the pork-pie hat who could be seen passing down the road, with the marionette-step of the habitual drinker, on the way to get a curative gin at Gleeson's as soon as the doors opened." Now he was surrounded by enemies. They were out to get him. "Too much contempt had soured his palate."

In a small notebook he wrote: "The meanest bloody thing in hell made this world.

June 1945, "Cruiskeen Lawn": "When the world is at peace, horror camps are not photographed." And, a year previously: "War is to be understood only in terms of man; man only in terms of war. There is no third war. There is only one war; and to think that it will cease within the bournes of humanity's tenure of the soil is to think as one thought in the nursery."

His view of the "coming Ireland" was not too sanguine: "I can see the new Ireland . . . The decaying population tucked carefully in white sterilised beds, numb with drugs, rousing themselves only to make their wills in Irish. Outside, not a stir anywhere to be discerned—save for the commotion of funerals hurtling along the vast arterial roads to the vast arterial cemeteries . . ."

On March 2nd, 1966, just a month before his death, he wrote: "If a man has the courage to raise his eyes and look sanely at the awful human condition . . . he must realise finally that tiny periods of temporary release from intolerable suffering is the most that any individual has the right to expect."

Suddenly, on April 1st, 1966, at the age of fifty-five, with his life in disarray, permanent release came to Brian Nolan.

CIARAN: It becomes horrifying, but I think that at that stage the second book, *The Third Policeman*, that he wanted to say, "Well, this could be reality." I mean, what are we to think about eternity, you have to begin thinking about that and so on, nobody knows what's in store. It could be frightful. The future hell, you know, is not just a matter of being burned, being used; it's something much more subtle, you know, and much more frightful you know. If you can try and imagine it, you know, the cyclical sort of business in which you're back again at the start of the awful pilgrimage. And you know it's a frightening thing, and people have described the book to me and said, you know, "It's terribly funny but, you know, it frightens me." Maybe it's meant to.

NARRATOR: His last years had not been happy ones. In the epigraph of the rejected novel, the one that would not see the light of day in his lifetime, life—human life—is seen as "comic maggot folly": "Human existence being an hallucination containing in itself the secondary hallucinations of day and night (the latter an insanity condition of the atmosphere due to the accretion of black air) it ill becomes any man of sense to be concerned at the illusory approach of the supreme hallucination known as death."

All Dublin turned up for the funeral in Glasnevin—it was packed out, a full house. Patrick Kavanagh wept. The Sage of Santry was going underground. Near his grave the hawthorn was breaking out, and there were whips of snow on the Three Rock Mountain.

ARTHUR POWER: He was in Mercer's Hospital covered in poultices. The nurse brought him another poultice on a tray. He said, "Look Nurse, I have enough poultices." She said, "This isn't a poultice—this is your dinner." (*Sniggering.*)

KEVIN: Finn and all those people who were revered figures . . . there's another way of looking at them. These people existed, you know. Sweeney and so on. As he used to say when he was nearly dying, "Being ill is no joke, you know." But he'd make a joke of things, you know.

BEN KIELY: Was it, I wonder, a real story or was it one of those fantasies that he might have developed?

NARRATOR: Let the last words be from O'Nolan, from the rejected second novel hidden for twenty-four years; the story of the revolving Irish-style hell, the novel from beyond the grave:

"Down into the earth where dead men go I would go soon and maybe come out of it again in some healthy way, free and innocent of all human perplexity. I would perhaps be the chill of an April wind, an essential part of some indomitable river or be personally concerned in the ageless perfection of some rank mountain bearing down upon the mind by occupying forever a position in the blue easy distance. Or perhaps a smaller thing like movement in the grass on an unbearable breathless yellow day, some hidden creature going about its business—I might well be responsible for that or for some important part of it.

Or even those unaccountable distinctions that make an evening recognisable from its own morning, the smells and sounds and sights of the perfect and matured essence of the day, these might not be innocent of my meddling and my abiding presence."

# Assassin

Sixty-minute play. First broadcast on BBC Radio 4 on the 6th of August, 1973. Stage version prepared for this edition.

# CAST

*The Hapsburgs*

ARCHDUKE FRANZ FERDINAND

ARCHDUKE AS CHILD

COUNTESS SOPHIE CHOTEK, his wife

EMPEROR FRANZ JOSEF

MAXIMILIAN

CARLOTA

THE KAISER

FIRST AUSTRIAN COUNT

SECOND AUSTRIAN COUNT

*The Opposition*

GAVRILO PRINCIP, the assassin

JOVO, his elder brother

PETAR, his father

PETAR'S SISTER

IVO ANDRIĆ, Yugoslav author

*Others*

BISHOP OF LONDON

BISHOP OF HERZEGOVINA

DR. EISENMENGER

NURSE

LADY BURTON

NARRATOR

FRENCHMAN

RUSSIAN

ENGLISHMAN

GERMAN

COCKNEY

BOSNIAN BEATER

THE PAST

CHORUS

•

# SCENES

Sources: Ivo Andrić, Saul Bellow (*The Adventures of Augie March*), John Berryman, Elizabeth Bowen (*Bowen's Court*), Galeazzo Ciano (*The Ciano Diaries*), Vladimir Dedijer (*The Road to Sarajevo*), Isak Denisen (*The Life of the Storyteller*), T. S. Eliot, Dr. Eisenmenger, Hans Magnus Enzensberger (*Politics and Crime*), Heinrish Friedjung (*Oesterreich von 1848 bis 1860*), Sir Edward Grey, Nadine Gordimer (*Something Out There*), John Hawkes (*The Cannibal; Death, Sleep and the Traveler*), James Joyce (*Letters*), Franz Kafka (*Letters to Milena, Blue Octavo Notebooks, Dearest Father, The Country Doctor*), Emil Ludwig (*July 1914*), Robert Musil (*The Man Without Qualities*), John Reed, Joachim Remak (*Sarajevo*), Bedrich Rowhan, Abram Tertz (*A Voice from the Chorus*), Seyton Watson, Virginia Woolf (*The Waves*), Jack B. Yeats (*A Charmed Life*).

# ENVOI

*At the front of the stage chairs are arranged, as if for an audience. As many of the cast members as are available enter and sit in these chairs, excluding* PRINCIP, ARCHDUKE, *and the two* AUSTRIAN COUNTS. *Brass band plays Imperial Anthem. German crowd, voices.* ARCHDUKE *and* PRINCIP *enter and address this "audience."*

PRINCIP: (*Narrating.*) After sunset on the 28th of August, 1914, the day Austria-Hungary declared war on Serbia, the German-speaking community crowded into the Piazza Grande in Trieste, where the Schiller Club flew the flags of the Triple Alliance from its windows, and a military band played the Imperial Anthem.

*Buzz of excited German-speaking crowd in square.*
*Imperial anthem becomes Gershwin's* Rhapsody in Blue—*near opening.*

ARCHDUKE: (*Narrating.*) On Appel Quay a breeze disturbs the leaves of the trees that line its embankments. And all that remains of those momentous happenings, so soon terminated, is a small museum, and outside, at the head of the bridge that bears his name, (*motioning disdainfully to his companion*) Princip's footprints immortalised in cement.

PRINCIP: (*Narrating.*) If you see a chauffeur-driven limousine go by today, the stout fellow lounging in the back seat is either a party boss, or a mullah.

"*Lush Life*," *Nat King Cole, 2–3 secs alone, then under to end. Two* AUS-TRIAN COUNTS *remove their chairs from the makeshift audience. They arrange themselves as described below.*

ARCHDUKE: (*Narrating.*) Reclining at their ease in baroque arm-chairs, long slender legs clad in soft light-grey trousers with razor-sharp creases, two comfortably-situated aged counts are sitting in the golden-and-red Chancellery of the Viennese Foreign Ministry. Occasionally, one of the two makes a move on a richly ornate chessboard.

PRINCIP: (*Narrating.*) A scent of limes from the Volksgarten is wafted through the tall open wind—

ARCHDUKE: (*Narrating. Interrupting, indignant.*) Still in Vienna at the beginning of July? Is something amiss? Have they no affairs of state to transact?

FIRST COUNT: Well, yes and no; we are discussing whether one can wear tussore or only grey.

SECOND COUNT: Court mourning in the summer is always a nuisance, and the black mourning-band on the tussore sleeve would look too much like the national colours.

ARCHDUKE: (*Drawn out of narrator role.*) In mourning? But who . . .

PRINCIP: (*Interrupting, he escorts* ARCHDUKE *offstage.*) . . . as they talk in low, reflective tones, each trying to impart a tone of sadness to trivial remarks, in the hope that the other will be impressed. (*From offstage.*) But as a matter of fact both are pleasantly excited by the events at Sarajevo.

FIRST COUNT: (*Smoking a pipe.*) It is pleasant . . . in moments such as these . . . knowing with certainty an approaching catastrophe, to view the whole incident that will probably extend over fifty years . . . not as the death of politics . . . (*reflective puff*) . . . not the fall of kings and their wives . . . but as the loyalty of civilisation; to realise that Krupp (*puff*), perhaps a barbarian, is more the peg where history hangs itself than a father who once spoke of honour.

SECOND COUNT: Streets in the sky! Citizens' moonlight zones! Where in the springtime of an idle life, on twentieth-story rooftops, behind high mesh netting, Modular Man can play tennis for ever and ever!

# Introduction

FIRST COUNT: (*Standing to address the audience. Brisk.*) Welcome to the Everyman Palace Theatre. The oldest theater in Cork.

SECOND COUNT: (*Standing to address the audience. Excited.*) As you can see, this beautiful six-hundred-and-fifty seat theater is a jewel of late Victorian architec—

FIRST COUNT: (*Clears his throat to interrupt. Annoyed. Waits until he has everyone's attention.*) The Everyman Theatre in cooperation with the Abbey Theatre, Dublin, brings you *Assassin*, a staged reading of a radio play by Aidan Higgins, directed by Joe Dowling.

Judiciously subtitled, "The End of the Hapsburg Empire, or History as Humiliation."

SECOND COUNT: Act I. Vienna, May 1914, a month before the assassination at Sarajevo. In the Hapsburg Palace, Archduke Franz Ferdinand stands alone, looking out over Vienna.

*Fauré's first sonata for violin and piano. Say 3–4 secs alone, then under following:*

FIRST COUNT: (*On echo.*) Nothing that ever happened, nothing that was ever willed, planned or envisaged, remains irrelevant today.

In the savage and austere light of a burning world details leaped out with significance.

War is not an accident. It is an outcome. One cannot look back too far to ask, of what?

As our forefathers thought, we act; and our descendants will act out what we thought.

SECOND COUNT: (*Dramatic.*) A curtain is opening on a play . . .

*Onstage audience abandons their seats (taking them with them) with a flourish. Woodwinds tuning up: trills and arpeggios. The effect should be that of a curtain opening to the real audience.*

# VIEW FROM THE SCHLOSS

*Fauré Sonata. 4 secs, then under.*

ARCHDUKE: (*Sotte voce, looking out window at Vienna.*) How dark everything has become! And yet it had been so bright before. Everything is (*Pulls at cigar.*) . . . quiet, as far as one can see. The anglers go on angling. The onlookers go on . . . looking. The children play football. (*Pause.*) The man at the bridge collects Kreuzers. (*Puffs, coughs.*) On looking more closely one discovers a certain nervousness. The people force themselves to stick to their work so as not to betray any of their thoughts.

*Offstage sound of troops of household cavalry trotting over cobbles, orders in German. Church bell.*

(*Gloomily.*) It's gloomy.
Sometimes it tries to rain. Sometimes the light of the clouds disturbs me while writing. Well . . . it's exactly as it is. Sad and heavy.

*Offstage: Pedestrians, feet, voices, church-bell.*

Sunlight has been dimmed not by clouds but by itself. Yet all the time the clouds do not disappear. How could they? I can no longer take one step. (*Puff.*) Suddenly everything becomes a lie and the hunted chokes the hunter.

ARCHDUKE *draws the drapes. The sounds of the city are replaced by the silence of the room where the grandfather clock ticks.*

Suddenly it happened. The lamp splintered into a thousand pieces. A strange man with a fresh light came into the room. (*Shadow of a person which might be Princip.*) I rose, my family with me. We greeted him. No notice was taken. Absolutely none.

*Gusting, window buffeted.*

(*Baleful.*) Thus the sad dream rolled over me. There was an intelligible hidden element of . . . rejection in it. I didn't mention it but cursed myself, and in so doing only pronounced the curse that lay on me. (*Indrawn breath, pacing parquet floor.*)

. . . I didn't know why this was unbreakable to me. Again and again, I couldn't help it . . . I had to pull him toward me with a question, and again and again I lost him through my own fault. (*Pacing.*) Giants too have their weaknesses. Even Hercules (*coughs*) I believe, once had a fainting fit. And the rest of the world I take like Münchhausen (*deep*) took the gun carriages of the Gibraltar Army and threw them into the sea. Or as Gulliver, wading, dragged the pygmy fleet off its moorings.

*Wind and rain, thunder.*

Either the world is so tiny or we are so enormous, in any case we fill it completely. (*Puffs.*) Of whom should I be jealous? (*Pacing, cogitating.*)

This wish for a comfortable death, this was already the wish for small children. Nothing more. I'm tired. When shall we see one another? (*Alertly.*) Where are you now?

*Seats himself, pulls open drawer, slaps documents on table during following.*

(*Glum.*) On the way to the village where the hut is? I'm also on my way there. (*Resigned.*) Whatever happens we are on our way. One can do no more than that. Where did all the trouble between us come from?

*Storm rattles window.*

(*Dreamingly.*) Yes, it's probably best that we meet. How long would it otherwise take before we could put things straight? And I could have stopped it long ago. The eye was clear enough, but the cowardice was stronger. The sick man is detested by the healthy. But the healthy one is also detested by the sick. And the doctor? Ah! The thought of the sick man brings a doctor, who is detested by both. And how can I be satisfied if the doctor doesn't find any trace? And is it really so serious?

*Roll of thunder and church bell*

(*Low.*) I am sick.

However I am not going to bore you with stories of my sickness. All sick stories are similar and differ only in degree. And are we not all sick, if it comes to that? A safe rule of conduct: mistrust the sickly. They only tell you lies.

*Closes drawer, shuffles papers.*

*Storm outside. Sad bell ringing.*

(*Low.*) Perhaps our lies are different to yours. Perhaps they are not lies at all.

The invalid's secret desire . . . is that everyone should be sick, like him. All sick ones are sadists at heart. But their sadism is acquired at a stiff price, its only excuse.

*Desk-phone rings, Vienna model circa 1910.*

(*To himself.*) Who was it spoke of the "ecstasy" of complaining? Some unhealthy Czech, no doubt. Some *Bulgar*!
(*Lifts receiver, speaks sharply.*) *Ja*! *Richtig. Gut . . . Mein Frau*? Ah!

*Pause as wife is put through. Sophie's high excited indistinct German.*

SOPHIE: Franzi, it is I . . . I have such trouble . . . (*Indistinct message, her laugh.*)

ARCHDUKE: Sopherl! (*Fondly.*) *Ja . . . ja*, it is I. I was this very moment going to write to you. (*Listens.*) *Ja*! Things have turned out well in Gilgen? (*Listens.*) Ohhh-ho? (*Listens.*) *Ja*! That's not so good . . . that's bad. (*Listens.*) But here too! (*Listens, wife being solicitous.*) I feel poorly and so-so, depending how you look at it. I hope my health will last a while into the autumn. (*Listens, wifely indistinct message in German.*) *Ja, ja*! *Richtig*! But even before I had finished reading your letter—towards the end you mention something similar—it occurred to me it might be possible . . . to arrange something along those lines. For you to stay there a little longer. As long as the autumn allows. Would that not be possible? (*Listens.*) No? (*Listens.*) *Ja*, I received your letter from Strasburg. (*Listens.*) . . . A hare in the snow? Ho-ho-ho! But here all the time it was raining, and outside it doesn't look as if it will ever stop.

*Storm as on cue, brief thunder.*

(*Listens*) . . . I have! I did. I will. (*Pause.*) What? All the rest? *Still telling lies!* I don't bel—

*Dinner gong, muffled drumstick on brass, an elaborate summons.*

(*Heavy eater, greedy, would end phone call, speaks more resolutely.*) . . . I wouldn't embark on . . . explanations just yet, not until I have considered all the . . . implications. (*Impatient.*) *Ja, ja-ja!* Just so. *Precisely!* (*Pause. Listening.*)

Now I better stop and go and eat. You may have just heard the gong. Warm love to you (*Tender.*) . . . to *mein Kinder. Auf Wiedersehen, Katchen!*

ARCHDUKE *replaces the receiver gently. Dinner gong ends in flourish. Music, Shostakovich Trio in E Minor, plucked violin at beginning and at end, under following.*

(*Low, rapid, resolute, his "politic" voice, a third manner. Conscience, wife, now fear.*) I'm travelling towards you now and nothing in the world can save me. One can get certain results, after all, if only one has the courage.

It is degrading, but what shall I do when instead of a heart this fear is beating in my breast? (*Pause.*) . . . What do they hold for me—today's night, today's day? Besides (*low*) . . . I like myself so little. I feel like the giant who keeps the public away with outstretched arms.

PRINCIP: (*As a ghost. Hollow, on echo, Serbo-Croatian.*) Our ghosts will walk through the Palace . . . frightening the Lords.

*Sophie-voice on telephone, speeded up.*
*Babies (two sons) bawl lustily in unison, abrupt cut.*
*Break of 4 secs silence.*
*Forest, peaceful.*

. . . And there's the night again. Inconceivable that one can breathe it . . . inconceivable that the chest can expand and contract sufficiently to breathe this air.

*Breeze brings in leaves.*

If one can perish from happiness, then this must happen to me. And if a person designated to die can stay alive through happiness . . . ? (*Racking cough.*)

*Mix to palace apartment. Storm faint, grandfather clock loud, then under.*

ARCHDUKE: (*Bossy now.*) There is a door in my apartment to which I hitherto paid no attention. It is in the bedroom, in the party wall between this and the next house. I have never thought about it; indeed I did not even know about it. (*Clears throat.*) And yet it can be seen quite plainly, though the lower part of it is concealed by the beds. It extends to a great height, almost not a door but a gate. (*Amused.*) Yesterday it was opened.

(*Takes out handkerchief, sudden blast of noseblowing.*) I happened to be in the dining room, which is separated from the bedroom by yet another room. (*Pause, putting handkerchief away.*) . . . I had come home very late. There was nobody left in the house, only the maid was busy in the kitchen. Then the noise began in the bedroom.

*Forest again, sawing of axe or crosscut.*

(*Narrative tone.*) I instantly hurried into the room and saw the door being slowly opened, the beds being pushed aside by some gigantic force.

I called out: "Who is that? What is wanted? Careful, look out!" and expected to see a gang of brutal and violent men bursting in. But it was only a slim young man who slipped in, as soon as there was a crack just wide enough for him to get through. He hailed me joyfully.

*Forest: small tree falling to crosscut.*
*Bosnian folk tune, 3 secs, then under.*

PRINCIP: I was overcome by something that was almost a swoon. I dropped the spade and went home. There were men sitting at table there, all eating out of the one common dish, and the two women were at the stove and the washtub.

I at once recounted what had happened to me, and while doing so fell down on the bench by the door. They all stood around me. An old man of proven skill was fetched from a farm nearby. While we were waiting for him children came to me. We took each others' hands, linked fingers.

*Bosnian folk tune.*

(*Tired.*) . . . To tell the truth, the whole affair does not concern me overmuch. I lie in the corner, looking on insofar as one can look on while lying down, and listening insofar as I understood him. And for the rest (*Heavy sigh.*) . . . I have for months now been living in a sort of twilight, waiting for the night.

CHILDREN'S CHOIR: (*From Kafka's "The Country Doctor."*) Unclothe him, unclothe him, then he will heal, and should he not heal, then kill him. He's only a doctor, only a doctor.

PRINCIP: (*Almost dozing.*) Like me for instance . . . when during the arithmetic lesson I saw the Professor up there . . . (*Yawns.*) Leafing through his notebook . . . and I compared my inconceivable lack of knowledge with that spectacle of . . . strength . . . terror . . . and reality.

I wished, half dreaming with fear, that I could go up like a ghost . . . flit ghostlike between the benches . . . fly past the Professor as light as my knowledge of mathematics . . . somehow penetrate the door, pull myself together outside and be free in the lovely air.

*Bosnian folk tune fades.*

## Evening in the Forest

*Bosnian folk tune.*

PRINCIP: We arise out of the graves and want to go roaming through this world too. (*Pause.*) We have no definite plan.

*Bosnian folk tune.*

In the evening, went to the forest. Confused day behind me. (*Pause.*) . . . Sick stomach. The pale moon rose as I made way through the trees.

*Forest wind.*

(*Lethargic.*) I lay sick. (*Pause.*) Dreams flooded over me. (*Pause, long indrawn breath.*) . . . The tormenting demon dwells in the forest . . . in the long-abandoned cabin dating back to the old charcoal-burning times.

*Rooks cawing.*

Quietly the forest murmurs are heard through the empty window. (*Pause, looking out.*) . . . Moon waxing. How lonely it is here and how well it suits me! Here in the corner I will sleep. Why not in the forest, where the air moves freely?

*Forest sounds.*

(*Dreamily.*) Evenings by the river. A boat in the water. Sun setting among clouds. A shout rises out of the river.

*Faint indistinct cry: "Gavrilo!"*

ARCHDUKE: (*Interrupts, from palace.*) Letting the head full of disgust and hatred sink, the chin upon the chest. But what if someone is throttling you?

*Neither hears nor heeds the other.*

PRINCIP: The worries that are the burden of which the privileged person makes an excuse in dealing with the oppressed person, are in fact the worries about preserving his privileged condition.

ARCHDUKE: Does he do it for the others' sake or because he believes that only with the others can he remain what he was, because he must destroy the world in order not to be compelled to love it?

PRINCIP: Sometimes I believe I hear nothing but the other voices and everything else seems to me only a dream. (*Pause.*) And it is as though I were just letting the dream go on talking at random.

*Forest and river sounds, cry off, fainter: "Gavrilo!"*

FIRST COUNT: Why do you compare the inner commandment to a dream?

*Ghostly gate bell rings. Jingle of harness. Knocking.*

PRINCIP: (*To himself.*) It was already late in the night when I rang the bell at the gate. (*Swallows.*) . . . It was a long time before the gatekeeper came out, evidently from the depths of the courtyard.

    (*Imitating rustic:*) "Master bids you come in," the servant said, bowing. And with a soundless jerk he opened the high glass door. (*Wonderstruck.*) . . . With an almost flying stride the Count hastened towards me from his writing desk, which stood by the open window. (*Pause.*) We looked into each other's eyes. I was taken aback by the Count's rigid gaze.

ARCHDUKE: (*Aghast, whispers.*) What do I carry on my shoulders? What spectres cling to me?

*Rooks taking flight, agitated.*

PRINCIP: Barren Fields. A barren plain. Behind the mists the pallid green of the moon.

*Hunting horn, pack preparing to move off.*

    I lay on the ground by a wall, writhing in pain, trying to burrow into the damp earth. The huntsman stood beside me and lightly pressed one foot into the small of my back. (*Indrawn breath.*) . . . Ah!

*Pack at the kill, close.*

    Already tired of me and eager for fresh action the hounds were running senselessly against the wall.

*Hunting horn, off.*

. . . The coach came. And bound hand and foot I was flung in beside the gentleman, over the back seat so that my head and arms hung down outside the carriage.

The journey passed swiftly and smoothly. Perishing with thirst, with open mouth, I breathed in the high-whirling dust. (*Sucks in breath*).

*Horse and carriage in Vienna, lady laughs, brief.*

ARCHDUKE: (*Awed.*) There were many waiting.

*Hubbub of large excited crowd at concert, orchestra tuning up. Brief.*

. . . A throng reaching further than the eye can see, extending away into the darkness. (*Pause.*)
What does it want?

*Hubbub still. Large orchestra begins* Die Fledermaus *hold say 3 secs, sudden cut.*

It is evidently definite demands that it is making. I shall listen to those demands and then answer. (*Orchestra begins again.*) But I shall not go out on the balcony. Nor could I do so if I wanted to.

*German music hall. Joke just ending, guffaws from packed house.*

(*Voice raised over catcalls in German, guffaws, fainter under following.*) In the winter the door to the balcony is locked and the key is not available. But neither shall I go to the window. I do not want to see anyone. I am not going to let myself be confused by the sight of anybody.

*Audience response tails off. Comedian begins another terrible joke.*

. . . There are many waiting. I said: "That's not so bad, they're all like this." But in this way only made it worse.

*Joke building up, shouted out.*

Because of the errors in my upbringing, I could not tell how it should be done differently. Not for the life of me.

*Music hall fainter, say 3 secs, sudden mix to Vienna woods.*

PRINCIP: When I came along the water at night, from the direction of the tower, now, every night, the dark water is slowly moved, almost like a body, under the light of the lantern.

(*Low, fatigued.*) At midnight I am always to be met with by the river. Either I am on night-duty and on my way to the prison . . . or . . . on day-duty and am going home.

Evening by the river. A boat on the water. Sun setting among clouds. A shout rises out of the river!

*Call (Fainter) "Gavrilo!"*

Moon waxing. How lonely it is here and how well it suits you! Here in the corner you will sleep. Why not in the forest, where the air moves freely? (*Pause.*) The tormenting demon dwells in the forest (*Indrawn breath.*) In the long-abandoned cabin dating back to old charcoal-burning days. Quietly the forest murmurs are heard through the empty window.

*Forest murmurs.*

ARCHDUKE: (*Testy.*) Letting the head full of disgust and hatred sink, the chin upon the chest . . . But what if someone is throttling you?

*Grandfather clock, storm outside, as before.*

(*To himself*) . . . Someone pulled at my clothes, but I shook him off. I was able to die, but not to bear pain; though my efforts to avoid it increased it markedly. I could yield submissively to death, but not to suffering. (*Pause.*) . . . I lacked scope for spiritual movement. Just as, when everything is packed, the tightened straps are tightened agonisingly yet again and again and the departure is not taken. (*Whispers.*) . . . The worst thing: pain that does not kill.

*Knocking on window.*

(*Low.*) There came a knock on the window! I started up out of my doze, pulled myself together, and said aloud: "*Es ist nichts* . . . ! It's nothing, the wind is shaking the window."

*Knocking on window.*

(*Horror-struck*) . . . There came another knock. I said: "I know it's only the wind." But at the third knock a voice asked to be let in. "But it's only the wind," I said, took the lamp from the cupboard and lit it, and drew the curtains over the window.

*Wind blows; high psychotic whine.*

(*Hollowly.*) Then the whole window began to tremble, and there began a humble wordless lamentation.

*Ghost-Princip on echo, voice from the grave.*

PRINCIP: I am on a journey, don't disturb me, open your shirt and carry me close to your body.

ARCHDUKE: (*Low, obedient.*) I did so. He took a long stride and disappeared into me as into a house.

*Music-hall din speeded up as nightmare, brief.*

I stretched out as though constricted. I was overcome by something that was almost a swoon.

*Forest noises, Vienna woods, resume.*

PRINCIP: . . . So deep in the forest, so restful in rest, that one doesn't really want to say anything but that up there through the trees the sky is visible.

*Music off: faint Serbian folk tune*

(*The failed poet, emotional.*) "The light advanced across the river . . ." (*Pause, changing tack.*) "The flower-decked corpses are following their toes to the open sea . . ." (*Pause, no improvement here.*) "Poor Chinese dead float out on the Yangtze . . ."

*Slow fade. Gusla, plucked string.*

*Panting of dying* ARCHDUKE, *his dying words.*

ARCHDUKE: (*Expiring.*) Sopherl! *Meine Lieber* Sopherl! . . . *Stirb mir nichts!* . . . *Bleibe fur meine Kinder!* (*Strenuous breathing.*)

*Silence.*

SECOND COUNT: Once Princip had tried to approach Ivo Andrić with some verses he had composed. Andrić told him to bring them to him. But Princip never did.

When Ivo asked him why he had not brought them, Princip answered casually that he had destroyed them.

ARCHDUKE: (*At last gasp.*) *Es . . . ist . . . nichts!* (*Expires.*)

FIRST COUNT: (*Bland*) Trembling like a child Princip brought out his poems about roses which were blooming deep in the bottom of the sea for the beloved one.

PRINCIP: (*Emotional, Serbo-Croatian.*) The garden is in mourning . . . (*Pause.*) The rain sinks coolly on the flowers . . . (*Pause.*) Summertime shudders quietly to its close . . .

*Silence.* PRINCIP *hums under breath, tries again.*

From a balcony a rose petal drops to the cobbles . . .

*Mix to: wheezing old* KAISER *exiled in Holland*

KAISER WILHELM II: (*German.*) The roses in my garden are blooming . . .

*Gusla plucked string.*

PRINCIP: (*Resumes.*) We found ourselves in the miasmic and spirit-ridden forest . . . (*Hollow cough.*)

Without a word we progressed hesitantly through the trees . . . deep silence. (*Pause.*) We struggled upward through the thick forest. We looked at each other, despairingly. A faint shudder went through my limbs.

*Forest sounds.*

(*Low.*) And in silence now we continued the upward march.

*Distant horn sounds; hounds at the kill.*

(*Low.*) We built a fire—the best sight I ever saw. No poet has ever . . .
(*Stops.*) My companions fell asleep around the fire. I could not. My
companions burrowed into the leaves. (*Racking cough.*) . . . My heart-
ache, my sorrow, my life—my visions and my illusions. (*Cough ends
section.*)

# THE HUNTING TROPHIES

FIRST COUNT: "The Hunting Trophies!"

(*Sarcastic.*) . . . Ah, the hunting trophies.

(*More explicitly to the audience.*) I wish I could persuade you to travel to Konopischt for a weekend.

This Konopischt is a hunting castle in Bohemia, near the town of Benesov, about fifty kilometres south of Prague. It's been kept intact almost as it was in Franz Ferdinand's day. To see the huge collections—three of them—at close quarters should give you a little idea of the strange atmosphere he lived in, when Kaiser Bill was his hunting guest.

ARCHDUKE: To shoot eagles on the lower Danube was the thing. Although my preference—as I believe with Tito and Franco before me—was for deer, preferably stag. *Waldmannsheil!* Lovely shooting weather down there in Bohemia.

BOSNIAN BEATER: (*Gap-toothed mumble, abject.*) Your royal and imperial Highness's most humble and devoted of servants, old Slobodan, begs to humbly report that 380 hares have been counted in the Kozli district alone. (*Sniffs, wipes nose.*) . . . All looking forward with unbounded joy (*indrawn breath*) . . . to the prospect of being shot by Your Royal Highness!

*Hunting rifle firing, distant cries.*

SECOND COUNT: His physician, Dr. Eisenmenger, made the conservative estimate that his total kill must have exceeded half a million specimens.

DR. EISENMENGER: (*Wheezes.*) At a most modest estimate: 3,000 stags, 272 hares, 511 gamebirds (including a cormorant and a brace of vultures) and two large monkeys while touring India and Ceylon. In Australia he surprised his hosts by shooting wallabies and even a duck-billed platypus.

ARCHDUKE: At Ringhoffen in Bohemia during one hunt I bagged 2,140 units of small game. And in Bluhnback I shot fifty-three chamois without hitting a single doe. Up to 1913 . . . (*faintly puzzled*) the year before my death . . . I had killed more than 5,000 deer (*fusillade off*) . . . even shooting them from the windows of moving trains. A Viennese taxidermist was always at hand to stuff and mount the slaughtered specimens.

SECOND COUNT: (*Blank, resumes.*) Another notion of his was for collecting objets d'art showing representations of St. George and the dragon. Over the years he had amassed nearly four thousand pieces bearing a likeness of the Knight and the Beast.

FIRST COUNT: He was proud, thin-skinned, a misanthrope. And rather a religious bigot; somewhat miserly, short of breath *and* of temper.

ARCHDUKE: (*Dressing down his chamber officers, thunderously.*) Do I look like a man who can be made to suffer? (*Stunned silence.*) Well, DO I?

*Murmurs from officers.*

Gentlemen, I can give you my answer here and now! (*Pause.*)
It will be: incompetence! Gross incompetence! No other word for
it.
I came to the manoeuvres at five A.M. and saw nothing. I waited an
hour—*still* nothing! On the Bohemian plain.

*Murmurs from officers.*
*Mix to dawn chorus on Bohemian plain. Horse neighs.*

(*Voice up.*) Gentlemen, is this the way to conduct manoeuvres?
(*Pause, trenchant.*) Is this the way to conduct war? (*Pause, iron will.*)
Just so. Is this the way to conduct *anything*. (*Raps table with knuckles.*) I THINK NOT, Gentlemen! . . . I think not!

*Murmurs from disgruntled officers.*
*Fusillade off, German shouts.*

SECOND COUNT: The Archduke did not go in for shooting *dangerous*
animals—lions, tigers, leopards, jaguars, pumas and suchlike. Perhaps out of deference, fellow feeling; he preferred game that wouldn't
hit back.
The scattergun for sandgrouse, the hunting rifle for Bohemian
stags, broadbrim tera hat with fish-eagle feather protruding from
leopard-skin puggaree, stout calves in thick woollen stockings tucked
under lederhosen. Blazing away in the buttes, at the battue, thinking,
knowing—

ARCHDUKE: (*Arrogant.*) Here I am, where I ought to be.

*Hunting rifle on echo, grouse flight.*

FIRST COUNT: That, in a certain sense, was the man. He saw that the old times after all . . . could not be wiped away, and always contain possibilities that can come to life.

SECOND COUNT: It sounded well. What he meant was: Let it all continue as before. Let Bosnia *accept* her servitude. And Bohemia. *And* Herzegovina. And of course Serbia. Let Princip not exist.

*Distant hunting rifle firing twice on echo.*

But for every Gavrilo Princip you cut down, forty more will spring up, an unkillable hydra-headed monster spitting fire; or like wheat in the spring, with the poppies and the crows.

*Disturbed flock of crows rising from wood.*

FIRST COUNT: *His* life was to end as it had begun, among servants and attendants. Franz Ferdinand died as he had lived, in the proximity of guns.

SECOND COUNT: Of course, he *suffered*. Bigoted choleric men in positions of unlimited power often do. The people did not like him. That too was part of his suffering. "Always lording it and never making sacrifices," they said. The act does not permit anything else to exist beyond itself. This martinet would tolerate no slackness in those placed under him; and all Austro-Hungary was placed under him.

FIRST COUNT: (*Weakly.*) I cannot take to the man, and to be honest, it was always so. And as for taking his arm, I should as soon think of taking the arm of an elm tree.

ARCHDUKE: Discipline began early . . . in the nursery.

ARCHDUKE AS CHILD *and* NURSE *enter.* ARCHDUKE *throws toy to the floor, breaking it into several pieces.*

ARCHDUKE AS CHILD: (*Loss.*) Awwww . . .

NURSE *smacks his bum.*

NURSE: (*Heavy German accent.*) That's naughty!

ARCHDUKE AS CHILD: (*In pain.*) Awwww . . .

NURSE: (*Continued smacking.*) Very . . . very . . . VERY naughty!

*Wail on beaten child, self-willed, angry.*

ARCHDUKE: (*Aggrieved forty-eight-year-old.*) Everything was mixed together from morning until evening, one hour after another. We were allowed only once between two lessons to go out like good little boys, holding the hand of the Chief of the Household, for a short walk.

(*Aggravated now.*) . . . My education, let it be said, was exhaustive, haphazard, and superficial. The outcome was that we were pushed to learn everything, and in the end to know nothing thoroughly . . .

SECOND COUNT: A good father and a loving husband—what the Viennese call a *Pfikke* . . . He made this great collection of hunting trophies together with an armoury of guns. You never saw such slaughter in your life. Only one trophy he failed to add to his collection—Gavrilo Princip.

*Silence.*
*Moan of wind on Bohemian plain.*

ARCHDUKE: (*To* ARCHDUKE AS CHILD.) Can you whistle me a tune from Mozart's *Thamos, König in Ägypten?*

*Wind risen.*

Precisely. I could cheerfully wake up each morning to the strains of a military band.

*Sitting, and taking out quill and paper.*

(*Composing letter to beloved.*) Someone had said you were tall. I received an impression of firmness and neatness. (*Amorous growl.*) A chestful of breasts, a rural burr, the body of a breeder. The mother of my sons.

You would take me in a carriage to a place in the country! (*Delighted.*) That was your gift. No one ever before offered me that peace. (*Softly.*) To disappear, be born again, and lose oneself in the ineffable (*low*) softness of another. The reflection of your dear face in the window, amid the children. "Kiss me," you whispered. "*Gibst me ein Kuss, Franzi.*" I did so; I kissed you.

*Passage of time. Changed tone.*

(*Anxious. Standing and looking in the distance.*) I am waiting for you, as always, nervous and anxious. Will you arrive on time? I find myself in a field, a hay-meadow to be exact.

Coming towards me I see a sort of hay wagon packed with tall flowers, white petals, deep blue delphiniums and cornflowers, I imagine, pink blooms, outspread high and splendid as a . . . fountain, or a peacock's fanned-out tail.

Two female heads appear on either side of this contraption, this floral magnificence; an oldish woman of the people who drives the horse, and to the left, leaning out, you, my dearest. (*Wonderstruck.*) . . . A gift of flowers! You come in, breathless, face not quite yours, smiling at me. Your face . . . hardly seen; presence of . . . love. You are nameless in the dream (*fondly*) but I knew it was my Sopherl.

*Sitting again.*

(*Moodily signing papers.*) Isn't it the natural thing to leave the place where one is hated so much?

The heroism which consists of staying on in spite of all is that of the cockroaches which alas cannot be exterminated from the ballroom.

*Vienna street sounds.*

(*Gloomily.*) I have signed my name already twenty—sixty times: I and again I. Franz Ferdinand, Archduke, Emperor. Clear, firm, unequivocal, irrefutable; there it stands, my name: Franz Ferdinand.

Clear-cut and unequivocal am I too. Yet a vast inheritance of experience is packed in me. I have lived thousands of years. I am like a worm that has eaten its way through the wood of a very old oak beam. But now I am compact; now I am gathered together this fine morning.

*Pushes back chair, walks (spurs/jangle) to window. Increasing noises of Vienna. A church bell.*

The sun shines from a clear sky. But twelve o'clock brings neither rain nor sunshine. The hatchet must fall on the block; the oak must be cleft to the centre. The weight of the world is on my shoulders. (*Walks to desk, spurs, sits, sighs.*) Here is the pen and paper; on the letters in the wire basket I sign my name. I, I, and again I . . . Franz Ferdinand.

(*Scratching of pen.*) In theory one would think that power belongs to brute force. (*Stamp of seal.*) Authority must have death behind it, to make it work; otherwise it is not, strictly speaking, authority.

At my desk—that is my place. My head in my hands—that is my attitude.

FIRST COUNT: The finger writes and moves on.

SECOND COUNT: But what if you were to meet men from another century dressed strangely; who would seem more the ghost—you or them?

*Pop of champagne cork ends scene.*

# A Medical Check-Up

*Heartbeat.* ARCHDUKE *is having a medical check-up. His personal phy-sician,* DR. EISENMENGER, *is at hand to auscultate.*
*Slow heartbeats (slight amplification), sluggish, heavy.*

DR. EISENMENGER: (*Wheezy, timid of his patient, ear pressed to arch-ducal chest.*) H'mm ... H'mmm.

*Heartbeats.*

ARCHDUKE: (*Gloomy.*) Sometimes I think I have too much blood in me. Once, in the autumn I think it was ... or possibly in the spring, I'm not certain; I heard it roaring (*deep intake of breath*) ... It was a very hot day, I recall.

*Heartbeats.*

DR. EISENMENGER: (*Listening, rapt.*) H'mm ... *say nein und neunzig bitte.*

*Heartbeats, regular and slow.*

ARCHDUKE: (*Ruminates.*) Through all these years I had done every-thing demanded of me mechanically, and in reality only waited for a voice to call me.

*Distant hunting rifle, cries of beaters.*

(*Echo.*) Until finally the illness called me from the adjoining room and I ran towards it and gave myself to it more and more . . . (*Pause.*) But it's dark in that room and one isn't quite sure that it *is* the illness.

DR. EISENMENGER: (*Listens.*) Say *neunundneunzig* . . . *bitte.*

ARCHDUKE: (*Testy.*) You spoke, Eisenmenger?

DR. EISENMENGER: (*Conciliatory.*) *Nichts*, Excellency. It's only the oppressed breathing of the oppressed chest. Nothing more. Nothing less. (*Putting away stethoscope.*) . . . You must eat less, that's all. (*Resolute.*) You must diet, Excellency. Dispense with the Gabelfruhstuck. (*Weak laugh.*) One good Austrian breakfast per diem should be sufficient. (*Pause, weak wit.*) Two is too much. (*Clears throat.*) . . . Grapefruit and black coffee. Cut down on those cigars, *ja?* (*Helping patient to dress, wheezing.*)

ARCHDUKE: (*Gloomy.*) Nothing more?

DR. EISENMENGER: *Tchh-tchh.* (*False teeth.*) Excellency is in rude health. A little overweight perhaps. Blood pressure perhaps a leetle suspect. But the constitution, strong as . . . an oak! Unsinkable as a battleship! Nothing to concern us there. (*Pause.*) But cut down on those cigars!

ARCHDUKE: (*Sour.*) I smoke in moderation, Eisenmenger.

DR. EISENMENGER: (*Rubs hands.*) Ach, *Gute, gute.* Excellent! *Unt* alcohol, Excellency?

ARCHDUKE: (*A sore point here.*) Well . . . h'rrmph!

DR. EISENMENGER: (*Diplomatic.*) *Ach zo* ... (*Changing subject.*) Dr. Schwe-
ninger, Bismarck's own physician, remarked to me only the other day—

*Heartbeats rapid.*

ARCHDUKE: (*Violently.*) Bismarck! A fine shot! A magnificent glutton,
and a heavy drinker ... likes nothing better than to make a regular
pig of himself. (*Chuckles.*) A serious man and a good father, but a true
Prussian. (*Pause.*) A true *Pfikke*, as we Viennese say. (*Pause.*) Was
he greater than Ludendorf? (*Rhetorical.*) Ludendorf, it is said, played
games with the dead.

DR. EISENMENGER: (*At basin, tap run, nailbrush, hygienic.*) Bismarck,
the hero of Tannenburg!

ARCHDUKE: (*Sour.*) Bah! He slept through it. (*Pause.*) He remarked
to me once: "One knows where a war begins (*thoughtful*) ... but not
where it ends."

*Heartbeats slow and regular. Slow fade.*

DR. EISENMENGER: (*Nervous, abrupt.*) The sinister disease that was
sapping the Archducal strength found vent in ... occasional fits of
ungovernable rage, bordering at times upon ... (*cannot bring himself
to say it*) insanity.

*Rapid fusillade, cries of alarmed beaters.*

The symptoms were most marked at shooting parties ... (*cries can
be heard*) where the Archduke fired indiscriminately at anything that
moved within range, and was an object of general terror.

*Flock of crows rising in general panic.*

Brosch thought that the Archduke acted "explosively rather than impulsively" and that he was "often sharp and strict, and sometimes a little too fast."

FIRST COUNT: In his veins flowed the bluest of blue blood, from no fewer than one hundred and twelve aristocratic families. Among them German, Polish, French and Italian.

*Music, build medley,* Tanhauser, *Prussian anthem, Austrian requiem, "Prince Eugene's March."*

SECOND COUNT: (*Loud.*) He was related to many European dynasties. His forefathers included Wittelsbach, Nassauer, Hessen, and Hohenzollern, and no less than ten Savoyard princes!

Franz Ferdinand inherited much of the temperament of Bourbon ancestors on his mother's side. She was Maria Annunziata, daughter of King Ferdinand of the two Sicilies, nicknamed "La Bomba"—for ordering the bombardment of his own town during the rebellion of its citizens. Maria Annunziata died when Franz Ferdinand was but a boy.

Languages were not his strong suit. He spoke broken French and a few Magyar words. He did not like the Hungarians.

ARCHDUKE: (*Growls.*) *Kut-cha . . . Kuuuu-cha! Disz-no . . .* (*Pause.*) *Dizz-no*! (*Pleased, spits out.*) *Fatt-chu*! (*Pause, vehement.*) *Akasztofavirg*! BULGAR!

Through which terrain are you slinking, Bosnian skunk? Hyena! So distant, it seems, that it is too far for any signals to be transmitted.

## MAYERLING AND MAXIMILIAN

SECOND COUNT: Emperor Franz Josef's prospective successors had died before him, three by violence. His son Rudolf became Crown Prince on the day of his birth and held this little title until his death in January 1889, at Mayerling.

*Pistol shot, female scream, second pistol shot.*
MAXIMILIAN *and* CARLOTA *enter. Action mimed, as follows, with the two* COUNTS *standing in for Mexican emissaries.*

FIRST COUNT: Ferdinand Maximilian Josef was dispatched with his wife Princess Charlotte—renaming herself Carlota—to Mexico, as a puppet of Napoleon III, to further his dreams of a second Empire in the New World ...

After their Civil War, America began arming Juarez, and in the guerrilla war that followed in Mexico, Maximilian was captured.

MAXIMILIAN: (*Voice blown about by high wind, coming and going.*) As for myself ... guided by my honour as a Hapsburg ... I shall try to make arrangements ... (*garbled*) with my countrymen ... placing my life and service at the disposal of my new subjects.

FIRST COUNT: But his new subjects had other ideas.

*Jackpot hit on fruit machine, cascade of coins.*
*Firing squad.* MAXIMILIAN *cries* "Viva Mexico!"

There had been the usual protest from the Vatican, but it did not save Maximilian. Carlota returned to Europe, where she believed her only friend was the Pope . . . and refused to leave the Vatican, drinking water she had herself fetched from the Trevi Fountain . . . or eating chickens that she kept in her rooms and had killed there.

*Squawk of chickens.*

She lived on until 1927 and died insane.

SECOND COUNT: The progenitrix of all this Hapsburg misery, the Empress Elisabeth, had met her death at the hands of a dangerous lunatic, an Italian by the name of Luigi Luccheni, who was accused of being an anarchist.

FIRST COUNT: The third heir apparent, after Rudolf's death, was the second-youngest brother of Franz Josef, the Archduke Karl Ludwig, father of our hero.

He was quiet, a very pious man by nature. His confessors were Jesuits, diplomatic busybodies. In the spring of 1896 he went to Jerusalem on a pilgrimage, and died of typhoid after drinking the contaminated waters of the Jordan.

*Passage of time.*

Now the old Emperor was tired. Not exactly senile yet, but feeble and worn out . . . older than his years would warrant.

Grown old and cold, he was the end result of commands coming down through the years.

*Indrawn breath of* EMPEROR *amplified.*

SECOND COUNT: He felt that people bowed as he passed. He sought to be that image: potentate of the north. He scowled upon his subjects: the trees, the chips of broken glass, brass casings and broken fuse ends . . . but, alone, he smiled on the castle walls.

He was the last living representative of a Europe that no longer existed. Perhaps it had never existed; or existed only in the minds of the rich and privileged, the entitled ones, in surroundings of festive costume and bright lights.

Wherever he was, the place was dark and close as a sickroom. All Europe was beginning to be that sickroom; that Krankenhaus.

## GAVRILO PRINCIP

*The two* COUNTS *change their outfits, becoming two bishops, and now, behaving as stagehands, quickly assemble the three sections of a First-Class Smoker. And sit facing each other by the window; the chess set is between them, and during various pauses, they continue the game. Steam whistle.*

*They are travelling from Zagreb to steamy Fiume (later Rijeka) on the Adriatic coast; the assassination year is some time in the future. The two play-acting counts are gaitered and in glistening black barathea, pectoral cross on the breast, a touch of purple at the throat. They are drinking Turkish coffee laced with slivovitz. Seated at their ease in the rococo comfort of their First-Class Smoker, puffing at thumping great King Edward coronas. Outside, ignored by them, the impoverished splendour of . . . Karlovac, beyond the Sava.*

*Serbian folk tune.*

FIRST COUNT: Gavrilo Princip was born in the summer of 1897 in the city of Obljaj in Serbia, a little over a decade before the annexion of Bosnia-Herzegovina into the greater Empire of the Hapsburgs. The reason why, seventeen years later, Princip would join the Young Bosnians and set out to assassinate the Archduke, who, the year before Princip's birth, had become heir apparent, on the death of his father, the pious Karl Ludwig who had drunk contaminated water from the River Jordan while on pilgrimage to the Holy Land.

The Princips lived in an old family house made of wood, with a steep-pitched black roof; a building style that had not altered for hundreds of years . . . like Serbian poverty itself.

Jovo Princip was the elder brother of little Gavrilo-to-be.

JOVO: (*Rustic, aged thirty, deferential; he speaks to the two* COUNTS.) The doors were small and low. You could only enter the house by bowing the head, your Honour.

SECOND COUNT: (*As judge.*) Speak up!

JOVO: (*As before.*) It has no windows. Only the beaten earth, instead of a wooden floor, your Lordship. Smoke rises through a hole in the roof above the open fireplace. The only light in the house comes through it. Life was hard.

FIRST COUNT: (*As solicitor.*) In such conditions, without doctor or midwife, the newly born had fifty-fifty chances of survival.

JOVO: (*Swallows.*) Yes, your Honour. It was a very hot day, your Honour. Our mother had been working in the meadow, gathering grass which had just been cut. She had to make big bundles of hay, each weighing about thirty kilos. She felt labour pains and ran towards the house . . . falling to the earth by the open hearth. She gave birth. The young one lying on the stones formed around the fireplace.

*Water pouring into basin. Thin sorrowful wail from infant* GAVRILO.

Petar—our father—was not at home. He was at his work, your Honour. Late at night he returned.

PETAR *enters whistling "The Roses are Blooming in Picardy" or some equivalent Serbian or Bosnian folk song.*

PETAR'S SISTER: (*Off.*) Petar! Petar PRINCIP! (*Wildly excited, approaches, laughing.*) A shawl for me and a son for you! (*This in Serbo-Croatian.*)

FIRST COUNT: (*Still the solicitor.*) He is a simple man: a postman on a bicycle, but in rural Serbia . . . a winged Mercury! He brings good news and bad with equal impartiality. He is a man who knows everything that is written on any postcard, and in every sealed envelope, and parcel he carries, not because he reads with these eyes, of his, the postcards, nor by experiences and deduction, makes the covers of the rest translucent.

SECOND COUNT: It is simply, that he doesn't care, and so the messages inside screech to him.

*Thin wail.*

PETAR: (*Pacing, babe in arms, fondly.*) My own . . . my own!

FIRST COUNT: For him and his like history is pitiless. Spoils go only to the victor: Prince Esterhazy's pearls!
   Handsome couples dance all night in each other's arms to Viennese waltzes. Battleships protect the Adriatic.

SECOND COUNT: Such Theatrum Mundi was not for Petar Princip, postman, but for the well-appointed, the well-born. It was something that happened to the rich, passing the poor by, ignoring the kmets. Poverty was something to be ashamed of, particularly by the poor themselves.

FIRST COUNT: They were scarecrows in a field harvested for the master. They drank vinegar, water, tears. For clothing they wore sacks; they had no system of their own. Their lot was hard. Is he a good father? Perhaps he is a good father to the dead; from a family of nine, six have already perished in infancy. He is fourteen years older than his wife, and now this great unhappiness has come upon him, been thrust upon him. He has a son: Gavrilo the assassin-to-be, the saviour of Serbia. He who will put out all the lights in the Schloss Belvedere, put an end to the Hapsburgs, create two orphans, the sons of the Archduke who will spend the coming war in Ravensbruck concentration camp.

PETAR: (*Hoarse with emotion.*) Long life to little Gavrilo Princip!

*Serbian folk tune.*

JOVO: (*Low.*) Gavrilo left Grahovo Valley at the age of thirteen, when he had finished primary school. He was christened Gavrilo by the priest because he had been born on the feast-day of St. Gabriel. At school he was nicknamed "Gavrica"—little Gavrilo—but he wanted to be "Gavroche," like Victor Hugo's boy-hero in *Les Misérables*.

He was tormented by his friends for being a student at the Merchants School. Among them the idea of being a merchant, a money-maker was . . . well—

FIRST COUNT: In August 1910 he went to Tuzla, a town in northern Bosnia. He passed his exams and was enrolled in the fourth grade of the high school. The first morning he attended his new school he carried a copy of Cesar's *Commentaries* under one arm.

JOVO: Poor Gavrilo was never in the best of health. He missed many classes. About twenty in the first two months. He graduated from the fourth grade in June 1911. He was seventeen, and his way of life changed. (*Sly.*) From the Tuzla railway station there was a direct line to Sarajevo.

SECOND COUNT: (*Urbane.*) No doubt, no doubt. We know that history at all times draws the strangest conclusions from the remotest causes.

*Steam train leaving, distant.*
(*Sister's laughter, screech . . . "*A son for you!*")*
*Train whistle, derisive.*

## ANDRIĆ AND DUČIĆ

*Bell of Sahat-Kula clock tower.*

PRINCIP: (*Grimly.*) Kolkrabe the Raven greets you! Shaking out his feathers, stropping his beak, hiding his food, first under one stone, then under another.

*Distant sound of dinner gong in palace.*

The aged poodle whines all day behind locked doors. This summer is already endless. Life gets excessive; that's its way. Now the grave-diggers are on strike. People who were not born then will find it difficult to believe, but the fact is that even then time was moving faster than a cavalry camel.

But in those days no one knew what it was moving towards.

FIRST COUNT: Nor could anyone quite distinguish what was above and what was below; between what was moving forward . . .

PRINCIP *fires Belgian automatic pistol at wooden target, close, sound of impact.*

SECOND COUNT: . . . and what backward. (PRINCIP *fires again.*)

FIRST COUNT: History is what one age finds worthy of note in another previous age. A servant sharpening knives? A plate of caviar garnished with cyanide?

The grave-diggers may be on strike, but Princip the assassin has reached Sarajevo with his death-dealers, some still schoolboys— Mehmedbašić, Chabinovitch, Čubrilović, Popović, Grabež . . . It's June 1914, and for Princip it's the end of the line.

SECOND COUNT: Aged seventeen. His co-terrorists are mostly under age, primed with pistols and home-made bombs, to dispatch despots. For themselves, cyanide. For none mean to return to what they came from, Bosnia, Serbia, Montenegro, Herzegovina. They cannot go any further. They are set, primed.

*Catholic church bell in Sarajevo.*

PRINCIP: I think of walking along by the river, but my whole body is like dry wood. My willpower leaks away. I turn down the street in my dream . . . a wide street blue and empty. Empty sidewalks as far as I can see. The light tells me it is summer. A summerlike light in which the heavy buildings stand, the balconies overflowing with flowers.

ARCHDUKE: . . . The Viennese Hausfrau likes to hang red bedcovers over balconies, throw open windows, hang out birdcages. One smells coffee . . . purpose. Austria. (*Yawns.*) I am always awake long before the city stirs, before Vienna awakes; pulled from sleep by disturbing dreams that release their hold upon me most reluctantly. I awake early, shaken by them, warned . . . threatened? I am making an extraordinary record of this city. I am discovering it, bringing it to light. It almost seems the work of . . . sick men. It has a radiance, a *tubercular* charm.

*Vienna, children calling out*

The children playing by the fountain will become old men, but nothing of this will have changed. I try to find darkness, a void. But the buildings are too luminous, the white sky burning behind them. It's all bitterly real: a frozen fiction for which a place already existed. Suddenly it is quite clear how *acrobatic*, how dangerous, everything is.

*Cries of children (in Serbo-Croatian) at play*

... The soufflé sank, the duck was dry, the peas were like bullets. It could have been a disaster. But it wasn't. The important thing was that you (*fading*) chose the right wine ...

FIRST COUNT: (*A slight re-costuming, indicating he is reverting to the role of* COUNT.) It seems not to be his own life he is living, but another, the life of some victim. Suddenly he is filled with intimations of being found somewhere, of being seized and taken away.

ARCHDUKE: (*Dreaming.*) Her mouth feels warm. She knows how to make things come true.

SECOND COUNT: (*A slight re-costuming, indicating he is reverting to the role of* COUNT.) He doesn't even have a chance to talk to her. They are separated. They are lost to each other. He tries to cry out of his coalescing dreams, to tell her where she should go, what she should do, but it's too complicated. He cannot.

ARCHDUKE: (*In recurring nightmare.*) Sopherl! . . . Sopherl! (*Low.*) *Stirb mir nichts!*

*Second shot, fatal for Sophie.*

SOPHIE: (*As if admiring a surprise gift just opened.*) Oooo ...

SECOND COUNT: (*Bland.*) She lies asleep, her pale arms fallen, her lips . . . parted. They talk of the past . . . there is nothing, the days have fallen everywhere; they have collapsed like cards. The past has vanished and he fears the future. His money is lying on the table.

ARCHDUKE: (*Dreaming.*) . . . The model numbers are cabalistic, the prices seem terrifying. The symbols are ugly.

The Ace of Spades seems to be running. The hearts have turned blue.

Buried among other buildings, deep in the town, there are alleys one can pass by, cats know the way. Above the level of trees and foliage, the movements of branches, in a room filled with the same cool air of evening. And what days they were: summery, vast. The light failed slowly. The world was filled with blue cities.

I finish this letter now, because the sleeping pill I took seems to be pulling me down, as if with chains. And, as always, I am painfully longing for you.

(*Fondly.*) . . . There is no cure for that.

*A votre bon coeur* . . . my Sopherl. Your . . . Franzi.

*Sephardic/Ladino lament, voice and guitar (Yekoram Gaon). Lament for dead Countess Chotek under following.*
*The two* COUNTS, *fully costumed, reclining once again at their ease.*

FIRST COUNT: Light, as in an aquarium tank of greenish blue hues, a glaucous green shaft of sunlight on boxwood maze shines on the figures perambulating in slow motion, as if sunk in thought, digesting some unsavoury facts, no verbal greetings exchanged, all heads bowed, some smoking cigars—the Czech Parliamentary Delegation pace up and down the Ilidža gardens.

*Lament alone, say three secs, then under.*

SECOND COUNT: Through them moves the white-veiled Countess Chotek of Chotkova and Wognin, all in white; white kid gloves and buttoned boots, white parasol, bustled, a white rose on corsage; a veiled ghost-figure perambulating in the Ilidža gardens.
To her they give way, bowing.

*Fade lament.*
*Music changes: Fauré sonata.*

The corpse of the assassinated Emperor is laid out on a billiard table in Sarajevo. Their bedroom is empty at Ilidža in Bohemia. They walked hand in hand down an avenue of armed assassins. To her they give way, bowing.

*Hotel taps running. Toilet flushing.*
*Fauré sonata under following.*

FIRST COUNT: The place with the sources of the Bosnia River near Sarajevo is called Ilidža.

*Flushing toilet ends.*

These sources are really small ponds. Huge fat placid trout swim in them. The place seems to have been an official enclave for ages. Even the Tito government used it when they put up high-placed official guests. The first time I happened to get there with a Czech Parliamentary Delegation, I had the privilege of sleeping where the Archduke and his formerly shapely Sophie spent their very last night before the assassination.

*Berlin hurdy-gurdy. Brief, then under following.*

SECOND COUNT: 1900 was the period of the paterfamilias, large families, buhl-inlaid fire screens in With-Drawing-Rooms; hard cravats about flushed male necks, dyspepsia, feminine "nerves," hot flushes, corns and water-cures, monumental marble toilet seats, the Cornish Water Wheel, surgical appliances and spats; the Boer War.

*Hurdy-gurdy. Puffing steam train.*

FIRST COUNT: Steam trains.

The acetylene lamp had just come on the market and the Browning revolver had been invented. One could observe the blood pressure rising.

The Princess of Wales, not as yet twenty-seven years old, was suffering from a form of deafness sometimes brought on by excessive childbearing.

*Steam train receding.*

At a luncheon at Claridge's given in his honour, the rigid Imperialist Lord Milner spoke of "panoplied hate, ambitious, inimitable ignorance"; referring not to matters local but to that perennial thorn in the English flesh—the Boer General Botha.

*Toot from distant steam train*

SECOND COUNT: It was the last year of dear old Queen Victoria's exceedingly long reign. The "flatulent old bitch" herself was over in Dublin on a recruiting campaign, attempting what her recruiting sergeants had signally failed to do—namely, present Spion Kop in an attractive light. Her Imperial Majesty went about "wearing horn-rimmed glasses on a livid and empty face."

*Distant brass band play airs from "Norma."*

FIRST COUNT: The implacable foe, President Paul Kruger, was seated in an easy chair on a shabby patio hard by a large comatose stone lion. Mafeking had been relieved after a seven-month siege—a cruelly extended constipation.

Whores were considered comic, as was the United States of America. It was widely believed that De Beers millions would finance the ultimate recovery of the United States of America as an "integral part of the British Empire." Ho-ho-ho!

History had some unpleasant surprises up its sleeve. Summer was a-coming in.

*Distant brass band. Crows cawing. Summer sounds. Menacing, Bora begins to blow.*

And Trieste? (*Fake patio.*) . . . ah Trieste! If the Austrians gave a ball, the Italians threw a bomb into the middle of it. (*Pause.*) The Imperial Family was always received with bombs.

LADY BURTON: (*High, acid, peevish.*) Bombs in the railway, bombs in the garden, bombs in the sausages. In fact, it wasn't at such times pleasant.

*Distant crump, cries.*

(*Sour.*) The climate is *detestable.*
Varying from arid heat in summer to a succession of continental gales in winter. Ugh!

*Bora, rising.*

SECOND COUNT: These "continental gales" are best characterised by the *bora*, a north-westerly wind which besieges the Adriatic coast in summer in devastating three-day blasts. Bringing clear skies, white light and foul tempers.

*Bora closer, high, psychotic.*

The bora is responsible for violence far worse than any perpetrated in civil disturbances. (*Amused.*) One of the few cases in history when the elements become more destructive than man.

*Bora, maximum. Hold say 3–4 secs.*
*Mix to methodical heavy breathing of sleeping* ARCHDUKE.
*Breathing say three secs. Sound of Sarajevo night.*
*Catholic church bell striking 2:00* A.M.

FIRST COUNT: On June 8, 1912, two years before the assassination, the Yugoslav author Ivo Andrić noted in his diary—

ANDRIĆ: (*Rapid, as if dictating to his diary.*) June 8, 1912. Long live those who secretly—with a few words—are scheming new rebellions. But—unfortunately—I am not one of them. Anyone who spends one night in Sarajevo—sleepless on his bed—can hear the strange voices of the Sarajevo night.

*Sarajevo night.*

Heavy but steady strikes the clock on the Catholic cathedral—it is 2:00 A.M. More than one minute will pass—exactly fifty-five seconds I counted—a while after—with hoarse faraway voice—the Sahat-Kula near Beg's Mosque declares itself.

*Sahat bell begins to strike 11:00.*

It strikes eleven times. The eleven ghostly Turkish hours—according to some strange alien part of the world.

*Sahat bell, fainter, and snorts from dreaming Archduke.*

The Jews have no clock of their own to strike the hours—but only the good God would know what is their time . . . according to Sephardic and Ashkenazic calculations. And thus even during the night—when everybody is asleep—in this counting of the hours—the differences which divide these sleeping beings has been emphasized—

ARCHDUKE's *methodical heavy breathing.*

Beings who will—when they rise—rejoice and mourn—entertain and fast—according to their four different hostile calendars. And who will send all their wishes and . . . (*listens*) prayers.

*Two pistols shots on echo. Cries at assassination.*

(*Composed, ignoring sounds.*) Send all their wishes and prayers up to Heaven. And this difference—sometimes openly and visibly—sometimes invisibly and basely—approaches hatred—often indeed identifying with it.

*Listens, silence, resumes.*

The whole of our society is snoring ungracefully—only the poets and revolutionaries are awake. (*Pause, listening.*)

*Archducal snoring.*
*Brief whistle of steam train.*
*Mix to interior of carriage, ta-tappata of onrushing wheels over points.*
*The two* COUNTS *make only the slightest adjustments to their costumes, again becoming bishops.*

*Warning whistle, approaching tunnel.*

FIRST COUNT: (*Bland, referring to his companion.*) The amiable prelates are Dučić, poet and Bishop of Herzegovina.

SECOND COUNT: And Arthur Winnington-Ingram, educated at Marlborough College, Oxford.

*They take their seats.*

(*Hoarse as crow.*) Karlovac!

*Rattle of train.*

FIRST COUNT: (*Shouts.*) How fortunate you are in your people, Bishop. I am told they are very devoted.

*Onrushing express.*

SECOND COUNT: (*Shouts.*) Very . . . ?

FIRST COUNT: (*Loud.*) Dee-VOTED. (*Guttural.*) AAAhh! Yes, in Serbia we do not trust too much to God. We prayed to Him for five centuries to free us from the Turks, and finally took guns and did it OURSELVES!

*Prolonged screech of steam whistle as express enters tunnel.*

# THE CRACK IN THE CEILING

*Strauss's* Vier letzte Lieder *on a faulty old 78 RPM recording, quavering female voice.*

> In dammrigen Gruften
> Traumte ich . . . *etc.*

FIRST COUNT: (*Redressing himself as Count.*) Sarajevo. Early summer 1912, two years before assassination.

*Sarajevo street.*

SECOND COUNT: (*Redressing himself as Count.*) The city gives off its summer fumes—olive oil, Turkish tobacco and coffee, menthol and pine, garlic, sweet alyssum and slivovitz. Goat cheese, rough red wine in goatskin bags. And something gone rotten, on the turn—the rancid aromas of Macedonia and the Levant.

*Sarajevo street market, cries of traders.*

FIRST COUNT: Cedary smells too, as of scented polish. A drunkard is sleeping on a pile of melons near the harbour where the coastal launch is just leaving for Cavtat and Mlini.

*Market noises.*

SECOND COUNT: On Appel Quay a breeze stirs the leaves of the trees that line its dusty embankments. Below the parapet the riverbed is dry. The site itself conveys nothing especially grandiose; quite the contrary. The scale is small enough, history's pomps are toylike.

*Traders, shouting.*

It is a day in the last of the high summers of Europe. A day like any other day. A day like today.

*Fade market.*
*End on female voice singing Strauss Lieder through all this.*

FIRST COUNT: The crack in the ceiling exudes a foul-smelling liquid. On the shelves the morocco-bound volumes with tolled spines are out of order, uncataloged, leaning at a tilt. The state papers are in disorder. On the wine-stained chessboard the chessmen lie scattered. The game is over.

*Music.*

Liquid caca drops heavy as mercury, quick as vulture-dung, as the crack in the ceiling widens, releases this sickly effluvia onto the carpet below. Black the stench! Outside, a kind of tower. Dark clouds. It happens as you see it. You'd better believe it.

*Mix to "Prince Eugene's March." Hold, then under following.*
*Vienna street in period.*

SECOND COUNT: The clouds of war gather once more over Europe. Marching through them come the Great Men of Vienna: Strauss and

Schnitzler, Schoenberg and Schönerer the anti-Semite, Klimt and Kokoschka, Egon Schiele and Camillo Sitte, Otto Wagner and Josef Hoffmann, Lueger and Herzl. Not forgetting Old Father Freud himself, fishing off a jetty, being closely observed by a little boy.

*Music and street.*

History has taught a certitude about the future, for the bourgeoisie, for the Hapsburgs. All around them in the city of Vienna, in the monuments, in public policy and upward social mobility, in water and sewage works, they witnessed the success of what they knew to be their own specific historical mission; their destiny, their Schicksal.

They were wrong.

*Street cries, Vienna circa 1913.*

FIRST COUNT: (*Bland.*) Friedjung the historian interpreted the architectural transformation of the 1860–1880 period as "a redeemed pledge of history . . . [where] power passed, at least in part, to the bourgeoisie."

SECOND COUNT: (*Eager.*) Encircling the inner city, home of the First and Second Estates for centuries, ran the Ringstraße; and along it those mighty monuments to middle-class culture and aspirations—

*Antiphonal.*

FIRST COUNT: The City Hall and Burg Theatre . . .
  The Bourse and University . . .
  Schloss Belvedere and Parliament . . .

*Vienna street, period.*

SECOND COUNT: . . . With the green parks in between, the lungs of Vienna, City of a Thousand Melodies. Outside, the blue Danube, the famous woods.

FIRST COUNT: Wealth and power are shifting from the land and the old ruling class to the cities, the banks, and the bourgeoisie. The old rural world was about to be taken over.

SECOND COUNT: A favourite subject of Austrian painters and writers throughout the nineteenth century had been the garden, a symbol of the Protected World. One's safe childhood there, the past seen as secured, property; Vienna, that Austrian garden, secure forever. It was only a dream.

FIRST COUNT: For, outside the garden, in far-flung parts of the Hapsburg Empire, in Serbia and Bosnia, dissent was at work—the unkind forces of human hydrostatics were already thickly plotting—all within the eight-inch diameter of the human skull.

*Postman's double knock.*

SECOND COUNT: . . . Some sort of long official document hung with the Hapsburg seal is being forced through the letterbox—alarming as a foot-long tapeworm expelled from the lower bowel through the anus. Prognosis? . . . Cancer!

Fantasy is toxic—the private cruelty and the world war both have their start in the heated brain. Similarly the schemes hatched by terrorists and would-be assassins.

*Fade voices, traffic.*

FIRST COUNT: (*Ecstatic.*) Ah, Vienna! The bed into which the common people climb, docile with toil. And out of which the nobility fling themselves, ferocious with dignity.

*Brief wind-gust, derisive.*

PRINCIP: (*Sad.*) I am not strong enough. One must be selfish. It's like entering the past. Nothing is altered. It is all bitterly real, a frozen fiction for which a place has always existed.

Nothing makes a noise. A night, a long night in which I am held captive, is beginning. A vast malicious calm prevails. All over the world a deadly silence seems to presage bad news. The sunlight of that icy morn falls on my face through enormous windows.

*Distant church bells, Sarajevo.*

. . . through flats of glass with tiny flaws, purified by bitter, Sunday silence.

*Bells.*

. . . and then one day the clock is wrong. The hands are frozen. It is ended. The blunders are all there, as in a chess game, just waiting to be made.

FIRST COUNT: (*Dressed as* FIRST COUNT *but in character as bishop—as if having given up continually changing his wardrobe.*) The agitated melancholic cannot keep track of his own appointments. Hasn't he even gotten used to being frustrated yet?

It doesn't look like it.

PRINCIP'S *TB cough.*

SECOND COUNT: (*In the character of second bishop, guilty, makes only the smallest of concessions to his bishop's costume.*) The patient's mental horizons and interests keep shrinking. (*Pause, listens to cough.*) He does not realize he is ill and has no wish to be cured.

A lonely and difficult childhood, parents at odds with each other, and always poverty, *grinding* poverty. An abattoir of injured feelings. All that produced this malcontent you see before you now. A dangerous person, he holds freedom in his hands: a Belgian automatic.

PRINCIP: (*Ill.*) In every changing vision I see other worlds. *Better* worlds. (*Pause.*) Is not all guilt punishable here on earth?

As we distinguish our stains we lay off our masks. There comes a day when our game is at an end. No stains, no masks, and no audience either. We have overrated our secrets, the energy of our miseries.

*Sarajevo street, morning market.*

FIRST COUNT: Venus is burning in the morning sky over Sarajevo. She rises about 5:15 now, and gradually later. It is a brilliant object of magnitude 4.2 dominating the eastern morning sky, although in a rather low declination.

The monotony, the dream, the town that was so much less than its glow. The Pope, though indisposed, rose up from His sickbed in the Vatican, in order to bless a great congregation of the faithful who had assembled that morning, kneeling in St. Peter's Square.

PRINCIP: I have a message from nowhere. (*Pause.*) I am a message from nowhere. I cannot explain or hope.

My name is No Name . . . (*repeats in Serbo-Croatian, Hungarian, Russian, Greek, Czech, Polish.*) . . . that is my name. (*Deep breath.*) My name is Black Heart . . . (*Repeats in Spanish, French, Gaelic, Arabic.*)

A disease of the spirit that strikes without warning all those who put things off.

(*Grim.*) Kolkrabe the Raven greets you.

FIRST COUNT: (*Still acting as first bishop*) You go under different names then, if it suits?

PRINCIP: (*Rapid.*) I go under forty different names, if it suits.

SECOND COUNT: (*Still acting as second bishop*) What does this mean? What are you saying, Princip?

*Silence.*

Well? Expand.

PRINCIP: Weevils in the wheat.
　　Rat-droppings in the bread.
　　Bugs in the blankets.
　　Fleas in the kitchen.

FIRST COUNT: What does that mean?

PRINCIP: The food in our stomachs!
　　The clothes on our backs!
　　The boots on our feet!
　　The roof over our heads!
　　The poverty of our life! (*Rising intonation.*)
　　The Hapsburgs in Vienna! (*Crescendo.*)
　　(*Grimly.*) On Friday the 6th, 1888 the price of sugar rose from forty-two Kreuzers a kilo in Imperial Vienna. At a quarter to twelve precisely the gates of the imperial Palace swung open and . . .

SECOND COUNT: (*Interrupts.*) 1888! But you weren't even born then! What are you complaining of?

PRINCIP: Pickings. The parasitic vague half-life of half-employed persons, or of persons living on pickings. When everything, even the most commonplace thing, such as being waited on in a restaurant, can only be got with the assistance of the police . . . This robs life of all . . . spontaneity. Yes?

ARCHDUKE: (*Hollowly, on echo.*) I have suffered more from bad dancing than from all the misfortunes and miseries of life put together!

*Passage of time.*
*Almeida, "Cajita De Musica."*

FIRST COUNT: (*Returning with relish to his role as* COUNT.) Authority was in control for a little longer. In the heavy shadows of that last summer the actors, in their dreams, moved circumspectly, as behoves actors, or condemned persons under sentence, or somnambulists sleepwalking.

*Hunting rifle.*

SECOND COUNT: (*Relieved to be back in his role as* COUNT, *he allows himself a glass of wine.*) In the shivering woods the hunters were banging away, and driving home with dead animals. The gun-smoke was slow to rise from the wood's edge.

The Emperor Franz Josef is growing old. He is eighty-three, the oldest Hapsburg and the oldest reigning European monarch. The Belle Epoque ends with him, to a final burst of ribald laughter from the Gunroom.

EMPEROR: (*Senile quaver.*) If nothing happens—as I fondly hope—I won't say a word. But still I cannot feel easy (*Salivates.*) . . . *Is weiss nicht . . . isweissnicht.*

If our kind is fond of someone, there'll always be some pedigree to block the union. That's why, with us, man and wife are related twenty times. The result is that half the children are idiots. Dynastic law compels us to do terrible things . . .

SECOND COUNT: The Emperor is old and weak. His mind must be weakening too.

EMPEROR: (*Rising, quaver.*) VICTORY!

FIRST COUNT: Victory! Sit down, you old fool, the war hasn't started yet.

EMPEROR: (*Petulant.*) *Nein nein*! I must water the roses. Where's the railway station! I must, I must. *Soldat, rauss.* (*Exits, pushed in wheel chair.*) *Wasserraum, schnell*! (*Voice fades.*)

SECOND COUNT: The world has always been in the hands of old men, and their ideas are different. In exile in Holland the Kaiser was cultivating roses.

KAISER: (*Excited.*) My greetings to all . . . and a *Handkuss* for Sophie!

FIRST COUNT: The killing of the Archduke led to the outbreak of the First World War by a series of quick and irrevocable steps. The end came to four Empires and to the ancient Hapsburg, Romanov, Hohenzollern and Ottoman dynasties which had ruled them for hundreds of years. This war changed the map of Europe more than any previous war in its history.

SECOND COUNT: Europe was torn limb from limb as a consequence of the murder, while Sarajevo itself was scarcely scratched. Bosnia suffered. Orthodox Serbs fought against Catholic Croats and Muslims. Croatian terrorists murdered 30,000 Serbs in Bosnia alone during the Nazi occupation of Yugoslavia.

Josef Brosz, who was to become Marshall Tito, founded his Peoples' Republic of Yugoslavia. One of the bravest Partisan commanders was Slobodan Princip, a nephew of the assassin.

*World War II soundtrack under.*

FIRST COUNT: The first and second Balkan War began and ended.

FRENCHMAN: (*Heavy French accent.*) Ideas are changing.

RUSSIAN: (*Accent.*) The world is changing.

GERMAN: (*Accent.*) The world is whirling.

ENGLISHMAN: (*Cockney.*) Not 'arf!

SECOND COUNT: The Successor was calling a halt all along the line.

CHORUS: (*All on stage.*) All along the line!

FIRST COUNT: He does not want war against Russia! Of Serbia, he wants not one plum tree, not one sheep!
   (*Forlorn.*) Baaa.

SECOND COUNT: He just won't think of it.

ENGLISHMAN: Not 'im . . . not bleedin' loikly!

GERMAN: Victoria of England passed away—

FRENCHMAN: To be succeeded by her son—

RUSSIAN: A greybeard of sixty!

FIRST COUNT: The Governor of Bosnia was assassinated, by a bomb thrown in a bouquet of flowers.

CHORUS: (*As above.*) A bouquet of flowers!

*Distant crump.*

RUSSIAN: Amphibious manoeuvres were held in Ragusa.

CHORUS: (*Merrily.*) Held in Ragusa!

FRENCHMAN: A train passed through Transylvania without stopping.

RUSSIAN: (*Puzzled.*) Without stopping?

FRENCHMAN: Faces were pressed to the windows.

CHORUS: To the windows!

FIRST COUNT: Gentlemen, enough of this horseplay! (*Tap of cane on desk.*) An election campaign was raging in Hungary.

ENGLISHMAN: (*Low, insubordinate.*) In 'Ungary . . .

SECOND COUNT: Spring manoeuvres at Troppau . . .

GERMAN: (*Low.*) Troppau!

FIRST COUNT: Moving lights were seen in the sky. (*Pregnant pause.*) . . . German Zeppelins floating over Belgium.

*Screech.*

FEMALE VOICE: (*High.*) Europe is burning!

FIRST COUNT: He says that on the street remains a pillow-sized bloodstain. *Auf dem Straße bleibt bloss ein Kopf kissen grosser Blutflect.*

He says he sees the eyes of hyenas. Schicksal, destiny, is hard to bear, particularly if one be born a Hapsburg. Schicksal becomes Schniksal—something ridiculous, even dirty.

. . . The distant cry of some furry animal. The great round luminous eyes of an old stag collapsing and sinking rear end first into a pool of slime.

ARCHDUKE: (*To himself.*) I remembered that grief is only another form of derangement, and that my innocent childhood had been filled with it.

*Brass band plays, Vienna 1900.*

Sooner or later the young child discovers that he cannot account for himself. As soon as he becomes inexplicable he becomes unreal. Immediately everything else becomes unreal, as one might expect. The rest is puzzlement. (*Pause.*) Or terror.

*Mutti* is an invention of necessity, no matter where you were born. (*Brief guffaw.*) . . . Before we were born we old babes knew our mother's heartbeats. How could we not? "Love" means: I want you to *be.*

THE PAST: Naughty . . . very, VERY naughty!

*Smacks and wails.*

ARCHDUKE: (*Glum.*) I heard the sudden hiss of urine . . . a small red naked face appeared ready to burst. And the straw, the rust, the scattering of grey feathers, the pile of bare bones, the droppings, the distant cry . . . Ah!

The world cannot change its appearance without causing suffering. The truth-telling eyes see distance clearly, and nearness in a haze.

*Brass band in distance, period airs, melancholy.*

My constant companion . . . fear, the basis of all nastiness. The woodcock can dress its own wounds. Partridges travel in pairs, like policemen, and sleep with one eye permanently open. Male rats are better at finding their way about a maze than female rats.

The Chinese, more observant than most, maintain that a rat changes itself into a quail, and the quail into an oriole. And the female of the muskrat, as everyone knows, is the mother of the entire human race.

*Pushing open window, to noises of Vienna circa 1910.*
*Again he is looking out from the palace.*

Below in the square, in the park, people on crutches, mostly young men in steel crutches, feet in plaster, crossing the street.

The alcoholic woman moves slowly. An old lady feeds the pigeons. A cat carrying a bird away to kill it, down Carpenters' Lane, its forelegs straddled. The bird twitches in its mouth.

*Schubert Duo in A Major, violin and piano, old 78.*

A young woman fainted when a piece of human flesh, flung through a shop window, struck her in the face. She had gone to buy herself a dress. Outside it rained. The scene was like a crystal in which, while one was looking, a shadow formed.

*Schubert, Vienna street.*

Some had found shelter under the arcades of the square, which thousands of umbrellas coloured with an (*deliberating*) . . . "autumnal hue."

*Vienna street.*

A lawyer parked his Bugatti near the cemetery.

(*Rubs hands.*) Judge of his horror the following morning when, en route to work in the Brinkgasse, he saw something which he took for a log of wood in the driving seat.

On closer inspection it turned out to be a blackened male corpse, minus its head. (*Glum.*) Presumably needed to contact spirits of another world. It was not black magic. Oh no.

PRINCIP: If you open a lead coffin, it's like opening a tin of sardines. (*Pause.*) But if you were to question a fish about its life, the one thing it couldn't tell you about is water.

*Vienna street cries.*

FIRST COUNT: Now he understands that a man never knows for whom he suffers and hopes. He suffers and hopes and toils for people he will never know and who, in turn, will suffer and hope and toil for others who will not be happy either . . . for man always seeks a happiness far beyond that which is meted out to him.

SECOND COUNT: The onerous daily struggle absorbed him. This was what he had been born to do. The daily struggle with duty he perceived as a struggle for universal order . . . order with Hapsburgs at the helm of course; his birthright.

He had his own inexhaustible supply of honour. The high and mighty idea of being all things . . . and nothing in particular. He saw the daily struggle as a struggle for *Ordnung*, not exactly Brotherhood. Not *Kamaradschaft*. The people—his servants—were not supposed to like their rulers; it was right and proper that they feared them. And fear induced respect. Certainly they were given few enough reasons to like him.

*Cavalry troop passing on cobbles, as before.*

FIRST COUNT: The evidence that was presented to him every day but which, quite naturally, he refused to recognise—the dislike and even hatred that many of his people bore towards him—this was resolved in the hunting-field. The battue became a battlefield.

SECOND COUNT: (*Rhetorical.*) You ask me about Franz Ferdinand and Princip? They came and they went. (*Blows nose.*) So much for the high and mighty Hapsburgs and their fabled Lip.

And Sophie Chotek? They went hand-in-hand down the regular avenue of assassins. They did not intend to come back; hand-in-hand they entered history. (*As boxing commentary*) . . .

Čabrinović threw his bomb, but high and wide, before swallowing cyanide and jumping into the river. The cyanide didn't work, the Drina riverbed was bone-dry. He was arrested at once. Handcuffed, thrown into prison.

Mehmedbašić never even threw his bomb. Instead he saw the entourage pass and then ran to the railway station where a train—providentially—was just leaving for Montenegro. He jumped aboard and disappeared from history.

Now the schoolboy Čubrilović had been told that if Mehmedbašić threw his bomb, he was to finish off the work with his revolver. He did nothing, since Mehmedbašić had done nothing. Neither did the other schoolboy, Popović. In the excitement he had taken up a strategic position alongside a policeman.

So. One assassin was already en route to Montenegro. Two had fled. One was in custody. Only one remained, armed and free. The most resolute: Princip.

FIRST COUNT: Dr. Kafka was suffering from a raging toothache that summer, in Prague, arranging for the publication of "The Metamorphosis" with the publisher Kurt Wolff: the story of the dutiful Jewish son who finds himself turned overnight into a bug. You know it, of course.

SECOND COUNT: Kaiser Wilhelm told his troops: "When the leaves fall, we will have peace."

FIRST COUNT: (*Flatly.*) The Kaiser was wrong.

KAISER: (*Senile.*) The roses in my garden are blooming, held together with the help of glue that might not work.

*German troops cheer (archival).*

# The Austrian Counts

FIRST COUNT: (*Interrupts, gloss.*) The success of Serbia, Greece, Bulgaria and Montenegro in the 1912–13 war, ending the centuries-long rule of the Ottoman Empire in Europe, was seen in the Stock Exchanges of European capitals as the victory for Schneider-Creusot and Vickers-Armstrong over Krupp and Skoda.

*Clock-tick, brief, stops. Distant thunder.*

*Nearer thunder without, darkening. Enter ghost of* SOPHIE *in long white nightdress as at Konopischt, with dried abdominal bloodstains. She paces to and fro behind Baroque armchairs of the two elderly* COUNTS *who ignore her throughout the following exchange.*

SOPHIE: (*On echo, spookily.*) The clock's ticking on, Franzi. (*Pacing.*) Once again the sad dream rolled over me. I loved him, light came from his face. He was a young man once. Not any more. (*Pacing.*) Look at him now!

He began to grow old in his early forties. (*Low.*) Now he is a dead man. (*Pleads.*) Franzi! (*Pause, louder.*) Franzi!

*Exits.*

*Storm receding. Clock-ticking resumes.*

FIRST COUNT: It was a grey soggy morning in Vienna when this grimly serious, mournful act was performed.

*Gun-salute firing at spaced intervals, then mix to imperial anthem.*

SECOND COUNT: "Until death do you part," the old Dean said, joining their hands under the stole. The Imperial Anthem was the only indication that this was a marriage of an heir to the throne.

FIRST COUNT: It seemed as if more had been signed away than honours and titles and the claims of unborn children. No door had been locked, no entrance barred, there was no reception line. In the galleries town officials and employers, servants and chambermaids sat looking down.

*Thunder and anthem mixed.*

SECOND COUNT: It was June 28, 1900, with an old Pope of ninety dying in the Vatican, and an old Emperor of seventy on the throne of Austria.

Fourteen years later, to the month, to the day, to the hour, on a sunny morning after days of rain, both husband and morganatic wife were to die at the hands of the Serbian assassin.

FIRST COUNT: (*Thoughtful puff.*) But the Hapsburgs themselves had been executing Czech patriots ever since the Battle of White Mountain. So there were snubs for the Morganatic One. They were forbidden to make a private visit to the theater together. When the Archduke was on manoeuvres in Bohemia the sentries were withdrawn from outside Schloss Belvedere.

SECOND COUNT: They were snubbed by every royal court in Europe. Only one court accepted them. The Court of St. James's. They were invited to Windsor and treated as equals by the King and Queen of

England. (*Pause, dryly.*) Of course the Empirical English may have had their own, good empirical reasons for this kindness. A splendid example of English fair play . . . or Hanoverian diplomacy.

*Wind of the plains. Music.*
*Enter ghost of slain* ARCHDUKE *in long white nightshirt, nightcap with tassel, slippers, gutting candle in candlestick, which he elevates to peer into the room. The throat-wound has stained nightshirt to navel.*

ARCHDUKE: (*Hollowly.*) Where is that Serbian swine? (*Peers about.*) The gentry must not abdicate . . . *cannot!* *Der clan versammelt sich:* *Hyanen!* (*Aghast.*) . . . *Wohin man sicht: Augen! Auf dem Straße bleibt boss ein Kopf kissen grosser Blutflect!* (*Horror-struck.*) Sopherl! (*Coaxing.*) Don't die. Live for the children! *Bleibe fur die Kinder!*

*Exits: puff of wind.*

SECOND COUNT: (*Ignoring interruption, blandly.*) What were this fellow's motives, and who were his instigators . . . if any, and his accomplices?

FIRST COUNT: (*Affable theorist.*) The ruler's *idée fixe* of being irreplaceable infects his opponents. They take him at his word, though this had only been a delusion on his part. Individual terror is based on the conviction that history is made by Emperors, Kings and Presidents . . . (*Chuckles.*) A conviction that is shared by Emperors, Kings and Presidents. No bomb thrower can change the great and anonymous social forces. It is for this reason that no modern assassin has become truly famous; even the two gunmen of Sarajevo were only pawns in a larger game.

The actions of bomb throwers remain *anecdotal.* (*Thoughtful puff.*)

*Clock-tick.*

(*Resumes, pedantic*). . . Anecdotes, however, if they have a fine point, can be made more expressive than whole volumes. Assassination becomes a historical allegory . . . (*Clears throat.*) One can detect social outlines even in the tendrils of their plans, in the artistic detail of their assassination attempts, which have not been completed to this day.

The element of Utopia is present even in their operatic attitude, and has not been disproved by all their failures.

SECOND COUNT: His crime has been called "the perfect political murder," as if there ever could be such a thing—the spark which detonated the mass of hatred with which the world had long been charged, and which destroyed the precarious balance of power among the empires which had long dominated Europe and divided the world.

The world will never know what lay behind this murder. Probably there is not, and never was, any one person who knew all there was to know.

FIRST COUNT: The sky over Vienna was the colour of warm lead, yet the atmosphere was full of a latent silver-greenish light; it was as though it were about to snow, in June!

SECOND COUNT: (*Sotto voce.*) The shadows in doorways, the empty spaces of open windows, took on their greatest power of suggestiveness. An imperceptible smell of sulphur hung in the air.

FIRST COUNT: The stench of corpses in the Somme mud! Death becomes a rotten green smell . . . a sweetish smell—gangrene. Dysentery.

## The Last Days

*The two* COUNTS *enter in full bishop regalia; as if on a train.*

FIRST COUNT: There were no eyewitnesses to Princip's last days. His chest was covered in tubercular ulcers a hand-span wide and full of pus. The doctor who put dressings on him every second day had to use more bandages than would have been required to dress five wounded soldiers. It was not intended that he should ever leave Theresienstadt; and to survive, as he did, three years in the dungeons, under penal conditions that would have put paid to a man of stronger constitution, speaks for itself, or for his strong Bosnian constitution.

PRINCIP: (*Low, ill.*) The wet logs of the open fire gave the only light to the closely packed kmets, and their slow breathing could hardly penetrate the heavy curtain of smoke . . . (*Racking cough.*)

*Wheeze in ventricle, voice reduced to whisper, short of breath, rattle of chains.*

The most that I could see were the eyes of the human beings, numerous, sad and glaring, with some kind of fluid light coming from nowhere. Also (*coughs*) . . . some kind of reproach—even threat—radiated from them. And many times since—many, many times—have they wakened me from my dreams.

SECOND COUNT: Heavily bandaged and in chains, what was he thinking of, this doomed man just come of age? It is impossible to look into his eyes, into the photo taken during the first interrogation; his eyes do not meet yours.

The disease has destroyed the elbow-joint of his left arm, later amputated. Tuberculosis of the bones was given as the cause of death. He never complained, except for the lack of writing materials which effectively silenced him, one more part of his punishment. Secretive grows the disappearing soul!

Princip was disappearing all right; he was being cast down among the kmets, the serfs, perhaps the poorest of the European poor.

We know that he came from a family of nine, of whom six died as babies. His father was a postman.

PETAR: (*Hoarse with emotion, on echo.*) . . . my own! (*In Serbo-Croatian.*)

FIRST COUNT: He too had had trouble over a girl he loved; as had the Archduke, whom his son was to assassinate. Both Emperor and Serbian postman at one time were tubercular.

Under the microscope Franz Ferdinand saw his sputum teeming with bacilli. He had TB of the lungs, which was cured. His killer, laden with chains, and at about the same age, had assumed the dead man's tuberculosis. No attempt was made to cure *him*.

PRINCIP's *heartbeats, sluggish, faltering, under.*

PRINCIP: (*Listens.*) H'mm . . .

The death certificate has been preserved. It states that I, Gavrilo Princip, aged 21, died on the evening of April 28, 1918 at six-thirty P.M., in Room 33 of the closed wing of Theresienstadt Hospital.

*Sluggish heartbeats.*

SECOND COUNT: (*Listens.*) H'mm . . .

He never complained of the conditions, except, as I said before, of the lack of writing materials. A poem was scratched on the cell-wall in his hand. It said

*Heartbeats very loud on echo.*

PRINCIP: (*Calls out in Serbo-Croatian.*) "Our ghosts will stalk through the Palace, frightening the Lords."

*Heartbeats, faltering.*
*Concorde over Mexico City, Carlota's demented laughter. Say four secs.*
*Sudden cut to heartbeats.*
*Heartbeats stop. Slam of heavy cell door.*
*Ornette Coleman, "Sadness."*

FIRST COUNT: When they finally came, with much purposeful jangling of keys, to unlock your cell door, they found nothing there. You had flown. Had become a pretty blue Bosnian butterfly, or a night-moth fluttering near battlements, or a church bell ringing over the sleeping Serbian countryside. You had become that.

Or you had become a shadow of prison bars cast down on the floor of the cell, moving as the days moved, with atrocious sloth, all 1,430 or so of them—very slowly. Your lingering death made you part of a company, a sorry part of European history; as one bullet from a Belgian automatic pistol fired not quite four years previously had also made Franz Ferdinand a part of that company, a part of our sad history. (*Idiot voice.*) "Do you believe, Sirs, that the dead will rise again?" . . . No? People keep worrying. (*Brightens.*) Life teems with quiet fun.

# The Tomb of Dreams

IRELAND IN THE LATE SEVENTIES.

Sixty-minute play for radio in two parts.

*Natures wrung by obscure abstract hatreds must come by the most devious ways to mayhem, with us almost a family affair; and all in the name of thwarted love.*

—A.H.

# CAST

ANNOUNCER

DEEP VOICE

DUBLINER

JAMES JOYCE

NARRATOR

MALE VOICE

T.Y.W.

FIRST WOMAN

FIRST MAN

SECOND MAN

THIRD MAN

SECOND WOMAN

THIRD WOMAN

UNSOBER GAEL

LECHER

MOTHER

MALE SLOOGER

FEMALE SLOOGER

PATHETIC ONE

TIPPERARY MAN

HUSBAND

PAULINE

DERRYMAN

FIRST GAEL

SECOND GAEL

AN ASSERTIVE GAEL

OLDISH DUBLIN WOMAN

COQUETTE

DUBLIN WOMAN

COUNCILOR

GROOM

UBS

FIRST MAN IN BAR

SECOND MAN IN BAR

THIRD MAN IN BAR

FOURTH MAN IN BAR

CONFIDENTIAL MALE

BOY

HISTORIAN

STATISTICIAN

ANGRY FATHER

IRISH T.D.

ENGLISH TORY

GARRULOUS BOOZER

DANE

BARMAN

THE ORANGE FOE

PATRON

TAXI RANK

Sources: James Joyce (*Ulysses, Finnegans Wake*).

ANNOUNCER: In September 1978 the Irish-born author of *Langrishe, Go Down* was awarded the American-Irish Foundation Grant of $7,000 on condition that he spend ten months in his own country. Aidan Higgins, after sojourns in Johannesburg, Berlin, Spain and London, returned to his homeland, to live for half a year in Bealadangan, West Connemara, through the coldest winter since 1840.

This is his account of the most westerly country in Europe . . .

*Crows, loud rookery (5–6 secs).*
*Mix to tape. Sounds like Middle English: Henning Mortensen recites "Auld Lang Syne" in Jutlandic.*
*Crows (fainter).*

DEEP VOICE: (*RTÉ recording.*) A school of turlehide whales stranded in hot noon . . .
BLOOMSDAY 1983.

*Sandymount Strand. Summer. Voices, gulls under following.*

Then from the starving cagework city a horde of jerkined dwarfs, my people, with flayer's knives, running, scaling, hacking in green blubbery whalemeat.

*Medley of voices, children calling.*

Famine, plague and slaughters. Their blood is in me, their lusts my waves. I moved among them on the frozen Liffey . . .

*Dublin traffic under.*

. . . that I, a changeling, among the spluttering resin fires. I spoke to no one: none to me.

*Chiming doorbell (pause) grand canal lock-gate. Wind in trees (brief).*

DUBLINER: (*Broad.*) The traits featuring the *chiaroscuro* coalesce, their contrarieties eliminated, in one stable somebody similarly as by the proverbial warring of heartshaker and housebreaker and of dramdrinker against freethinker our social something bowls along bumpily, experiencing a series of prearranged disappointments, down the long lane of generations, more generations and still more generations . . .

*Wind in trees. Crows (brief).*

JAMES JOYCE: (*Recording.*) Teems of times and happy returns. The seim anew. Ordivoco or viricordo. Anna was, Livia is, Plurabelle's to be. Northmen's thing made southfolk's place, but howmulty plurators made eachone in person. Latin me that, me Trinity scholard!

*Feet of pedestrians in Grafton Street (hold). Crows (closer).*
*Pause.*

## PART ONE

NARRATOR: The city.

*Pedestrians in Grafton Street. Gull-cries over O'Connell Bridge. Traffic, train arriving, bar sounds and human voices. (Toner's Pub, Davy Byrne's pub, Shelbourne Bar.)*

I am in Dublin. Everything tells me so. The shabby buff-coloured city seems to convey the overall impression: *Make the best you can of what there is . . . There's nothing more.*

The environs abound with unpleasing innovations (music in buses) as well as pleasing old familiarities. The illuminated Bovril sign over College Green is gone, but immortalised in *More Pricks Than Kicks*; Magill's remains. "Feeling only so-so," they used to say forty years ago; "fair to middling"; proper health was very much an off chance.

The Liffey hasn't changed much. Anna Livia smells as before; the stench of stools, diarrhoea, coalslack and sulphur, oilslick under the Corinthian Cinema, neon lozenges in the water; the Arctic flowers that do not exist. Sluggishly stinking she crawls on, dragging effluents out to the bay.

By the shell of the old Grafton Cinema the flower-sellers are offering bunches of siempre vives, flowers of the Andes also known as immortals. The dead Hound Dog is howling over Dublin. "Forty-two years on this earth," the young newscaster announced with passionate conviction, "and he'll be remembered forever."

The tall blonde blue-eyed woman who had just left her French lover and his skipping-rope, is being accosted by a stout Italian businessman outside the Dublin Savings Bank. Clubs or tulips?

Tired of walking in the dream I have returned to the country where I was born half a century ago. It doesn't feel like that anymore; it appears to be very dreamlike itself. "In my dreams I wept," wrote Heine. No matter.

Great grey-backed gulls squall over O'Connell Bridge where thin itinerant children beg. So much for the waste and futility that was our world.

Turned fifty this year. Basho's age when, ill (dysentery?), he undertook that last marathon hike into Japan in 1694. A year younger . . . move on three centuries . . . than Jane Bowles, who died of a heart attack in Malaga, capital of sorrow, where in a snail-bar in the brothel quarter I chanced upon the shabby ghost of Terry Butler, late of Bologna (and never shabby in life), who failed to recognise me, darkened by long tramping in the Sierra Almijara.

There are days when we do not properly belong to ourselves, assailed by mysterious sundowns, endings of certain omen-filled days, tormented by our star-signs, auguries. The tall blonde recently returned from Bangladesh and the Amazon is now leaning over the bonnet of a parked car outside what used to be The Sign of the Zodiac in Harry Street, being broadly propositioned by a stout Italian businessman.

DUBLINER: "I Tried to Make It Look Like Rape."

NARRATOR: Were the memories of things better than the things themselves? I say things but I mean times and persons. The city is changing, has changed, in my long absence, though I never knew then how these things would end.

The Libyan wives are leaving Emor Street, baffled by the English as spoken by the Irish, by Dubliners in particular. The computer-expert husbands will follow in a month with the Peugeots. The student from Honduras is studying a book on venomous snakes in an effort to improve his English. A fellow practices scales on the bagpipes all through one long wet afternoon.

On a television mast at least twenty metres tall a blackbird sings *Aujourd'hui! Aujourd'hui!* over Emor Street, above the home of the RTÉ producer just returned from a short winter break in Benidorm. A deranged boy is breaking up the newly laid crazy paving in his narrow back garden.

All's well in the Liberties! A discoloured sun sinks behind the brewery chimney. Leaning across the narrow deal counter, Mick the chain-smoker studies the racing form. Sunk in thought, the washed-out blue watery eyes follow the print, the last third of a damp fag glued to a pendulous wet underlip. The puffy features are unhealthy, the body bloated like a frog. Smoke gets in his eyes. Mick's lad is in the Guards.

DUBLINER: Little Bitty Tear (J. Roe up) beat the odds-on favourite Minnie Hawk (T. J. Murphy up), running away from Napper Tandy and The Bugaboo at Leopardstown. Charlie Haughey's colt Aristocracy won the Donnybrook Handicap. U-Be-Quittius was well down the field.

NARRATOR: I record for posterity the trivia of our time in Emor Street in the Liberty Ward near the South Circular Road: Bagpipe music droning in the night. Corrected proofs of a book written twenty years and more before, then called *Felo de Se*, now *Asylum*.

One Sunday outing to Straffan and swam in the Liffey.

One Saturday we bought a length of felt as under-carpet for my officina, from one Christy Bird near Portobello Bridge, for 1£. The sign BIRD out in the rain; the prams chained together, sign of the times.

The annex at Emor Street had been put up by the builder and some-times Chief of Staff of the IRA, who had done fifteen years "inside."

All one Saturday afternoon the church bells rang, the Protestant more persistent than the Catholic, coming on the breeze, mixed with the sound of the bagpipes from three gardens away. Sparrows in the overgrown hedge against the wall, gulls wheeling high up, sun all day.

*Bar hubbub.*

MALE VOICE: (*Conspiratorial.*) How he was makin' out I do not know . . . He was like a god to her.

*Bar hubbub.*

NARRATOR: The Trinity Professor wears fishnet stockings, suspender belt and bustier, a Cupid's bow painted on the lips with the reddest lipstick and hair tied back with a scarf. He-she likes to mingle with the Ballyfermot rough trade drinking tea in the kitchen of the whore-house and they have been told to call him "Mary" and not to laugh at him in "her fishnet stockings."

When he-she isn't mingling with the hard men in the kitchen she-he has to do housework, and the Madame is strict. The house can never be clean enough with this sloven Mary sighing and scrubbing the toilet bowl with her bare hands, thinking of the hard men in the kitchen.

But it won't do, it's not clean enough, not half clean enough for the mistress who has no choice but to whip the arse off this slutty maid, the dirty thing.

Dublin was infested with mice in the twelfth century. In the mid-seventeenth century there were wolves in Wicklow. A public wolf-hunt was ordered in the Ward of Castleknock, only six miles from Dublin.

Dung-heaps, free-roaming swine, hog-styes, noxious stenches from the slaughter of cattle polluted the air in the thirteenth century.

There are thirty abattoirs in Dublin today. Slaughtering goes on at night and at weekends. In summer, in hot weather, two ladies in Rathmines keep their windows closed and avoid the garden humming with bluebottles.

The Trinity Professor has not had a natural erection since he was systematically beaten as a boy by the Christian Brothers who made him what he is, the sloven Mary in the whorehouse who crawls on hands and knees, in fishnet stockings and falsies, and cleans out the lavatory bowl with her bare hands, and is beaten by her angry mistress.

Never before such disparity between those who have and those who have not.

The Dublin pimp takes up his position. Hidden from sight in the deep hanging cupboard he unzips himself and applies his eye to the small peepholes he had bored at eye-level and holds his breath.

In the bedroom under observation his whore-wife performs fellatio and unnatural acts with her grunting clients, unaware that she is under observation. She earns £700 a week. The husband in the dark, watches, sucks in his breath, stands stock-still, as the exiled Emperor at Longwood House on St. Helena spied on the English watch coming on and off duty.

On the window ledge outside the back bedroom at Emor Street, the weighing scales fidget in the breeze.

All night they fidget in the breeze and by morning the little pans are half-full of rainwater.

Then the traffic on the South Circular Road starts up and the early jets come in, whereupon the neighbour's dog howls. The mother spanks her little daughter. The child weeps.

The hidden pimp neither drinks alcohol nor smokes but treats himself to expensive clothes, runs a Citroen. When his whore-wife goes off the game he beats her, plugs up the peepholes with cigarette filters.

The hidden *prompter* just couldn't believe his eyes or ears, no longer recognised his own bedroom nor his own dear wifey, silly Milly O'Callaghan that was; for both bedroom and spouse had undergone substantial sea-changes, as covertly observed from the *trou du souffleur*, become movie-set and porno star in a blue movie.

"Call me Gus."

"I'm Imelda."

"My pleasure, I'm sure."

"This is our new bedroom, Guss. Do'ya fancy it? Fancy a drink, a snack or anything? Peckish Guss?"

"Ah Melly, I cudda eatcha!"

The sleazy dialogue is spot on, the bedroom transformed, the bedclothes thrown back and the drapes drawn, the door locked, the TV pushed to one side, the carpet Hoovered and obese client and whorewife already buck naked amid the cut flowers. Gus is blowing out his cheeks like a bullfrog unsober enough to act brave and bold, be outspoken about his requirements, gazing down complacently upon his own particular hairy grossness.

He lies on the bed as though it were his own, his greasy poll subsiding onto the pillows as he gazes down in a stealthy way, a glass of Paddy balanced on his hairy chest; a heavy-breathing adenoidal type with unhealthy skin white as ebony, matted with curly black hair like a ram, a regular forest darkening the armpits.

"If I said I wouldn't come in your mouth wouldn't I be tellin' a lie, like saying the cheque is in the post."

The hidden husband is rigid as a hare in its secret form. How did such abasement come? In the close hanging-cupboard he can neither blow his nose nor clear his throat nor hardly blink his eyes, riveted to the peepholes. Oddly enough here is another Fergus, unless the client is sailing under false colours and using an assumed name at the altar rails.

"Ah now Melly. Smelly Melly."

"Ah now get along with you."

"Go down on me, Mell. Blow me."

"Anything to oblige."

Trousers about his knees, grasping a fistful of tissues and breathing shallowly, his eyes fixed on the action, the concealed pimp is tense and rigid as a hare confronted with a hound.

How teasingly adroit she has become, his shameless Milly professionally started up, that is to say provocatively undressed to velvet black choker about the neck suggesting bondage, one snappy scarlet garter about the bulging thigh, false eyelashes on eyes heavily made-up, rouged nipples, the works, and all to pleasure this Walkinstown slug with hands clasped behind his neck, exposing the dark forest, as if casually sunbathing on the Sandycove seawall.

The pimp-husband whose name is Fergal grasps himself and applies dilated pupils to the twin peepholes, preparing to ejaculate along with the client who now is reduced to uttering a series of great hollow sealion hootings as the kneeling whore-wife, stilettos sharp as daggers, works upon him.

As the bedroom seems to expand and contract he utters a great hollow staglike bellow, a terrifying mating-call, and plunges both hands into her hair, fuzzed up, crimped and dyed black.

In a trice the cork train has departed from Platform 2, sucked into the void leading to Ballybrophy, Thurles, Mallow. Emelda Lurcan will never be found.

Two lapsed Republicans were shot dead in Dublin as a salutary lesson for the rest. Seamus Costello, Chairman of the Irish Republican Party, had absconded with party funds from a train robbery at Sallins. When John Lawlor, the Ballymore Eustace haulier, revealed the whereabouts of hidden arms dumps to the police he had signed his own death warrant.

"We Irish think thus," *pace* Bishop Berkeley, the tar-water expert. We think as we do because we do as we think; but who do we think we are? My late philosophical friend Arland Ussher phrased it more elegantly: "As our forefathers thought, we act; and our descendants will act out what we thought."

Tame perks everywhere, Dog Agility Courses, Ho Chi Minh Walks, Crazy Prices, Chinese and Italian take-aways, dual carriageways to all points, Golf Ranges, Heritage & Interpretive Centres, Safe Houses, Cat-Homes, Dawn Meats, Premier Piggeries, Hare Coursing and Alfresco Benediction; a time clock for every oven and a big fat bun in every one. A jumbo-fridge for the stout O'Hanrahans and a jumbo-jet to foreign parts for the nice Miss Kerrigans.

Client and whore-wife are buck-naked as if about to try a few falls at all in wrestling or undergo a medical examination; her fingers sink into his soft yielding flesh as into plump blancmange. Obese and hairy Gus wears only black socks, perhaps ashamed of hammer-toes or for some passing whimsy of his own, an act of sheer bravado.

It is the last day of a curious year.

A grudging daylight is already fading by three in the afternoon. The weather neither good nor bad; an overcast grey day, with a frugal grudging daylight leaking away, just as before, as I seem to recall from the days of my youth. It's this melancholy climate that makes the Irish what they are: Farsoonerites to a man.

Typical Dubliner weather, you might say. Sea-fog and river-mist mixed; turning to drizzle in the late afternoon.

Turned fifty this year.

Basho's age when, ill again (dysentery?), he undertook that last marathon hike into Japan in 1694. A year younger than Jane Bowles, if you will be good enough to move on three centuries, when she died of a heart attack in Malaga, Capital of Sorrow. In a snail-bar in the brothel quarter I came upon the ghost of Terry Butler late of Shanganagh Bridge and Bologna (and never so shabby in life) who failed to recognise Rodrigo de la Sierra darkened by long tramping in the Almijaras.

Why, blustery brothers and tittery sisters, there are days when we do not know ourselves; the days when we do not properly belong to ourselves; assailed by mysterious sundowns, the cattle bawling in descant on Gorumna; those gory endings of certain omen-filled days, tormented by our star signs, by comets passing in the night sky overhead, by dire diurnal auguries.

Tired of walking in the dream I have returned to the country where in I was born half a century ago; it doesn't feel like the place I knew anymore; it appears to be most dreamlike itself, sailing away. "In my dreams I wept," Heine wrote.

Great greybacked herring-gulls squall over O'Connell Bridge where thin itinerant children beg, as their mothers before them, as theirs before them, and other mothers before them. So much for the waste and futility that is our world. The gulls giving loud calls release their heavy loads.

The Liffey hasn't changed much. Anna Livia smells as before, oilslick and Godknowswhat flows by the Corinthian Cinema, its neon red lozenges reflected in the river are "the Artic flowers that do not exist." Sluggishly stinking she crawls on, dragging her affluent out into the bay. I am in Dublin again; everything tells me so.

The shabby buff-coloured city conveys the overall impression (a shrug of the shoulders) of "Make the best you can of what you have, it's all there is, there's nothing more." "Feeling only so-so", they used to sigh forty years ago; "only fair to middling." Reasonable health was very much an off-chance.

The environs abound with unpleasant innovations (piped Muzak in buses) as well as pleasing old familiarities: the illuminated Bovril sign over College Green has been taken down, but immortalised in Beckett's *More Pricks Than Kicks*; Magill's remains in Johnson's Court.

Are the memories of things better than the things themselves?

The city has changed in my absence, you never know how these things will turn out. Within the airless precincts of the modern lounge in what was The Sign of the Zodiac sits a man of double deed in grey suiting and bow tie, perched on a high stool with drink in hand, smoking a cigar and immersed in *True Detective* ("I Tried to Make It Look Like Rape"). The lounge is ruthlessly modern in a chintzy way with metal scrollwork in curlycues, phallic beer pulls with hunting motifs and Las Vegas-type cash registers for ringing up the change.

Renaults, Cortinas and a Mercedes wait in the reserved parking lot of the Meath Hospital, with a surgeon's squash racquet thrown into the back seat of the Mercedes. The country-bred nurse shouts loud personal questions of an intimate nature, as though interrogating halfwits.

Porters stand about in green smocks. A dead man is pushed in on a stretcher.

Wishing to be well, when not exactly ill. Wishing to be ill, when not exactly well, I want everything to be still and at the same time everything to be in constant motion. And I want both to happen at the same time. Can that be arranged? The cock always crows at one o'clock on the third day of March every year, for me.

Nico's in the evening.

"Were you at the Curragh today?"

"I was."

"Had any luck?"

"I had."

Pause.

"Is Tom inside?"

"He is."

Longer pause.

"Tell him Micky wants Jewish macaroni. Macaroni from Jerusalem. Tell him that."

I am in Dublin. Everything tells me so.

The sound of the weighing scales moved by the wind on the sill of the back bedroom window. The sweet sound of the bells. Catholic and Protestant mixed, the drone of bagpipes. Did not our happiness lie there?

My constant companion: Fear (the basis of all nastiness), which has always been with me, as child, as boy, young man, husband, father, grandfather to be. In the old days a man would sometimes let his horse choose the way. Now, no horse. No way. A third of one's address book contains addresses of those gone elsewhere, those no longer friends, dead friends. Perhaps three forms of the same condition: Absence.

The dead are everywhere; very dear friends all gone home. We cannot escape them, even if our memory only retains images of them. Dreaming of them, as we must; this is the price we pay for our "rest." The dear departed are with us still, walking around, attending to their own business, whatever it may be.

*Grafton Street pedestrian way. Voices.*

I ride through time. Dead times and places return to life, the dead walk again. Two in particular, a man and a woman. Peter Alt was killed stepping on to electrified railway tracks somewhere in England, en route to academic tenure in Holland. Gerda Schurmann (née Fromel) was drowned in the Atlantic attempting to save her son Wenisisclaus who had got into difficulties in the water off Mayo Beach.

I see them walking around Dublin with set faces, seemingly ashamed of themselves and as if under punishment, condemned in some way; averting their eyes they hurry by, never together, always alone, in a hurry, furtive, as if ashamed. Are they being punished? The man and woman may have met through me. Now, as if suffering some punishment, condemned in some way, they hurry by with head averted. Some of their *horror vacui* infects me.

*Grafton Street pedestrian way. Voices (brief). Quick fade to:*

. . . Death is a silent picture, a dream of the eye; such vanishing shapes as the mirage throws. But then horror is something perfectly natural. Somehow *our* history is not as others know it; never was.

*Flies.*

A green lounge infested with flies: O'Donovan's Arms! Down a step and the house-flies are thickly assembled. Gallagher complains. We leave immediately. Outside; a band of silver, wheeling gulls, moving air. The River Shannon!

*Shelbourne Park greyhound track. Crowd, race, Tannoy.*

Old Puffy Face, look forth!
Not that Mick is old; he must be about my age, but he looks bad. A bloated cushapooka suppurating in damp after-grass. Mick reads, squinting: "And in that tomb of dreams, the losers' dressing room, melancholy has claimed all for her own. It is always a sad cavern, but it is sadder still when you feel you have been beaten in a battle where for some strange reason you fought with only one hand."

*Uproar at dogtrack.*

Doughy Daw! With narrowed eyes Mick now reads of the bizarre events at Shelbourne Park when Mrs. Elisabeth Lewis's brindle bitch Glen Rock literally staggered from the No. 2 box and failed to reach the first bend.

DUBLINER: . . . Had the prize-winner been interfered with? Urine tests had been taken, following an even-more eccentric performance in the English Derby at White City, when Glen Rock hit the fukken rails.

NARRATOR: . . . The permanently worried, permanently watering blue eyes follow the close print. Customers come in for loaves of Boland's bread and bottles of Lucan Dairy and Mick serves them absently, lost in the dream where Glen Rock is hitting the rails at White City or coming drugged from the No. 2 box. His shop smells like a country shop in the country of my childhood (King's in Celbridge) when everything alarmed me.

*Dogtrack, cheering (brief), under.*

"Man Held for Pub Murder" proclaims the *Evening Press* headlines. The Ballymore Eustace haulier John Lawlor had been shot—"executed."

A pretty auburn-haired girl in a green pullover cycles with folded arms down Rathmines Road through the lunch-hour traffic.

*Rathmines traffic.*

. . . The gasometer, the ebbing Tolka, the filthy tide, the pull of weeds, skeletons of abandoned bikes, sodden bread, grey-feathered half-grown gulls squalling.

*Rathmines traffic.*

"SMASH U.S. IMPERIALISM!" painted along a wall in Bath Avenue. Mick, looking dead-beat, covers his face with a soft stubby hand, the index finger stained to the joint with nicotine.

Now once more the air begins to nip and bite.

*Fade.*

One grey morning in Timmon's pub I fell into conversation with a garrulous returned Native Son who had lived for many years in a poor part of New York and was now back in Dublin, where he found employment in St. Brendan's, formerly Grangegorman Lunatic Asylum.

In his high apartment he had paid sweeteners—bribes or protection money—to the Costa Rican garbage collectors. Otherwise your garbage wouldn't get collected, or they'd do something unpleasant with it. Speaking of garbage, he had thrown out Tennessee Williams once, very drunk, who had come with one of his bum boys. The playwright had taken Brendan Behan to be a . . . shy man. I could have told him otherwise.

One night he had to throw out an even drunker Burl Ives. He had seen Cassius Clay (Muhammad Ali to be) in the ring fighting Spinks. "Clay took a blow from Spinks in the solar plexus that could be heard in Pittsburgh." He repeats the story; Pittsburgh now becoming Phibsboro.

He tells stories of suicides in the mental home. "As sure as you're putting that cigarette in your mouth," the awful yarns are true. A Third World War would not occur, he believed; instead, Famine: "Ireland has forgotten too soon about Famine."

Six bullocks are being driven by two herdsmen in dungy Wellingtons, what the Germans call Blücher, into the abattoir in Swan Alley, for it's slaughtering time again. One of the herdsmen in a crushed hat, seen from the back, is a dead ringer for my late friend Paddy Collins.

*Brief lowing of cattle.*

A young bloodstained burglar was caught red-handed at three in the morning attempting to jimmy his way into Rosita's sea-green Morris Minor. She had thrown on a shirt and run out, armed with a bicycle pump, snatched up. The robber had a screwdriver in his hand and explained that he had been chased by a gang from Kelly's Corner. He was looking for the Meath Hospital. "Well this isn't the fukken Meath Hospital; this is me fukken car," said the Contessa in a great wax.

The blood-stained burglar was most apologetic and staggered off into the night.

*Night approaches.*

The bus crews are drinking pints in Agnew's. Spent cartridges in William Street gutters, shattered windscreen glass and clots of blood presumably human in Dawson Street, opposite the Royal Automobile Association. The renovated Mansion House resembles a Christmas tree stiff with icing. There is no beauty that has not some strangeness in the prescription.

The postmen and the garbage collectors are on strike. All the phones in pubs have been taken over by gabby girls.

Fifty percent of the public phone booths are vandalised, all the directories lifted. Mick is out of briquettes. The little black cat Danny La Rue is lost, run over, gone elsewhere, strayed, done in. And that fellow plays scales on his bagpipes all through one damp afternoon, droning. The Parisian actor Pierre, late student of Grotowski, has left behind his skipping-rope, and his heart.

The sudden shadow of a flock of wheeling pigeons cross the patio of sunflowers, circle above Avoca Road and Orinoco Street, settle on the ridge of the roof of the City Building Suppliers opposite Mick's shop.

The old lady scatters Marie biscuits in her cramped backyard fetid with their droppings. Two hundred of them line the roof above, keeping an eye on her; you can smell them when the breeze blows in the wrong direction.

The drone of bagpipes, the blackbird singing, the low shifting clouds, all tell you it's Dublin, shower and shine.

In Searson's snug, opposite the humpbacked Portobello Bridge, behind glass, Virginia tobacco fumes lie dense. Jack Yeats (God rest his soul) recuperated in the Nursing Home opposite after a one-man exhibition at the Waddington Gallery. Here was once a landing-stage for the canal hotel. Now it's a region of Saunas, massage parlours, whorehouses.

The Antiquarian Bookseller uses the snug as his office. He is on the phone to a client in Killiney. A thick bunch of keys depends from his waistcoat pocket. Now he replaces the receiver. Now the door closes behind him. A truculent young worker with lime-stains on his overalls is telephoning his Mammy:

T.Y.W.: (*Gruff.*) Hullo Mammy. Can you put on my dinner right now. I'm just after walkin' in this min-yute.

*Receiver being replaced.*

DUBLINER: (*Derisive.*) Does your Mammy know you're out?

*Makem and Clancy, "Peter Kagan and the Wind."*

FIRST WOMAN: Action for Lesbian Mothers . . .
   An all-female *Waiting for Godot* showing at The Studio in North Great George's Street . . .

FIRST MAN: Flikkers Gay Disco, 10 Fownes Street . . . Legion of Mary . . .

FIRST WOMAN: Lesbian Line . . .
   Proust Study Circle, Goatstown . . .

FIRST MAN: Personal: Gay Male, 22, well-built, hairy with moustache, like to meet same, 25–40. Photo if possible. Very sincere.

SECOND MAN: Tenor sax in perfect condition, with velvet-lined sax-case and accessories. What offers?

THIRD MAN: Transvestite shy male (25) wishes to meet ladies of any age willing to work in house for free in exchange for company.

FIRST MAN: Gentleman (30) good-looking and TV seeks discreet relationship with petite feminine lady who is perhaps gay.

FIRST WOMAN: Camden Health Studio. Private Suites with Showers Adjoining. Qualified Female Masseurs. No appointment necessary.

SECOND WOMAN: (*High.*) Apollo Health Centre. Massage, Solarium, Showers. Staffed for your personal attention.

FIRST WOMAN: Atlantic Health Centre: relaxing massage. Pleasant masseuses.

FIRST MAN: Baytree Health Studio. Thöner sauna. Private facilities. Phone Avril or Jill.

UNSOBER GAEL: (*Sotto voce.*) You wouldn't happen to have the phone number of Ford's of Dagenham?

*Donkey bray.*

LECHER: Would you sit on my face for a fiver?

*Phone receiver replaced.*
*Gulls. Ship's siren of the Liffey.*

DUBLINER: (*Elegiac.*) The weather was neither good nor bad, an overcast grey day. Typical Dublin weather, you could say. Sea-fog and river-mist mixed; turning into fukken drizzle in the late afternoon.

*Dublin zoo.*

NARRATOR: Yellow monkeys with permanently shocked faces are attempting half-hearted congress from behind in their dungy cages in the Dublin zoo.

DUBLINER: Ah, will you look at the little monkeys!

MOTHER: . . . if they are monkeys.

NARRATOR: Two young whores have their beat by the back gate of the Phoenix Park, hard by the People's Gardens. The spiked tips of the railings have been removed, filed off, and the stumps painted patriotic green.

A chimpanzee is screeching on the island. The seals are barking to be fed. The clouded leopards pace their cage.

*Zoo medley, peacock screech.*

(*Bland.*) An alternative life that never existed anywhere, at any time . . . except in the scheming of ad-men. . . is being considered; "real life" as such is over. It's a perpetual buying spree. The adman's dream of perfectly matched well-dressed dupes, with no thought in their head but buying, has at last come true.

The make-believe of actors performing chores thought out for them by others . . . that ideal and unreal Consumer Existence is now yours.

By mid-morning, the lazy young wife, in a bikini, is leaning over the garden wall, at Foxrock, Glenageary, Dalkey, Howth. The garden is untended, her children fed on tinned foods chosen from television commercials.

Television advertising insists on a showy leisured lifestyle, pretensions to gracious living; and the new suburban Ireland would aspire to that. L-plates everywhere.

Now a word on Sloogers. Derivation of the word uncertain. A stock type, new to Ireland, very common elsewhere in the "Free" World. Possibly related to farmyard slurry, liquid manure, cow shit or pig dung. Ideal topdressing on cabbage.

Sloogers are much given to a promotional smoothness of address, chat-up lines from the soap serials: they speak familiarly of "ongoing" situations, "pressurised states." "Viable" alternatives. Sloogers speak always in intense and compromising vagaries. "Initially," they say; they speak of "relationships", and even "intense relationships"; of being "involved," or being "crazy" about some person acquisition. Doing their "thing." Getting their act together.

Sloogers are, in effect, polished peasants; social climbers with some country cuteness still adhering. Ideal Slooger address: "The Rise," Mount Merrion. Slooger marketing: Quinnsworth's. The thickest concentration of Sloogers, after the capital, can be found in Limerick and of course Cork. A word now about Slooger modes of dress, habitats, Slooger art and slang.

Male Sloogers favour hacking jackets with single or double vents covering the behind. Female Sloogers wear sunglasses on top of the head, even in the darkest bars in the depths of winter. Silk scarves are threaded through shoulder bags, and French wines mispronounced in skintight provincial accents. Car keys are carried ostentatiously in the hand into public places; or, a daring touch, clenched between the teeth in a leather thong. Female Sloogers order "Vodka and white," never half pints of Guinness.

Slooger meeting-places: Davy Byrne's, the Shelbourne Bar and Saddle Room, the Hibernian Buttery and Dining Room, the Bailey . . . a very thick concentration here.

O'Sullivan's coffee-bar in Dawson Street is a favourite venue for country Sloogers up for the day. The Athenaeum near Portobello Bridge and Nico's in Dame Street are favoured Slooger dining places or Caesar's opposite the Olympia. Bojangles, Hatters and Sachs are

Slooger nighteries. The preferred Sloogertipple is Bacardi, Greek wine, Nuits St. George. Or the most expensive drink on the menu. Slooger Food: Mousaka, prawn cocktails, avocado, steak ta-ta. Slooger smokes: slim panatelas. Slooger art: Talboot's Box ("You are getting religion, plus"). Slooger art centres: the Abbey, the Peacock. Slooger reading: Strumpet City, the Year of the French.

*Athenaeum around midnight.*

Slooger specials: Greek dinners, Irish Coffee.

MALE SLOOGER: Different aspects of the situation, *of course.*

FEMALE SLOOGER: I'm not saying it's necessary, *but.*
Could we have some service here, *please!*

MALE SLOOGER: Okay, you're doin' very fine.

FEMALE SLOOGER: Like, everyone has to *eat.*

MALE SLOOGER: Thank you *very* much!

FEMALE SLOOGER: I'll accept that!

NARRATOR: (*Relentless.*) Slooger heavy reading?

MALE SLOOGER: Maeve Binchey.

NARRATOR: Slooger *light* reading?

FEMALE SLOOGER: *Image Magazine.* A feminist organ with touches of *Tatler* and *Sketch.*

NARRATOR: Slooger radio?

MALE SLOOGER: Pardon?

NARRATOR: Slooger . . . solecisms?

FEMALE SLOOGER: Pardon?

NARRATOR: (*Patiently.*) Slooger solemnity. You know, *verbals*?

FEMALE SLOOGER: Typical!

NARRATOR: Pardon me.

FEMALE SLOOGER: (*Impatient.*) Typical! Typical, for God's sake!

NARRATOR: (*Nonplussed, resumes.*) Slooger artefacts, bangles on male wrists, a bunch of keys worn at the waist. A comb passed through the disarrayed windblown Slooger hair, hand following to settle the Slooger quaff, in a public place.

A most Sloogery ploy, on entering public places such as bar or restaurant or foyer of Abbey or Peacock, is to be in full Slooger conversational flow.

MALE SLOOGER: (*Dictatorial.*) The trouble with the shoulder is, once you dislocate it, it's out.

FEMALE SLOOGER: (*Gushingly, bright.*) It's always cheaper in September. (*Long pause.*) I don't know why.

MALE SLOOGER: (*Faint.*) Typical!

*Grafton Street pedestrians, footsteps, voices under following.*

NARRATOR: (*Afterthought.*) A good Slooger Christian name please?

MALE SLOOGER: (*Proudly.*) Manus!

*Pop of cork.*

NARRATOR: Female Slooger name?

FEMALE SLOOGER: Mandy. (*Pause.*) Manus and Mandy O'Callaghan.

MALE SLOOGER: Do you know what I mean?

FEMALE SLOOGER: Let's forget what I just said.

MALE SLOOGER: A textile company in *Longford!*

FEMALE SLOOGER: I find it a bit dry myself.

MALE SLOOGER: THANK YOU VERY MUCH!

NARRATOR: (*Bland.*) I see an ivy-covered wall. In an upstairs window the starched white stiff caps of staff nurses, making considered nurse-wifely gestures, perhaps at a bed. It's the blood bank building; above it the Pelican House flag flies in the breeze over Leeson Street.

VOICE: (*Low.*) Soft day, thank God.

MALE SLOOGER: (*Faint refrain.*) THANK YOU VERY MUCH!

NARRATOR: I see a couple of turps drinkers with purple faces squatting in the doorway of disused premises off Liberty Row.
News headlines are full of their own brand of intense and com-

promising vagaries. "ETHIC CRUX . . . IRISH BISHOPS . . . BOY FOUND IN FRIDGE!"

Lavish Jail Fare Angers Welfare Man!

DUBLINER: Mystery Fire in Cinema!

NARRATOR: The habitual drinkers are sweating like suckling pigs. Stink of the shambles in the airless, cigarette-fouled air. Someone is pouring abuse into an attentive hairy ear.

*Bar hubbub.*

"Stand up there, you little fucker, until I contradict you."

"I have a vague hazy recollection."

"Kilcullen at nine!"

"*Litherally* brilliant."

"The Doctor said, 'Go out now an' have a good slash.'"

"It's a bad wind that doesn't blow someone good."

"Ah not-a-tall, Tess!"

On the outskirts of Athlone a little boy lost is weeping bitterly in the rain.

PATHETIC ONE: (*Abject.*) It's all gone, Lil.

*Timmon's in Essex Street. Hubbub*

NARRATOR: Timmon's is now closing for the Holy Hour. I see no bloodstains on the floor or on the counter. Here Lawlor was murdered one lunchtime in September by the man he had arranged to meet, his murderer, the Provo "hit man." The nameless one, the faceless one. But he has a face and an Irish name . . . a Catholic name, no doubt. He carries a gun.

I finish my tot of Jameson, screw my *Irish Times* into a scroll, prepare to leave. A man sitting in a corner by the counter asks me "What do you read that for?" For my own amusement, I inform him. His hand goes for an inside pocket ... Is he going to pull a gun? ... but draws out nothing more alarming than a crumpled copy of the *Daily Telegraph*.

He's a *Daily Telegraph* man.

We arrange to meet later.

*The Chieftains, "Mná na h-Éireann Seán Ó Riada."*

I tell you a thing. I could tell it otherwise. A few pictures emerge into light from the shadows in me. I consider them. Quite often they fail to please me.

So what now?

I recall the voices that spoke within me.

TIPPERARY MAN: (*Oracular.*) What is your personal opinion about the Astral Body?

*Hubbub.*

LECHER: (*Lugubrious.*) Pauline and I had a platonic relationship.

*Loud hubbub.*

HUSBAND: (*Sour.*) What's your definition of platonic?

*Hubbub.*

PAULINE: (*Brightly.*) I wasn't, chaps, like that. I *became* like that from being on my own.

*Cork extracted.*

*Squawk of gulls outside. Gulls over O'Connell bridge, Dublin traffic, ambulance or siren under.*

NARRATOR: A group of Consciousness Raising ladies are holding a meeting in a fine mansion overlooking the so-called Gents Bathing Place at Greystones. Below the first tee a dark-visaged man is sleeping at Greystones Golf Club; around his unconscious head flutter white butterflies.

*Dublin traffic.*

The Dublin pimp takes up his position early in the deep hanging cupboard, fixes his eyes to small peepholes bored at eye-level, holds his breath.

In the bedroom under observation his whore-wife performs fellatio and other acts, unaware that she is under observation. She earns £700 a week. The husband holding his breath, watches, as the exiled Emperor at Longwood House spied on the English watch coming on and off duty on St. Helena.

The Deviant Professor (who has not had a natural erection since he was beaten as a boy by the Christian Brothers), called "Mary" here, crawls on hands and knees. In fishnet stockings and falsies "she" cleans out the lavatory bowl with her bare hands, is beaten by her angry mistress.

Never before such disparity between those who have and those who have not. The hidden pimp neither drinks nor smokes; he treats himself to expensive clothes, runs a Citroen. When his wife goes off the game he beats her, plugs the peepholes with cigarette filters.

*Emor Street. Blackbird sings.*

On the window ledge outside the back bedrooms, the weighing scales fidget all night. The little pans are half full of rainwater. I hear the traffic on the South Circular Road, and the early jets going over. The neighbours' dog howls. The mother spanks her little daughter. The child weeps.

There are depths of grey out there that a man might capture. Duffy's Circus has come to Booterstown. Marcel Marceau, the famous mime, to the Olympia, on his last Dublin visit.

No more will Dubliners see Bip as Don Juan, master swordsman and tireless lecher, with sticky fingers, sharpening the point of his sword as a snooker-player the point of his cue, prior to dispatching a rival. There is no death in his work; Goliath returns to life for the encore. The Earth-loving fallen angel is making a perfect pig of himself in a nightclub.

His senses seem far sharper than ours . . . as lemur, badger, marmoset, barn owl. Pierre Verry presents the cards, still as a sundial; a seventeenth-century figure preserved in aspic.

Met a tall shy man who kept covering his face with a huge paw in the Oak Lounge . . . Con Houlihan!

In the vestibule of the Olympia, that gilded emporium of earthly delight, a deaf and dumb couple are tick-tacking at each other.

It is August the 16th. St. Hyacinth's Day. My youngest son's twelfth birthday. On August 16th 1850 died Dora Dickens, the author's ninth child, of convulsions in London.

It is the fifth anniversary of the death of the Hound Dog Man, the American multi-millionaire Elvis Presley; grown obese, who died of drugs and dissipation in his mansion "Graceland" at Memphis, Tennessee.

It is the thirty-third anniversary of the destruction of Hiroshima. At 8:15 A.M. in 1945, 200,000 Japanese people died, a city wiped out.

Predatory birds sometimes drop strange objects from the skies. The natural flight of the human mind is not from pleasure to pleasure but from hate to hate. Private infamies proceed from political turpitude, and it's impossible to take a step without stepping on something unclean.

Two lapsed Republicans were shot dead in September and October here in Dublin: Seamus Costello, Chairman of the Irish Republican Party, who absconded with party funds, from a train robbery at Sallins. And the unfortunate John Lawlor, the Ballymore Eustace haulier, who exposed arms dumps.

DERRYMAN: (*Broad accent.*) He told me he was interested in buying a horse. I advised him to go ahead.

*Hectoring in house of commons, ending oration.*

NARRATOR: The long unhealthy winter is ending. Hot toddies in hand, the Countess and I watch a coffin being loaded into a hearse outside the Maam Hotel in the Joyce Country. The river nearby is free of cannibal pike, but the salmon infected with disease. This was formerly a coaching inn designed by the ingenious Scots architect John Duncan Nimmo, who opened up the West.

The trees in the Mall at Castlebar, planted in Lord Lucan's time, are being pollarded. Lime and chestnut mostly. A big wedding is leaving Nenagh, haunt of dreams; the klaxons of the motorcade blaring, passing out of town for the grand reception.

GAEL: Never leave your country. My ship is going to Ballina. Nora is not below at the well; she is above on the cliff. My eye is blind. The fire is hot now. The place is cold but wholesome. God is generous.

*Leopardstown races.*

(*Pedantic.*) If the upper part of the tongue be pressed against the back of the upper teeth while the English word "low" is being pronounced, a thick sound of "il" will be heard. This sound does not exist in English.

(*In Gaelic.*) Do not praise a slow horse. There is a large green tree at the well. Con is blind. Art is not blind. There is no bread on the floor.

The heavy boat is on the land. The field is soft. Una is young. I am hot and the big well is dry yet . . .

AN ASSERTIVE GAEL: (*An epistle from Letterkenny.*) Sir, being a Catholic, I am never activated by spite or malice, I am merely concerned with principles. For me Neil Blaney personifies all that is clean and wholesome in Irish public life, a model of moral rectitude, and he embodies the qualities of patriotism, idealism and dynamic leadership so sadly lacking today.

*Dáil in session. Approval (grunting) of senators.*
*Pigs grunting.*

NARRATOR: All the municipal dumps are closed; the nearest one in operation is out at Lusk. Two postal deliveries a day. Two garbage collections a week. Sign of the times.

The number of tourists visiting the Republic is up 14% while revenue has jumped by 32%. Managerial salaries have increased by 19.6% in the year ended 1st April. The Bank of Ireland returned pre-tax profits of £20,832 million for the six months ending 30th September.

The banker's families of Ireland are large, as befits an expanding Catholic economy. A breakdown of managerial families reveal that twenty couples have four children, eighteen couples have five, seven couples have six, three couples have nine, and the Chairman of the Ulster Bank, ten.

*Fiddle.*

Eight inches of mud engulfed the Scout Jamboree in Woodstock, Co. Kilkenny, yesterday. Despite the mud and overnight rain the 4,000 parents and friends who visited the camp found the 2,000 Cub

Scouts in good spirits, and the Camp Chief danced with Girl Guides from Vienna. French Scouts cooked crêpes suzette, Ringsend Scouts dispensed cockles and mussels, and some Dutch Girl danced in clogs in the mud.

Then the sun came out to provide a beautiful setting for an open-air Mass celebrated by Dr. Birch of Ossary.

Elsewhere archaeologists and patriots joined in a search for the grave of bold Robert Emmett. They never found it.

Two-thirds of the rainfall normal for the month of August fell in the Inner City alone. In several places there was thunder and lightning. Holiday weekend traffic had to be diverted by the Gardai.

The Pope died in the Vatican, and the German pre-Socratic thinker Martin Heidegger passed away in Messkirch, his home-town, aged eighty-six. He had been influenced by Hölderlin, Heraclitus, Parmenides. He argued that Being cannot be thought, but remains the all-important question raised by thought.

Farewell the old fart.

Also passed away this year: Cearbhall Ó Dálaigh, ex-President of Ireland, and Dr. Micheál MacLíammóir, thespian and linguist.

The bagpipes played mournfully all through one miserable damp afternoon in Emor Street.

PATHETIC ONE: It's all over, Lil! (*Weeps.*)

*Rain of street.*

DERRYMAN: You're a young lad now an' mebby you wouldn't understand this . . . but do you know who I'd fancy? (*Pregnant pause.*) . . . The Queen Mother!

GAEL: (*Sotto voce.*) You wouldn't happen to have the phone number of Ford's of Dagenham on you would you?

OLDISH DUBLIN WOMAN: (*High voice.*) It's desperate to be livin' in a flat.

*Council flat hubbub of children screaming, feet on stairs, etc.*

I was out in O'Connell Street the other day an' the wind was goin' through me.

NARRATOR: Casement was horrified by what he witnessed in the West around 1910. The poverty and degradation of his poor countrymen and women. "White Indians," he wrote in his report, recalling the skinking Congo. "This enduring Irish . . . *Putumayo!*"

COQUETTE: (*Donegal.*) I am on the pill and I have put on a lot of weight. (*Pause.*) Can I change to another form of pill? (*Pause.*) I am twenty.

DUBLIN WOMAN: (*Rough.*) I think I'm pregnant.

COUNCILLOR: (*Soothing, low.*) What makes you think so?

DUBLIN WOMAN: (*Rough.*) Well . . . I don't know. But when he came into me I felt it shootin' up to me fukken eyebrows.

NARRATOR: Outside the Cathedral of the Immaculate Conception in Sligo, our patron saint is standing on what appears to be a dragon or toothed iguana . . .

*Cobbled yard. Mare being groomed. Groom whistling through teeth, mare fidgeting.*

GROOM: (*To himself.*) Grand day, thanks be to God!

*Grooming, hoof stumble on cobbles.*

 Whoa there, me beauty! (*Spits.*)
 Grand day for a big blonde! (*Explosive, meaty slap of hand on haunch.*)

*Gull over O'Connell Bridge, derisive calling.*

NARRATOR: Dublin was infested with mice in the twelfth century. In the mid-fourteenth there were wolves in Wicklow. A public wolf-hunt was ordered in the ward of Castleknock, only six miles from Dublin.
 Dung-heaps, free-roaming swine, hog-styes, noxious stenches from the slaughter of cattle polluted the air in the thirteenth century.

DUBLINER: What's wrong with your man? What's he on about? What's eaten him? The curiosity is killin' me. (*Pause.*) Jaysus, he's a gas man altogether!

DUBLIN WOMAN: (*Rough.*) There's a grain of truth in what he's sayin'.

NARRATOR: In 1847 during the Great Famine the natives of Dingle were living on periwinkles.

DUBLINER: Sairtenly your woman was nearly in tears.
 Will Emelda Lurcan please go to the kip-house!

*Steam-train, scrambled Tannoy.*

 Will Emelda Lurcan please go to the ticket orifice!

NARRATOR: The first of the Grand Hotels were opened in 1785 at Sallins. By 1804 those at Shannon Harbour, Tullamore, Robertstown and Portobello were built.

*Somebody whistling "Isle of Capri."*

The ghost of my dead father, thirsty and garrulous as in life, his two younger lads snug and safe enough on a seat in the vestibule of the Grafton Picture House, is just stepping into the Sign of the Zodiac for a ball of malt. Guinness's draymen go there for pints. The coloured rhomboids of the stained glass in the door cast a familiar, almost holy light into the dim interior.

In the Auld Dubliner in Anglesea Street light evening meals are served 'till dusk and all your favourite potables served in sumptuous surroundings, now under the personal supervision of Eddie Doyle.

Agnew's is packed with bus-drivers and conductors off duty, unsober ballad-singers, one of whom latches on to me, insists upon giving an imitation of Elvis Presley.

"A dreeem, just a dhreem," he intones with eyes closed, aquiver with strong emotion, humming like a radiator, the lips scummy from Guinness. The voice of the dead Hound Dog man is howling over Dublin.

UBS: Whooze th' greatest singer in th' world?

NARRATOR: Alfred Deller.

Some of the few remaining constants in a changing capital: the squawking of great gulls between O'Connell Bridge and the Ha'penny toll bridge, across which W. B. Yeats as a youth was too poor to go, but walked it to O'Connell Bridge.

The "crack" . . . formerly "great gas" . . . of extempore colloquiums revolving around off-the-cuff non-sequiturs as like as not; elliptical thinking . . . *feeling*, rather expressed in colloquial ellipsis.

The feral reek of the Gent's Toilet in the bowels of the National Library; doubtless the inspiration for Mr. Joyce's "sulphur-dung of lions." All of that.

The demented piper practising scales. The bloated herring-gulls heavy in the air, about their business, squawking among themselves. The phone booths occupied by gabby girls. The Lord Mayor's Mansion House a Christmas cake lit up. Searson's snug packed to overflowing, the regulars all lit up; a rare treat for connoisseurs of buffoonery.

*Antiphon.*

FIRST MAN IN BAR: Hold on a second now.

SECOND MAN IN BAR: Kilcullen at nine.

THIRD MAN IN BAR: Stand up there now, you little fucker, until I contradict you!

FOURTH MAN IN BAR: You're as far out as the wind that dried your first shirt.

SECOND MAN IN BAR: (*Derisive.*) Does your mother know you're out?

FIRST MAN IN BAR: Do you know where he was? . . . in fuckin' *Alaska*!

NARRATOR: In the Bailey Bar a flushed toper is leaning his right elbow on the counter, ball of thumb pressed under nose, listening to the young barman who is discussing Squash techniques.

FOURTH MAN IN BAR: Litherally brilliant!

NARRATOR: In Searson's back bar a heavy-breeched, bull-necked man is pulling on a thick cigar, his gingery brows drawn fiercely together, drinking Paddies while immersed in *The Clare Champion*. It's coming on to the New Year in Dublin city.

An unsober little elderly man, unsteady on his pins and cocky as a bantam is clutching a broom handle . . . a late Christmas present, perhaps . . . and whispering hot abuse into the hairy ear of the Clareman, who orders another Paddy in dumbshow. He's not treating the bantam, who is now staggering towards the Gents.

FIRST MAN IN BAR: The Good Shepherd!

SECOND MAN IN BAR: That happened on the eve of Christmas Eve.

NARRATOR: The tobacco fumes are dense as fog, or a gas attack. Hot Paddies are carried past on a tray. The little angry man with the broom handle has left the Gents and is now tacking across the Lounge, as if punting, smiling an enigmatic smile. The regulars are taking half ones with their pints. The thick-set man is deeply immersed in *The Clare Champion*.

CONFIDENTIAL MALE: She's not a bitch nor a dog. She's an in-between. She's an incubator bitch.

OLDISH DUBLIN WOMAN: (*High voice.*) Is that a fact now?

*Pause.*

CONFIDENTIAL MALE: A cat once gave her an awful dig in the head. She's never liked cats after. (*Pause.*) I think she thinks cats is rats or something. She's a great little ratter. At the crack of your finger she'd kill them.

OLDISH DUBLIN WOMAN: Is that so now?

*Pause.*

CONFIDENTIAL MALE: The Kerry Blue is the best dog to draw the badger. (*Pause.*)

Mind you, I don't hold with the so-called sport of puttin' the Kerry Blue into the burra to see who comes out.

OLDISH DUBLIN WOMAN: No, I suppose not.

NARRATOR: An intense voice is telling tales of Christy Ring performing miracles at Croke Park in the year of the Eucharistic Congress. In Harry Street near the closed-up shell of the old Grafton House the ghosts of Anglican clergymen and their tweedy wives gather to see Deanne Durbin in *One Hundred Men and a Girl*. The flower-sellers are offering bunches of siempre vives.

*Bar hubbub.*

In Searson's snug by the long window, a husband is looking daggers at an old suitor of his young wife: a stout smiley man leaning forward. Packed between them with her nice legs crossed and sipping gin-and-tonic sits the effervescent bone-of-contention: Pauline. The suitor dips his lips into his pint. Pauline is glowing, delighted with herself. The husband is lowering, afraid to go to the Gents and leave Pauline with the old suitor, who is not so old, leaning forward now, talking of the olden times. There is a strong suggestion that Pauline may be thrown into the canal.

The fumes are thickening.

A Dutch coaster is drifting in heavy seas off Rosslare Harbour. The German trawler *Kiel* got a line aboard the crippled ship; the English tub, *Englishman* is standing by. Shipping alerted in the southern Irish Seas.

FIRST MAN IN BAR: I was over in that bar . . . whaddyacallit . . . Eagan's.

*Pause.*

SECOND MAN IN BAR: He's a funny little man that runs it. A couple of fellas wanted to go out into the jax an' begob he wouldn't let them.

THIRD MAN IN BAR: Signs are he keeps a good little house.

FOURTH MAN IN BAR: Oh I'd say he was a stickler for work altogether.

THIRD MAN IN BAR: I was up there yesterday meself.

NARRATOR: Men with weak red-rimmed eyes assemble in an airless pub in Rathfarnham; the curates too have bad eyes.

SECOND MAN IN BAR: Kilcullen at nine?

FIRST MAN IN BAR: I have a vague, hazy recollection.

THIRD MAN IN BAR: In Dublin they say, "Buy now while the stock lasts." In Belfast they say, "Buy now while the shop lasts."

SECOND MAN IN BAR: I was up there yesterday meself.

NARRATOR: Hot Paddies are carried past. An affable little smiley man talks to a total stranger in the long narrow bar in Wicklow Street; a little tan-faced woman in black, drinking JJ and cider. He tells her how he caught and tamed a wild cat "on the outskirts" and brought it up as a dog.

I am deep in one of those daydreams which overtake even the wretchedest of men, such as myself, here in Dublin. I'd tell you no lie.

## Part Two


ANNOUNCER: The Country.

*Sean at Heuston Station. Tannoy announcement, train leaving, voices.*

WOMAN: There's poor Sean dartin' back!

MAN: (*Anguished.*) Paddy . . . I'm over here!

VOICE: (*Derisive.*) Safe journey!

*Wild Atlantic shore.*

NARRATOR: (*Sombre.*) Ireland is the most westerly country in Europe. It is twice the size of Switzerland, but not itself a part of Europe, geographically nor any other way.

"Thus separated from the rest of the known world," wrote Geraldus Cambrensis, "and in some sort to be distinguished as another world."

Of the four fertile provinces of Ireland, Connacht is the most westerly, and Connemara the most westerly and way-out part of Connacht. One more foot and it would have been into the Atlantic. It's as far out as the wind that dried your first shirt.

The Protector, as is well known, tried to confine the entire Irish race there. It was the first act of genocide . . . east of the . . . Parallel.

It is in some respects a melancholy place.

Melancholy . . . the projection of a psychic state. The sun is low there. Winter is long. The days are short. The nights are black and endless. Day breaks reluctantly again . . . The clouds dripping rain. High water and floods everywhere, swamped fields, the snow reluctantly melting off the Maamturks, the bars closed, the cornerboys clustering.

Ireland is dithering, the swans are leaving the flooded fields.

The marbled eyes of drenched mountain sheep. Even the toilets are overflowing. The whole country is flooded. The cornerboys of Connemara, Costello Cross, Carraroe, do not go to Mass anymore, but stand in the lee of the newsagent's, like sheep in a storm, pawing *The Sunday World*, the semi-nude model girl smirking on the cover in flaky colours, her skin pigmentation the colour of the summer that never came.

So. Seaweed drying on the fretwork walls, a *pucán* rotting in the harbour, the moon down behind the Maamturks, the wind getting up at 4:00 A.M.

The sycamores trembling. In the pubs of Galway an obsession with maggots and worms prevails.

*Galway bar.*

FIRST MAN IN BAR: They do live on maggots.

SECOND MAN IN BAR: Are you goin'?

THIRD MAN IN BAR: I y'am.

FOURTH MAN IN BAR: Cockroaches an' lizards an . . . snails.

THIRD MAN IN BAR: What's that . . . *schnails* is it?

SECOND MAN IN BAR: A small little fellow altogether.

FIRST MAN IN BAR: *Schnails?*

THIRD MAN IN BAR: Slugs is alright.

FOURTH MAN IN BAR: I'll not take another wan . . . by God no!

SECOND MAN IN BAR: A fine big duck . . .

THIRD MAN IN BAR: Turkey's eggs now . . .

FIRST MAN IN BAR: Ho-Ho! The bloody burgers!

SECOND MAN IN BAR: Startin' to lay now . . .

FOURTH MAN IN BAR: Dark it will be until this month is out.

SECOND MAN IN BAR: Turning out bad . . .

FIRST MAN IN BAR: Getting very windy . . .

THIRD MAN IN BAR: That was the time you'd fly home by nine o'clock.

SECOND MAN IN BAR: An' still they were happy . . .

FIRST MAN IN BAR: There was nature in the people then.

NARRATOR: (*Resuming.*) A soft, crooked boreen? Corn is growing. The lock is in the door. The bog is . . . wet. Though the Atlantic climate may be cold and wet for most of the year, this is more than compensated for by the fraudulent warmth of the natives. Shannon shallys are rented out to Germans and Scandinavians at exorbitant rents. But romantic scenery abounds around every bend.

The land itself, never a spent force, in its turn the instrument of a distant past. Eyes of bullfrogs straining, veins in the neck pulsing, the twittery beat of the banjo.

*Frogpond.*

(*Ironic.*) Help Kerry's Mentally Handicapped Children. "The Rose of Tralee" sung at closing time. At Fermoy on the Suir, *Torso* and *Caged Heat* are showing at the Regal Theatre. Coming Sunday: *Oklahoma Crude.*

VOICE: You're as thick as the lid of a pot.

NARRATOR: (*Unperturbed.*) Above the Cathedral of the Immaculate Conception in Sligo a stone statue of St. Patrick stands on what appears to be a toothed dragon or iguana, in his right hand the Saint has a hold of the Holy Book; the left hand, broken at the wrist, has slipped down the crozier and come to rest by his left ankle. Jackdaws squall on the roof. A large stands diagonally opposite. I saw a low ill-designed school.

(*To* BOY.) Is this the front or the back?

BOY: The back.

*Silence.*

NARRATOR: Is the front any better?

BOY: (*Low.*) Worse.

NARRATOR: The boulders in the wall above the unused pier. The rotten *pucán*. Seaweed drying on the wall. A donkey-engine out on the bay. (*Reading news item.*) Dr. Brigid Rose Dugdale, daughter of Lt. Colonel J.F.C. Dugdale, who farms extensively in Devon, is reported to be angry at leaked information of his daughter's intended wedding to "Mad" Eddie Gallagher, serving a twenty-year prison sentence for his part in kidnapping Dr. Herrema the former Managing Director of Ferenka.

Dr. Dugdale is serving a nine-year sentence for receiving nineteen paintings stolen from Sir Alfred Beit.

The couple have a son aged three . . . (*Pause.*)

It is believed that the wedding will take place in Limerick Prison. (*Pause.*)

HISTORIAN: Sir, I am currently writing a book on William Burke and William Hare, the murderers, both of whom were of Irish birth . . . (*Bout of coughing.*)

NARRATOR: Tory Island and Inishboffin isolated by storms, seven of Mr. Haughey's workmen marooned on Inishvickaleen.

The high consumption of animal fats is resulting in cardiac conditions.

An aged sheepdog sleeps in the backyard sun. The injured St. Bernard limps about the hall of Hyland's Hotel, its back broken by cruel boys.

The howling dogs of Castleconnel give collective tongue when the elderly bell-ringer hauls on the rope and the church bell sounds the hour.

*Howling dogs, church bell.*

An infatuated young couple are glued together in an endless embrace near a wet wall on the outskirts of Kilkenny town, in the pelting rain.

Gorry Nally sits snug in his warm Conservatory at Kinvara. In the tidy living room of this neat Georgian house there stands a curious love seat painted powder blue; it's Lady Gregory's bathtub with one side removed and some cushions laid down. We sit there, drink Irish whiskey. A fourteen-year-old Pomeranian wheezes on the thick carpet.

*Pomeranian panting.*

On leaving, we are given bunches of grapes from the Conservatory: old-style Irish courtesy.

I recall: A poor pub run by a gabby little woman. Three masted schooners marooned in the silted-up harbour.

An ugly modern church in Silvermines.

A beautiful modern church somewhere between Ennis and Killaloe, the Pope John XIII Memorial Church, closed and congregationless. Over it flocks of crows.

Corcomroe Abbey, under the rule of the Cistercians since 1249, dissolved 1564, today a museum.

*Church bell.*

A huge hoarding on the Tipperary border proudly proclaiming:
 Kilcommon (My Home!)
 Land of Friendship, Freedom, History and Song!
 *Failte*: Welcome!
 Dare no man say that this is a barren land.

*Wild wind. Mournful curlew or plover.*

Rearcross . . . Scores of hooks in the ceiling of the pub, from which scores of gumboots hang. I talk to dowser and mystic Jim Armshaw who asks me . . .

VOICE: (*On echo.*) What's your personal opinion of the Astral Body?

NARRATOR: Evidences of a dead colonization. The church was shipped from Scotland. Up to 1820 there were no roads in the area. Up to 1887, no church. The old IRA burnt down the Police Barracks.

VOICE: (*Fainter.*) Hullo Mammy, will you put on my dinner right now?

*Connemara. Plover, wind.*

NARRATOR: One pale late November day in Maam Valley on the mountainside above Screeb, the white forms of sheep graze on the wet slopes, diminished to the size of lice.

The bear-like brown dog is tearing open a plastic garbage bag. A single court-shoe lying on the road to Carraroe. A butterfly emerges from the woodwork of the bed, sluggish as a moth in November. A rainbow appears over the boggy land on an extraordinarily still late November day. The snow-capped Maamturks are reflected in the estuary. Someone is hammering on a roof. Curlew cries.

Sawing on the roof; otherwise absolute silence. Now the Maamturks are reflected upside-down in the estuary where, thirty years before, Johnny O'Toole saw fifty hookers with sails set, fishing in the little lagoon beyond the bridge where today two seals hunt mackerel.

The grape-coloured and violet glacial mountains are all atremble in the estuary. Silence fills the little cemetery.

VOICE: In Loving Memory of Dr. William Hearn who was drowned in Camus Bay in the discharge of his duty, 13 November 1919, aged fifty-one years, together with his boatman.

NARRATOR: Age improves the headstones and the Celtic Cross. Mildew and weathering has reduced the pomposity of the gravestones. Camus Bay . . . little granite piers, docks, all built in famine times.

*Curlew cry.*

Who is it speaks of the void eternally generative? Occurrence as part of an infinite series. Reality: concreteness rotating towards illusion. The smaller the island the bigger the neurosis. The Irish were Picts before they were Celts. The world's older than we had supposed.

I remember: The Lake of the Blind Trout. You could throw a stone across it. We swam in it.

The inlets turn all colours as the sun sinks behind the clouds, the wind rises, and the last leaves flutter from the copse of trees.

The Maamturks materialise and dematerialise, uncannily freakish, as if playing games with the observer. The two seals are fishing near the bridge; one drives the fish towards the other waiting upstream as the tide floods in again.

*Wind on bridge, Bealadangan.*

One Sunday morning some tall unshaven and fierce-looking Dutch trawlermen in clogs were discovered picking blackberries near the sculptor Delaney's atelier.

Crystals of pink potash and feldspar embedded in granite, the boulders themselves as if pitched about in the giants' battles of prehistory. They loved fighting among themselves then down there. Bedad they did; first mythical battles, then real ones.

STATISTICIAN: Ireland of all countries in Europe has the highest percentage of babies born with abnormalities of the central nervous system.

*Loud bar hubbub (brief).*

. . . This can be directly related to the high number of Irish parents who use the rhythm or so-called "safe" method of birth control.

Birth abnormalities in Catholic families is four times higher . . . 2.79 per 1,000 . . . than that of orthodox Jewish families, where intercourse is only permitted at fixed times, when the wife is not able to conceive.

NARRATOR: (*Lyrical.*) Somewhere in County Wicklow the moon is galloping behind the trees. A stuffed fox, a duck, an open razor, behind the bar counter in Lawless's Hotel in Aughrim, County Wicklow. A stuffed six-pound trout in the Kingfisher's Rest.

In a laneway behind the Clubhouse Hotel in Kilkenny, on a damp afternoon, a clock is striking thirteen times, and an angry father is giving his little boy "what-for."

ANGRY FATHER: Listen!

*A blow.*

Are you goin' to walk with Daddy?
Are you?

*Second blow. Child wails.*

Are you?

NARRATOR: The rats are eating the insulating material from inside the oven door. One of them has electrocuted himself in the motor behind the fridge. He hung there for four days before I found him. The stench was unspeakable.

STATISTICIAN: (*Murmuring.*) The Deviant wears fishnet stockings, suspenders and bra, big falsies; a Cupid's Bow painted on his mouth and hair tied back with a scarf. The whore's house can never be clean enough with this sloven "Mary" scrubbing the toilet bowl with her bare hands, while the angry whore whips the arse off her.

IRISH T.D.: (*Speaking in Dáil.*) A man can't be in two places at wance, unless he's a bird.

*Dáil response.*

NARRATOR: It is sufficient to say, the scroll of Irish history is still unwinding . . . with its quota of *misery, blood and bluster.*

*Connemara. Plover cry. Wind (brief).*

ENGLISH TORY: (*Stoutly, bigoted.*) The custom of these savages is to live as brute beasts among the mountains. They live in huts made with peat . . . do not eat oftener than once a day, and this at night, meagrely enough . . . butter with oaten bread, sour milk. No water. On feast days they eat some flesh, half-cooked, without bread or salt.

They clothe themselves in light trousers and short loose coats of very coarse goat's hair, cover themselves with blankets and wear their hair down to their eyes.

They carry on perpetual war with the English, who keep garrisons for the Queen.

*Rowdy bar.*

GARRULOUS BOOZER: Do you know where he was? . . . in the fuckin' Armoury!

*A hanging. The drop. Heavy grunt (farcical).*
*Silence.*

NARRATOR: (*Benign.*) The English hangman Albert Pierrepoint, who runs the Help the Poor Struggler public house near Southport, was recognised yesterday at Royal Ascot. No photograph of him existed up to this time. He had just hung one John Fleming at Mountjoy. Fleming had killed his own wife, since they couldn't divorce.

*Curlew.*

It's hard to classify nice people. The Irish have a saying: "When the fun is at its height, it's time to go home."

GAELIC SPEAKER: (*In Gaelic.*) When the fun is at its height, it's time to go home.

NARRATOR: And the Danes, who built Dublin and Dundalk, and raped an unholy number of Irish girls, have this saying: "When the music is good and the girls are all pretty, then it's time to go home."

DANE: (*In Danish.*) When the music is good and the girls are all pretty, then it's time to go home.

*Henning Mortensen, "Auld Lang Syne" in Jutlandic (tape).*
*Bar sounds.*

BARMAN: (*Patiently.*) Are you away, lads? Okay then. Safe journey home.

NARRATOR: The gently rolling granite hills of Iar Connacht! In the present relatively mild oceanic climate west of Costello Cross lies a hundred square miles of island-studded water. There is no beauty but hath some strangeness in the prescription. Haunt of mallard and widgeon, ptarmigan and crow, cormorant and swan. Gulls of course. Hares on the beach.

*Connemara.*

In the cold kitchen we found rat-claw prints on the dried grease of the frying pan. In the chill bathroom, rats' teeth and claw-marks on the Pears soap. At night we heard them running races in the attic, enjoying rat-hoolies in the deserted kitchen, come drunk from the skips of the pub opposite. An Hooker was a haunt of hostile Gaelic-speakers in knitted woollen caps who shot pool: "spots" and "stripes" were their only English words. A few of them spoke English, but most reluctantly: the sad bachelor on an old and venerable bicycle who could name all the pubs on either side of Kilburn High Street. Sean Claherty the carpenter has come home after eight years in San Francisco.

In the wild side of life you don't get security. Prejudice . . . a state of mind brought on by experience. The safest cages have the cleanest straw. He has come home. Wouldn't you?

*An Hooker bar, Bealdangan. Pool game.*

The late-arriving Gaels were known as Milesians in the *Book of Invasions*. The first Mesolithic Man reached Ireland at the beginning of the sixth millennium BC (6,000 BC) across the narrow sea between the northeast and Britain. Even at the end of the Mesolithic Period (circa 3,000 BC) there may have been only a few thousand inhabitants on the island. The laws were not committed to writing until the seventh or eighth centuries, or thereabouts; in the ninth came the cruel Norsemen, hewers-off of Irish heads. The adaptable natives learnt to blind and mutilate their hostages, prisoners and rivals, in the Norse manner. Oppression breeds shiftiness, inbred cruelty, the long-deliberated vengeance of the oppressed. Inbred cruelty, the worst of all.

*Sanctus bell. Latin Mass. Priest's prayer.*
*Pause.*
*Screams of rabbit in snare, death throes.*

While Belfast is roasted by firebombs, Connemara is drenched by Force 10 gales.

The old Irish grievances take on a new reality here; the harsh violent breath of the past breathes upon the living—infected breath. The young seem surly and resentful. Cromwell's New Model Army marched with the bloody flux through Ireland; the tempers of foot-soldiers and dragoons never very sweet. Oliver Cromwell was forever chasing Piaras Feiritéar through bogs.

*The hunt. Galway blazers.*

In the attic the cavorting rats make no attempt to go about their affairs silently. Conditions were bad. They had always been bad; but now they were worse. The sanguineous bugaboos were wreaking vengeance; Seamus Costello had his head blown off with a shotgun, Lawlor despatched with a handgun while taking a pint in Timmon's of Essex Street. Thirty foxhounds were poisoned. Sinn Feinism, more deadly than a mad dog's tooth.

*Gas leaking.*
*Protestant congregation at prayer.*

Out of the medieval darkness came the first public lighting to Dublin in 1689. The population was then around 40,000 souls. By

1750 the population had grown to 130,000. By 1800 to 321,000. Gas-lighting came in 1825. By 1911 the population was 389,000. 26,000 poor families lived in 5,000 tenements. By 1927 nearly twenty-eight percent of the city's population lived in single-room tenements . . . the "house of decay" referred to by Mr. James Joyce.

"From house to house . . . went the nine o'clock postman."

DUBLINER: (*Broad accent.*) He told me he was interested in buying a house. I told him, no way. There was no chance. (*Pause.*)

*Muffled sound of falling masonry (abrupt).*
*Rapid-fire antiphony from two Gaels, to background music of Irish jig, fiddle and whistle.*

FIRST GAEL: (*Fierce.*) Art O'Connell is going to Granard, and Patrick O'Flynn is going with him. Patrick is not going to another country; he is sick . . .

SECOND GAEL: (*Resigned, passive.*) He is not sick; he is working on the road to Derry.

FIRST GAEL: (*Fiercely.*) There is a rock at the well, and there is a tree growing at the door.

SECOND GAEL: (*Passive.*) There is a fire on the road. Close the door. The day is cold. The fort is old. The whole field is green. Come with me to Kildare. Leave the young horse on the road and come with me.

FIRST GAEL: (*Fierce, eager.*) Nora and Mare are at the well. Mary is go-ing down to the meadow with a . . . pitcher. And Nora is at the . . .

SECOND GAEL: (*Passive.*) . . . barn. The grass is dry and heavy. The fresh grass is heavy yet. Una and Nora are going with you to Kildare.

Do not stand on the floor, stand at the door. I am going to another country . . . good-bye.

THE ORANGE FOE: (*Very fierce, sarcastic.*) Leave a big stool at the door. Follow me; do not follow Peter. The day is bright and dry, and I am going to Derry. Follow the man on the road. A clean road and a dry path . . .

FIRST GAEL: (*Rapidly.*) Do not follow the man on the road. Do not leave a big stool at the door. Do not stand on the road. Conn is going to Granard. Art is going with a young horse. I am not going with you to Derry, I am going with Conn to Granard.

SECOND GAEL: (*Confused.*) There is a shamrock growing at the well. I am going with you to Granard. There is a long road between Kildare and Derry. The spinning wheel is old and broken. The work is heavy and Mary is not strong . . .

*Curlew and plover-cry, wind.*
*Mournful Connemara.*
*Congregational responses at Mass (brief).*
*Protestant equivalent.*
*Howling dogs at Castleconnel.*

NARRATOR: It was the coldest winter in Connemara since 1840. There I was taken for an Englishman and as such insulted by Gaelic speakers . . . drunken young pups. There I spent six uncomfortable months.

Leaving it for the foothills of the sierras in Andalucía in August into the hottest summer in living memory. One-hundred ten degrees in Malaga and the birds died in their cages; no rain fell in months and the vines suffered. (*Pause.*) The children accepted me as a Frenchman.

*Gallows bar. Galway. Dialling.*

PATRON: (*Galwayman.*) Hellew there . . . wouldja send a taxi to The Gallows please?

TAXI RANK: Where?

PATRON: (*Patiently.*) The Gallows.

TAXI RANK: What's the name?

PATRON: Small.

TAXI RANK: Right you be, Mr. Small. I'll be right there.

NARRATOR: And he was good as his word. It was pouring with rain on Eyre Square as usual. (*Pause.*)
(*To himself.*) The White Rook is lost.
(*Pause.*) To whom do I address myself? (*Silence.*) You again. But who are you? (*Long pause.*) Begin again. Write on only one side of the paper, and confine yourself to essentials.
Am I or am I not the same person that I have always imagined myself to be? Taken myself to be. In that case who am I? (*Pause.*) Is the silence significant or just a lack of something to say? (*Pause.*) Is that significant? (*Long silence.*) What do you do when memory starts to go? (*Long pause.*)
I come here Fridays. (*Titter.*) What do you do?

*Latin Mass.*

# Zoo Station

**A BERLIN THRENODY FOR FOUR VOICES.**

Broadcast on BBC Radio 3 on the 19th of October, 1986. Recorded
and directed in West Berlin by Piers Plowright.

*The city of Sophronia is made up of two half-cities. . . . Here remains the half-Sophronia of the shooting galleries and the carousels, the shout suspended from the cart of the headlong roller coaster; and it begins to count the months, the days it must wait before the caravan returns and a complete life can begin again.*

—Italo Calvino, *Invisible Cities*

*I now again write what I have heard, what was confided to me. But it was not confided to me as a secret that I must keep, all that was directly confided to me was the voice that spoke, the rest is no secret, on the contrary, it is mere chaff; and what flies in all directions when work is being done is what can be communicated and what implores the boon of being communicated, for it has not the strength to remain lonely and quiet when whatever gave it life has slipped away forever.*

—Franz Kafka, *Dearest Father: Stories and Other Writings*

# CAST

NARRATOR

GERMAN

DR. HAHN

*Berliners*

MARTIN LINDERMANN

LORE SCHRÖDER

*Gasts*

NANCY WAKES

KILDARE WAKES

# SCENES

# PRELUDE

*Uproar in Nullgrab bar (brief).*
*Mix to: Schoenberg, "Modern Psalm" for speaker, chorus, and orchestra, Op. 50c.*

NARRATOR: (*Subdued.*) The Motorschiff Vaterland passes the Dampler Siegfried, the one outward-bound for Spandau, the other inward-bound for the Wannsee.

Their wakes join to become one, like a muscle, sending a shiver over the whole broad reach of the Havel. Dirty water is slapping against the Wannseebad shore where ill-tempered swans wade in the shallows, chocking themselves to death on the slops of bread cast there. Whole sodden loaves lie half-submerged on the shoreline stained a brownish hue . . .

*Swans, water.*

LORE: . . . How can I go without you? How can you go without me? The thought seeks a way out, as the prisoner in his cell: You are here, yet not here.

*Bundesallee traffic.*

. . . along the whole Bundesallee the blocked traffic can only advance centimetre-wise. Please judge of my . . . nervosity, my depressed feelings. I was . . . *Untröstlich!*

NARRATOR: The Divided City, like a woman, withholds its secrets. Unless she likes you. Then something can always be arranged.

DR. HAHN: (*Caustic.*) You should perhaps leave her alone . . . That is, unless you have already gone too far.

GERMAN: The father has eaten sour grapes and the childrens' teeth are set on edge.

## LORE'S DREAM

*Berlin Zoo, aviary, free-flying zone.*
Lohengrin *low on tape recorder.*

LORE: (*Low.*) One week ago I had a strange but somehow great dream. I was lying somewhere on a riverbank, then this mysterious light between day and night with hardly no colours.

*Zoo mixed with Kurfürstendamm.*

. . . a calm and peaceful atmosphere. The river was not very large, and surrounded by wonderful bizarre trees.

*Ku-Damm and Zoo mixed (close).*

. . . Suddenly I noticed a little island swimming down the river coming towards me and on it seven or eight huge grey elephants all very quiet and looking at me.

*Zoo.*

. . . I became afraid but thought that it would be best to keep very quiet and not to move at all, and to make myself very small.

Then the mysterious island stopped and the huge elephants moved towards me and went very slowing and carefully one after the other over me without touching me.

I saw the enormous heavy bodies above me.

And in this way these fantastic creatures arrived and passed me and they disappeared again. When I woke up I felt a great admiration for the very strong nature and its marvellous and peaceful and so-powerful creatures.

# THE EX-CAPITAL

NARRATOR: (*Didactic.*) 341 square miles in diameter, 250 acres left for agriculture and gardens, perhaps 19,000 forested, and six percent made up of lakes and waterways. It lies a hundred miles inside the DDR, prim inside a prison.

Blind Borges called it the ugliest city on earth. Undoubtedly ugly deeds were done there; but you tell me where they are not? It was a railroad centre in the last century; previous to that, a city of the Hanseatic League, a centre of the garment industry. It was probably first a trading centre, and has been settled since the New Stone Age (of 3,000 BC). Today it's an industrial centre processing partially finished materials, which are then exported as finished products.

The ex-capital today holds its own, as a rude Prussian should: at times charming, at others repulsive. It is known as the Mecca of Transvestites—a change of heart for the old garment industry.

The fringes of this half-city have a distinctive atmosphere: Lichtenrade, Teltowkanal, Marienfelde, fields of wheat waving around the village of Lubars, somewhere at an inn there Lindermann and Kildare Wakes are drinking a flagon of good Franconian wine, enjoying the cool breeze that sometimes blows from Arcadia.

The winters are protracted and severe. The lakes freeze over, the skaters come out, Klopstock and Jules Laforgue and Vladimir Nabokov as a boy, a brat I bet. Industrial salt is laid along the Allee verges of Dahlem and Onkel Toms Hütte, Potsdamer Chaussee and Kronprinzsinnen, on Podbielskiallee and Nikolassee, killing the overhead chestnut, mostly.

Down there lived the pallid composer Kaufmann with wife and family. His wife is blonde, Dutch as Delft, whereas he is silent and devious as an eel, a deeply suspicious man. We have a saying in my part of the world . . . but no matter.

He says either too little or too much, and I cannot say which is worse. Let him speak for himself if he will, or be silent, as he would likely prefer. I never heard his music, never wanted to. I imagine it might be rather like himself, glum, unattractive, halting, awkward, humourless, difficult.

"Nullgrab" is a city of the old. They say the young are coming back. I cannot do without them. The last widow-making war was more disruptive to its life and growth than the seven-year-siege of Veii. Every second citizen is over forty years of age and above twenty-five percent of the population are over sixty-five, with 13,000 more dying than are being born. 37,000 more expire each year. The place is a warren of graveyards, like the extensive ones below Rudow and Buckow, and another great megapolis of the dead between Britz and Steglitz, below the Südring. Klinikums and Krankenhauses abound, graveyards and Kurzgartens, so popular with old ladies.

Walter Hardiman lives in Steglitz, once a Brown District, with many of the grim Nazi-type villas and high walls, strange building styles.

Goebbels and Heydrich were married in the Lutheran church near Joachim Knepper Weg at the end of our road, Beskidenstraße, though not to each other, thank God. City of war widows, blinded veterans, night watchmen, brutal dogs, heavy eaters.

Difficult to imagine, yes, but once seen never forgotten. Hard to forget. The truncated metropolis depicted here and designated "Nullgrab" is of course only my own invention, and figures and descriptions may sometimes be more aromatic than exact.

# STEGLITZ

LINDERMANN: The reason I am writing today is that I had a dream last night in which you figured prominently. You and your wife were living in Nullgrab in a house located close to the Steglitz part of the Teltowkanal, the grounds adjacent to the backside of the Klinikum Hospital, which one could see from a window.

*Nature, wind in trees, Lutheran church bell. Hold under following.*

You and your wife and me stood eating Langnese ice cream in a bright room without any furniture. Your wife was tall, blonde and thin. You and me were arguing about your refusal to show me around the house. Your wife told me that you're only trying to hide your daughter from me. I said that I didn't know that you had a daughter. You assured me you had none. Your wife laughed and made some signs with her hands.

I left the room to walk about the house, you and your wife following me, your wife laughing all the time and gesticulating. I felt very tense. I opened a door to a room where a bunch of children of uncertain age and sex were playing a game. This room had no furniture either.

I discovered a steep staircase going down to a basement. I asked you, where does it lead to? You said, to the kitchen.

*Furnace, close, brief.*
*Lutheran bell, idyllic.*

. . . You produced a piece of paper from your pocket and began reading aloud. I didn't understand the words. I went down the staircase and your voice faded. I came to a corridor, the walls of which were all covered with photos showing you and a girl, you wearing sunglasses. The girl reminded me of somebody I knew and longed to see. The longing became so strong that I had to sit down on the floor, feeling quite sick.

The corridor led to a door which opened after some time and a beautiful dark-haired girl appeared, approached and sat down beside me. She wore a black dress.

*Nullgrab party, hold under following.*

. . . It was my Paris friend from Madrid. She said something in a language I didn't understand. We went upstairs and came to a garden. The house was gone. The garden went down to the Kanal.

You were working in the garden with enormous tools, wearing sunglasses. You didn't notice us. You were sitting there under a tree with a gun. One of those old cargo boats was going by on the Kanal. We swam to the boat and sat on it. We were floating down the Kanal, making love, when, passing the Hospital, my sister Ishie looked out from one of the windows, shouting, "It's war!"

*Cry in German. Mix to Schoenberg: hold under following:*

. . . We saw huge black airplanes approaching.

*Schoenberg under. Bombers flying. Hold under following:*

. . . They came towards us, right down the Kanal. They were firing and we were hit. Then I sat on a chair and somebody was standing behind me and repeating the sentence: "It's your fault. You will never see her again!"

*Spoken in German, middle distance.*
*Wind in trees: hold under.*

. . . I really felt sad this morning, like you do after certain dreams. There are no cargo boats on the canal anymore, they've closed it long ago.

*Nightmare, sounds distorted, the voice distorted. On echo.*

NANCY: (*Talking in her sleep, voice slurred.*) What's the meaning of these anti-snail eaters?

*Brief silence as if listening.*

(*Voice not her own.*) What's all this about barley fields and pink pigs ripening down your lane?

*Brief silence, deep sigh.*

. . . something funny's going on here!

*Silence, groan.*

(*Vehemently.*) I don't like it!

NARRATOR: The half-city is situated between two great rivers. Into the tributary of one of these—it might have been the filthy River Ine—an overflow from a chemical factory manufacturing a product classified as an organo-chlorine compound of persistent nature, capable of destroying four hundred different types of insects, in a few days in June

1969 killed 25,000,000 fish. Hoechst Endosu, lethal against insects, caught them below Bingen-Luch, and they never made the Nordsee.

Man comes in and turns the fishes out!

Imagine a city without a head, its limbs lopped off like in a fairy tale, German of course. It's true symbol should be the Wild Boar, with Berliner Schnauze, as they say with intense self-satisfaction of themselves, and just a pardonable touch of conceit. They are as attached to their quartered city as the Parisians to theirs.

In modern Germany, espionage has become another industry. Capitalism's function is to gorge itself and grow. Destroy itself. When fish die they begin to stink from the head. Similarly with Nullgrab.

Puzzled feelings, *Ziche-Zache*!

# From Within the Divided City (1980)

*Train (interior of carriage).*

KILDARE: The Poles are asleep. The West Nullgrab carriages arrive last. This express train goes on to Moscow, onto a different, narrower rail gauge, through Warsaw, into another time. Passports are checked at six A.M. in the dark, then an hour later, passport photos are checked against the originals, half asleep, always the faces of dead people. A small portable contraption *depends* about the bull-necked Saxon VoPo Guard, who is gravely suspicious. The toilets have already been searched. Alsatian guard dogs have snubbed about under the carriages. A sinister fellow in a trench coat is hugger-muggering with the uniformed guards in the corridor. We are ordered to rise so that the space below the seats can be checked. We are on the DDR border; for a hundred miles back into the darkness it is all Soviet-owned territory.

Potsdam drifts by on the left, as if seen underwater; a sports stadium, soccer stands. A stout officer in bulging Red Army breeches pedals a thin bicycle past a pile of upended street signs; en route, no doubt, to some excruciatingly dull official routine. Then a firing range, a pond, crows. A goods-train passes, carrying what appear to be tarpaulin-shrouded tanks, which on closer view turn out to be innocent enough agricultural machinery, bulldozers and tractors. A flock of pigeons wheel above a green dome. Potsdam, Potsdam!—Chateaubriand,

Jules Laforgue, the liar Malaparte, *Mädchen in Uniform*, garrison bells, pealing Glocken, rural weddings, old Europe, lost times. The same flock of wheeling pigeons fly from right to left over the green dome, a breeze brushes the water of the pond. Potsdam is passing, passing.

Now we are on sandy Prussian soil and no mistake, passing regimented lines of pines, distant wheat fields, clearer skies but still mournful DDR territory, Soviet-grey skies about the straight lines of pines planted there in rigid calmness with no undergrowth to distract; we are entering the land of the gnomes and witches and evil stepmothers of the *Brüders* Grimm, a part of Germany hidden within the DDR: Nullgrab, itself the lost city.

On empty platforms of deserted stations female station guards stand about in the early morning sun, their peroxide hair and slingback shoes invoke a Hollywood of the 1940s, Lili Marlene. On this line, time stopped in the spring of 1945. Two youths slick back their short hair as they walk to work; they want to look like Elvis Presley. German yet un-German, they would have been born in Soviet time. Their land teems with soldiers in Red Army uniforms, on the alert, prepared, trained for war. I see the sign for *Nikolassee* in old Sütterlin script and am almost home.

Approaches to Nullgrab are sinister. You know you are nearing the site of a great calamity. In the thinning dark the watchtowers loom out of the Prussian mist. The war may be ended thirty-five years past, but these wooden towers are not empty; a soldier in Red Army uniform trains binoculars on the Mittle Europa Express bound for München and just now pulling out, packed with degenerate Capitalist swine. A VoPo with bulging holster sets his Alsatian hound down onto the tracks, and in a surly early-morning manner watches it slink under the carriages where desperate ones have clung on and made their escape to the "free" West. This passes. Now Nikolassee Station and my ghost walking there, boarding an S-bahn from Wannsee, going to meet Lore.

Now Berliners appear in the corridor, the men shaving, engaged in methodical toilets; the women well dressed, good-looking, fresh, assured. It's eight o'clock on a thoroughly German morning; the express has halted in Bahnhof Zoo but the end carriages are beyond the platform. We are obliged to step down onto the tracks and walk into West Nullgrab.

The divided city seems unchanged. This is how it is. In the Nullgrab Zoo, the hippos consort with their young. Submerged to their huge nostrils in the dank cement ponds they masticate slowly, ruminatively, sluggardly, thick veal that stinks of cow, around them their pink active calves. A heavy avalanche of meat and gristle now subsiding into the man-made pond until only their exhaling nostrils and bulbous pachydermatous eyeballs show: to glaze over, sunken in the digestive mulch. They move ponderously in another time, far removed from their African swamps, these hippopotami of the Nullgrab Zoo.

*Die schonen Nixen, im Schleirgewant Ensteigen der Meerestiefe,* wrote Heine, who had made a lifelong study of the German nature. Only dreaming, he believed, lost in an ideal dream, does the German dare to give his opinion, which he has kept deep in his loyal German heart. Germany would last forever, Heinrich Heine believed, because it was a thoroughly healthy land, with its oaks and its linden trees, and its fine women.

Bahnhof Zoo is an odd place. A sort of Lido for German inverts; a sort of underground Nullgrab lavatory. Do not dally there. Around seven A.M. some poorly dressed cleaners are sweeping dirt away with heavy brooms.

The Americans are engaged in sporadic sharpshooting in the Grünewald by the border, the forbidden ground; you hear the fast heavy drilling of modern weaponry, a mailed fist hammering on a heavy door that will not yield. The woodpeckers are drilling too, around Krumme Lanke and Schlachtensee, into which a Lancaster bomber dropped during the war. French divers are recovering parts of it, laid out on a raft. Sonic booms break the double-glaze windows as MiG jets go through the sound barrier, with the express purpose of annoying Sir Roger Jacklin who is dining with the Bürgermeister. Sir Kenneth Clarke is reading a paper on "Sign, Symbol, Image." The pinched shocked features of Vladimir Nabokov stare insolently from the cover of *TIME* magazine. *Der Zirkus* is showing at the Capital. Young prostitutes, with weight thrown on one hip, pose in pairs near the Hotel Bagota. The SS officer from the death camp now works as political adviser for the Dresdener Bank. In Dahlem Cemetery there stands a tombstone with an English inscription, thoroughly Prussian in sentiment. "Life is Sweet, Brother. Do You Not Find It So?" Well, as a matter of fact, no, dead *Brüder*.

In the headlights of a parked car (not theirs) near the Spree in a snowstorm at two A.M. at the end of the Polish Week in the Akademie der Künste, two sad sodomites about to part, and frantic with betrayal, copulate in the snow. The long thin one comes running towards me, vaults from the bridge and disappears through the thin ice of the spree with a last scream: *Michel*! The air temperature being twelve degrees below zero and still dropping in that dead hour of an ironbound Nullgrab winter.

In an illuminated yellow phone booth Nancy despairs of finding a taxi and phones the police. The two lately copulating pederasts are now together in the frozen Spree and I have removed my overcoat and let it down as a lifeline. Something funny is going on between those two, having broken the ice, as it were, they struggle in the black water, reach out their hands, are swept away. Nancy saunters down, over the bridge in the snow.

## Arnimallee

LINDERMANN: Terrible weather here in Nullgrab, neither hot nor warm, just grey days, drowning in greyish shade, all colours dirty and everybody in an offensive mood under heavy winter coats. Fatima washing her car before Haus Hecht with a sour face, car radio playing "Jungle Boogie" by some jerks—Zappo and his Hot Cats—trying to produce rutting noises.

Fatima longing for the sun, dreaming of St. Moritz or Cortina. Once a week she goes to a stinking gym for ski-muscle training. She has a theory about her own skin, something about the smoothness of it and its brown pigments and its greed for the sun. Hates pullovers and winter clothes in the city, especially when there is no snow, feeling sticky all the time, her skin developing acne, rotting away. Has several anointings of Nivea Crème during the day.

I remember her being obsessed with some quite strange thoughts when we met first, for instance, her fear of kisses, due to her being a dentist's daughter, "All children of dentists loathe kissing," she used to say then, with her father always talking about people's disgusting dirty mouths.

Her Pappi, old Immin Kahn, is a strange, fierce-looking man with a wild life-story, calling all females "Püppchen," but also prone to sudden outbursts of anger, throwing knives and forks about. Or, when left by a girlfriend, walking around with a crutch and dark sunglasses. He has a hearing aid which he switches off when people talk too much. Something of him in his daughter.

When she was much smaller I saw her with her family in the Berliner Wald—a child with long hair, black fur like an animal, years before we came together. Exotics solemnly walking around the lake, old Immin Kahn leading the way, people staring at them, me on a bicycle behind a tree.

Sorry for not having written sooner, meant to unclench teeth first but guess I did just the opposite, spending an idle time with a blonde woman (divorcée) in her most corrupt thirties—turned out to be an especially *grässliche* experience, among other things being introduced into her snobbish wonderland, arts and thereabouts.

She is working in the Neue Nationalgalerie or rather that messed up thing they call the "scene," a nuthouse papered with money, huge sums circulating in there, spent on whatever imported vanities strikes their fancy. Vernissagen, exhibitions, grim lectures on the "grammar" of cars neatly decorated with some pig's bloody entrails. Bonn and Berlin in my opinion sponsoring so many wrongdoers and exhibitionists. Conceit, elegant gossip, bombastic atmosphere of so-called savoir vivre, would-be tarts and homos by the dozen, the flashy ones with their proud but nevertheless shrill self-accusation. Just the setting that promotes murder. Bad cut-up of life.

In Nullgrab now *LIEBE* splashed in aerosol on every second wall and the American Chapel announced a "Love Contest": send in a photo depicting your image of love. Don't suppose they want to see my picture. Parties crowded with multicoloured monsters and the inevitable wild Irishman who sits broodingly in a corner, casting wild glances around, as he is expected to do—Ireland being still very much à la mode; many young people going there to find out another of their illusionary "real things." In each and every pub the Dubliners roar out "You're drunk, you're drunk!" etc., most lustily.

Fatima left home some weeks ago for a boy who drives a Mercedes coupe and keeps telling her that he is a secret agent.

Last thing I remember of Blonde Disaster is drinking in her best friend's (homo) flat in Wielandstraße, thirty people talking at once, air full of poison, and she introducing me to French words I didn't understand, trios and quadros, etc. and me winding up alone in Berlinerzimmer without any furniture in it, unless you count an artish object by a certain Votzrello or Vostell, a pink penis in a glass case fucking a plastic brain.

Had some trouble for weeks getting rid of her, phoning me all day long, me swearing and menacing, and the ruder I became, the more persistent she became. Gave her a hint at last how jealous an Oriental buddy of mine is, Afghanistan knives and all.

I hated that Blonde Bitch after a month's time; but couldn't quite manage to get away at once, probably out of curiosity, and later I tried my best being stone-drunk all the time we spent together to avoid her false, theatrical ways in bed. Sure I am just a romantic idiot, but I know what I see in young girls, sense of beginning, not of rotting away. With Fatima gone, Liza hating me in Paris, I am fed up with the whole business at the moment. Expect you'll raise a mocking eyebrow. Nothing has worked out too well by now, but perhaps it just seems so. Trouble is, am always a little afraid to write to you about it.

# GEDÄCHTNISKIRCHE

*Billie Holiday, "Mean to Me." Hold under:*

NARRATOR: The Kaiser-Wilhelm-Gedächtniskirche, or Memorial Church, is a smelly place. There is a pool of piss in front of the plaque. Hippies and bums are having a good exhibition time on the steps during the warm months. They piss merrily away in the ruins next to embarrassed tourists. It is every Berliner girl's secret wish to be married from there. I saw no bride in white leaving in a white coach drawn by a white palfrey, pelted with confetti. Most of them are brunettes with dark inviting Latin eyes, (a new species) the *Schlussel-Kinder* of the war.

The ruins are the stump of a burnt-out tree struck by lightning: behold these blackened remains!

The old clock still works, the old Prussian heart still sound; hear the heavy ponderous chimes!

A nervous bride in white, holding white roses to her palely anaemic face, hiding her blushes in the white roses, plays in the ruins of this city of widows in sad hats, "who believe the heart is dead," hard vertical rain, serious men attacking thick steaks, ghosts in broad daylight. Its pre-war population has dropped to 2.2 million and the cultural heart moved some kilometres west, away from Unter den Linden to the Kurfürstendamm and the Opera, Schiller Theatre, IBM

Centre. City of legendary Teutonic overeating. Rabbits burrow for roots in the Tiergarten, moles are digging in the Rehwiese, a hawk flies down Schlüterstraße. Now that the country is being poisoned by chemicals, the birds and animals have moved into the city. Megapolis is coming.

(*Sotte voce.*) Built in the late nineteenth century, gutted in World War Two, but for the bell tower, and with a great hold over the nave, it stands there in a very permanent fashion, its blind wall eye looking crookedly down the Kurfürstendamm. A turret of blue stained glass has been grafted onto it, a modern church: Mie's fancy. There may be no more cathedrals built in our times, Gaudi's the last, in Barcelona.

Stand in the once-holy place, in the piss, study the plaque!

*Male church choir: Bach motet.*
*Tolling of KWG Kirche.*

GERMAN: (*Oracular, with pomp.*) *ZUR ERINNERUNG AN WILHELM I, ONIG VON PREUSSEN UND DEUTSCHER KAISER, WURDE IN DEN JAHREN 1891–1895 UNTER DER REGIERUNG WILHELM II AUS SPENDEN DES GANZEN DEUTSCHEN VOLKER DIE ERSTE KAISER-WILHELM-GEDÄCHTNISKIRCHE ERBAUT. WAHRENT DES II. WELTKRIEGES IN DER NACHT ZUM 23. NOVIEMBRE 1943 WURDE SIE BEIM LUFTTANGRIFF ZERSTORT. DER TURM DEN ALTEN KIRCHE SOLL AN DAS GERICHT GOTTES ERIN-NERN, DAS IN DEN JAHREN DES KRIEGES UBER UNSER VOLK HERINBRACH.*

*Bach, Mass in B Minor, final chorus* (Dona nobis pacem).
*Sudden silence, then roar from Ku-Damm.*

NARRATOR: As darkness falls over Nullgrab, heavy-winged crea-tures issue from the belfry and the great dark hold above the nave.

"Ganzen," "Erinnerung," "Nacht," "Turm," "Krieg," "Kaiser," "Luft," "Kirche," "Volk" ponderously fly out over Europacentre.

Hard by, in Wittenbergplatz, another monument proclaims:

ORT DES SCHRECKENS, DIE WIR NIEMALS VER-
GESSEN DURFEN: AUSCHWITZ, STUTTHOF, MAI-
DANEK, TREBLINKA, BUCHENWALD, DACHAU,
SACHSENHAUSEN, RAVENSBRUCK, BERGEN, BELSEN.
ERINNERN UND VERGESSEN.

The vendors in the kiosks do not bother to peer out from their kiosks, with all summer around them in the concupiscent glow of female flesh; as cold air from the Baltic streams in, and a perishing fog crawls along the whole length of Kurfürstendamm. Jules Laforgue is on the razzle, frequenting the low dives. He writes in his diary: "A Jewess with black armpits, a blonde made of wood, the red-faced English girl, unbelievable."

Father Corcoran from Ireland is studying pornographic displays in a sex shop nearby.

Step out of the Zoo, cross under the arched flyover, pass along the colonnade, experience the brassy clarity of evening, never exhausting. Hear the heavy, resonant chimes!

Something offered, something given, something lost, then retrieved, an element suppressed, something arrested. In Spandau Prison the ex-Nazi Arms Minister Albert Speer hears on the wind a cock crowing, the voices of children at play, and weeps.

Over the way someone is whispering in German.

Outside, a blue evening has fallen.

# A SATISFIED STOMACH

*Kurfürstendamm by day. Kaiser Wilhelm Memorial Church bell, pedestrians and traffic.*

NARRATOR: Along the Kurfürstendamm the kiosks reel under their burden of soft porn. In the winter months, when snow lies on the ground, a wind blows from the Baltic or, who knows, even from Siberia; then the rude models, all imperfections such as rashes and pimples and love-bites airbrushed out, glow like beds of begonias. The fine rain spends itself, *Chimrimiri (Cochonerrie?)* as the babbling Austrians put it. Bared female flesh was burning lushly through the long winter months, when the thoughts of the citizens turned longingly towards the sun.

It—bared flesh, the laughing mouth—stood for repleteness in the great consumer society, the sick society. Cleavage and cleft and wetted hair and smiling mouth were cheesily, cheekily perpetuated a thousand times, ten thousand; and differed only in degree from the photo displays set up behind glass in the foyers of cinemas where blue movies were shown, or the blatant attitude of the strip houses.

*Kurfürstendamm (close).*

GERMAN: *Rinderbrust mit Meerjellich sauce.*

331

*Pfannkuchen mit Weissbier. Oder . . . Eisbein.*

*Kassler Rippenspeer mit Bier. Schlachtplatte mit Brathering.* The food is solid and plentiful. There are five thousand restaurants in Nullgrab. Man is the only animal that can remain on friendly terms with the victims he intends to eat, until he eats them.

NARRATOR: Order: Boiled ham hocks served with plenty of soured Kraut, washed down with that highly carbonated green beer with the sour aftertaste suggestive of fresh vomit.

Puzzled feelings, *Ziche-Zache.* In the arcade near Bilka, a middle-aged woman buys the new issue of *Spontan.* Around the Bahnhof Zoo the lines of colour magazines are laid out head-to-toe on the wide pavement. The breeze lifts a page and lo and behold we are in a . . . *Wald und Weise* set-up: a pretty strumpet in her skin is smiling toothily at the camera, and a grinning fellow with *Knorpel* erect is feasting his eyes on her lush blonde charms.

*Car horn. Kurfürstendamm traffic rages by. Calls.*

A tall Negro with vest open to the waist, a single earring, cowboy boots, finds a gap in the oncoming traffic, crosses against the traffic lights, dances onto the far pavement.

The halted traffic, laid bonnet to boot, takes off like wild beasts stampeding towards a water hole in the dry season. Without looking back the Negro strides arrogantly on past the bullet-riddled Amerika Haus.

*Herbst, du bist Chic!*

In all the main cities the same feature film was showing, with identical posters, identical plugs, the hoardings identified McQueen and Dustin Hoffmann in *Papillon*, Henry Fonda in *My Name is Nobody* (sic). At the Palast Kine hoarding the long naked back of a brunette as big as a destroyer with rapt look and damply parted lips is looking over her shoulder with a shining predatory eye. Pressurised dream in lurid glow. The great lie: "The Sated Beast."

The originals of these healthy-looking nudist models walked around Berlin and Munich, Frankfurt and Köln. They came up on hoardings, blown up ten times life-size, photographed in ambiguous proximity to horses and grooms. You could ski down the slopes of their backs. These Brobdingnagian broads were ripe for eating, succulent morsels undressed for you. Nipples and white teeth were the salt and pepper; axillary and pubic hair the garnishings. Some of the breasts were excessive in size, with sore-looking roundels. Below all that the rich unshaven mound. And two wealthy movie actors unshaven and in chains, engaged in pseudo-suffering.

*Immer mehr, immer mehr!*

## An Invigorating Confrontation

*Title given in German, then English.*
*Hindemith Cello Concerto, solo until orchestra.*

NANCY: I had a dream the other night. I am leaning against a boulder. It's by the sea. Small waves are coming in and furniture being washed ashore, if you please. It's not any kind of junk, mind you, but really elegant period stuff. A child is holding my hand, looking up into my face.

A high-backed chair, then another, floats in, both encrusted with barnacles. A feeling of well-being pervades all. Don't ask me why.

NARRATOR: (*Ruminating.*) Afterglow. Then darkness. Fall of night by the sea. Then afterglow again. Then a phosphorescent shoreline with weak surf. Is it summer or winter? . . . *Sommer oder Winter?* No odours in our dreams, or temperature, so impossible to say. Autumn or spring, winter or summer, who can say?

## THE WALDKRIEG KRANKENHAUS ON FISCHERHÜTTESTRASSE

KILDARE: Opposite Krumme Lanke U-bahn station, the end of the line, stands a closed-down Kurzgarten; nothing sadder to see.

Across Argentinische Allee the *krankenhaus* is set back a little amid trees, evergreens as in a cemetery. On garden seats, on balconies, appear the anxious pale faces of incurable convalescents at windows, or sitting, seldom perambulating, or then on crutches or with nurses, anxiously leaning, wretchedly alive, lethargic as dying flies in winter, all hope and most of life drained out of them. Live for the hour!

Parkland nearby, meadows open out, a pond, a public park. Behind wire, the nurses' home. Bare nurses bursting out of their bikinis are sunbathing in the grass. The odour of pines from the aromatic wood, the odour of the nearby lakes, pervades all.

## KURZGARTEN, FISCHERHÜTTESTRASSE

*Zoo turnstile. War widows at Kaffee und Kuchen in Kurzgarten. Mix with Russian front warfare documentary.*

LINDERMANN: Many old people are found in the Kurzgarten now, down the way from Krumme Lanke station. They order *Kaffee und Kuchen*, they are addicted to this, it is somehow fashionable. It's also fashionable to laugh at them, all the old ladies who have seen so many things. But I do not wish them ill; I wish them well. I wish that they will not be run over, all the old ladies who have seen so many things. Admittedly they give off a peculiar smell. This is the true No Man's Land, this last heaven of the mothers of Wehrmacht heroes who perished on the ironbound Russian front; this *Kurzgarten* on Fischerhüttestraße.

*Kurzgarten: widows chattering.*

(*Recollecting tranquilly.*) I'm writing this in the Kurzgarten on a warm day in Nullgrab, sitting at the window, watching the exotic tree with the bean-like fruits and drinking chilled Moselle in a long-stemmed green-tinged glass as we did before. You—or a ghost—are sitting opposite me with a good Dannemann cigar, going well. The young married couple are still serving, the girl with the long hair. You are watching her taking an order in the garden.

# SCHLACHTENSEE

KILDARE: Boxer hounds with permanently disgruntled expressions of overfed elderly men, the worried faces of bats, the incontinent lurch of old men, waddle about after their masters as they take the air around the lakes, rarely bark though reputed to be good with children, surly brutes too. Their displeased faces with creased foreheads and weeping cataracts betray natures deeply unhappy. Their blueberry mouths have come to resemble their masters'. How that humid gaze does wander around, scarcely holding back the tears!

When I take a turn around the lakes, Krumme Lanke and Schlachtensee, Munge Pond and Gunge Pond, haunt of suicides, approaching by the Rehwiese, those sunken meadows below Argentinische Alle, seldom do I fail to meet him. No matter what time of day I venture out, meet him I am sure to, this Namenlose, a foreigner (Serb or Croat?) looking as if just out of bed (in the late afternoon!), not exactly fresh, quite the contrary, tousled and stale, with scum on his lips, gummy-eyed, troubled: his hindquarters slink along in a manner positively hyena-like; very unsettling to come upon. Maybe he has come up from Schopenhauerstraße by the hotel where the black-jacketed Hells Angels like to assemble, about to descend an endless flight of stairs leading nowhere. Vowed to secret ways, where he goes nobody knows. Brother, *Nichts für ungut!*

The calm evening casts the reflection of trees down into Schlachten-see and Krumme Lanke. We pass without formal salutation. What could we say? Silent as the grave passes, this hyena-man.

Yesterday I encountered him on the Rehwiese, the sunken mead-ows. The day before that outside Nikolassee S-bahn station. Tomor-row, who knows where? He moves about. He is everywhere, roaming far and wide.

The Keep-Fit-Fiends jog around the little lakes in singlets and ten-nis-sneakers, leaving behind them an acrid reek of human sweat. A red-headed maniac on a bicycle blows a bugle. I walk there as if new-risen in a dream.

When I walk by these two adjoining lakes, these small tributaries on the great Havel where we used to walk and which you liked so much, getting up a thirst for Moselle in long-stemmed green-tinted glasses in the Kurzgarten, I feel like a condemned spirit floating in free space.

I observe the citizens of Nullgrab, how solidly they go, so rarely alone but always with dogs or a dog, departing in different directions, breast out, seeking Nature's embrace, putting in time until it is time again for Kaffee und Kuchen. Why, their days revolve around good square meals. They look mightily determined, full of—well—them-selves. They make me sad. Faces from the days gone by, in the cold light of morn. Then I see myself in a broken mirror, badly repaired. Dr. Kafka began his death in this city, over by the Botanical Gardens. Milena Jesenská—his Milena—died in the hospital in Ravensbrück concentration camp in May 1944.

Freedom meant seeing again the first town, entering again the first forest; not for her. Not anymore. Germany's forests have been cut down, reduced to wood pulp for Axel Springer's empire of lies; the last third is dying, killed by the acid rain.

At the Ronisch kiosk on Argentinische Allee, late-risen surly drunks gather, lounging over the counter. Surly drunks dressed carelessly as

Confederate stragglers from Vicksburg or in fringed buckskins like Buffalo Bill, lounging around there where Freddi the spare-time gardener drinks.

Or it's day again and I encounter the warm air rising off the lakes. I see the people below, as I go down the flight of steps; couples walking clockwise or anti-clockwise, or with dogs, all avid for exercise, taking the air, sharpening hearty appetites, all ready for afternoon coffee and cakes.

Watch them pass by, these stout feeders, these bottom-feeders; they look gorged with life. And determined, as true Berliners should. Whereas I feel dead already within myself and far removed from this exercise-yard parade in such pleasant surroundings.

The trees go down to the water that reflects them back again and the clouds that pass over them and the jet-trails in the high sky passing to and fro as the wind shifts them, as the great passenger jets arrive and depart in the Templehof air corridor. I neither speak their language nor understand them: as blindness cuts people off from people and things or deafness cuts people off from other people.

*Ronisch kiosk on Argentinische Allee, traffic, kiosk sounds. Krumme Lanke pedestrians, Schlachtensee. Church bell ringing over Rehwiese. Bierstaube Musik, Ronisch hotel on Argentinische Allee.*

## NAKED NIGHT-SWIMMING

KILDARE: In the hot night of that summer, on moonless nights, naked couples cavorted unseen and swam in the lukewarm Havel lakes, tributaries of the old Fluss Flies.

Their cries and splashings produced an atmosphere quite Roman. Or do I mean Greek?

A legitimate nudist beach, known as the "Bullenwinkel," was laid out on the east shore of the Hundekehlensee, or dog-bathing place. Young naked males with fashionably long hair and the elongated shanks of Indian fakirs assembled there, sat watchfully on rocks, like so many Charlie Mansons, the murderer by proxy. Turkish and Greek *Gästarbeiters* dressed in awkward Sunday suits of the 1930s also assembled on weekends on high ground, to gape at the nudists below.

Lubricious model-girls were not much in evidence, only mounds of middle-aged female flesh gone past the sexually attractive stage, past the breeding stage, become functional *Mutti*.

It was the year the Social Democrats first came to office, led by Herr Willie Brandt as Chancellor, to the satisfaction of all right-thinking Germans. It was a year like any other year, as every year must be.

French frogmen dressed in black rubber suits with flippers dived into the Oxo-brown waters of Krumme Lanke—for it was there, not in Schlachtensee—attempting to recover parts of a Lancaster bomber shot down over the "Bullenwinkel" by Berliner anti-aircraft batteries,

Günter Grass among them, during the Kriegsjahren, the Todtendanz that had left behind a garrison of widows.

*Kurzgarten widows at Kaffee und Kuchen.*

. . . or maimed and blinded elderly males who wore yellow armbands and sat on public benches in Erlen Busch park in this country, this city, then so addicted to armbands and insignia. The Lancaster had gone down with or without its crew, no one knew. Small pieces of it were recovered by the French divers and these were laid out on a raft.

Meanwhile the "Popo look" had arrived from Japan, that chain of islands where they make golf bags from the prepuces of whales. Popo—the clever Oriental imitating the primitive African, dedicated admirers of huge female backsides. The erotic zones had been switched about: now it was the receding figure that was admired.

Denim slacks stonewashed and already with a worn look in the shop windows, were cut to cling, and cling they most certainly did, as though hands were convulsively clutching. Bosom cleavage had been supplanted on a grander scale by the cleft of the buttocks. *Die Stern* featured a corn-blonde model in the act of removing, unpeeling, a skin-tight corn-yellow singlet, her only article of clothing. On the nearside bare buttock was embossed the entwined circles of the XX Olympic Games about to be contested in Munich that August. I was going there, though not to the Games.

# MAUERKRANKENKEITZIG

KILDARE: I met her first at Frank Schwerin's tea party. It was a winter Nullgrab tea party that began with English tea in another room. The pale host wearing blindman's spectacles, preparing to go mad again, first introduced me to Mando Demotroupoulos, a poetess from Athens.

Then the lovely Berliner came dancing in, asking brightly "What language do we speak?" Then we were drinking Scotch, the three of us on a sofa.

Mando looked as if she would eat the lovely linguist. Then I was called away to be insulted by a strange woman who seemed a little demented. Then the party was breaking up and I was in the lovely linguist's wasp-yellow Karmann Ghia being driven like the wind down Kurfürstendamm to an all-night café frequented by young and not-so-young whores of the town.

Mando Demotroupoulos walked by the Spree. She suffers from insomnia. Some of the Berlin Wall isn't wall at all, she says. Some of it's the Havel (But what is the Havel but an overflow of the prehistoric Fluss Flies?). The Berlin Wall, Mando says, is Kafka's Great Wall of China. With missing parts that don't join up. Sibilant, brown-eyed, mock-serious, she stands close, perspires much. "Sphrr'ay!" she says, spitting it out, splashing me. "The Reds are coming!" They're at the door, she says, revealing the sceptical whites of her Greekish eyes.

The face is very odd, seen close to; the fierce mask of the Bogey Man, brown and damp as prunes—an overwhelming presence, probably dangerous.

"It's a city of keys. Everything is shut up after eight in the evening. You cannot get back in. They positively won't let you!" Here Mando released a mighty guffaw. She lived over in Wildpfad, near the Grunewald, the wooded border where the Americans were banging away at skulking imaginary Reds. "A city of frightened people carrying rings of keys. Communism begins outside the gates. It really puts the wind up them." Here another storm of guffaws left Mando speechless. Mando is most Greek.

She takes train journeys to Paris, otherwise she would go mad. One must get out of Nullgrab in order to remain sane. She is a political activist, with two undercover names, moving about. The working conditions of the Greek *Gastarbeiters* concern her, for they make no effort to learn German, cannot read warnings, are injured at work. Lost in the divided city they just wander about, window-shopping, live in a compound. Mando spoke up for them, listened to their grievances, worried about them, translated, took the train to Paris. Leaving behind the small lost bands of sallow-faced low-sized dark-skinned men with great mustachios wandering about under the revolving Mercedes-Benz symbol over Europa Centre, lost and miserable without a word of comfort, but they did not concern Mando.

She had witnessed Greek hostages being shot by the SS and had written a poem about it, in Greek; as had the troubled Professor Hollerer, in German, having observed the same scene from the safety of a Luftwaffen control tower.

Mando had translated some of *Ulysses* and parts of *Finnegans Wake* into Modern Greek and wanted to know what the Irish thought of Mr. Joyce.

"They have mixed feelings about him," I said. "They don't read him as a general rule."

Mando knew what was going on among the DAAD people; who was having it off with whom, which husbands and what wives were not hitting it off together—certainly not the Greeks—who was leaving and who arriving. English Armitage had left, advising me to watch my liver, and pale Per Olaf Enquist and entourage were expected hourly, coming from Stockholm. She had heard that no less a person than Mr. Beckett had arrived, and was indeed already rehearsing *Endspiel* in the Schiller Werkstatt where two German translators had been placed at his disposal, but Mr. Beckett had chosen the Dutchman, Tophoven. He was staying at the Akademie der Künste and was always first to arrive by taxi for rehearsals. He had been observed going up in the lift. All were delighted with his fluent German and charmed by his modest manner. He was *most* self-effacing, for a great man; although Mando herself had not seen him. She wished to interview Grass, Enzensberger and Bachmann. She laughed like a little innocent girl with all her life before her; she who had seen very bad things in the war in Greece.

She told us a story about Mr. Beckett. It was a true story. It happened in his Paris flat near Santé Prison. A Greek visitor had asked him did he ever think of Ireland, miss his own country or feel homesick, as a Greek would when out of Greece. Mr. Beckett had thrown one of his fierce looks over his granny glasses at the impertinent Greek, and had replied emphatically: "No, never." Frowningly. The Greek visitor said nothing, casting a glance around the room, and then looking pointedly at Mr. Beckett; all but himself (the Greek) present were Irish, Beckett's friends in Paris drinking John Jameson whiskey out of Waterford cut glass. He looked at Mr. Beckett and laughed. Whereupon Mr. Beckett himself laughed in a guarded way. They were all drinking good seven-year-old Irish whiskey.

I told Mando my dream about Mr. Joyce. I had dreamed it in Nikolassee, in the snow, in the quiet, with the sound of a distant train, maybe, coming into West Nullgrab, a fearful sound, for Jewish ears.

Mando folded her brown hands with their rings, rattled her bangles, and listened, her Greek knowledgeable eyes fixed on me.

In the dream, snowbound climbers, all of them Chinese, were trapped while attempting Mount Everest. Among them, but a little apart, Mr. James Joyce of Paris. It seemed he had just caught up with them, and now they were all trapped in a ravine. Above them, in a narrowing neck of exposed rock, a great turbulence of air and then thunder, by Jove! Mr. Joyce, being Irish and superstitious, dreaded thunder, as was well known. The silent Chinese climbers were caught in this profoundly deep defile or crevasse and Mr. Joyce along with them, turned into a petrified snowman.

In the dream, now hurrying to its enigmatic close, I watched them, their senses about to leave the white Chinese like sheep and the *very* white Mr. Joyce; they all stared fixedly into the blinding snowstorm, while above them the thunder rumbled on. Mando gave her high laugh.

"Poor, poor Mr. Joyce!"

"Poor Chinamen," said I.

"Yes, them too."

Mr. Beckett was seen later, ascending alone in the lift at the Akademie der Künste, wearing bottle-green trousers.

## Axel Schröder's Apartment

KILDARE: Wakes knew where it was of course, from seeing Lorelove home. A configuration of melting snow made a pattern on the side of the building where the wind had driven it; inside the furnaces were going. It was on the topmost floor. The last touch of her warm lips, the final embrace, and Lore the latchkey child who had grown up to be a fine tall brunette of twenty-nine, dipped into her handbag, unlocked the street door with one practiced turn of the wrist, blew a kiss and disappeared. What happened thereafter had been a mystery. Whether she lived in moderate comfort or in luxury, what were the dimensions of her apartment, for me these were unknown. One day she would show it to me, she promised. The entrance had no protective porch; it was a cold place to embrace in. Balconies projected from the top floor; the end flat was the Schröders'; in summer the weight of creepers and potted plants would be enough to drag it into the *Straße* below. It was their wish to remain hidden and anonymous. He had been the boss of a chemical works and now lived in deep retirement, willing himself to be old before his time. If he could be old enough he would be safe.

A stern-faced man, to judge from photographs, with a deep resonant voice. "Lore at Krumme Lanke," the deep voice said on the line. "She wait there for you." He did not say "Herr Wakes," although he knew who it was; he would prefer not to meet Herr Wakes, being too old to "start learning a new language." He had an ungovernable temper. Once he had beaten her. She stood up to him, furious as he; not flinching, her strong German will—*Prussian*—become hard as steel. "Inside I was on fire."

Mamma Schröder was most properly alarmed. "Stop, Axel, you will kill her!" His office was in the apartment; he kept in touch with the chemical works. I tried to imagine Pappa Schröder in carpet slippers, puffing a cigar, booming at his womenfolk, cracking heavy Prussian jokes.

One night, sure enough, I did see it. Pappa Schröder was taking Mamma Schröder to dinner at Kimpinski's after *Ariadne auf Naxos* at the Philharmonie. Lore phoned at an hour when Nancy was out. "You can come now. I am all alone here."

An hour and a half later I pressed the bell at street level. A disembodied voice from above asked in German who it was. "Eisenhower," I said. The door lock clicked and Wakes entered. I mounted to the sixth floor via a shadowy nondescript stairway with its smells; came to a heavy door, pressed the bell. It opened at once. Lore stood there with her lopsided smile. She took my overcoat, hung it on a wooden hanger heavy as a gallows, on which were hung expensive street clothes, waited to be embraced.

She took me by the hand and led me along a short carpeted corridor, murmuring "Pappa Schröder's room . . . Mamma Schröder's room!" threw open a white door and announced triumphantly: "*My room!*"

It was charming. A bower of bliss, a flowery grot, a bridal chamber. It was all white. She had the red wine ready. Her mandolin, her batik materials were for me to admire; the colours were of Mediterranean fruit and tropical flowers, colours from my childhood, colours of fever, in tones of bear-brown and orange and yellow. The heating was full on. Lore was very lightly dressed. Outside it was March and bitterly cold. Her bed was narrow. A wind from the Baltic was setting its teeth into frozen Nullgrab. We drank the wine. Pappa Schröder always had a stock; but it was her wine.

"And now, Mr. Eisenhower," she said gaily. "Being a good American soldier I suppose you would wish to rape me?"

"I sure as hell would," he said.

*Quick break here to suggest the passage of time.*

The Schröder apartment: Though situated on the sixth or topmost floor, it was like an apartment sunken in the depths of the sea. Trapped in the weeds below, a box for living in that could not sink further until one of them died. The intention was to remain hidden. It had a curious lifeless atmosphere, as if all the air had been pumped out. This shrouded place was home for the Schröders. It would last their time; it seemed to me that they begged for it to end.

# WIRTIN

KILDARE: Under an affably bland exterior, a gushing manner, our landlady Frau Meinhardt was a decidedly unpleasant woman. A war widow, she had left off her widow's weeds, ran a sports car, a Karmann Ghia like Lore's, flirted with the Master Butcher opposite. She said Nullgrab was dead, the old heart had been Unter den Linden (Chateaubriand walking there with Laforgue), and that was dead. All that remained was the fine house we were renting for a year; a woody area in Nikolassee near the Jochen-Klepper-Weg, the path through the wood to the Little Squirrel Inn. She never referred to her late husband, or told of how he had met his death, surely a violent one in Russia. She liked to flirt over the fence with the retired meat man. Out of his low chimney gushed thick black smoke; was he burning files? Incriminating evidence? Once in the snow I had seen a coal-black sweep in a tall black hat above a blacked face on the roof, working a brush up through the flu. The Dutch couple Van der Zee from the Nullgrab Symphony Orchestra lived next door, next to the Pan-Am pilot and his family, the red setter barking every morning at the stout cyclist who delivered the post, barking and hoping to eat the leather patches off her arse. Beyond the retired butcher lived the ex-SS man from the concentration camp who was now a political adviser for the Dresdener Bank. I had drunk with him, he had lent me money, he seemed a reasonable type; provided you kept off the subject of Karl Marx.

The Wirtins of Nullgrab, the professional landladies, had worked out a graded scale for tenants, based on nationality. First came the Japanese so small and quiet, composers like Ishii. Then the Americans, bursting with dollars. English and French were alright. Italians might just pass muster, but Greeks were suspect. As for the Irish they were an unknown factor. "You are the first Irishman in our DAAD programme," Nicholas Born told me. Professor Kildare Wakes and family were seeking quiet accommodation for a year in Nullgrab, paid for by Bonn. The honorary title was Herr Born's idea. "It makes a good impression." That was to change not long after we took up residence. I did not hit it off with Frau Meinhardt, who took to spending extended weekends in the long attic with her two Airedales.

Frau Meinhardt owned a flat in Weisbaden, that haunt of four-square Hausfrau. She drove the Airedales about in her low-slung green Karmann Ghia, the boot packed with tinned food, water supplies; took her vacation in Malta, a change of air for the dogs; but they hadn't liked Malta. No shade: bad for dogs. One was called Aya, a classical allusion; mother and daughter were inseparable. She liked to currycomb the bitches on the balcony of a morning and fine reddish hair floated into our coffee cups. She seemed to be spying, her eyes fixed on various household objects which had been moved or, worse, removed. Landlady and tenant were not in accord.

The "Professor" sat unshaven after breakfast on the terrace, smoking a cigar, ignoring his landlady in a pointed way, staring critically at the dogs. "That one has fleas—she scratches too much."

"Ouff!"

Frau Meinhardt demonstrated how to operate the vacuum cleaner, a Vampyre model. The snout could get at awkward parts of the armchairs and sofa; it got up an excited whine when dirt was discovered, the snout setting to in an avid devouring of dust, crumbs, hairs; the bag became quickly inflated, swelling up in a self-important way, whining towards climax. It functioned well, could do a number of specific tasks. It was all snout and stomach, a true German machine. Nancy switched it off. Frau Meinhardt clicked her teeth and flushed.

She had no English and the "Professor's" command of German was halting, tending to be as low as German (*Berliner Bierstaube*) could get, Berliner slang picked up from friend Lindermann. Nancy's late father, the crusty old family lawyer Gottfried, had been born in Germany and his daughter had a smattering of the language. The Professor left polite conversation to his wife. When he spoke, Frau Meinhardt listened with a pained set smile on her thin lips, sipping a blue liqueur, which we called Vogel Caca.

The German verb constructions, Frau Meinhardt agreed were not easy. No laughing matter. All nouns began with a capital letter and all sentences ended with a verb. The definite article had sixteen forms and could also be employed as a neuter noun. Berliners spoke the purest German. The nice blonde Swedish lady, Frau Enquist, spoke "almost perfect" German and might have been a Berliner. The language was especially rich in compounds; the long sentences a form of grammatical warfare and no fun at all for beginners.

In West Nullgrab every second citizen is over forty years of age, and more than twenty-five per cent over sixty-five, with thirty-nine thousand passing away each year, thirteen thousand more dying than those being born. In a way that no other city could be, Nullgrab belonged to the dead. To every third citizen one dog.

By 1972, there were 63,705 dogs registered in West Nullgrab, or one dog to every 32.8 inhabitants. By 1982, 90,000 dogs.

The old heart of the city was dead, Frau Meinhardt said, sipping Curaçao, a vile blue concoction. Two of her friends had been reduced to giving up their flats, fine apartments with eight or nine rooms; and were now sharing one flat near the Opera. One lady worked late; as one retired the other rose up. They would manage somehow.

Frau Meinhardt dined at Alexander's and Kimpinski's, slept with the Airedales in the attic, in what had once been servants' quarters, currycombed the bitches, sat with legs crossed in the living room and sipped her Vogal Caca. Birdshit to you.

# THE OMINOUS LITFASSSÄULE

KILDARE: Certain dwellings, even certain ruins—and perhaps they most of all—are the essential Nullgrab. As, for instance, the blackened ruins of the gutted Soviet Embassy left standing as a monument; as the ruined Gedächtniskirche with its oddly worded plaque at the end of the Kurfürstendamm near the Romanische Café where George Grosz drank with his friends, near the ice rink where Laforgue skated, and Nabokov as a boy with teeth braces, a brat I bet. It was not far from the Schröders' apartment.

Lore showed me the Soviet shell darkened by a fire long gone out; indicated it as if unwillingly, when we chanced to walk by it. It was something that had to be seen, though not something a Berliner could be proud of; those spoils, that booty? *Nein!* Some of her political prejudices she had inherited from Pappa Schröder. Beliefs had to do with fear of communism. She voted CDP, very conscientious in casting her vote.

"Unsound," Lindermann declared into his long-stemmed green-tinted glass of Moselle. "Mistrust German politicians who come from Bavaria. Regard that wild man Strauss."

Always Lore showed me the ruins of her city with this strange diffidence, simultaneously proud and ashamed. It was all carved up; the Reds had the eastern part with the lakes around Kopenick, the Americans the high ground overlooking the Havel; the French had their sector; the British had a slice; what little remained was for the Germans.

The shuttered Italian and Spanish Embassies faced the Tiergarten, that haunt of whores; empty now as beehives when the bees had flown, or a wasps' nest when all the wasps had been destroyed. Purposeful, even grievous, presences, abandoned but not yet dead. A curious still atmosphere surrounded them; centres of finished ambitions as Stonehenge and Tara; the Alhambra or the great megapolis of Allied dead at El Alemain. Goebbels and Göring were on the line, Himmler was expected; jaunty adjutants were conveying briefcases and memos, telephone lines were hot. All that hectic activity had suddenly ceased; the absolute stillness was perhaps a shocked silence; as though that time of gross splendour and nationalistic fervour could begin again any day, resume its fierce tenor, its cruelty, its Nationalist Socialist storm.

In a linden-lined side street stood the Litfasssäule. One of those essentially Nullgraber constructions that are truly German in the way Paris pissoirs are truly French. Here one seemed to feel the real Axis soul that had fled from the twin embassies and huddled hereabouts, a little way from the gutted embassies, safe among the copse of trees; sitting squarely there, a little furtive.

On its defaced surfaces a patina of proclamations well-weathered by time had been destroyed back to the acid; not as the fungus on trees, a natural growth of decay, a natural dragging down; for no hand had removed the ordinances, the propaganda become threatening even against its own people. Consumed by the passage of time, brief enough, the paper had laid down its propagandist life; its purpose sinister as the hidden pillbox, the anti-tank gun emplacement at the turn of the cobbled road where it dipped down to the Rehwiese's sunken meadows; rotted back here into a decayed repose.

Beauty is the projection of ugliness (the muzzle of the anti-tank gun behind camouflage netting), I must have read it somewhere; the notion sounded definitely French. By developing certain monstrosities we obtain the purest ornaments. And if that house was me, what part of me was buried in those graves?

"Let's move on," Lore said.

In the Tiergarten some wildly excited shirtless Serbo-Croatian Gästearbeiters were playing a rowdy game of *fußball.* Above the excited Slavs the Friedensengel rose up golden into the clear blue Prussian sky.

Calm grey clouds were passing over Europa Centre and the Mercedes-Benz revolving star. Grey elephants still as rocks in their compound by a dry moat, thoughtful-looking brutes and strict vegetarians that can go berserk when provoked, these prehistoric beasts who move in their own time. Jackdaws squabbled in a tod of ivy, free as air. Three doleful snow owls dozed in their cage. It was a wet afternoon and few people were about in the Berliner Zoo, walking between the cages and the compounds.

Outside, the Allees were alive with action, a peaceful demonstration march winding through the regulated streets. From behind wire mesh the riot squads waited in paddy wagons in side streets. The police watched, took names, photographed, made records, waited. Amerika Haus was bullet-riddled.

The constants remain: traffic raging up and down Kurfürstendamm, the heads and shoulders of savage Alsatians with lolling tongues fixed in car windows, the hairy Hippies with trinkets set out on the wide pavements like primitive tribal artefacts in a jungle clearing. Bahnof Zoo's unbanishable stench. Two Frenchmen insulting a German waiter at a table outside Alexander's. Time running out in a circle. In a cigarette-smoke-fouled second-class *Raucher* a young couple sits together, the man makes a joke about East and West winds. They exchange a meaningful look. The window of the carriage is closed fast, the air foul; the train will take us across the DDR, the Forbidden Ground, to Frankfurt. Speed suggests something very like fear,

Tacitus thought. Depression arises from the absence of alternatives, the inability to conceive of alternatives. Turbidity reigns, the calmness of those who have given up. Marching, it is rumoured, will replace people soon. Woe to the conquered! Oh execrable world, it isn't easy to draw good from you! The Mercedes-Benz star revolves. The owls fidget in their wet cage. The people go by.

So what now, comrades?

# THE OTHER DAY I WAS THINKING OF YOU

KILDARE: The other day I was thinking of you. Or rather of Nullgrab, that quartered city you love so much; it amounts to the same thing. When I recall Nullgrab I remember you, or vice versa. Go quietly, the ghosts are listening. Is it even possible to think of somebody in the past? Or is the memory of things better than the things themselves? I say things but I may mean times. I say things and times but I mean persons and places. I may be just thinking of you; your name at the end of the world. One replaces another in what you call *Herz* and the light goes out.

Your voice again. Your eyes in the shadows. Reddish tints in your hair in the Augustinerkeller under the dripping arches of the Bahnhof Zoo in the snow. Or in the Italian restaurant Rusticano with the waiter who always remembered us. Or in the hothouse dining room at the Yugoslav Hotel with a view of a snow-clad dome and Slivovitz on the table and outside Mexikoplatz on which the Schnee lay deep. Or in the well-heated Greek place with the retsina. Our night refuges.

Today is your name-day; you a Gemini like the ill-fated Kennedy ("Ich bin ein Berliner"). The Nullgrab children call: *"Nullgrab, der Datum wess ich nich, ich jlob et hees verjib nich."* Snotty French kids go: *"Je te tiens, tu me tiens par la barbichette. Le premier de nous deux qui rira, aura une tapette."*

Your smile, a smirk: liquid glue, a lopsided smile. Your English expressions were charming indeed. You said: "The Hollands" . . . "trouts" . . . "copulations" . . . "intercourses." You asked in high dudgeon: "What do you take me for—an animal in a box?" You were no animal in no box. "Yus," you said in a throaty siren's voice, "yus . . . Oh quatch!" It was another language. Another World. There I couldn't follow you.

Do you recall the Isar flowing in the wrong direction and an invisible deer crashing through the undergrowth in *der* Englischer Garten and the goose shit around the pond and the tattered tribes of Hippies with their unstrung guitars below Minopterus and the fine clouds over München and the grand flat in Jakob-Klar-Straße? I felt giddy under a tree, the sky whirled above us, it was the beer, the wine and cognac of the night before in Schwabing. It was the air, the Föhn, the Bavarian day, the clouds. The trees danced, the earth moved, the air was all a-tremble in a manner well calculated to bring on nausea. I lay on my back on a public bench but it was no good, the earth kept moving, the clouds passed swiftly overhead as though I did not exist, the leaves were tittering. I said "Oh quatch!" and laid my head on your warm lap, you laid your cool hand on my heated brow, and I was anchored to the earth again; the sky drew back, the leaves stopped tittering, earth and sky stopped their whirling, the giddiness departed. I was with you. Your cool hand, your calming presence, the warmth of your thigh on my neck.

Luitpoldstraße was dug up; they were preparing an underground system for the Olympic Games, the killings to come. Our pillow-book was a yellow copy of *In Wassermelonenzucker* which you translated back into Brautigan's English outside a restaurant in Schwabing, or in the big bed in the airy flat. On the balcony opposite the retired boxer sat all day; his good Frau—reduced to an arm—handing him out mugs of *Bier* all day long. Your brief silence meant that you were changing German words back into American Hip-Talk, lively

English. You bought a minute bikini, in café-au-lait. For me it was always a giddy time with you, my dearest *Schmutz*, walking and linking the bright sunlight and the air with an earthy odour in a very lush Bavarian spring.

You suggested a *siesta*. In German you said it was called the little-shepherd-hour. How twinsome the *Poshlust*! You drew the long wheat-coloured drapes; in the room become a shadowy wood we removed our clothes and with them our inhibitions, if we ever had any. The caterpillar's function is to gorge itself and grow.

Afterwards we walked in the Tiergarten (flown from München), all the boscage burnished in that Berliner way (it must be something in the soil) and I offered to take you in the bushes. "Yus," you said . . . "yus." It was our day.

You were a child in a city selected for destruction; in a way that no other city could be, it belonged to the dead.

The maid hid an expensive ring in a bag of flour; the horse was shot standing between the shafts; the Red Army were coming, the bombing was terrible, the earth trembled. The Schröder family hid in the village while the Red Army had its way with Nullgrab females. It belonged to the dead, the burnt-out capital was theirs; and they were everywhere, not only in the civilian cemeteries between Mariendorf and Britz: Russian and German dead were overwhelmingly present.

I had shown you something that you considered shameful once. I opened my fist and in my hand the unspent cartridge I'd found in undergrowth by water near the Jagdschloss.

"Throw that away," you said.

It was something shameful I showed you once.

I am reading Heine again. About the lovely nixies all dressed in green. Today, stricken with longing, I am thinking of you.

## KURFÜRSTENDAMM

*Hurdy-gurdy, Ku-damm traffic, muted. Under.*

KILDARE: The face on the hoarding walks the streets. The individual as such is disappearing, only intent remains, in a milieu grown progressively grubbier; become irredeemably foul. The world's capitals have become pissoirs.

Everything is oversold, overheated, overstocked, over-praised; fraternity too has become a hell. The cities are splitting up from within. Supermarkets and car parks replacing cathedrals and concert halls. Overpriced and largely useless commodities are sold by ingenious advertising campaigns, in a war not on want but on abundance, plenty. Shoppers passive as fish and stunned by piped music ascend and descend escalators in Kee Dee Wee, Bilka, Peek and Cloppenburg.

On fine summer evenings long cinema queues wait to see a violent surrogate existence flicker on huge screens. Their own life has ceased to interest them. Huge coloured graphics on hoardings display a Redskin brave naked from the waist up, advertising mens' shampoo.

Rock cellars throb, their lurid entrances leading down into an inflamed throat, permanently wide open: the mouth of hell itself. Horsetail, Skullcap, Asafoetida gum, Hungarian camomile, Strained Passion Flower, mushrooms for addicts, bananas for the sick, kola nuts for one and all. Syrian rue, fly agaric, Yohimbe, these were all popular. In Absurdia the poor drank the urine of the high rich.

Informed heads, *Tagestraumers*, trippers, might tell of the so-called Jackson Illusion Pepper, with a lit cigarette at one end and a hole in the opposite end, through which the entire contraption might be smoked to provide colourful and elaborate hallucinations. Road-hippies on endless round-trips sold their blood in Kuwait; took overdoses, "split," observed the "way-out" regions, the teeming poor of the Deprived Nations. Lost ones blew their brains out, the only way to admit in some sense at last.

A huge organ played at noon in a department store. Alcoholic professors of history taught their own versions of progress and colonisation; how the world had gone wrong, was going insane. The students were apprehensive to leave the University grounds. In the surrounding woods maniacs prowled all night, whistling. The young debated much on their "development," always making schemes. Schedules were drawn up, considered, debated about, abandoned. Mad youth leaders sprang up, spouted reams of drivel, were listened to, went out of favour, were gunned down.

They seemed to be exclusively concerned with drugs of one sort or another, hard politics, gris-gris, voodoo, India-Buddha teachings highly corrupted, changed; claptrap about "Freedom."

(*Bombastic.*) The American myth is dying. Things are not going better. Instead history seems deranged. We have lost our way.

To free the world and dream, that was their dream; a sourceless craving now externalised, brought close. For them it would always be *Sperrmuell Tag*: Throwing-Out Day.

On high cinema hoardings over Kurfürstendamm the braced bodies of huge female nudes proclaim in no uncertain fashion, *luxuriant*; in hay, in or near water, in rustic barns reserved for venery. A nude girl crawls on all fours into a tent, a brunette ready for anything while out camping becomes a beast in her lair; a lecher crawls after her; in a movie still, posted at ground-level.

High over the savage growl of the fast traffic a cut-out of the murdered Sharon Tate gazes indifferently on the human clotting below;

the sandwichboardmen advertising the strip joints, the hurdy-gurdy man cranking out an old tune, the beard-plucking Hippies on the prowl, their beads and bangles set out on the wide pavements as if in a jungle clearing.

"Pigs" her murderers had scrawled on the Polanski death house. Manson's tribe. Disordered thoughts, exposure, civil disobedience, lewdness, drugs, hallucinations, murder; *Kaos oder Anarki* in the here-and-now. Karl Kraus had once defined German girls: "Long legs, obedience." Not any more.

Two enormous Sapphic heads with frantic blue-tinged eyeballs swooning, regard each other, lecherously, steadfastly across a movie façade. Something funny is going on between those two. *Der Zirkus is* showing at the Capital. Bullet-proof glass protects the ticket office in the vestibule. The pace is set to hedonism, gluttony. Some tall beauty with the seductive name of Lore is being escorted home by the solicitous Doctor Hahn; having danced the night away in the Akademie with Sweaty Peterson, the Grey Man, the Platonic Lover, the Beast, and Frank Schwerin, who is about to go mad again, be put inside again.

Professor Wakes, as though fishing for big bass at night, is pulling two pederasts out of the frozen Spree. The time is two A.M. at the end of the Polish Week in the Akademie der Künste. The air temperature: ten degrees below freezing.

*Mournful zoo noises, cries. Monkey house and aviary.*
*Rock Cellar (loud, brief).*

NARRATOR: Down here in this bedlam I smell sulphur. The asinine cacophony is deafening. It goes on relentlessly. In this cave they are reverting back to savages. It must stink enough to smoke the Angels out of Heaven. They like to be stupefied by tumult, exulting in din as bluebottles in dung. Noise, Cioran thought, is the direct consequence of Original Sin. But what happens if you don't believe in Original Sin? You still have noise, racket . . . (*Pause.*) Bedlam.

On the streets their style of dress is both haphazard and predictable, a baffling mixture of Orient and Occident. Hindu priests in sandals pace gravely along, wrapped in thought; mendicant medieval friars with begging bowls, Red stragglers from Vicksburg and Bull Run.

And everywhere, of course, the jaundiced features of the Pseudo-Saviour, a tortured mixture of Ernesto "Che" Guevara and Charlie Manson, the insane murderer-by-proxy. A sad procession shuffling along Schluterstraße, Jesus holding aloft an olive branch, of all things, with many Mary Magdalenes in tow.

Paranoia is perhaps the normal state of mind in savages. The psychotic mind is all deep melancholy and distrust. They do not look for a new Saviour but for totems. Idolatrous animism! In the clutch of the obscene, hell is noise.

Rousseau wrote in his *Confessions*: "Perfect beings do not exist; the lessons which they give us are too remote from us."

LINDERMANN: (*Sepulchral.*) *Der Traumer, die Bilder, der Vergangenheit herauf . . . Krankenende Mutter!*

In a small garden in Lichtenrade, close to the Wall, the air is permeated with noxious fumes from the paper factory next door. An old lady sits in the garden and polishes some well-worn dwarfs who smile all the year, and all the years will go on smiling. She is afflicted with morbus pictus. In Lichtenrade, in Lichtenrade!

*Screech of vari (Zoo).*

NARRATOR: In Nullgrab Zoo the snow owls screw their heads about 360 degrees, to stare fixedly upwards, the predatory eye fixed in its socket. The young ones drift down from a low perch to pick the red eyes out of white mice. It is difficult to assess the mood of these owls.

The eyes of the white mice are red as rubies. The scream of the Madagascar vari in the night is said to make the heart stop . . . twice. As I mentioned once before.

They say you go to the Zoo to see yourself in the animals. There aren't enough animals in the world to see ourselves in, wrote Saul Bellow.

In this year, 1972, there were 63,705 dogs registered in West Nullgrab, or one dog to every 32.8 inhabitants.

A grey steel engraving set down here on the edge of the Prussian Plain. Phantasmagorias of snow, light, and glittering void. Nullgrab!

The bluish shimmer and hardness of an old steel engraving, set down at the edge of the great Slavic plain.

# BESKIDENSTRASSE

*Debussy Arabesque No. 1 on harp. Sounds from Nikolassee woods.*

KILDARE: The coming year was like a wall in front of us. The quality of stillness is everywhere. We seemed to have come to some agreement, wordless yet binding, never again to speak the truth to each other or tell our innermost feelings. We began to turn away from each other.

The house had everything that you could reasonably expect, and more, in the way of home-comforts. The low-ceilinged Master Bedroom had a veranda overlooking the garden; down there a hammock hung between cherry trees. Grapes and strawberries grew there. Our neighbour to the right was stone deaf. Herr Wind had no small talk at all. He loved his little son Gunter Wind, took him out on a rubber boat on Krumme Lanke. His dumpy good-natured Frau resembled to a striking degree Queen Juliana of the Netherlands. They had a tree in their garden that was nurtured on milk. It had curious luminous yellow-green leaves and must have come from China. The older daughter had long auburn hair and looked as Lore must have looked when she was studying dancing at Bernadottestraße. She also ran a Karmann Ghia, green, and had an adoring boyfriend. They were pleasant silent neighbours.

The tennis courts were near the church and the graveyard. The Pan-Am pilot and his wife played tennis. The Dutch couple did not go in for games, tinged with that slightly ceremonial Dutch reserve. They kept to themselves.

There was a wood traversed by a path, the Jochen-Klepper-Weg; it led to a bar, the Eichhörnchen, The Little Squirrel Inn. I used to drink there with Baldur Braun. He told me his real name was Jerusalem; his father had been Russian. We drank beer in a number of dark places, including the Gamba Staube, and he told me all over again how he was not hitting it off with Gudrun. He was mad about Karl Marx.

The Dutch couple were issueless. The wife was blonde. He was a dull fellow too. A couple from the low land of dykes, tulips and clogs. Muskrats are barren in captivity and if they breed they devour their young. The female muskrat, as everyone knows, is the mother of the entire human race.

The Chinese, more observant than most, maintain that the ordinary plump rat changes into a quail and the quail changes into an oriole.

Strange birds that I never heard or saw before roosted in the surrounding woods and made odd calls at unusual hours. The nights were silent as the grave, apart from the sound of distant trains. Squirrels passed over the roof in their passage from one part of the wood to the other.

Sometimes they fell to the ground, but darted up the bark of a tree again, their claws digging in. They were mostly silent.

There were no rats around, unless you counted our immediate neighbour, a consumptive whose manner was decidedly creepy. He took care of the heating when our house was empty. He went out at odd hours with a net shopping bag and came back with it still empty.

The silence of the night was something; it positively crepitated. I could not sleep. Our son slept in a wooden cot. I heard the few late wayfarers that pass on the road below. And Dr. Baldur Braun coming and going on his Bier-trips. He walked to Ronische kiosk on Argentinische Allee, by the Ronische Hotel closed by the Health Authorities.

His gait was sprightly when going (sober), stumbling when return-ing (unsober). I heard the drone of his pacifications and the sceptical voice of Gudrun Braun raised again. Then silence again. Night fell.

Trains enter Nullgrab by night, crossing the Forbidden Ground. It can hardly be a soothing noise to sleepless Jewish ears; nocturnal trains passing through, dragging their great weight on the sleepers, waiting for the lights to change, then pushing on.

The nights were mercifully free of barking dogs. In the morning the golden retriever sets up a great din against the stout mail-delivery woman with leather patches on the seat of her britches; the first post was delivered at 10:30. The garden was full of singing birds. I went to my workroom. The deaf man was mowing his lawn. He spoke hardly at all. It was a dry summer.

Sometimes Dr. Braun had cronies in, and we were invited out for drinks. There would be Busche and Udet, Hunde who shot deer in the Harz Mountains. Freddi the part-time gardener. A grim company.

# The Mushrooms of the Havel Lakes

*Under: Havel water lapping on Wannseebad, sounds of swans gobbling.*
*Wind.*

NARRATOR: The famous Swiss author and playwright Max Frisch is dining with the young Günter Grass in the latter's place in Friedenau. The older author praises the mushrooms, gathered that morning, who knows, near the Havel by Anna Grass or the host himself. Mushrooms have many names that might bear a vulgar application. Hard to translate such multiple innuendos, though not for a true Berliner, progeny of the beer-swigging, life-loving, Hofmachen Zille, the great cartoonist.

GERMAN: Dattel and Ding, Bruntrutsche and Fotze, Furchel and Muschi and Loch, Pussi and Punze, Ritze and Rille, Pfefferbuchse and Fickritze, Saftpresser and Schwanzschlucker—

*Havel, gobble of swans closer.*

—Vogelkiste and Steckdose, Klemfotze and Klemme, Hohlweg and Zwicke, Schwanzklammer and Schnappfotze, Nille and Alte Tasche, Altes Haus and Ente—

*War widows at Kaffee und Kuchen. Mix to Zoo sounds: flamingos feeding* (*close*)*. Under:*

—Aquarium and Mulltute, Waschwanne and Schneunentor, Planschbecken and Bubikopf, Lustzapfen, and Kitzler, Fotzenwarze and Kofferdeckel, Zitternadel and—

*Zoo, lion roar* (*close*)*.*

(*Emphatic.*) —Rubikon and Eisener Vorhang.

NARRATOR: These are but a few samples of mushrooms that grow by the Havel, in the water-meadows, or gathered perhaps in the dewy morn near the nudist camp called Bullenwinkle over from the Hunting Lodge.

Mushrooms abound in the woods after rain. I saw a beauty with long brown legs and thighs in the briefest of red shorts collecting them in a trug above Schlachtensee as I passed by on the path below; a while later she passed me, as I went slowly back to see her again, so lovely there, and met an old woman with a little basket of mushrooms, the beauty grown old in five minutes in these magic woods where an opera singer, a fine coloratura, is practicing arias, walking on the rides, hidden in the pines, where I once took you, Lore.

Evenings of such calmness. Clouds reflected in water, in the depths of which is buried a Lancaster bomber lost in the mud of Schlachtensee. Walking there on the sandy paths you expect lions and lionesses to come down from the woods to drink. The evening ducks are skidding in. The sound they make, hitting the water with their webbed feet. A woman is humming to herself; I hear a dog bell in the wood above the path, by the gazebo. A stout middle-aged Frau is bathing among the ducks. All around us Prussia. Prussian soil, the earth of Germany, the heartlands lost. Brandenburg sands. The good times gone.

Theodor Hosemann painted it; the hands clasped, the horses, the lantern, the winter trees, the potato-seller by the Brandenburg Gate when the city was one. Now the Brandenburg Gate is lost as Potsdam, both as if submerged under clear water, still visible on cloudless days.

GERMAN: (*To himself, ruminating.*) *Mein Inneres. Crimson-rosen. Ein . . . Hubsches Lied. Den Komt Du . . . ? In Gemauer pfiff der best Wind. Guten Tag, Monsieur Ich!*

NARRATOR: Married couples of a comfortable age are asleep on the fine Wannseebad sand carried from the North Sea shores. Their dog snoring with them; all in more or less the same key, snoring and twitching.

Things are never as they appear at first glance, and when we look closer we find strange and even unknown aspects; so that of our first impression sometimes not even the memory remains.

Such is the way with faces we imagine, with cities before we know them, which we picture in such and such a way; only to forget all our fancies at sight of the real thing.

Such is the way with Nullgrab, a spoiled city left over from another history, another time.

A scene of social existence like any other, did I hear you murmur? Well, *Ja und Nein.* Nothing is typical of course. Everything changes. The only constant is finding and losing again. *Dattel* and *Ding,* finding and losing, nothing else. You have to search. Nothing is given free gratis and for nothing except hardship. To learn is to have something done to one.

So perhaps one fine day you will find yourself again in this bracing city, half-city, drop your luggage in Nullgrab and never leave again? Leave your heart here, find love again in the arms of an obliging Nullgrab girl.

NANCY: I had a dream the other night. About this man whose mouth was full of gold teeth. He came into the Self Service in Beskidenstraße in shorts and said in a very angry voice that he'd ordered half a dozen Schulthaus Pils and why had they not arrived? The depressed service-woman with the mildewed fingernails took the order. The stuff had never arrived. He was very angry. His gold teeth positively flashed.

NARRATOR: A scene of social existence like any other, did I hear you say? Nullgrab exists for me: beyond itself, always beside itself, proud of itself, shocked by itself, divided up against itself, set against another Self it cannot see, is never permitted to see, will never be permitted to see . . . as long as there are handguns in holsters and Apen in Asia.

Only a lurid glow in the sky, a red eye winking at the tip of the Funkturm like no sanguine animal-eye, where another panting quest for the Impossible, more difficult, more purposeful, goes on. And on, and on, ad infinitum.

So perhaps one cold day you will lose yourself in this leftover city, drop your luggage in Nullgrab and never leave again, leave your heart in lonely Nullgrab, find Liebe again in the arms of some obliging Fraulein. As did Dr. Kafka . . . twice.

Perhaps.

# Vanishing Heroes

Broadcast on 20th June and on 25th January 1983 on BBC Radio 3.
Directed by John Theocharis. Prix Futura, 1983.

# CAST

ANNOUNCER

AUTHOR

THAI GIRL

FRENCHMAN

VOICE

ALVAR LIDDELL

VOICE OF THE PRESS

AUGUSTE PICCARD

JACQUES PICCARD

KIPFER

VOICE FROM THE GROUND

WONDERSTRUCK BAVARIAN

NATIVE OF GURGL

AMERICAN NEWSCASTER

SALVIO

OLD PICCARD

ENGINEER

CENSOR

RECHNITZER

REPORTER

NASA VOICE

NEIL ARMSTRONG

WALSH

VOICE FROM PAST

# SCENES

PART 1: THE ASCENT

(*Conquest of Space*)

PART 2: THE DESCENT

(*Conquest of the Depths*)

Sources: Auguste Piccard (*Earth, Sky and Sea; Between Earth and Sky*), Jacques Piccard and Robert Sinclair Dietz (*Seven Miles Down: The Story of the Bathyscaph* Trieste), Auguste Piccard and Claude Apcher (*Between the Earth and the Sky*), A. J. Allen and Elija White (*Ten Years in Oregon*), Hans Magnus Enzensberger (*Mausoleum: Thirty-seven Ballads from the History of Progress*).

*Metallic sound merging into voices.*

ANNOUNCER: Vanishing Heroes. Impressions for radio by Aidan Higgins on the theme of exploration—past and future. In 1931, Auguste Piccard ascended ten miles into the troposphere above Augsburg, in the enclosed gondola of a balloon. In 1960, his son Jacques descended ten miles (or near enough) into the Challenger Deep off Guam, in a bathyscaphe. Between these points in time and space, man is observed groping his way into the future.

## PART 1: THE ASCENT

### (*Conquest of Space*)

*Cross fade music to sound: Altimeter ascending. Close breathing.*

AUTHOR: Can't you see that this room, though closed, is endless? The labyrinth it pictures is your consciousness. That's why you're dizzy—because you're looking into your own brain. But we do not know what the brain is, nor what consciousness is.

St. Basil wished the middle of the night to be for the solitary what the morning is for others; so that he might profit from the silence of nature. (*Pause.*)

*Krupp Steel Works. Furnaces. Up, then muted.*

The earthball is slowly twirling, dragged around the foolish moon.

Ocean tides are forced against continents, dragged away on the further side . . .

It will be day again soon. For the other side, darkness. Competition is one of the essentials of life. The earth—the centre of which, we are assured, is of liquid fire—is turning. Twirling. This muckball on which the sublunary orbs cast their excrements.

*Close, Krupp furnace.*

The long slow centuries of stone, imbued with all the poignancy of things, have taught us nothing. Nada. (*Breathing.*)

The past is mortality's dreamland: there nothing need be, can be done. (*Pause—then establish breathing rhythm.*)

A lovely Thai girl is giving herself to a bearded student in the commodious toilet on the second floor of the Grand Hotel de la Loire, below the Sorbonne in Paris.

*Flushing of toilet.*

The sound of water in the mist? In the Café Tournon, *Pied Noirs* are playing a mysterious game of cards for hidden stakes.

*Organ music continued.*

THAI GIRL: (*Breathless.*) This world and all others belong to the future . . . Orientals, Germans, Hindus, French, English, North Americans, Italians, Greeks, all at the source to see their future cultures!

AUTHOR: In the Jardin des Plantes a two-foot, pencil-slim green tree-snake is pretending to be ivy. It wavers before a gap three hand spans wide. Its forked tongue spits silent curses. The prehistoric cold eyes watch.

*Zoo sounds, Aviary.*

Slowly it bends across the gap that spans the divide, as wavering ivy in a forest breeze, like Eternity passing, liquid green, patient. Slowly it bridges the gap, becomes snake again. Man is the most intelligent of living beings.

*Baboons.*

He cannot act for himself or show what he likes. To escape his memories, he spreads out into Europe and Africa.

*Lion close, growls. Korngold Violin Concerto.*

FRENCHMAN: (*Bombastic.*) A*ux deux cent mille morts dans les camps! Un mémorial de la Déportation! Martyrs Français de la Déportation! Aux deux cent mille!*

AUTHOR: Over the corrugated roof in the great heat of early July I hear the feet, animal feet and claws of birds, I fancy. Was it the snake passing again? Probably a bird, or a squirrel more likely. The noise is like an old man in poor health dragging himself along. It stops. I listen. Nothing. It goes on.

Bull-faced Lully, Keeper of the King's Musick, believed that creation was a book in two volumes.

*Krupp Steel Works. Blast furnaces.*

The first volume of which was (*blast of factory whistle drowns out word*) . . . I forget the second.

*Ragtime, Tin Pan Alley,1931.*

ALVAR LIDDELL: (*Over Radio.*) On the 27th of May, 1931, wireless messages in both hemispheres brought to an astonished world one of the most sensational news items in the history of aeronautics: Auguste Piccard, a Swiss citizen and a professor at the University of Brussels, had conquered the stratosphere.

*Babble of news bulletins in French, Italian, Arabic, Greek, Russian. Rise to crescendo. Silence.*

*Teletyping.*

VOICE OF THE PRESS: (*French accent.*) Wrapped in silence and shrouded in the folds of night and helpless before fate, the Piccard stratospheric balloon is floating aimlessly above the glaciers of the Tyrolean Alps, out of control and occupied only by the dead!

*Radiophonic background.*

PICCARD: (*In stratospheric cabin, very calm.*) What altitude, Kipfer?

KIPFER: 51,200 feet, Professor.

PICCARD: In less than thirty minutes we had risen above nine miles. Around us the sky. The beauty of this sky you have never seen; it is sombre, dark blue or violet, almost black. Were the air transparent, we should see the earth over a radius of two hundred and eighty miles and our visual fields would cover 246,000 square miles, or more than the surface of all France.

*"The Little Saxophone" under following:*

Beneath the stratosphere there is the troposphere, whose upper limit on that day was about seven and a half miles. Below us the Bavarian plain.

*Echoes from below of "Sieg Heil."*

(*Unperturbed.*) Even if we look vertically down, the picture is blurred as in a bad photograph. Between us and the earth there is nine-tenths of the atmosphere. Almost as much as if, at sea-level, we were looking at the moon. (*Pause.*)

Only the mountains emerge from the foggiest regions of the tropo-sphere. At first hidden by clouds, they reveal themselves: a summit, then another. At last, all the Bavarian Alps and the Tyrol, covered in snow, which we are approaching gradually. (*Pause.*)

In the near-vacuum of the stratosphere, the gas has expanded ten times. The mercury barometer reads 2.92 inches, instead of the usual sea-level pressure of thirty inches.

*Stratospheric cabin. Hiss of escaping air.*

KIPFER: The balloon is drifting horizontally.

AUTHOR: The pull-rope for releasing gas was fouled and it was not possible to valve off part of the hydrogen! They could not descend at midday as planned. It would turn colder towards sunset. They could only hope, then, to be still over land and not over the Adriatic Sea. Following their ascent before sunrise from Augsburg, they had tra-versed at high speed those zones where the temperature lies between fifty and seventy-five degrees Fahrenheit below zero. The walls of the cabin were then very cold and its interior was rapidly covered by a good layer of frost.

PICCARD: (*In cabin looking out of porthole.*) We were inside a drop of crystal.

*Radiophonic crystal sound.*
*Distant echoes of "Sieg Heil."*

VOICE FROM THE GROUND: *Irgend etwas ist mit dem Ballon nicht in Ordnung.*

*German song.*

AUTHOR: From seventy degrees Fahrenheit the temperature climbed to over one hundred. They sat as low as possible in the cabin. Kipfer discovered a spring—fresh water, clean and distilled, flowed along the wall, on the shady side. (*Pause, morosely.*) There was not much of it.

KIPFER: During the afternoon the balloon turned around, and we no longer had to suffer from the heat. Towards two in the afternoon we began to descend very slightly. We calculated that it would take fifteen days to get down . . .

*Breathing in cabin—radiophonic stratospheric sound.*

(*Looking out porthole.*) Eight P.M. Altitude seven and a half miles. At last we have left the stratosphere. We are passing into the troposphere.

PICCARD: (*At porthole, to himself.*) Below us the twilight is flowing through the valley of the River Inn.

WONDERSTRUCK BAVARIAN: Der balloon, still in the sun's rays, appeared brilliantly against the dark sky. Only the planets and the moon have been lighted up in this fashion.

AUTHOR: The illuminated balloon appeared in the form of a crescent. It even had a halo.

(*Amused.*) A year later, in August 1932, the reverse took place: the friends of Piccard, following in a car, were speeding in the direction of Venus, which they mistook for the balloon.

*Car taking corner, faint cheers, gear changing.*

PICCARD: (*Low.*) The sun now disappeared below the horizon. We descended more and more rapidly. Kipfer watching the barometers.

At 15,000 feet he announced equal pressures within and without. We opened the manholes immediately and put out our heads. (*Sound effects, voice in cabin, then in open—strong wind.*)

After having been shut up for seventeen hours we were at last in the open air. Above us the starry sky. Beneath us the Alps. Snow and rocks in moonlight. Two small clouds were lighted up from second to second by stormy discharges. But we saw no lightning nor heard any thunder. We prepared our parachutes. But luckily drifted away from the stormy zone.

KIPFER: A glance towards the horizon: it still formed a straight line. Soon silhouettes appeared. Mountains. We were already lower than the highest peaks.

*Wind.*

We were in the high mountains near a pass covered with ice. On the south side it appeared to lead rapidly down towards the plain. But we were drifting northwards. We dared not cast away any ballast, because of the danger of ascending again to ten miles with the manholes open. We touched a very steep hill of snow.

*Gondola scraping snow.*

The balloon bounced and flew over a glacier. We saw the lights of a village and Professor Piccard flashed a signal towards it with a torch.

NATIVE OF GURGL: (*From ground level.*) At Gurgl we saw it. *Ja!*

KIPFER: But the village disappeared in the valley. At last we approached a flat place free of crevasses.

PICCARD: Now, Kipfer!

KIPFER: I pull the strap of the ripper panel. The balloon begins to empty. We touch the glacier. The cabin rolls a little.

*High Alps, breeze, wind, distant waterfall.*

PICCARD: We had landed at an altitude of some 8,700 feet, but where? Switzerland? Austria? Italy? We bivouacked where we were. It was bitterly cold.

KIPFER: Wrapped up in his balloon material, Professor Piccard went to sleep. I woke from time to time, disturbed by the sound of a waterfall, which in my dream I took to be the whistling of an air leak.

*Waterfall—wind.*

At sunup, linked by a double rope, testing the snow at every step with a bamboo found in the rigging of the balloon, we reached the edge of the glacier. Picking our way across the rocks we went down slowly towards the valley. At midday a party of skiers found us. We were in the Tyrol, at Gurgl.

*Cheering.*

PICCARD: (*Stoutly.*) A few days later, at Zurich, the President of the Swiss Aero Club, Colonel Messener, congratulated us and expressed the hope that the world altitude record which we had just set up would not be beaten for many years. I was obliged to disagree with him.

*Zurich, Swiss Aero Club, crowded large chamber.*

(*Addressing an audience.*) It will be a fine day for me when other stratospheric balloons follow me and reach altitudes greater than mine. My aim is not to beat and above all not to maintain records, but to open a new domain of scientific research and of aerial navigation.

*Murmurings of approbation, applause.*
*Explosion.*

AUTHOR: Accidents have occurred. We know of two cases of balloons bursting in the stratosphere.

AMERICAN NEWSCASTER: On the 28th of July the Explorer 2 took off from the Black Hills outside Rapid City in South Dakota with a crew of three aboard.

*Gradual sound effects—squall, envelope, flames, etc.*

At an altitude of nearly 18,500 metres the envelope was torn, frictional electricity was produced, a squall ignited the mixture of hydrogen and air underneath the balloon, which was instantly destroyed.
The balloonists escaped by parachute at the last moment.

*Distant concussion.*

The cabin came down in Nebraska.
(*With relish.*) Not so fortunate were three Soviet balloonists in January of the same year. The balloon became separated from the gondola at a height of 17,000 metres. The crew had parachutes but the gondola had only one manhole, its door fastened by twenty-four bolts. During their dreadful fall the balloonists had time to remove seven nuts.

AUTHOR: On the 18th of August 1952, Professor Piccard, accompanied this time by Cosyns, took the FNRS to an altitude of 16,200 metres, or 10 miles. The world's record for Switzerland.

*Saxophone.*

We live in the troposphere. It is here that all meteorological phenomena take place. The seawater evaporates; sucked up by the sun, it soars up in the sky, there to be seized by the winds. In their frantic whirlings they carry it over the oceans, over continents; never does it find peace.

*Wind.*

Sooner or later the water condenses, forms clouds, rain, snow or hail, and a sudden plunge ends its aerial journey. The winds, meanwhile, continue their aimless wanderings—sometimes as gentle breezes, sometimes as hurricanes, rising as cyclones, descending as anticyclones, whirling to the right, to the left. Never can a stable position be reached; it is an endless circle. This is where we have to live; in the troposphere, a layer surrounding our planet. (*Pause.*)

Above this lies the stratosphere. There all struggle has ceased; there are no vertical movements. Each portion of air is satisfied with the position it has acquired, without altering its altitude, it pursues its journey.

No vertical motion induces moisture, no condensation occurs. Nothing disturbs the clearness of the atmosphere, no mist, no cloud. It is unchangeable fine weather, an eternal peace.

*Music continues.*

A bright sun rises over the horizon and travels across the violet sky. No sooner has it set than the stars light up and sparkle as no earthly spectator has seen them.

This land of dreams, this paradise, is the stratosphere. Twenty minutes, half an hour's ascent in a free balloon separates us from it. That is all; but it is a great deal.

*Wind buffeting foliage.*

(*After pause.*) Cyclic astronomical events beat out the tempo—the night and day spinning of the earth on its seasonal revolutions around the sun.

*During above reaper-and-binder merges into sound of turbo-prop engine.*
*Organ grinder.*

PICCARD: We passed over Cadiz, Toledo, Madrid, the Bay of Biscay, Arcachon. We could see the Straits of Gibraltar and the Rock, Morocco and the Atlas Mountains and beyond, the Mediterranean. All looked exactly as on the map. And yet the map was drawn long before any human eye was able to see all these places as a group.

*Fade . . . Radiophonics.*

AUTHOR: (*Resuming.*) Bees maintain straight courses by offsetting the sun as it passes across the sky. Plants flower and bear fruit according to the length of the day. All life responds to rhythmic time—all life, that is, excluding the denizens of the deep. Astronomical tempo does not reach below the deep-scattering layers of the Twilight Zone.

*Whale sounds.*

In the abyss there are no days, no seasons. Only the sperm whale ever plunges below the Twilight Zone. This huge toothed mammal plummets two-thirds of a mile to forage on squid, and has been found ensnared in marine cables at depths in excess of . . .

*Fade . . .*

(*Resumes.*) With no ties to land, only water-striders, the so-called "Jesus bug," live a purely pelagic existence, walking about at mid-ocean, supported only by surface tension.

*Rapid fade . . . Sounds for mid-ocean, surface.*

Wild trout in a stream have a home spot and kill off intruding planted trout from a fishery.

Owls hoot at night to proclaim ownership of a specific group of trees—and of the mice underneath them. Notwithstanding . . .

*Fade . . . Owl hooting, squeak of animal in death throes.*
*Aggressive apes.*

(*Resuming.*) Great apes with their harems establish rigidly drawn territories. Notwithstanding . . .

*Fade . . . Radiophonic music.*

The life cycle of the eel is a puzzle, and so too grunion in the spring along the South Californian beaches.

*Dense gathering of insects, humming.*

PICCARD: Insects are the only invertebrates not represented on the open sea.

*Radiophonic music.*

(*As before.*) Nothing is ever lost. There is no hurry. The Sahara on a moonless night. In the darkness we could scarcely distinguish the dunes. In the east Mercury was visible. In Europe one can never see this planet so clearly. But now notwithstanding . . .

*Fade . . .*
*Echo of whale song.*

AUTHOR: Certain species of crab place a single sand pellet in their ear, to establish their vertical orientation. But if the crab can be induced, in an aquarium, to replace the grain of sand with a magnetic particle and a strong magnet be then placed on top of the tank, the crab will lead an upside-down existence. Nevertheless . . .

*Fade . . .*

(*Resumes.*) In the abyss all fishes are brown, black or deep violet; but many of the shrimps are coloured brilliant shades of red or purple. Why, no one knows. Living in complete darkness, one might suppose the creatures would have become blind and bleached. (*Voice fading on following.*) Resembling the fauna of caves . . .
Mariners a century ago fancied the sea embalmed their dead.

*Bosun's whistle.*

Sewn up in his hammock with two cannonballs secured to his feet and readied on the gangplank, the body of the dead seaman was consigned to the deep after mustering all hands on deck by the bosun's call to bury the dead. The cadaver settled, still erect, in the ooze of the seabed, embalmed and beyond the reach of decay—a perfect human form to survive through the ages.

*Penderecki.*

Time passes. World War Two is over and two and a half million gross tons of Allied Merchant shipping have joined 785 U-Boats in Davy Jones' Locker—5,150 ships, of which one and three-quarter million tons lie in the North Atlantic, over one million in the South Atlantic, one and three-quarter million in the Mediterranean, the same in the Indian Ocean, one and a third million in the Pacific. Whole ships' companies have joined the sixteen million Allied and Axis dead in the period September 1939 to May 1945. The number having swollen considerably since the ninety-nine perished in the ill-fated submarine Thetis in Liverpool Bay in June 1939.

*Sea waves. Song.*

## Part 2: The Descent

### (*Conquest of the Depths*)

PICCARD: (*Twenty-two years older.*) In the spring of 1952 my son Jacques and I accepted a proposal received from Trieste to build a new bathyscaphe. We are indebted to . . .

*Fade.*

SALVIO: (*On telephone.*) You are going down. The deck is under water . . . the tower is half under . . . we are disconnecting the telephone cable. *Buono fortuna!*

JACQUES: *Arrivederci!*

*Tachometer for descent. In cabin.*

PICCARD: (*Low.*) From now on we are left to ourselves. There is nothing to cause us anxiety. Neither my son nor I could believe in the possibility of a fatal accident.

*Tachometer.*

(*Peering out porthole.*) It must be admitted, seeing the light decrease while the gauge indicated increasing pressure had something impressive in it. The light grows less . . . little by little the shadows . . . thicken. The portholes alone are still visible: grey-blue discs four inches in diameter . . .

Slowly the colours blur . . . All becomes grey, then dark grey . . . Black . . .

Schiller's diver speaks of a purple darkness and Beebe of a violet light . . . One thing is certain: eighteen inches of water already absorbs a great part of the red light. Beyond some hundreds of yards the darkness must be complete . . .

JACQUES: (*Low.*) We are in absolute darkness.

PICCARD: Pressure forty-five atmospheres indicates that we are almost at two hundred and fifty fathoms . . .

*Tachometer, breathing of Piccards.*

JACQUES: (*As before, looking out of porthole.*) In this darkness true plants cannot live . . . At all levels, animals lie in wait for dead bodies going downwards . . . They also eat each other . . . All life in the sea is dependent upon the upper layers lit by the solar rays . . . Small fish and crustaceans feed on living or dead algae, or on diatoms . . . Then, in their turn, they become the prey of larger creatures . . .

Each depth possesses its particular fauna . . . At the bottom there is a world apart—flat fish, crustaceans, spider crabs, shells filtering the water to get out of it anything that is edible . . .

PICCARD: (*To himself.*) Three thousand fathoms . . . As the petrol contracts the *Trieste* becomes heavier. And its speed increases progressively.

*Tachometer.*

JACQUES: (*Warning.*) Steady!

*Seabed at 3,540 feet, 1,080 meters.*

PICCARD: We touched so gently that we were not aware of it. Five hundred ninety-four fathoms.

*Deep sea radiophonics.*

An oceanographer told me that the sedimentary deposit increased not more than 1/25 in a year and that, at the end of several centuries, the mud solidifies and becomes rock in a thousand years. Down where we are; south of Capri, far from a river mouth, I expected only a small deposit . . .

JACQUES: In a state of equilibrium we drift slowly along near the bottom . . . Years ago the wind brought a large palm tree down here . . . There it is, covered in mud . . . One can hardly guess its shape . . . All's well . . . We're at the bottom . . .
(*To his father.*) What can you see?

PICCARD: (*Looking out of his porthole.*) Some sand—an empty shell . . . Nothing much . . .

*The Piccards chuckle together, old man high, son deep. Tachometer silent.*

A SEA ANEMONE! Its tentacles perhaps . . . sixteen inches long, waving gently in search of prey. The creature is a lemon-yellow colour . . .

*Passage of time.*

The silence is total. A real silence of the tomb.

*Dead silence.*

JACQUES: At the end of a quarter of an hour, thinking it useless to prolong our sojourn at the bottom, we decided to go up . . .

*Tachometer, ascent.*

Turned on the projectors for the greater part of the ascent. We saw several phosphorescent creatures, sometimes in a group, then once more the opaque shadows closed around us. We cut the light and ascended in absolute darkness.

*Tachometer indicates increasing speed. Hiss of oxygen, hum of instruments, breathing of Piccards.*

PICCARD: I see a creature more brilliant than the others. It looks like a planet in misty weather. Jacques lights the 5,000 candlepower projector, its beam directed downwards. A quantity of small bodies appear, luminous dots standing out against a dark background. The water is admirably limpid.

*Ascending tachometer, hum of electronic instruments, hiss of oxygen.*

(*Low voice, addressing himself.*) We are still in darkness. But for the instruments we could still have believed ourselves at the bottom.

*Tachometer. Bring in radiophonic music under following:*

(*Undertone, calm as before.*) The first gleams filter through the portholes. Little by little the illumination grows. There are no more phosphorescent fish. Soon it is light enough for us to recognise the objects in the cabin, with all the lights out. The daylight increases and the portholes take a bluish light. The cabin begins to sway. We have reached the surface

*"Qui Sotto," sound effects for surface. Wind and wave.*

(*To son.*) Jacques.

JACQUES: Salvio?

SALVIO: (*On the telephone.*) *Allo! Va tuto bene?* Everything okay? How far down?

JACQUES: More than five hundred fifty fathoms.

SALVIO *whistles.*
*Tachometer silent. Radiophonic music up. Vary range of register: baritone against bass.*

AUTHOR: (*Different register.*) The sunlight of that icy morning falls on my face through little portholes, through flats of glass with tiny flaws, purified by bitter silence.

CENSOR: The sea is rising. Drop by drop the glaciers are melting. So what of the forecast?

AUTHOR: The Swiss igloo, with Plexiglas holes!

CENSOR: Absurd! Quite absurd! It almost seems the work of a sick man—work of a great patience and simplicity. It has a radiance, a tubercular charm.

*Children at play.*

Children playing about the igloo will become old men, but nothing of this will have changed. There are periods when I am certain that duration is everything, the passing of time, one knows it instinctively; such statistics make the brain reel.

*Wind, ship's hooter, seagulls, factory whistle, sound of steam, etc.*

There are seagoing tankers stuck in the channels. The wind blows, the great clouds are white. Through the pale sun of the streets the living make their way towards the factories.

AUTHOR: Tall stacks, a filthy artillery, fire silently into the Sunday sky with beautiful bursts of smoke.

*Steam whistle.*

The acrid smells of gas refiners get into your lungs like a spear.

*Bagpipe requiem: "He'll No More Wi' Us."*

CENSOR: There is no future. There never was any future. What is known as the future is the greatest of lies. The true future is today. What will become of us tomorrow? There is no tomorrow.

*Radiophonic music.*

(*In derision.*) The future, hard to mark, of a world turning in the dark . . .

AUTHOR: So the day went. It turned into dark night. It was finished.

CENSOR: In a hundred years all this will be forgotten. The names of everybody today will be obliterated from the earth and be remembered no more, named no more.

AUTHOR: The hero knows who he is, who he wants to be, and only he and God knows it. The rest of mankind scarcely know either who they themselves are—for they do not really desire to be anything—nor do they know who the hero is.

*Jeri Southern, "You Better Go Now," under following.*

CENSOR: It's snowing, and it looks like a mad dance.

AUTHOR: In Tokyo the streets smell of sulphur. In Chicago the air is bad. A brown air, more gas than air, crosses the lake from the great steel-and-oil complex . . .

*Hooter, mournful.*

CENSOR: In the West Forties in New York in summer carbon monoxide is thick.

*New York traffic.*

AUTHOR: In San Juan the lagoons bubble and smell like stewing tripe.

*Music.*

CENSOR: Though carp and catfish still live in the benzene-smelling ponds.

*Music ends—applause.*

PICCARD: While the *Trieste* was resting on the bottom of the Tyrrhenian Sea under a pressure of three hundred and twenty five atmospheres, I carefully examined the great joint of the cabin. I did not find a single drop of water in it.

VOICE FROM PAST: The sky, a comet graveyard. Miracles of technology. Precision engineering may be a branch of psychology.

CENSOR: Or vice versa.

VOICE FROM PAST: Precisely.

JACQUES: The successful ONR trials in the Mediterranean brought the U.S. Navy into the *Trieste*'s future. It seemed a fine prospect to me when the Naval Electronics Laboratory at San Diego was indicated as her future base. Off Southern California, water a mile deep is only fifteen miles away. The weather there is good and . . .

*Fade.*
*Bring in trade winds gradually.*

AMERICAN NEWSCASTER: Guam is a steaming tropical jungle drenched with warm rain and buffeted by the trade winds. Uplifted coral, deeply corroded by the acid humus of the soil, provides a backdrop of weird sculpturing. The corrosive salt air reduces any exposed metal to a pile of rust in a few weeks.

*American artillery.*

Trinian Island on the north has reverted to tangan-tangan boondocks. A single Navy commander occupies the former HQ of General Curtis Le May with the ghosts of 110,000 enlisted service men.

*Artillery.*

As for the Jap occupation of three decades, only the imported giant land snails remain to infest boondocks and abandoned air strips. Windrows of their empty shells are strewn over the bomber apron where the first B-29 atomic bombers took off for Hiroshima and Nagasaki.

*Remote explosion—trade winds—death throes of rabbit.*

Guam is good!

*Penderecki.*

PICCARD: (*Persistent.*) So many questions, so many mysteries. It is only by going down ourselves to the depths of the sea that we can hope to clear them up. How is that to be? I cannot say. But the fact has been proved many times already. All scientific research sooner or later bears fruit. (*Pause.*) Exploration is the sport of scientists.

*B-29 in flight.*

(*Raising voice above bombers.*) Variable and harsh conditions, not constancy, quicken the ascension of life!

AUTHOR: (*Subdued.*) Over the lakes, steel mills twinkled. Lamplight showed the soot already fallen on the leaves of the wall ivy.

CENSOR: (*Subdued.*) In the street the air was bad.

AUTHOR: In San Juan the lagoons bubble and smell.

CENSOR: Lake Geneva is turning septic green, poisoned by the sewage from the rich canton of Valois.

AUTHOR: Soot on the leaves of Piccard's fine blue cedar!

CENSOR: Over the lake.

AUTHOR: Into the lungs like a spear! (*Brief pause.*)

It is requested that the Office of the Chief of Naval Operations authorises assistance and logistic support for a bathyscaphe (*Trieste*) operations (Project Nerton) in the Marianas Trench, between November 1959 and February 1960.

The *Trieste* purchased by ONR from the Piccards is being modified for dives in the deepest known submarine trench in the world—the Marianas Trench. A new and stronger sphere has been procured by ONR and the buoyancy hull is now being enlarged to provide the greater lift required. The modified craft with new sphere in place is scheduled for shakedown dives late July through most of August 1959 off San Diego.

A period of favourable weather conditions in the Marianas normally exists during November, December and January . . .

RECHNITZER: Rechnitzer speaking. The dive commenced at 1015. We are diving fast. Already at 1019 we are at one hundred and ninety-five meters . . . We have stopped at two hundred meters for an equipment check. At this depth the light is diminished and the colour of the water is deep blue.

Lewis, Lewis, this is the *Trieste*, we are now at five hundred fathoms. Lewis, we are now at five hundred fathoms at 1050 hours. Over.

AUTHOR: On January 23, 1960 Jacques Piccard and Lt. Don Walsh descended 35,800 ft. into the Challenger Deep.

*Apollo 11 liftoff.*

REPORTER: Lift. We have liftoff . . . Red flame and white smoke goes out from beneath the giant Saturn Rocket. You can hear it blasting into the sky. There it goes; beautifully straight up. Destination Moon. Driving straight up. It's a beautiful sight!

*Cross fade Saturn liftoff to atmosphere and commentary on moon-landing.*

NASA VOICE: The touch of his left foot on the lunar surface marks the opening, symbolically and in fact, of a new era for mankind. The accompanying words are simple and stark and poetic.

NEIL ARMSTRONG: That's one small step for man . . . one giant leap for mankind.

*Low hum with tick—cut to bathyscaphe tachometer.*

JACQUES: 1144 hours, 29,150 feet. Now we are as deep under the sea as Mount Everest is high above it. This is a vast emptiness beyond all comprehension. There is, perhaps, a mile of water still beneath us. I push the ballast button. Slowing us down to two feet per second. Then, to one foot per second, as decided before we dive.

*Inside* Trieste. *Tachometer, breathing of* PICCARD.

The echo sounder returns nothing on its six hundred foot scale. The bottom is still beyond one hundred fathoms. The echo sounder makes a long smudge on the graph from the iron ballast just released . . .

(*Murmuring to himself.*) We are clearly in the axis of the trench and most probably will miss the rocky walls . . . 1206 hours, 32,400 feet.

*Strong muffled explosion.*
*Inside* Trieste. *Breathing, controls.*

WALSH: (*Anxious.*) Have we touched bottom?

PICCARD: (*Calm.*) I do not believe so.

*Switches off UQC. Silence.*

(*Low.*) Without formal discussion, we continued down.

*Tachometer. Sonar sounder.*

WALSH: 36,000 feet, descending smoothly at sixty feet per minute. Suddenly there are black echoes on the graph! Sea bottom is forty-two fathoms below us.

JACQUES: Even as we settle in the final fathom, I see a wonderful thing.

*Radiophonic whale song.*

Lying on the bottom just beneath us is some type of flatfish, about one foot long, and six inches across. Indifferent to 200,000 tons of pressure, he regards us from two round eyes situated on the top of his head. The floodlight that catches him is the first real light ever to enter this Stygian realm. Moving along the bottom, partly in the ooze and partly in the water, he disappeared into his night.

*Jeri Southern, "You Better Go Now" under following:*

AUTHOR: (*Elegaic*) Can't you see that this room, although closed, is endless? You dream. That's no brain. Soon you yourself will resemble the insect reeling over the endless stairways, balancing on the parapets.

What you see on these engravings is another world, and we do not know what it means.

*Fade music. Prolonged silence.*

# Winter is Coming

Adapted into prose by Aidan Higgins from material initially commissioned by the BBC and broadcast on Radio 3 on 23rd September 1983, repeated 7th April, with Spanish location recordings by Antonio Jésus Fernandez. Directed by Piers Plowright.

# SCENES

THE VILLAGE

THE PEOPLE

THE BRIDGE AT ARANJUEZ

THE RITUAL OF THE GOATS RETURNING

## The Village

Winter is coming.

A warm humid night tonight, one of the rare ones that got lost or were left over. I don't mind it. Little else to say now because I find myself daydreaming, going back and thinking of this and that, of no importance. Remembering things and people—like the old woman I used to look for every morning. Not worth mentioning. I vacillate between deep despair and high resolution and if I have any hope it is only that I end up like Zeno, though not to the point of kissing a jackass. I think I even made resolutions once. I don't anymore—because they only end up by embarrassing me. Other things too. *Otra vez.*

Above me, above me on the rock, a lizard with a stone eye regards what he sees with reservation. Lizards, many of them, eat our mosquitoes, screw with crazy tails upthrust yet flagging, and occasionally get into the rat poison. They perish without a fuss and leave a neat corpse that doesn't rot, but quietly, odourlessly, dries out; a papery substance which scratches along, out of sight, in the first wind.

They rustle about, live in abandoned burrows and crevices in the walls, suffer accidents, grow new tails which don't match. Lizards never look you in the eye; never have and never will. They come before us; they are not our friends. Do they even see us? Doubtful.

Generally speaking, liars never look you in the eye either. Lightning has blasted a tree in Berkshire. Did you know?

It has rained here for the past fifteen days straight. Drizzle interrupted by torrent. In the garden below a mild growth of weeds proliferates and becomes, daily, a jungle. The view from the window is pure *View from the Artist's Studio, Le Cannet* by Bonnard.

We have this apartment on Calle de las Angustias, in a house built upon the estuary of a great prehistoric river that carries boulders from the distant mountains into the near sea on Calle Carabeo. Near enough. The Street of Sorrows is named after the Patroness of the village, the Madonna de las Angustias. Her effigy is carried about the village on her name-day, carried into the sea to the sound of fireworks going off, shooting their homage to the Blessed Virgin, the most approachable of the entire heavenly host.

In the back garden the figs ripen and fall into the sopping earth; weighed down by the rain, they drop onto the tin roof above the chicken coops.

There's a low wall enclosing our lot and last week Olivia spotted a great humpy rat with rain on its pelt skittering along the top. A few days previously a silent brother had come into the sala where she was sewing. I was out at the time, in one of the bars; and when I came in she heard me and, peering palely from behind a curtain, asked if it was me in the sweetest, softest voice. Olivia hates the rat, bearer of the plague.

The outer shutters of the narrow balcony are almost closed. The white cotton cross-stitch coverlet with a long rent in the side is thrown back.

Admonitions! Rain in the garden of 68 Calle Italia, sometimes called Carabeo, where the relatives of Federico García Lorca live in the smell of open drains. Screens of falling showers. Raining in the intervening gardens. The feria on the plaza. In the damp morning, a feria by the sea. Illuminated by night, the music blown by the wind. The sodden booths, the obligatory fireworks.

In the morning the rain falling, persistent, on the outstretched rubbery palms. Veils of streaming rain. Noise of the rain. Stormwind.

The small birds are scattering from the gardens by the sea. The trees shed them like leaves. Some drunk or madman with a set purpose (death to pests and waste) is blasting them out of the trees. The little birds scatter, leaving garden after garden, but keep coming on. The gun follows them—blasting away. Now they are in the fig tree outside the window, where I write this.

Salutes from the Plaza Balcon de Europa for the President of the Patronate His Excellency Don Ramon Castilla Perez! Salutes for the Civil Governor of Malaga, Don Antonio Garcia Rodriguez-Acosta! Volleys of gunfire!

The little birds keep scattering; they have lost their heads. The wind carries the sound of the volleys, a repeated delusion (like the repeated deceptive second stroke of the church bell, the after-tone, a reprieve for criminals). In Antonio Cerezo's dim bar on the Puerta del Mar the electricity has failed again. A line of candles are lit and illuminate a stuffed lizard the size of an otter that hangs upside-down on the wall behind the bar. On the duckboards Antonio of the circumflex eyebrows plays pocket billiards, rising on his toes and rolling his actor's dark eyes at me, whom he calls Carlos. The cognac advertisement shows the old cognac-imbiber with white spade beard and wormy hands clutching his glass and staring blearily at me as he has been doing for years and years, it seems. All over Nerja the lights have failed again and the town plunged into darkness, but for the flickering candles in all the bars. Outside, the night is pitch black, with rain imminent.

Now a downpour of sudden heavy rain drums on the roof, falling vertically from a great height—mountain rain. The open mouths of the gargoyles spew rainwater that tastes of granite. The narrow Puerta del Mar is awash and more candles are lit in Antonio's dim bar. "El Hiquito" has played soccer for Malaga. He does not encourage campo workers or fishermen in his bar, preferring extranjeros, foreign trade, languages he does not understand.

Indeed he does not encourage anybody, which suits me fine. I spend long hours here, standing at the end of the bar, looking away at the sierras with plantings of fig trees still small as bushes, by order of Generalissimo Franco. I see a cleft chin in candlelight, a hostile face in the gloom. It's the conman Brodey, that base Americano, that twister.

Now the lime-green shutters of the window are ajar on the narrow balcony and the wrought-iron window-guards stand out blackly against the white wall like a firing squad lining up. The white coverlet of the bed is thrown back and blank rolls of canvas and cartridge-paper, lightly sketched upon, lie in no particular order on the faded maroon blanket, which is stained on the side.

The sounds of the South are loud, particular to themselves. Human voices carry a long way in the dry air. Nature is different here, peculiar to itself, the Mediterranean littoral. After Aix-en-Provence the roof-tiles are convex, no longer concave, now faded by the sun.

Now an airy brownish-white mountain of clouds hangs suspended over an unnamed mountain range, image upon towering image. It will remain there all day, more or less stationary. On the tableland above Burriana beach a strong-flowing stream of brown water is splashing over the bed of rocks giving on the beach. A path meanders off diagonally into the campo, to reddish mire where the cane-brakes thicken, to scents of thyme and rosemary. The path leads into a narrow ravine. Here parasites grow, hardy scotch grass; olives and oleander afford some shade there in the olive groves.

Now the shutters on the small cast-iron balcony are thrown wide apart and the room receives the last light and warmth of the expiring sun which, much enlarged (an optical illusion), is going down redly in a haze at the head of the valley. Its late raking light fills the room, as in a bell jar, immutably fixed. Some light, but not much, is reflected in the glass of the double window. Its brilliance, which seems fixed, is in fact already on the wane; and in less than an hour it will receive no more light.

In the glass of the window is reflected: a roof of concave tiles sprouting weeds and grass, a whitewashed wall splattered with a wash of ochre-coloured light, a calm upended cloudy evening sky teeming with feeding swallows.

At the eaves there is no pipe nor any wooden apparatus known as gableboard. A few blades of grass deposited here and there on the sun-bleached tiles, by the wind's auspices. An occasional drip falls, radiating out and spreading once detached from the tiles, dropping heavily as if it were mercury, to penetrate all around the dampened compactness of the earth.

Murky days. Hanging on. Chill before October's out. Clouds hanging over the head of the valley and over the village, the pueblo. The narrow gorges of its streets radiate out from Calle Pintada like the ribs from the central vertebrae. Coming in from Malga one sees it, a pillar of cloud.

In the evening (and how calmly), the passing bell. Someone has died, passed away. First the statement, then the counter-statement further back, half muffled and as if with campanile half averted, like a face turned away; the other side of the belfry possibly; sweetly sustained in the air, prolonged but not mournful, a clearly modulated dingdong of doom and Time.

Pause and delay, go and stay; mixed with the sound of the sea, and a bird calling between casually spaced strokes; how sweetly sometimes comes the semitone! One questions, the other replies, and real life is over—to the wash of the sea and a commotion of alarmed birds heard between casually spaced strokes (as if the bellringer was thinking of something else).

Swifts and swallows go flittering about the belfry and a foreign lady all dressed in lime green goes walking home with lowered head. Mary Diamond.

It is cold all over Europe this winter. The coldest winter England has seen since the black frost of 1740, say the records. In freezingly sedate London the men come out in strange and outlandish headgear, with Russian earflaps.

Lightless morning after a night of torrential rain. Indoors all day, working. Blustery and cold without; carbon fires within. A few kilos of the stuff weighed solemnly on small scales, taken home in a basket, lit in the brasero, the old Moorish chafing dish. Winter is coming.

# THE PEOPLE

In this village or pueblo (population ten thousand) or fishing place, there are three Antonios and all three run bars; as there are three *casas* all numbered 77. Antonio Montilla (Antonio *primero*) of the sickly hue is given to overcharging in a most blatant way; certainly he does not enjoy the best of health, and has a young wife as sickly-looking as himself. They run the old bar at the head of Calle Italia where it joins the Puerta del Mar where "our" Antonio (Antonio *secundo*) has taken over his father's bar on the corkscrew bend. His younger brother Rafael, a prune-dark bogeyman with the slanted nipples of a gorilla, is a collector of bad debts and seems to have taken a dislike to me. Perhaps it is because his elder brother *has* taken to me? Rafael would like to dose my beer with cyanide. I remember their father, an old man in carpet slippers, taking the sun as it declined in the evening, outside the bar.

Then there is the stout, choleric, dark-jowled, dewlapped, sluggish-eyed, big-beamed son (Antonio *tercero*) of the owner of the Balcon de Europa bar, whose surname I never heard spoken. His old granny, aged one hundred and two, carries vessels of goats' blood up steep stairs to an upper room where they make blood sausages that taste of string and soap and give you the Spanish Shits, or violent diarrhoea.

## The Warholes

Blurred images, shapes that might be the Warholes, are standing together on the paseo, deep in conversation, leaning on the railing and looking, apparently, in this direction, at me staring back at them, from the mirador of No. 68. As far as one can tell of stationary objects a kilometre away.

My binoculars bring them into closer range. It's the Warholes alright. Standing talking to a stout lady-friend or amiable visitor in hunting pink. After a while she takes her leave of them with much waving of hands (Warhole flaps his like a seal). I recognise Warhole by the unbalanced way he turns on his heel and begins to move away, his feet as if sticking to the ground, his shoulders up, twitchy. He has been giving directions or offering advice to the party in hunting pink. Now they turn back to the railing, the Warholes. They do not lean on it but stand close together talking very intimately. Scrutinised closely through binoculars they seem in continuous agitation. He is talking very persuasively and she responds to this, by moving closer to him. He lays his hand briefly on her shoulder, then drops it—jumpy and restless. They move like insects in a hurry—the turmoil of small creatures enclosed and darkly surrounded and outlined by the shape of the object I peer through, as if peering down a tunnel or into a crevice (my own peacocktwittering eyelashes visible in it too), the right lens useless, blind as Sartre's right eye.

They move jerkily, uneasily, insects under the microscope, early emergent life. Or, better, they float into view bunched in close-up, two-dimensional objects in a three-dimensional world, their movements tremulous and watery, flattened, brought into focus by telescopic sights, on spindle legs rushing away. Now dwarf jockeys brandish whips; begoggled and becapped, bunched in terrific close-up on the bends, mounts with blinkers and knee-pads float out of the eyepiece, the enlarging lens, in frantic laboured action but quite soundlessly and strangely foreshortened.

Now they seem to contract and expand—the disorder of teeming insect life under the microscope; or the order of insect life, tumultuous, flickering—the constant agitation of insects always threatened. The needs they must satisfy quickly, on an admittedly small scale, with their feelers and pincers, consider that.

Now the outlines blur. They seem to float away from the railings, seen through intervening leaves all agitated by the rising wind, they coalesce and part, Warhole leading the way (that's usual), walking on spongy boots with his toes out, screened now by leaves, by palm trees, a parody of his abrupt bodily and manual gestures, shoulders hunched, walking somewhat stooped, his dome of a balding head and gingery beard quite clearly recognisable. A New York "concrete poet" quite vain of his small talents, which reveal bland ignorance of the true function of both poetry and concrete. But let that pass.

She follows him, a docile doe, very upright, with her short frisky stride—a small neat female person who once modelled hats in a New York department store, perhaps Bloomingdale's. Or again, the agitation of silent characters in an old movie (say Chaplin's Keystone period), or even further back in time—the agitation not merely of human characters in movement trapped, but animate objects (horses, dogs) also, throbbing and pulsating on worn film stock diffused by chemicals and light-leakages—and inanimate objects as well, grainy, contracting and expanding with their own troubled life.

### Melissa Dário

That perfect blue day in early October when most of the visitors had gone (taking the lady in hunting pink with them), there on the windswept mirador adjoining ours, her hair and skirt swept up by the Levantine blowing a half-gale and tearing the leaves off the white mulberry tree above her head, stood Melissa Dário. She and another.

The Levanter was blowing so hard that I saw them as it were dissolving in moisture. It was a strain to see these two figures two gardens off, huddled under a tree, merging and then separating from each other; movements difficult to follow, more difficult still to understand.

Her good-looking sister is weeping copiously. Leaning against Melissa, hair all over her face, the Levanter lifting it by the roots and sweeping it away. She confides in her sister of her hopeless love for Dan Delahunty, through this, in a wild rush of tears.

Melissa Dário of Cordoba, youthful, beautiful, wistful, sits upright, listening, for she loves and is loved. She tries to console her distracted sister, but her words are blown away. They sit with their heads close together, the wind, rising all the time, presses their thin dresses against their bodies. The good-looking sister of Melissa Dário weeps and weeps.

But now it is Melissa's turn. Now Melissa herself weeps. The best-looking of four good-looking daughters, because brokenhearted, for love, bending down, hair blown about her face, into her mouth, her skirt blown up to reveal a long brown thigh. But she doesn't care, weeping and weeping, her face down on her mother's lap (for it's the *madre* who is there now, not the thwarted sister, they have altered their positions; I see clearly that it's the mother who strokes her daughter's hair).

But her beautiful daughter is sobbing her heart out, as the wind lifts her skirt, exposing her thighs, lifts the distracted mother's dark long hair.

But the mother is now quite impassive, stroking her lovely daughter's long brown hair, consoling her, the daughter, lovelorn, bending down, sobbing. The Levanter explores her thighs and hips, but she doesn't care, she is beyond that, weeping her heart out.

But now, my eyes full of moisture, strained, staring (and I can distinguish only by difficulty), it's the mother herself who weeps, beyond consolation. She weeps because of her daughter's behaviour. Misbehaviour. With the dark Fossy youth who owns an Alsatian. Or for some unkept promise. She weeps for something her daughter has done or refuses to do, it's all the same. Melissa sitting bolt upright, quite composed, strokes her hair.

But now she is leaning down and pleading with her mother. For whatever's done cannot be undone, and whatever's not been done, she will not do. Or she is promising to mend her ways, bending down, trying to console her mother, their hair and light summer frocks blown together.

No, it's difficult to say who consoles whom, and for what. It could be anybody or anything. For now it's not even the mother who weeps, not even Melissa, not even her competitor in love, the other unattractive daughter (unattractive only in comparison with Melissa, for all four are stunners). No, but for the less attractive tall auburn-haired sister. She weeps because she considers herself plain.

Or because Melissa has cut her out. Or because she is ignored by the dark Fossy youth, who prefers Melissa, who prefers Delahunty.

But now the unit reforms once more. A daughter and a mother again, two females from a very united Spanish family (alfresco lunches with wine-imbibing padre in Panama hat at the end of the mirador) cling together and weep, turn and turn about, a couple of good-lookers clinging together, one weeping, one consoling.

The Levanter, risen to even greater force, in a furiously risen crescendo now goes howling through the white mulberry tree, lifting a skirt at random here, raising hair from a head at random there, blowing the voices away (but not their deep troubles).

Solarium!

Indentations of many thousands of bare feet mark the sand where the sunlight filters through the *cana* of Pepe Gomez's *merendero*, scores of bare feet, heels and toes. An engaged couple sit with their heads together at a table. (So it wasn't place, it was him, it was he, I was here, he wanted to go there. So I went there. Not there, but here. Not then, but now. Here is the sea. There are the pair. I hope you are well.)

She is small, dark, rather plump, pretty, with rats' tails from swimming, still in her togs, with legs crossed.

He is young, dressed in a blue suit. He peels small pears and offers her the halves speared on a toothpick. They sit with their heads close together, eating small pears, getting used to each other sitting at table, eating small pears.

You say "I haven't quite gotten used to being frustrated yet." *No me estoy totalmente acostumbrado todavia a estar frustrado.* I haven't yet got the hang of accommodating misery. But this refers to another, to Harriet, wife of a friend.

Now they are getting accustomed to seeing each other undressed for swimming, or eating small pears under the cana shade near the changing cabins, facing each other, now drinking cerveza, their undressed bodies close to one another, his hands about her hips. They are sitting on a towel laid out on the sand (now he clasps her back, her soft valorous young back, in the submarine light of Pepe Gomez's merendero on Playa de Torrecilla).

Her hips seem to widen as she enters the water, her hair comes undone, she swims, a graceful breaststroke, her head up, hair spread, a well-made girl. Her stern manner, flesh-tones, hands and eyes (shining like a cat's in the street on the night they went in a group to Raymon Fossy's Cine Olympia), disposition of allure, her shoulder-blades in motion (now she is dancing the Twist—all the rage then—with its Afro emphasis on arse, the poco-disco throbbing on the rocks at Carabeo Beach), spied on by the hunchback servant peering through binoculars, from under the white mulberry tree, keeping tabs for the mother, watched by Another with sketchpad on knee.

I don't hear the throbbing music below. It doesn't reach me here on the mirador. I hear the Alsatian barking. I see her dancing alone. Her arms before her, bent at the elbows, moving her hips, her hands shaping her body's curves as she turns in the dance, dancing alone, with pointed toes in the sand. The knowing thrust of the hips, as she turns with the music I cannot hear, looking over her shoulder, the curve and soft strength of her bare back, a broadbeamed Andalucían, sways me. Oh body swayed in music, oh brightening glance! How can we know the dancer from the dance?

Coming up the path in the glare of day, in the great heat of August, by the excrements of the children and the dogs (the fishermen crap on the beach and cover it in sand; but you stand on it), distantly infatuated, hotly disturbed Delahunty.

Drawn by impulsive necessity (she never had very much on), plumpcheeked pulchritude with probity approached, sweetly declined; ever so sweetly declined. I bring to you an anxious habit, an anxious mind and heart.

Here you come willing, not touching.

I felt myself much drawn to her. First impressions allay later suspicions. Voluptuousness is a quality little ambitious, say the old books; "it holds itself rich enough to itself without any access of reputation, and is best affected when it is most obscured." (Burton?) I was drawn to her, her colouring, her semi-nudity, the density of her limbs (suggesting later amplitude; she would grow into a heavy matron), her Spanishness, the familiar and the strange a compelling combination. Colour plays such a part in the beauty of the women here; a special charm lies in the tone of the flesh rather than the shape.

Her hair came undone in the water. She swam, head up and hair spread wide, laughing, being spied on by the hunchback on the mirador. She rose a little out of the water and with a quick movement of her arm seemed to point to the house on the hill, a white house in the distance. There, there—the cortijo de Maro, now locked up and empty, on the summit of the terraces of olive mixed with almond above La Luna—a house of assignation for us?—and then falling back, laughing, her hair like sea fronds all about her. Life Class models are always naked.

But a pick-up, a liaison, in Andalucía? In the olive groves at night with a good-looking girl from Corboda, well-chaperoned, spied on by the hunchback servant? Absolutely out of the question. Put it right out of your mind. Movie romances, wisps of passing fancy, wispy mare's-tails, cumulous. I am aware of a world, spread out in space endlessly, and in time becoming and become (Heidegger? Husserl?).

I'd known fallen days, fallen fortunes, suffered from *Anxietas tibiarum*—all-night twitching of the limbs—in far-off frozen London.

She must have known she was being spied on by the hunchback servant through binoculars, spied on by the father and sisters, spied on by her mother. She was acting up for Delahunty, on the beach below, watched from the mirador of No. 68 Calle Italia, as she came up the path from the beach reeling in the great heat of August, wearing a wide-brim sunhat with a broad blue band.

One morning early, maybe five A.M., I saw her two gardens across from me on her crazy mirador and wanted to call across but I didn't know her name then. She had come straight from bed, from sleep, the most distant country there is, in a shorty nightdress that left most of her bare, came for a breath of air onto the hazy early-morning grotto of the mirador under the spreading white mulberry tree.

She remained there some time and then went back into the house, as silently as she had come, not looking across, not knowing I had seen her, not knowing what turmoil she had created in my anxious breast.

One last image of her seated in the sheets of a rowing boat rowed in a muscular fashion by dark young Fossy; she was trailing one hand in the water, like a young Queen from a previous age, with extraordinary eyes, moving past the great boulders overgrown with marigold and Delahunty watching from mirador above; as now as before, as always.

I found out her name when the family had left for Cordoba again. Melissa Dário. I asked Olivia to bribe the hunchback servant with postage stamps and show us over the empty house. I saw her bed-room, one of the beds was her bed; on some of those hooks she had hung her summer clothes, in that bathroom she had undressed to shower, in that kitchen she had helped her mother or the hunchback to prepare breakfast.

Her father was a businessman, one of four brothers; she took his family, the four lovely daughters, to the house on Calle Italia every summer.

Oh Melissa Dário, where are you now?

# The Bridge at Aranjuez

It was a narrow bridge.

The arms came down as spans to lift it out of the water. There were wooden catwalks for pedestrians. Young lovers were leaning on the parapet, staring at the water flowing by under their feet.

I had been in the Prado in Madrid and had come down to Aranjuez, the old royal stud or retreat of los Reyes Católicos. The elms were fine as those from Kildare. Its strawberries and cream were mentioned by Pliny. Don Carlos had bred a *garañón* from the union of an ass and a mule—a colossal beast exceeding fifteen hands in height.

In the Royal Palace I looked at indifferent paintings by Mengs and Giordano, and had enough of art for a while. I walked across the Plaza de Armas, admired the stands of elms imported from England by the luckless Philip *Secundo* called Philip the Fair, who had died after drinking a glass of water following a game of tennis. The widow hauled his shrinking corpse about the dusty roads of Spain until she could bear to entomb him in some convent. A cognac had been named after him, he has that immortality at least.

I crossed the dusty bridge over the coffee-coloured river and boats on their moorings. It reminded me of Richmond on the Thames, but I preferred Aranjuez on the Rio Tajo. I stayed at the hostel Principe where a calm woman showed me a large room with four beds in it. The rates were most reasonable in the off-season. I washed myself and went out for a meal.

At the end of a wide boulevard there stood a sandstone church inundated by evening light; one of those beatific evenings that recur so regularly in Spain. A crowd was clustering about the open door of the church. The stone was tinged with the reddish pyrogallic acid of a spent summer's day. What Spanish King had ordained that ten thousand Masses be offered up for the repose of his royal soul? One of the Philips?

For months on end the shrinking corpse of Philip the Fair had gone jaunting after the unhinged widow, Juana la Loca.

I crossed the bridge again.

It was dark now, darkness had fallen as I came onto the bridge. It was dark there, as in a wood, and the lovers were still embracing, as if cast in stone, become part of the bridge.

I looked down into the muddy waters of the Rio Tajo. "Freshening the sweet tempe of Aranjuez, clothing the gardens with verdure," wrote the Englishman Richard Ford. Some disease had emptied the royal stables. I entered the Rana Verde Restaurante overlooking the river, a place of creepers and glass, empty of diners at that time of year. I ordered a tortilla and a bottle of white Valencia. *Sana, sana, culito de rana.* The tortilla was good, the wine cold and dry.

A peaceful scene presents itself by the river Tajo at Aranjuez: lovers (immortalised in sandstone) embrace fondly, for eternity, on an unlighted bridge near where the pleasure-boats are moored at the closed summer retreat of the Spanish royal pair. The elms were imported from England by the farsighted Philip the Second. Pray observe the colour of the stone in the Plaza de Armas in the evening light. Outside Hostel Principe not much is stirring. I saw a church half a kilometre away, lit by the evening light. Those evenings that recur so often in Andalucía, sand-coloured tinged with red, pumice stone tinged with pyrogallic acid, and worshippers clustering at the open maw of the church door flung wide open, and a sad bell tolling.

Now a young woman came strolling. A passing car stopped and two men got out, leaving their doors open; her friends, I thought. Until I perceived her to be a *puta*, attractive and black-haired in high-heel black shoes. When one of the men familiarly touched her rump she struck his hand away. No touching without paying for the goods on sale. After a great deal of palaver the three got into the front seat, the *puta* in the middle, and drove away from the church still tinged with its beatific threatened evening light, and the worshippers going in.

On the unlit bridge the lovers were still entwined as I passed them, going and coming on the narrow catwalk, the second time I was puffing an inferior cigar. After a good dinner at La Rana Verde Restaurante I had crossed the bridge, saw the entwined lovers cast in stone. Now I was looking for a tobacco kiosk, found it and was sold a dummy cigar that fell to pieces in my mouth as I passed the lovers again, still entwined on the unlighted bridge above the pleasure-boats moored on either side of the arches, bobbing hull to hull on the muddy water.

# The Ritual of the Goats Returning

It is fine weather now, the sun very hot during the day and cool in the evening. You can see the blue currents in the Mediterranean some forty kilometres away, down below us at the entrance of the Valley beyond the hill village called El Clot (where they cast stones at strangers), Ab Oxú (poor lighting, little water) and Nulles (where they throw stones at each other, being inbred and demented). And the sun goes down very fiery.

Darkness falls earlier, the two buses coming home with their lights on, ascending all the time, around the two hundred curves. One mistake and over you go.

The colours of the October sky change all the time, minute by minute. When the sun sinks behind Ab Oxú a breeze starts up and the light drains out of the sky, the mountains darken, the *gorriones* end their chittering and depart for their nesting-place, leaving droppings like small burnt worms on the terrace where we take our sundowners. Then begins the evening ritual of the goats returning, one heraldic beast leading, a bearded ram with a tangled span of horns, the progenitive parts protected in a dirty leather truss. In among the goats are some stray sheep and pigs, like the animals hurrying to the Ark.

They become more and more hesitant as they near home, pushing forward only to hesitate the more, advancing with vacillating threats, only to stop. All uneasy they draw near their sheds, as if uncertain of their whereabouts or their welcome, emitting dry anxious farts.

Below in narrow Calle Rueda, how soon the voices cease and evening silence falls! Among the group on the wall below, waiting for their evening meal, the stories become bolder as darkness comes on; and it comes suddenly here. Two glasses full, two empty, both refilled, here on the terrace; below, they drink nothing. Now comes the turn of the planet Venus.

"Marie, Marie! *Mira me!*"

"*Nada, nada.*"

"*Mira me*, Marie! *Mira me!*"

Soon they retire and the wall is empty. Even the cuckoo in the olive tree behind the house falls silent. Do cuckoos call at night? Always silent by night? A curious lone bird; when one calls, is it to its mate or for themselves alone that they call with the strangest of all bird cries, more like a death-rattle than a declaration of love, in these hills at least? Odder even than the fig-pickers who whirr in the air through October.

Messiaen heard an unknown bird calling in Persia in the evening and put it into his devotional work as the voice of the Almighty, not thunder but a voice close to silence and therefore closer to God, one might assume.

The silence that now on the terrace falls, and on Atepmoc below in the darkness, is an intimation of the great silence that will one day descend and never lift again. The globe and its wretched burden of history was only a dream, a bad dream only in God's head, on an off-day long past, now whirled into space, and us with it, back into the nothingness out of which we came.

Darkness falls like a dark cloak on Atepmoc. Even the dogs are silent.

Winter is here.

# Texts for the Air

62 CALLE RUEDA, COMPETA (MALAGA), SPAIN.

Broadcast on 13th June 1982 on BBC Radio 3.

# CAST

VOICE 1 (baritone): Speaks Monologues 1 & 8.
"The Retired Ones of the Twilit Zone" and "Amory Over England."

VOICE 2 (tenor): Speaks Monologues 2 & 7.
"Baptist Funeral Without Cortege" and "An End-of-Season Cricket
Game (An Open Letter to Harold Pinter)."

VOICE 3 (f. soprano): Speaks Monologues 3 & 5.
"The Lady Genevieve Goodsward" and "Rudyard."

VOICE 4 (bass): Speaks Monologue 4 & 6.
"Public Phone-Box or Public Transport (The Inside Story)" and
"Hoyle's Deadly Aerosol Squirt."

GHOST-VOICE

TANNOY

PRINTER

AUDIENCE and AUDIENCE MEMBER

VOICE OF BRIAN JOHNSON

A VOICE

ARLOTT

Rapid staccato delivery for all voices.
All voices divided by seconds of silence.

*Sound of distant resonant dinner gong, struck twice and echoing.* VOICE 1 *over, slightly increased pace.*

VOICE 1: Like fish immobile in a glass tank they stare at the foolish movies—

VOICE 2: Lady Genevieve Goodsward (or Godesward), who comes from an ancient and highly respected line known to Mysore—

VOICE 3: A new "concept" thought up by the Transport crowd, or more likely dreamed up—

VOICE 4: I once met Kipling with a group of young people at his place at Burwash—

*Fainter dinner gong, on echo.* VOICE 1 *over, pace increased.*

VOICE 1: They seem tired of life in a way no fish can be, save dying fish—

VOICE 2: Wife of the decorated poet, snobbish as a Whitwell, with a severe hairstyle that makes her long face—

VOICE 3: Copywriters being men more often than not are out of touch with reality as we know it—

VOICE 4: Somebody asked him about the British in India—

*Fainter dinner gong, on echo.* VOICE 1 *over, pace increased.*

VOICE 1: As though this incessant viewing of foolish movies was depriving them of even—

VOICE 2: A black Austin hearse with old-fashioned spoke-wheels and—

VOICE 1: The faithful, by definition, need no conversion—

*Fainter dinner gong, on echo.* VOICE 1 *over, pace increased.*

VOICE 3: Stroking a large comatose dog that lies half-buried on her—

VOICE 4: Curious jugged *hokku* of text and picture now solemnly presented to the public—

VOICE 3: "You want to know how we got the British Empire?"

VOICE 4: The windows of this top-floor flat, through which a Luftwaffe bomb—

*Distant dinner gong.* VOICE 1 *over, pace increased.*

VOICE 2: No mourners gather and the church door remains closed—

VOICE 4: Windows arranged along all one side of the living room, which is the end—

VOICE 2: A ghostly end-of-season scratch-game in every sense of the—

VOICE 4: I can tell you that I've seen some pretty strange sights—

*Distant dinner gong, on echo.* VOICE 1 *over, pace increased.*

VOICE 1: Fish immobile in a glass tank—

VOICE 3: Lady Genevieve Goodsward (or Godesward)—

VOICE 1: Ruddy faces, thick ears, nothing daunted—

VOICE 3: Once I met Kipling—

VOICE 2: A black Austin hearse—

VOICE 4: A new "concept" thought up by the Transport crowd—

VOICE 2: The faithful, by definition—

VOICE 4: A Luftwaffe bomb passed clean through—

*Dinner gong, close, gentle tap.*
*One voice over another; pitch rising.*
*Hold for say 5 seconds, abrupt silence.*
*Dinner gong, very faint.*

GHOST VOICE: (*Sepulchral.*) "The Retired Ones of the Twilit Zone . . ." the Quiz Programme.

*Horse-laughter from studio audience.*

"The *Retired* Ones of the Twilit Zone."

*Studio laughter fades out rapidly.*

VOICE 1: Like fish immobile in a glass tank, they stare at the foolish movies. They seem tired of life in a way no fish can be, save dying fish, as though this incessant viewing of foolish movies was depriving them of even curiosity, that force which makes the young to grow.

In the foolish movie, the movie-of-the-day, one of many, always the same; one more day of all the identical dull days spent in that stale-smelling Viewing Room where they congregate, now it is the old, old story of the father and the son. The story of the ambitious father who cannot let his son be.

The father is played by Malden and the son by Perkins. The father, you must know, played for the famous Boston Red Sox. See him deteriorate, I beg your pardon, demonstrate, with all the zeal of prosography, the grip, the stance, as he faces the pitches, to demonstrate most unconvincingly, standing and holding the bat limply in a fashion thought to be resolute, nothing deterred, just standing there facing the unseen pitcher.

Perkins and Malden play son and father respectively, in the foolish movie. Both idiots in their respective ways, Perkins and Malden.

GHOST VOICE: "Baptist Funeral Without Cortege . . ."

*Mocking studio laughter.*

"Baptist Funeral Without Cortege . . ."

*Fade embarrassed studio laughter.*

VOICE 2: A black Austin hearse with old-fashioned spoke-wheels and running-board stands before the brownstone Baptist Church in pouring rain which will not let up. No mourners gather and the church door remains closed, though the hearse is packed with flowers.

The weeping printer has slipped into the rathskeller off the premises and is dosing himself with Mild & Bitter in the gloomy public bar, looking about him furtively with scorched eyes. Dracula's black hearse glitters outside like an infamous joke as the mourners gather about the closed church door and stare up like fish at the brownstone edifice. Tell me, why do Baptists favour orange brick faced with grey pebbles from the seashore, in their oddly shaped places of worship, so unlike the sombre grey granite of High Anglicanism with their uplifted spires in perpetual memory of Luther's eternally upraised admonitory finger, the gesture of a stiff rationalist ever hostile to Roman Catholic hocus-pocus?

*Brief silence.*

GHOST VOICE: (*Lugubrious.*) "The Lady Genevieve Goodsward . . ."

*Burst of studio laughter abruptly terminated.*

"The Lady Genevieve Goodsward . . ."

VOICE 3: (*Soprano gossip, telling the story at speed, terminated by abrupt silence, swallowing, then on again.*) Lady Genevieve Goodsward or Godesward, who comes of an ancient and highly respected line known to Mysore and Delhi and the hill stations, in the life before our time, wife of the decorated poet, snobbish as a Whitwell, with a severe hairstyle that makes her long face a mask, sits in an armchair, stroking a comatose dog that lies half-buried on her lap, of a species not readily determinable.

Absently she pulls at its matted hair, palping the beast as though it were her worry beads, and speaks of the rights of vanished traditions in a stiffly upper-class voice, fwaithf'lly naice.

Sir Wilf is thought to sleep with his teddy bear Archway but would much prefer to chain himself to area railings of period lamp-posts or even period pillar-boxes (symbols of an extinct past once glorious) or rope himself to trees in parts of the city given over entirely to the modern automobile, in a manner made popular by suffragettes . . . (*Swallows, deep breath, continues at full tilt,* con amore.)

. . . Master of the softly-spoken aside, lover of the commonplace, at least in his poetry, descant signing over secluded Quads, Georgian chanting in school chapels, boys in distant playing-fields engaged in rough games in the rain, avid beer-drinkers not yet pickled in Old Bushmills; lover of the Worcester sauce bottle placed squarely on the spotless linen tablecloth, good breeding (a pure-bred golden retriever savaging its fleas, a pedigree bull scraping its neck on a gate, a beetle in the morning tea; a tiny coda, large as all England). (*Swallows. Brief pause. Continues pell-mell.*)

Of all this Sir Wilf is greatly enamoured; doing good or with a will towards doing good (not quite the same thing) in the style that smacks of a curate's useless ways, of men in cassocks walking in glebe lands and offering the soft hand at the rectory gate, softly imparted advice to subdued parishioners, to the sound of a quiet bell tolling and a vision of clouds over the Weald, the memory of a bottle of Worcester sauce triumphant on the now slightly stained linen table-cloth; the softly spoken rebuff. Dead England—an inward-turning trouble.

. . . Wearing gloves, stout walking-shoes, a sturdy walking stick, a decent hat, the old trusty gabardine, stumbling forward (always with a kind word). Now walking swiftly and resolutely towards an unseen destination: searching behind furniture for the object lost or mis-laid, fetching up heavy sighs, drawing aside drapes, all period stuff, the living room alive with dogs, faithful animals dangerous to stran-gers but good when you know them, all family heirlooms pickled in Old Bushmills, the dining-room choked with chintz, the bedroom a

familiar terrain of unknown battles, well-beloved objects, decanters,
Archway tucked in.

*Caesura.*

. . . Now wearing gloves, hatted and gabardined, the lost object
retrieved (a pipe); inane expression of grim resolution, the light rain
ceasing to fall and gabardine discarded for light-tweed overcoat,
thrown casually over the shoulders as a cape, rubber galoshes sometimes known as gum boots or overshoes, from the time of spats.
. . . Striding forward now courageously into the teeming rain, followed by a pack of dogs, expression of the most absolute determination fixed on the flushed face, the unlit pipe clamped in the jaws; to
the pedigree bull glaring hotly over the gate, the Weald obscured for
the nonce in drizzle. Onslaughts on the commonplace, pathogenic
bacteria. (*Swallows, brief pause.*)
. . . Or: quite paralysed from the waist down, over the brave display handkerchief in the breast-pocket, leather for the tweedy elbow,
flower in the buttonhole, fixed expression of the most absolute determination, pipe clamped in the jaws, as if struck by lightning in South
Africa or was it Ind'ja. Perhaps Cape Town or Krishnapur, Kimberley
or Mafeking it might have been (I see a heavy fan revolving sedately
and coloured bar-waiters in scarlet rat-catchers sedately placing little
bowls of salted peanuts on an oaken table beside a gin-fizz, taking a
quietly-spoken order), slowed by premature but quite crippling rheumatism, the English disease.

*Brief sound of English hunt, the "gone-away" sounded on the horn, bay-
ing of the pack. Voice over the winding horn, at full speed.*

. . . Behind it all once the lost herds, the holy cows, the Untouchables,
remittance men with drink problems to put it mildly, the long lines
of the destitute, descant song (surely not *there?*); the lost goldfields,

the afflicted ones of another colour and creed, the bullwhips of a Rhodes or a Kruger, men of destiny with public parks named after them; goldfields now in other hands, their wise policy-making now land-settlements, deeds of possession now in banks, all finished now, given once with the left hand (the hand that wavers); horrible opposites. *Most* unctuous rendering of "Sarie Maria" at closing-down time, with setting sun over rolling wheatlands that stretch forever but now reduced to a tiny pinprick and then darkness. But now the mug of Horlicks and a flood of wordplay or fatuous alliteration calculated to stun the clever mind and obscure the meaning, if any, or worse still, distort it, granted any meaning there in the first instance.

. . . Gone the carnation in the buttonhole, toppers at Ascot, straw boaters at the Oxford-Cambridge race, river-craft of the most various kind hooting in open derision, gone the upsetting wake disturbing the banks; toffs at Lord's, strawberries and cream at Wimbledon, wisteria clasping itself in an almost human almost painful way on the river-wall at Richmond. So much for the *Guardian's* middle pages.

*Ship hooting on Thames.*
*Orchestra tuning up, conductor's baton for silence.*

GHOST-VOICE: "Public Phone-Booth or Public Transport (The *Inside* Story) . . ."

*Polite applause from small audience at music.*

"Public Phone-Booth or Public Transport (The Inside Story) . . ."

*Heavy Rain. Brief.*

VOICE 4: A new "concept" thought up by the Transport crowd, or more likely dreamed up by the advertising agency that handled the account, agency copywriters being men more often than not out of touch with reality as we know it, to judge from the curious jugged *hokku* or text and picture now solemnly presented to the great public at large.

To put it at its simplest, we are being urged to use single-decker buses as readily as we do the public telephone service, even though a good third of the latter service is permanently out of order, more than that in certain rough areas, where the wild young like nothing better than destroying all public amenities, whether they be telephones in booths or young saplings planted in Wandsworth Common. Whereas the single-decker buses are manned by single morose fellows of uncertain temper, very prone to sudden walk-out disputes, that is to say, going on sudden strike.

Full-colour advertisements in the Sunday supplements and on Tube hoardings underground, must have cost a pretty penny; the message being driven home to the hilt by presenting the side of the red single-decker bus as a red letter-box (the postal services are not, of course, top-notch by any manner of means), a happy thought for foreigners or illiterates.

The opposite arrangement springs irresistibly to mind: why not use a public phone-booth as you would a single-decker omnibus? Supposing narrow seating accommodation was provided by the Transport people, one could bring in a favoured newspaper and sit there smoking a pipe in perfect peace, complacently gaze out at the long queue waiting patiently for an opportunity to use the telephone for the purpose it was intended.

TANNOY: Train departures between Windsor and Eton Central and Yatton, as also to Worcester and Crun Hill, will operate with skeleton staffs, due to industrial dispute; but the services between Evesham may arrive from nineteen to twenty-three minutes earlier; while the Slough train will be delayed until 8:01. But for our Didcot customers an extra commuter service will be laid on . . . (*The rest scrambled; hold for say three seconds.*)

*Gush of escaping steam from old train.*

VOICE 4: Without more ado I left the "station" and sprang into a stationary double-decker that was moored outside and just then on the point of imminent departure for destinations unknown (it turned out to be Mortlake garage) . . . Where I descended and, feeling the need for a sobering drink, plunged into a local hostelry, where who do you suppose was laughing his head off in a corner but the Baptist printer, drinking wallop and short ones in the gloom of the Public Bar that was all mirrors.

A small newssheet was set out before him. Open at the page devoted to the nude of the day, and there she was, all spread out, looking deadly serious and naked as two plums—a sullen-looking baggage, that is the approved erotic style now, a suggestion of *Wieb* and whip.

"THREE BABIES IN RIVER," I read. "MURDER PROBE." I ordered a round of drinks and informed the Baptist printer, who was far from sober, that the trains from Paddington were being delayed to all Western Regions . . .

TANNOY: The trains to Paddington are being delayed to all Western Regions, the Reading service will be thirty-five minutes delayed, but Oxford on the hour and Worcester in two hours eighteen minutes . . . (*Scramble rest of announcement: hold for say 3 seconds.*)

VOICE 4: Over his bowed shoulders I read the oddest headlines. He was devouring the paper with gusto, well accustomed to getting the hang of the odd morphology employed by the Yellow Press—a kind of passacaglia or montage of capitals in heavy type, devoted to local and regional and then European and Global calamities. "INSIDE STORY," I read. "PEACE SHOCK TALKS." "HOW GRIFFITH GAGGED THE COMPANY GASBAG." "CASTLE ROCKS AS TOP MAN QUITS." (Had the Duke left?) "TOMATO ISLE FIGHTS BACK."

The Baptist printer was breathing through his nose, eyes like saucers fixed on the crossword puzzle.

PRINTER: (*Cockney.*) Blimey, mate, I've just got the windowsill of a ship!

VOICE 4: I stared at him, at a loss for a word. Who was he, this mysterious Baptist printer, who certainly got around, staring before him now with compressed lips? Now he wrenched his hands apart, which he had been holding convulsively clasped and drawing the paper to him commenced making notations in the blank squares, as though another Greater Power guided his crabbed, ink-stained fingers, setting off with absolute confidence amidst its manifold tomfooleries, as if impelled—a very bad sign.

*Uproar at pop concert, maximum volume.*

GHOST-VOICE: "Hoyle's Deadly Aerosol Squirt . . ."

*Uproar.*

VOICE 4: Sometimes I, not too complacently, stare out of the front windows of this top-floor flat, through which a Luftwaffe bomb passed clean through during an air raid; the windows arranged along all one side of the living room which is the end-wall of this block of flats, this being the fourth floor (it's really the rear of an old galleon); and I can tell you that I've seen some pretty strange sights—what the disturbed ones can get up to when they fondly imagine they are not being observed, although that would not deter them, lathe-turners on the spree.

. . . One afternoon who did I spy but little "Curly" Hoyle gliding through the traffic that circles the public toilets of the Broadway, a public service used by drug-pushers for making contacts, and as a sort of open-air gymnasium for coloured youths practicing karate chops and kicks outside and indeed inside, the women's section.

Did he remind me of dog, hare or little boy about my own son's age, and his best friend, his only friend in all the world? In short, was he chasing (hunting) or being chased (hunted), or was he perhaps a mixture of all three: the hunter running, the hunted fleeing, or the little boy lost, running after the others? For, caught up in some dream, and far away, surely he did not know himself? Dog or hare or little boy following (pursuing); or a mixture of all, being the fourth state. Or, in the fifth state, more confusing than the first, a mixture of all four preceding: dog, hare, boy lost, hunter found, observer observing (like a fellow attempting to play the piano with his nose)? A treat for the chronically bored.

. . . He moved wraith-like (was this the sixth and last state—the wraith?) through this region of incessantly circling heavy traffic; a place of Old Peoples' Homes in the side-roads of what was once country. A Senior Citizens' twilit zone with hospices for the dying, all under the kindly auspices of the Borough Council.

In a little while his innocent fancies will harden to something coarser, become belligerent; little Billy ("Curly") Hoyle grown older, in boffer boots and with convict's shaven skull, a soccer supporter ("Arse Rules"), will set about the attack on this relatively green haven of parks and ponds, where Rhodes's friend Dr. Johnson walked by the stand of beech saplings. Here the ponds proper to a seafaring race who now fish for minnows in stagnant or dead water by sewage plants and gasometers; fishing patiently and as like as not by night (for I have seen their lights under the umbrellas), below the defunct Palace by the abandoned racetrack where no horse has run since the start of the century; now a grassy area for training police dogs.

By the empty Palace, empty of Royalty that is to say, for Indians hold banquets there and the middle-aged tango on Sunday afternoons, watched by a worker in overalls who is ostensibly cleaning the stone lion's mane, and appears to be combing it, Hoyle will begin his defacing attack with his trusty aerosol gun hidden in his seersucker, squirting his hasty message on all likely surfaces.

HOYLE RULES!

. . . Come to join all the other feverish imaginings (phrases of impatience, thud of William Blake's wings of excess) put out by the noctambulists with little or no regard for grammar, leaving behind their white dripping spoor of "full frontals" and hopelessly entwined lovers' initials, notes on themes of ardour and faithlessness, where a sullen Japanese girl waits for a No. 9 that comes with "YAMAHA" advertised on its bodywork.

. . . A desperado with convict's skull and intent look, carries a bundle of old newspapers into the toilet of the Cock in Edmonton, where felons hung from a gibbet in the old days, on the site of what was once the Cockerel Tavern, near where Lamb walked; and before that, was a Roman thoroughfare to Peterborough, but which now is merely the largest and oldest Ind Coope pub in London.

. . . I see the word EMBRYO painted in black on a clapboard fence near the Employment Exchange, and "Alec the copper is a spider loving cunt" scrawled on the roof of a bus bound for Barnet and Leyton Whipps.

THUG-RULES is scrawled everywhere. Thug-Rules and Punk-Rules and Suck, Screw, Cane, Cunt, in the angry idiom of . . . The Tit-Bum-Cane cry of the disgruntled brigade who operate by night; the Tit-Bum-Cunt cry become by some curious alchemy "Paps, Seas-Nature"; the instinct behind it all—baffled human nature at odds with itself—become pure. Even "CURLY'S HOLE RULES OKAY!"

IMMANUEL KANT RULES! I read on a broken hoarding. "The Scrots are Sick in the Winkle." Elms Road had by some simple adjustment become BUMS ROAD. And a desperate non-patriot had squirted on the side of the steps below the dead Palace: PUKE ON THE DUKE!

But below it all and above it all and through it all, sometimes in the oddest places: HOYLE RULES!

*Brief silence. Crows in elms. Polite applause at country cricket game.*

GHOST-VOICE: "An End-of-Season Cricket Game . . ."

*Brief studio laughter.*

"An Open Letter to Harold Pinter . . ."

AUDIENCE: Ewwwwww!

GHOST-VOICE: "An End-of-Season Cricket Game . . ."

VOICE 2: *Celebre Dramaturgo!* The faithful, by definition, need no conversion. Last weekend I witnessed a ghostly end-of-season scratch game, in every sense of the term, that would surely have gladdened your cricketing heart. The event took place at Crouch End. They now have a new pavilion almost as charming as the old one, the 1920s structure gutted by vandals, presumably soccer yahoos opposed on principle to cricket. They even burnt down the temporary structure that replaced the original and broke into a nearby pavilion to make a bonfire of the bats.

Our dreams cannot last long, someone sang sweetly. 'Twas a fine afternoon in early October, the mellow Rowlandson oak and beech turning to autumnal colours around the boundaries, and a Pentecostal calm in the air. Lovely batting weather. I counted only seven fieldsmen and none of them robust. A tiny spinner was tirelessly delivering long hops to a heavy batsman who changed ends when he had scored a single. The Commentary Box was sadly deserted; nor did I see the florid features of that face which for me means summer, Brian Johnson of *Down Your Way* fame . . .

JOHNSON: Umpire Dicky Bird trots back with mincing little steps . . .

*Applause at Test. Lord's.*

VOICE 2: We were spared the I-would-have-thought and the I-should-have-thought of a most tedious commentator who shall be nameless, but once one of England's Great Stone Walls. It was a dreamlike scene, Sir.

The Umpire was lame and held the score-book to his chest, as a Charge Hand might a scratch pad or clipboard in a factory where nobody works any more. He answered all appeals, no matter how dubious.

AUDIENCE MEMBER: (*Loud appeal.*) How WAS he??!

VOICE 2: (*Unperturbed.*) With upraised finger. With a stabbing of the air that would have done credit to the late unlamented Herr Hitler emphasising some oratorical point. Or even Emperor Napoleon himself, of whom it was said (by Chateaubriand I think) that all his gestures wiped everything off the table. At every turn he had to create facts.

The umpire seemed anxious to keep the game going at all costs, this last game, and the fielders were also batsmen. It was an all-fielding team playing against itself. Sufficient to say the traffic to and from the pavilion was brisk, despite the obvious poverty of the attack.

. . . The double of Cecil Beaton (now I understand yclept *Sir* Cecil) stood at square leg, wearing a floppy sunhat. The same haunted face, same small delicate gestures; who presently took a turn at bowling slow long hops.

A grossly corpulent medium-pacer (how he permitted himself to get into *that* condition I do not know) who resembled to a marvellous degree the fabled Billy Bunter of Blackfriars, then took a turn, but was accorded scant respect by the only fit-looking man on the field, who enjoyed a brisk knock of fifty odd, including three sixes in one over, this against an erratic pace-man with a queer green stain on flannels none too clean in the first place.

What with this tawny bronze-leaf colours, the rare strokes of some suavity recalling the Nawab of Pataudi, but here the static figures, not all in flannels, and a general air of benign incompetence, the umpire's unraised finger, all was a sober joy to behold. A bit of the old Maecenas and no mistake—*vita dum superset bene est*, what? While one's alive all's well, nothing but well and fair.

How *duced* pleasant, *Celebre Dramaturgo*, to watch the shadows lengthening, shoulders (no matter how incompletely) being opened for the last time, the vapour trails above in the last Saturday peace of this summerlike October day! The last yowls . . .

AUDIENCE MEMBER: (*On echo.*) OOww Waazzzee!

VOICE 2: (*Unperturbed.*) . . . those curious rhetorical imperatives. The last "Well bawled, Sir!" ringing out, and the final loud guffaw from the pavilion which up till then one had supposed empty—for the batsmen came down to field as soon as they had . . . unpadded.

Not forgetting the gentlemanly handclapping, absolutely de rigour at these polite affairs. A small coloured batsman who looked well set was run out attempting a quick one that was not on. Acorns were thick in Queen's Wood (sign of the end of the world?) in this autumn of conkers, and the squirrels careless of hoarding their nuts. I thought of you.

You should have been there, a well-knit figure striding to the crease with a Middlesex cap drawn down in a threatening Boycott-like manner over the hooded eyes. Discipline on the field was lax, but who cared; the figures had become effigies, emblematic. Playing or rather say conducting themselves at a game whose rules and quaint terminology . . .

AUDIENCE MEMBER: (*Fainter.*) How WAS he?

VOICE 2: (*Unperturbed.*). . . had barely changed in the course of its long and pleasant history. At least five matches were played at low tide on the Godwin Sands in the nineteenth century.

A game of detailed records, the keeping of records, which is not quite the same thing; which undermines boasting and must thus offer a strong appeal to the modest English character, being itself a form of hyperbole. Records, after all, cannot lie. There can be no appeal against the umpire's upraised finger. Cricket, a game played in the mind.

A VOICE: Which end, Alf?

ARLOTT: That one went clean through him. . . as if he had a hole in him like a Henry Moore statue.

A VOICE: Which end are you batting, Alfred?

VOICE 2: Such punctilio! An off-drive from the batsman with his eye in was a quicksilver flourish on the flute. *Arlott* should have been there, sipping Muscadet and recalling great figures and times of the past, never to return again. Hobbs and Sutcliffe, Compton and Edrich, Voce and Bowes, Bradman and Ponsford.

Are you, perchance, familiar with the work of Richard Jeffries, favourite author of naturalist Williamson? In *The Story of My Heart* he could tell the variety and categories of all the weeds in a given hill. He would have been in his seventh heaven at Crouch End Playing Fields, for the pitches are densely weedy.

A line of Heine came to mind. You may know it. "*Ich hab im Traum geweiner.*" "I hath in mine dreams wept" might be the more favoured Englished version. Of course the Froggies and the Huns couldn't play cricket for nuts. It's not in their natures; heavy doses of déjà vu.

Believe me ever the admirer of those early stage pieces of yours, Landscape and Silence; would that be correct?

I have the honour to sign myself,

Amory.

(*Pause.*) P.S. When are we going to see a bit of *action* in one of your plays?

GHOST-VOICE: Amory Over England . . . !"

*Factory recreation gathering, loud dissonant clamour, raspberries blown.*

(*Persistent.*) "Amory Over England . . . !"

*Clamour as above, louder.*

VOICE 1: Blown spume, ruddy faces, thick ears, nothing daunted, briney smells, kippers and herring, shelly seafood, sinking tides, semen-stench of the great heaving Ocean. Tars puking their guts out from the rigging, gulls a long way from home, jolly sea shanties in the steamy fo'c'sle, here-today-gone-tomorrow philosophy of a livelier time. A time of sea kale, jugged hare and cherry tart, the sailor's hornpipe, the vigour of Rowlandson. Cuckolds all awry, the old dance of England.

"I would rather be blown up," Lady Astor once confided to Harold Nicolson (later Sir Harold), "than suck up."

"I believe this to be true," Harold noted with a perfectly straight face in his diary, without a hint of sarcasm or *noblesse oblige* . . .

. . . Bankruptcies up thirty percent, a new record, one shouldn't be surprised; and one more species of butterfly (pale blue) extinct. I shouldn't wonder.

Saw a tall well-made girl grimacing with embarrassment as she led her tall old father, bent double and grinning, across a crowded way. A sense of public distress not too common; not since Dickens's day.

Another wasted day, did I hear you say? Oh no, Sirs. Never! Never a wasted day, in the strange withdrawn world of the Fish.

A Pearl of Days!

*Medley of voices (scrambled) as at beginning, say 2 seconds. Studio laughter, 2 seconds. Reverse both, superimpose, hold for 2 seconds. Slam of heavy door echoing, lock shot home. End.*

*Allow some interval of silence before announcer.*

# Uncontrollable Laughter

## CHARLES LAMB AND HIS TIMES.

# CAST

NARRATOR

LECTURER BOY

VOICE

BACON

SCOT

MRS. COWDEN CLARKE

WOMAN

COLERIDGE

LEIGH HUNT

DRAYMAN

BOY 2

REV. FIELD

BOY 3

REV. BOYER

ANCIENT LORD

BYRON

LE GRICE

CHATEAUBRIAND

HOTEL MANAGER

DE QUINCEY

CRABB ROBINSON

FOOL 1

FOOL 2

COBBETT

HAZLITT CRITIC

ENGLISH HISTORIAN

DUTCH HISTORIAN

VOICE 2

VOICE 3

VOICE OF DOOM

FEMALE VOICE

OLD WOMAN

SCOTSMAN

OLD WORDSWORTH

EMERSON

OLD MAN

FRENCH CRITIC

WASHINGTON ALLSTON

WILLIS THE YANKEE

MARY LAMB

Sources: Saul Bellow (*Herzog*), Robert Burns (*Complete Illustrated Poems, Songs, and Ballads of Robert Burns*), Lord Byron ( *Selected Verse and Prose Works Including letters and extracts from Lord Byron's Journals and Diaries*), Chateaubriand (*Memoirs*), J. C. D. Clark (*Revolution and Rebellion: State and Society in England in the Seventeenth Century*), William Cobbett (*Rural Rides*), Samuel Taylor Coleridge (*Biographia Literaria*), Thomas De Quincey (*London Reminiscences, Recollections of the Lake Poets*), Ralph Waldo Emerson (*English Traits*), Jean Genet (*The Screens*), Leigh Hunt (*Autobiography*), James Joyce (*Finnegans Wake*), Francis Kilvert (*Kilvert's Diary*), Charles Lamb (*Selected Essays, Letters, Poems, The Essays of Elia*), E. V. Lucas (*The Life of Charles Lamb*), George Moore (*Principia Ethica*), Henry Crabb Robinson (*Diary, Reminiscences, and Correspondence*), Olive Schriner (*The Story of an African Farm*), Raymond Williams (*Culture & Society*), W. B. Yeats (*Autobiographies of W. B. Yeats*).

*Lecture hall. Stir of students.*

LECTURER: (*American.*) A strong common sense, which is not easy to unsettle or disturb, marks the English mind.

*Student stirrings.*

There is a hygienic simpleness, rough vigour . . . (*Rapid fade.*)

BOY: (*Aged 12–14, public school; rattles off illustrious names as if reading out cricket teams.*) Donne, Bunyon, Milton, Taylor, Evelyn, Pepys, Hooker, Cotton . . . (*hesitates, slight stutter*) m-m-Macaulay . . . (*Rapid fade.*)

*Lecture room. Stirrings. Packed hall. As before.*

LECTURER: . . . and closeness to the matter in hand, even in the second and third class of writer. And, I think, in the common style of the people, as one finds it in the citation of wills, letters and public documents, and in proverbs and forms of speech.

*Stir of students. Reaction.*

I could cite from the seventeenth-century sentences and phrases of edge matched in the nineteenth . . .

BOY: (*As before.*) Camden, Usher, Selden, Mede, Gadaker, Walton, Burton, More, Bentley, Bacon, Sydney, Herbert, Browne, Spencer, Chapman, Crashaw, Norris . . . (*Pause.*) Berkeley . . . (*Fade.*)

*Polite middle-distance applause at country cricket match.*

VOICE: George Borrow summons the Gypsies to hear his discourse on the Hebrews in Egypt, and reads to them the Apostles' Creed in Romany. "When I had concluded," quoth he, "I looked around me. The features of the assembly were twisted; and the eyes all turned upon me with a dreadful squint. (*Voice receding.*) Not an individual present but squinted."

*Taproom laughter.*
*Silence.*
*Purcell, "Music for a While." Alone, then under following, muted.*

EMERSON: (*On echo, speaking in large chamber.*) As we find stumps of vast trees in our exhausted soils, and have received traditions of their ancient fertility to tillage, so history reckons epochs in which the intellect of famed races became effete . . .
    They exert every variety of talent on a lower ground and may be said to live and act in a sub-mind.

*Fade.*
*Playground. City. Children playing near high walls, cries on echo.*

BOY: (*Age 8–10 Comprehensive School, North London accent.*) When Dido found Aeneas would not come (*halts, begins over*) When Dido found Aeneas could not come, She mourned in silence, And went Di Do Dum.

SCOT: (*Not sober.*) The night drave on wi' songs an clatter, and aye the ale was growing better . . .

*Brightly.*

MRS. COWDEN CLARKE: You ask me if I knew Charles Lamb?

*Barrel organ.*

(*Resigned.*) He dined here on Monday night at five. By seven he was so tipsy he could not stand. Martin Burney carried him home.

*Laughter, faintly.*

NARRATOR: Lamb was born at the Temple, London, in Crown Office Row, on February 10, 1775. (*Bow-bells*). He died at Bay Cottage, Edmonton, on December 27th, 1834. (*Edmonton church bell.*)

*Benedetto Marcello, Concerto for Oboe & Orchestra, under following.*

VOICE: (*French.*) Verseau.
Uranus. Air. *Non conformisme. Goût de l'expérience. Solidarité, délictasse, réalisme, sens de l'amitié, idees revolutionnares . . . (Pause.) travail de'équipe, esprit scientifique. Destin en dents de scie. Le Verseau travaille pour la collectivite et pour l'avenir.*

*Mooing of cow, lugubrious. Roll of thunder hard upon. Gust of wind.*

(*Irish, not sober.*) And bullvolley answers volley-ball!

*Hurdy-gurdy.*

(*Ghostly.*) Whither can I take wing from the oppression of human faces! Would I were in a wilderness of Apes, tossing cocoa nuts about, grinning and grinned at!

*Squall of rain hitting tin roof. Wind.*
*Bach, Toccata and Fugue in D Minor (J. J. Grunewald). Wind over Bach.*

NARRATOR: Stendhal was of the opinion that a secret principle of unhappiness undermined the English character. (*Pause.*) Melancholy is perhaps the natural emotional habit for an island people whose climate even in summer suspends the landscape in a perpetual haze. (*Distant foghorn.*) Melancholy, the projection of a psychic state. (*Hiss of escaping steam.*)

*Music as before, fainter. Voice over:*

COLERIDGE: (*Stout, middle-aged, ill-tempered.*) By deep feeling we make our Ideas dim; and this is what we mean by our life, ourselves.

*Foghorn.*
*Horse-drawn carriage over cobbles. London street cry. Young rose-seller. Purcell, "Music for a While."*

NARRATOR: Charles Lamb was born in the Inner Temple at No. 2 Crown Office Row on the 10th of February 1775—the youngest of seven children of whom three survived: himself, his brother John, and their sister Mary.

By profession Lamb's father was a scrivener; though his principle employment for many years was that of servant and assistant to Samuel Salt, a bencher of the Inner Temple.

The Lambs came from Lincolnshire. The mother's maiden name was Field. Little money could be spared for the education of the children. They used to visit their grandmother (*sheep-shearing leaks in here: clippers, tumult of baaing lambs and sheep*) who lived near Ware and acted as housekeeper and custodian of an old mansion.

*Sheep-shearing. Frantic baaing.*

Many years later Lamb wrote: "The oldest thing I remember is Mackery End. When the currants and gooseberries were quite ripe, grandmamma had a sheep-shearing. All the sheep stood under the trees to be sheared. (*Tumult.*) They were brought off the field by old Spot, the shepherd. I stood at the orchard-gate and saw him drive them all in.

When they cropped off all their wool, they looked very clean, and white, and pretty; but, poor things, they ran shivering about with cold, so that it was a pity to see them.

*Sheep-shearing, fainter.*

I can assure you there was no want of either roast beef or plumpudding after the sheep-shearing. My sister and I were permitted to sit up till it was almost dark, to see the company at supper.

*Convivial gathering.*
*Hertfordshire ballad under following:*

The common supper we had every night was very cheerful. Just before the men came out of the field, a large faggot was flung on the fire.

And then the crickets, for they love the fire, they used to sing. The milk was hung on a skillet over the fire, and then the men used to come and sit down at the long white table."

*Fade.*
*Leak-in sounds of schoolyard. Rough area. Boys shouting.*

In October 1782, Charles Lamb, a little boy between seven and eight, entered Christ's Hospital free school. Another new Bluecoat boy was to become his life-long friend: Samuel Taylor Coleridge. Coleridge was ten years Lamb's senior. Leigh Hunt was enrolled two years after Lamb left.

LEIGH HUNT: Our routine of life was this.

*Draws deep breath.*
*Pachelbel's Canon, up and under following:*

We rose to the call of a bell, at six in summer, and seven in winter. (*Distant handbell, sounded over music.*) And after combing ourselves and washing our hands and faces, went, at the call of another bell (*bell*), to breakfast. All this took about an hour.

From breakfast we proceeded to school, where we remained until eleven, winter and summer, and then had an hour's play. Dinner took place at twelve. Afterwards was a little play till one, when we went again to school, and remained until five in summer, and four in winter. At six was the supper. In summer, then, we played till eight. In winter, we proceeded from supper to bed. On Sundays, the schooltime of the other days was occupied in church, both morning and evening. And as the Bible was read to us every day before every meal, and on going to bed, besides prayers and graces, we rivalled the monks in the religious part of our duties.

*Fade.*

BOY: Prim Betsy Chambers
      Decayed in her members
      No longer remembers
      Things as she once did.

*Schoolyard cries.*

DRAYMAN: (*Somerset, dense.*)
      When Ardnose was a man
      He could not be pealed
      At the old sport he wan
      When Ardnose was a man
      (*Belch.*)
      And now he neither may nor can.

*Arrow hitting target. Second hard upon first.*

LEIGH HUNT: The Under Grammar-master, in my time, was the Rev. Mr. Field. He was a good-looking man, very gentlemanly . . . He had the reputation of being admired by the ladies. (*Pause.*) I believe he once wrote a play. (*Pause.*) A man of more handsome incompetence for his situation perhaps did not exist. He would come late of a morning, and went away soon in the afternoon.

*Schoolroom.*

BOY 2: (*Alto.*) Are you not a great fool, sir?

*Pause.*

REV. FIELD: (*Absently.*) Yes, child.

BOY 3: (*Tenor, cheeky.*) Isn't your daughter a pretty girl?

*Pause.*

REV. FIELD: (*As before.*) Yes, child.

*Class tittering.*

NARRATOR: The other master was the Rev. James Boyer.

*Crash of cane on desk.*

REV. BOYER: (*Furious.*) Sirrah, do you propose to set your wits at me?

LEIGH HUNT: (*Sotto voce.*) This to a poor trembling child with the maternal milk hardly dry upon its lips.

*Door violently opened on rowdy class.*

REV. BOYER: (*At limit of patience.*) Od's my life, Sirrah, I have a great mind to whip you!

*Boyer exits, door slammed. Diminished uproar. Door opens immediately to expletory yell from Boyer.*

(*Violently.*) AND I WILL TOO!

NARRATOR: (*Urbane.*) He adopted a method of whipping a boy and reading the Debates at the same time. A paragraph and a lash between. (*Sounds for this.*) Which in those times, when Parliamentary oratory was most at a height and flourishing, was not calculated to impress the patient with a veneration for the diffuser graces of rhetoric.

BYRON: Will you erect a gibbet in every field, and hang up men—

*House of Lords.*

—like scarecrows? Or will you proceed—as you must to bring this measure into effect—by decimation? Place the country under martial law? Depopulate and lay waste all around you? And restore Sherwood Forest as an acceptable gift to the crown, in its former condition of a royal chase and asylum for outlaws?

*Stirrings in House of Lords. Byron's maiden speech.*

(*Raising pitch of oration.*) Suppose this man—and there are ten thousand such from whom you may select your victims—dragged into court, to be tried for this new offense, by this new law; still, there are two things waiting to convict and condemn him; and these are, in my opinion, twelve butchers for a jury, and Jeffreys for a judge!

*Prolonged applause at Prom concert, Albert Hall. Brief. Cut to hanging. Chaplin's prayer. Trap opening, victim on rope. Sudden silence. High ascending note on piccolo for soul launched into eternity.*
*Leak-in: Accolade for Byron (House of Lords). Cries of "Here, here!"*

ANCIENT LORD: (*Disgusted.*) Sticky wicket.

*Boy, homesick, snivelling.*

REV. BOYER: (*Thunderous.*) Boy! The school is your father! Boy! The school is your mother! Boy! The school is your brother! The school is your sister! The school is your first cousin, and your second cousin, and all the rest of your relations! (*Crescendo.*) Let's have no more crying!

*Silence.*

*Haydn, Nocturne in F Major.*

NARRATOR: (*Calm.*) Coleridge in his *Biographia Literaria* wrote of the terrible Boyer—whom he calls, with characteristic inaccuracy, Bowyer.

COLERIDGE: (*Choleric, middle-aged.*) At school I enjoyed the inestimable advantage of a very sensible, though at the same time a very severe master—the Rev. James Bowyer. He early moulded my taste to the preference of Demosthenes to Cicero, of Homer and Theocritus to Virgil, and again of Virgil to Ovid. I learned from him that poetry, even of the loftiest, and seemingly, that of the wildest odes, had a logic of its own, as severe as that of science.

*Hiss of escaping steam.*
*Bach, Piano Concerto in D Minor. Up, then under following harangue:*

REV. BOYER: (*Somewhat distantly, subdued.*) Harp? . . . HARP? Lyre? Pen and ink, boy, you mean! Muse, boy, Muse? Your nurse's daughter, you mean! Pierian spring? (*Fainter.*) Oh aye! The cloister pump, I suppose!

LEIGH HUNT: His clothes were cut short; his hands out of the sleeves with tight wristbands as if ready for execution; and as he generally wore grey worsted stockings, very tight, with a little balustrade leg, his whole appearance presented something formidably succinct, hard, and mechanical.

NARRATOR: Coleridge studied under Boyer; Lamb, under the Rev. Field. The characters of the two masters were as divergent as that of the inhabitants on either side of the Pyrenees.

*Whipping. Bawling of victim.*

The same might be said of Coleridge and Lamb, who were to be drinking partners in the Salutation and Cat. (*Pause.*) Another Christ's Hospitaller, Charles Valentine Le Grice, remembered Lamb . . .

*Fade.*

LE GRICE: His eyes were not each of the same colour. With an expression which might lead you to think that he was of Jewish descent.

His step was plantigrade, which made his walks low and peculiar, adding to the staid appearance of his figure. I never heard his name mentioned without the addition of "Charles"—although, as there was no other boy of the name of Lamb, the addition was unnecessary. He . . . stuttered, and was indulged by his schoolfellows and masters on that account. He stole along with all the self-consciousness of a young monk.

NARRATOR: The "King's boys" were the mathematical pupils. Bred for the sea, they were the terror of the other boys. Frequent and severe chastisement was designed to make the lads hardy and to give them early sea-habits. All for the fugitive Monarch, Charles II, who, dressed as a lady's servant, makes a fleeting and curious appearance in Kilvert's Diary.

VOICE: No occasion for laying on the lash was ever let drop. There was one Higgins: this petty Nero actually branded a boy with a red-hot iron (*brief scream*), as the boy had somehow offended him.

Lamb was a good Latin scholar but because of the poverty of his family and of a defect in his speech was denied the opportunity of an academic education.

VOICE 2: (*Deeper.*) Around 1791 he obtained a post in the South Sea House, where his brother John already held an appointment, and in 1792 was promoted to clerkship in the accountant's office of the East

India Company, in whose service he was to continue until 1825. This post gave him economic security, on a modest scale, for the whole of his life.

*Pachelbel, Chaconne. Alone, then under following.*

NARRATOR: On the death of Samuel Salt in 1792 the Lambs had to give up their home in the Temple and move into lodgings in Little Queen Street where they struggled along on Charles's small salary—£40 per annum after three year's non-paid probation, plus a bond of £500 as a security for good behaviour—and his sister's earnings from needlework.

*Music out.*
*Feet dragging, close-up breathing, heavy sigh.*

By 1794 the four pound London loaf cost 6d ha'penny, in a population of two and one-third million. A year later the same loaf was up to one shilling. Following a fit of temporary insanity midway through the year, Lamb was confined for six weeks in Hoxton lunatic asylum. His sister Mary was now supporting a family of four. In September 1796 Mary, in a sudden outburst of psychotic rage, stabbed her mother to death with a table knife. And the four pound London loaf had risen to one and tuppence. By 1800 it was one and four pence. In the same year income tax was introduced to pay for the French war (Broadside). Abolished with the peace, it would be reintroduced in 1841 by Robert Peel, at 7p in the £.

In 1782 Walpole could write: "I know nothing, for I live as if I were just arrived from Syria and were performing quarantine. Nobody dares stir out of their own house. We are robbed and murdered if we do but step over the threshold of the chandler's shop for a pennyworth of plums."

*Distant cannon.*

VOICE: Highwaymen were particularly busy that summer. Gambling at Almack's could involve a thousand meadows and cornfields staked on one throw. There was a fashion for suicide. Mill's "softening of manners" had not yet come in.

*Mournful ship's hooter downriver.*

NARRATOR: Wheat, at 60s. a quarter in 1794, had risen to 142s. by 1800. And, since bread made up one-fourth of a poor family's budget, the consumption of flour fell by a third in London.

In 1844 the railways came in. (*Early locomotive crossing viaduct, whistle blowing.*) By 1848 the British Empire (*introduce Elgar recording of "The King's Hunting Jig," ending; Albert Hall 15/8/74*) was reckoned to contain 222,000,000 souls—perhaps a fifth of the total population of the globe, compromising a territory of five million square miles. And forty million of those were of British stock.

*Ovation for Elgar. Encores. Hold as long as possible. Abruptly cut.*

VOICE: Chateaubriand has very impudently laid the blame for the start of the French Revolution on an Englishman: a certain Mr. Folkes who was staying at the Hotel Royal.

*Debussy, Arabesque No. 1.*

CHATEAUBRIAND: The July Revolution began badly. Then a shot from the Hotel Royal (*champagne cork popping*) in the Rue des Pyramides decided matters.

A certain Mr. Folkes, an Englishman staying at the hotel, had taken it into his head to fire on the Guards below. (*Second cork popping.*)

The soldiers replied with a volley (*volley, muted*)—and Mr. Folkes (*contemptuously*) and a couple of servants fell dead.

*Arabesque intervenes briefly.*

This is the way in which the English, who live a sheltered life on their island, take revolutions to other nations. Provided they can sell a piece of calico, what do they care if they plunge a nation into calamity? You find them in the four corners of the world mixed up with quarrels which are no concern of theirs.

HOTEL MANAGER: What can you expect of a man ou ees al-ways inspect-ing ees teeth in ze look-ing glass?

*Subterranean tapping on sewer pipes, distant. Dripping water, close. Debussy under.*

CHATEAUBRIAND: In Paris a rumour spread that an army was arriving by way of the Montmartre sewers.

*Sky-rocket going up at fireworks display, cut before the burst. Aerial sizzling.*

VOICE: A ditch had been dug in front of the colonnade of the Louvre, and a priest in surplice and stole was praying beside it. The dead were being laid to rest there.

*Tolling bell, Paris.*

CHATEAUBRIAND: In a crowded cafe near the Palais Royal I was dying from the heat. There was a man wearing a jacket with the sleeves turned up: a man with black hands. A sinister face, such burning eyes, and he kept trying to come up to me. I had seen him before. I never learnt either his name or what he wanted of me.

*Doleful bell.*

*Paris church bell. Couple of seconds. Mix into Parc du Princes, England-France international. French score. Crowd wild. Hold for full effect. Rapid fade.*

(*Tired.*) Moments of crisis produce a reduplication of the life of men. The breaches of the laws and the disruption of daily life all add to the interest of this disorder.

*Music under: "Ô ma tendre musette."*

The Revolution would have carried me with it if only it had not begun with a series of crimes. I saw the first head carried on the end of a pike . . . in my eyes murder will never be an object of admiration, or an argument for freedom. I was horrified by these cannibal feasts.

*Music as above briefly. Then under.*

Have I not met in France the whole of this race of Brutus, in the service of Caesar and his police? The levellers and cut-throats turned into valets and spies, and even less naturally into Dukes, Counts and Barons. How thoroughly medieval! (*Rapid fade.*)

*Arabesque again.*
*River flowing. Oars. Hold.*

NARRATOR: In the winter of 1804—or possibly the beginning of 1805—the opium-eater De Quincey, then aged nineteen, first encountered Lamb.

DE QUINCEY: I had been told that he was never to be found at home except in the evenings. And to have called on him then would have been, in a manner, forcing myself upon his hospitalities, and at a moment when he might have confidential friends with him. Besides that, he was sometimes tempted away to the theaters. I went, therefore, to the India House . . . (*Rapid fade.*)

*Kumar Sharma's "Improvisation," Purcell Room recording 25/5/73, towards end. Hold for 3–4 seconds, then under following:*

. . . After some trouble, I was shown into a small room, or else a small section of a large one, in which was a very lofty writing-desk, separated by a still higher railing, from that part of the floor on which the profane—the laity, like myself (*very dissipated voice in ruins*)—were allowed to approach the *clerus*, or clerk rulers of the room. (*Pause.*)

*Music, as above.*

Within the railing sat, to the best of my remembrance, six quill-driving gentlemen . . . who were then driving it in act as well as habit, as if they supposed me a spy sent by some superior power to report upon the situation of affairs as surprised by me . . . they were all too profoundly immersed in their oriental studies to have any sense of my presence.

Consequently I was reduced to the necessity of announcing myself and my errand. I walked, therefore, into one of the two open doorways of the railings, and stood closely by the high stool of him who occupied the first place within the little aisle.

I touched his arm, by way of recalling him from his lofty Leadenhall speculations to this sublunary world. And, presenting my letter, asked if that gentleman—pointing to the address—were really a citizen of the present room, for I had been repeatedly mislead, by the directions given me, into wrong rooms. (*Pause.*)

"*Improvisation.*"

The gentleman smiled; it was a smile not to be forgotten. (*Pause.*) This was Lamb.

The seat upon which he sat was a very high one; so absurdly high, by the way, that I can imagine no possible use or sense in such an altitude, unless it was to restrict the occupant from playing truant at the fire, by opposing Alpine difficulties to his descent.

*Guarded laughter of clerks.*

CRABB ROBINSON: He related a droll history of a clerk in the India House suspected of living on human flesh.

*Subdued laughter of clerks.*

VOICE: Following a heavy bout of drinking, Tommy Bye, the India House Petrarch—his poetry resembled Petrarch's, Lamb said, if Petrarch had been born a fool—awoke the next day to find his salary docked by one-sixth, after thirty-six years tolerably good service.

*Expiring laughter of clerks.*
*Atmosphere for Waterloo.*
"*Ca ira.*"
*Pierre Jugell, "Spell."*
"Veni Creator," *adolescent solo.*
*Wind blowing in heavy foliage.*
*Juxtapose under following text.*

VOICE OF DOOM: (*Rapid delivery.*) The clerk coughed in the church and two girls in grey dresses passed quietly through and moved about among the graves on the north side.

Then a woman in deep mourning moved slowly down the path and the clerk began to ring the bell for service.

Hannah Gore was born with six fingers on each hand but not with six toes. Her feet were all right. The sixth finger was cut off on each hand.

*Draws deep shuddering breath.*

. . . William Wordsworth was a tall man. Dorothy was short and square. Towards the end of his life he could not bear the act of writing. He was very absent and had been known to walk unconsciously through a flock of sheep without perceiving them. (*Sheep-fold, repeat.*) He did not care much for society and preferred the society of women to that of men . . .

*Insane female laugh.*

(*Drawing breath before launching hurriedly into text.*) Went to Cabalva in the teeth of the bitter east wind and the ground freezing like iron. They were grinding apples. Some ragged men were cutting the golden green mistletoe boughs out of the Cabalva orchards where they grew in thick bushes and bunches on the apple trees, and carrying them away.

An inch of snow fell last night. (*Pause.*) As we walked to Draycot it began again. As we passed Langley Burial Church we heard the strains of the quadrille band on the ice. The afternoon grew murky and when we began to skate the air was thick with falling snow.

The Lancers was beautifully skated when it grew dark and the ice was lighted with Chinese lanterns and the intense glare of blue, green and crimson lights and magnesium riband made the whole place as light as day.

Then the people skated with torches.

I went to see old Isaac Giles. He lamented the loss of his famous old pear tree. He told me he was nearly eighty and remembered seeing the Scots Greys passing through Chippenham on their way to Waterloo. They looked very much down, he said, for they knew where they were going . . .

*"Home Sweet Home," oldest possible 78 RPM.*

FEMALE VOICE: Many small articles make up a sum, and hey ho for Caleb Quotem, oh!

*"Home Sweet Home" continuing under following:*

BYRON: Fine day—few mares' tails portending change, but the sky clear, upon the whole. Rode—fired pistols—good shooting. Coming back, met an old man. Charity—purchased a shilling's worth of salvation.

*Horse galloping over grass.* BYRON's *pistols fired. Horse approaching in a lather of sweat, heavy equine panting, hooves on sodden ground.*

(*Urbane as ever.*) Returning, on the bridge near the mill, met an old woman. I asked her age.

OLD WOMAN: (*Italian.*) *Tre croci.*

BYRON: I asked my groom what the devil her three crosses meant. He said, ninety years . . . and that she had five years to boot! Ninety-five years! (*Rapid fade.*)

*Wind in summer trees. Distant cannons of Waterloo.*

VOICE: (*Historian, ultra-bland.*) One century was expiring; another being born. But there were overlappings and stretchings. The lifetime of Blake might, in general, be considered the decisive period: 1757 to 1827. Or from the publication of Adam Smith's *The Wealth of Nations* in 1776 to the Peterloo riots. Waterloo intervening . . .

*"Veni Creator," solo. Up and then under following:*

CHATEAUBRIAND: On 18th June 1815, I left Ghent about noon by the Brussels gate. I was going to finish my walk alone on the high road. I had taken Caesar's *Commentaries* with me and I strolled along, immersed in my reading. I was over three miles from the town when I thought I heard a dull rumbling. I stopped and looked up at the sky, which was fairly cloudy, wondering whether I should walk on or turn back towards Ghent for fear of a storm. I listened. I heard nothing more but the cry of a moorhen in the rushes and the sound of a village clock.

*"Veni Creator" ends. Begin Wagner, Siegfried solo from* Gotterdammerung, *singer about to enter cave.*

I had not gone thirty steps when the rumbling began again (*thunder over Wagner*) . . . now short, now drawn-out, and at irregular intervals.

Sometimes it was perceptible only through a trembling of the air, which was so far away that it communicated itself to the ground as it passed over those vast plains . . .

*Wagner and ominous roll of thunder.*

The detonations, less prolonged, less undulating, less interrelated than those of thunder, gave rise in my mind to the idea of a battle. I found myself opposite a poplar tree planted at the corner of a hop-field.

*Wind in poplar tree.*

I crossed the road (*footsteps on road*) and leant against the trunk of the tree, with my face turned in the direction of Brussels.

*Fade-out Wagner. Fade-in Viennese waltz. Under following. No break in delivery.*

A southerly wind sprang up and brought me more distinctly the sound of artillery (*distant waltz, breeze, artillery mixed*). That great battle, nameless as yet, whose echoes I was listening to at the foot of a poplar, and for whose unknown obsequies a village clock had just struck, was Waterloo!

*Village clock striking two.*

(*Close, emotional.*) Was not every sound that reached my ears the last sigh of a Frenchman?

*Brief silence.*

CRABB ROBINSON: (*Crusty, writing up diary.*) December 21st, 1816 . . . proposed to Cargill, as the day was inviting, a walk to Highgate.

*Grandfather clock beginning to strike two melodiously under following. Diarist pauses, listens, scratching of quill as he continues.*

We enjoyed the day out of town, though within was a thick mist. We found Coleridge at home, and we enjoyed his conversation for an hour and a half. He looked ill, and indeed Mr. Gillman says he has been very ill. His bowels have been diseased, which he says is a family disease.

He explained at our request, and as I had anticipated, his idea of fancy, styling it memory without judgment, and, of course, not filling that place in a chart of the mind which imagination holds, and which in his *Lay Sermons* he has admirably described as the "reconciling and mediatory power which, incorporating the reason in image of the sense, and organizing it as it were (*voice rises as confusion grows*) the FLUX of the senses by the performance and self-circling energies of the reason, gives birth (*rather lost here, fading*) to a SYSTEM of symbols . . ."

NARRATOR: At Waterloo, for not so many hours one day, 200,000 soldiers fought. 65,000 were slaughtered, 15,000 English falling before lunch. (*Pause.*) Was it a sunny day?

*Polite scattered applause at country cricket game.*

Eleven months later Byron rode over it and was surprised how small the field was. The ravages of that day were again obscured by growth.

BYRON: (*Lordly.*) It is singular, how we lose the impression of what ceases to be. I allow sixteen minutes, though I never counted them, to any given or supposed impression. From whatever place we commence, we know where it all must end. It is all a mystery. I feel most things, but I know nothing . . . (*Fade.*)

VOICE: (*Rough, mocking.*) Many small articles make up a sum, and hey ho for Caleb Quotem, oh!

LECTURER: (*American academic, sourly.*) After Napoleon fell, the ambitious young man carried his power drive into the boudoir. And there the women took command.

*Macaw screech, zoo.*

VOICE: (*Irish: high, nervy, up and down emotional scale.*) If, as I think, minds and metals correspond, the goldsmiths of Paris foretold the French Revolution when they substituted steel for unserviceable gold, in the manufacture of the more expensive jewel work, and made those large flat steel buttons for men of fashion wherein the card-sharpers were able to study the reflection of the cards. (*Pause.*) All is hatred and bitterness: wheel biting upon wheel, a roar of steel or iron tackle, a mill of argument grinding all things down to mediocrity.

(*Welsh.*) The lords of yesterday will tell the lords of today that nothing must be protected as much as a little heap of garbage. Let no one throw out all the sweepings. One never knows. Keep a little mudpile in reserve, in a corner.

(*Scots.*) When will society disappear? What accidents will suspend its movements?

*Cock crowing.*

. . . To mention but one point in thousands.

*Children wailing.*

(*Warming to theme.*) That man sees his countless furrows ripen; this one will never possess anything but the six feet of earth lent to his grave by his native land. Now how many ears of corn can six feet of earth give a dead man?

*Amplified on echo: laughter of the clerks.*

. . . As education reaches down to the lower classes, the later gradually discover the secret canker which gnaws away at the irreligious social order.

*House collapsing, slow motion.*

... The disproportion of conditions and fortunes was endurable as long as it remained concealed; but as soon as this disproportion was generally perceived, the old order received its death blow.

*House of Lords. "Here, here!" Repeat.*
*Arabesque, repeat.*

CHATEAUBRIAND: An escutcheoned old lady and an emblazoned old baron, watching over the last of their daughters and the last of their sons in a feudal manor, appeared in the guise of what the English call "character." There was nothing provincial or narrow about that life, because it was not ordinary life.

*Delicate blowing of nose.*

... In summerhouses and palaces (*hunting horn*) scattered around the Crown Forests, long-haired Kings were engaged in mysterious pleasures.

*High-pitched male giggle, girl's laugh, door closing. Giggle and laugh behind closed door.*

VOICE: Wordsworth had a theory that homes should be the same colour as the soil.
(*Irish.*) Their one great poet who, after brief blossoming, was cut and sawn up into planks of obvious utility.

ENGLISH HISTORIAN: (*Ignoring interruptions above, sonorous delivery.*) Separated from the Continent by a long war, the English at the end of the eighteenth century preserved their national manners and character. There were still only one people, in whose name the sovereign power was wielded by an aristocratic government; only two great classes existed, bound by ties of friendship and common interest: patrons and dependents . . .

That jealous class called the bourgeoisie in France, which was beginning to arise in England, was yet unknown: there was nothing between the rich landowners and the man who plied a trade. Everything had not yet become machinery in the manufacturing professions . . .

*Spinning jenny.*

. . . folly in the privileged classes.

*Baying of foxhounds.*

CHATEAUBRIAND: They hunted the fox or shot pheasants in the autumn (*shotguns*), ate fat geese at Christmas, shouted "Hurrah!" for roast beef (*cooking on spit*), grumbled about the present, praised the past, cursed Pitt and the war, which sent up the price of port, and went to bed drunk only to begin life all over again the next day.

They were convinced that the glory of Great Britain would never fade as long as they sang "God Save the King" (*brass band opening up with national anthem, muted, then under following*), maintained the rotten boroughs, and secretly sent hares and partridges to market under the name of "lions" and "'ostriches."

FOOL 1: (*Upper-class playgoer.*) I say, whom do you prefer, Pitt, Disraeli, or Burke?

FOOL 2: Sheridan.

*Guffawing.*
*Geoffrey Burgon, "Golden Eternity," Vesuvius Ensemble. Hold for 5–6 seconds; fade choral under following then piano full strength as before.*

NARRATOR: But where is Charles Lamb in all this? (*Pause.*) The Emperor Napoleon—previously a "lion"—has, in Chateaubriand's estimation, become a "hyena," It is not known what the employee of the India House thought of the Battle of Waterloo, or of the man who lost it.

*Footsteps on country road. Call of high plover.*

CRABB ROBINSON: (*Crusty as before, tedious, writing up diary, quill scratching.*) I supped with Mrs. Thornthwaite and read Wordsworth's ode. It has heavy passages. The verses on the Russian winter are, perhaps, the most delightful in the volume . . . (*Fade.*)

*Continuing, footsteps on country road.*
*"The Sentry" from Peter Maxwell Davies's* Eight Songs from a Mad King, *recording by The Fires of London.*

NARRATOR: Bach, it is said, walked two hundred miles to hear Buxtehude play. Wordsworth in his lifetime tramped between one hundred seventy five and one hundred eighty five thousand miles, before pedometers were invented. Dorothy Wordsworth would think nothing of walking from Brinsop into Hereford, six miles and back, for a thimble. Lamb averaged twenty miles a day, to his sister's fifteen. And De Quincey, on first meeting Coleridge, walked twenty miles by night . . . (*Fade.*)

*Solitary footsteps on country road.*
*"The Sentry," as before, under following:*

DE QUINCEY: About ten o'clock at night I took leave of him; and feeling that I could not go easily to sleep after the excitement of the day, and fresh from the spectacle of powers so majestic already besieged by decay, I determined to return to Bristol through the coolness of the night.

The roads, though in fact a section of the great highway between seaports so turbulent as Bristol and Plymouth, were as quiet as garden walks.

*Fade-out music.*

. . . Once only I passed through the expiring fires of a village fair or wake. That interruption excepted, through the whole stretch of forty miles from Bridgewater to the Hot Wells, I saw no living creature, but a surly dog who followed me for a mile along a park wall, and a man who was moving about in the halfway town of Cross.

The turnpike gates were all opened (*turnpike gate opening*) by a mechanical contrivance from a bedroom window. I seemed to myself in solitary possession of the whole sleeping country. The summer night was . . . (*brief cough*) calm. No sound, except once or twice the cry of a child as I was passing (*cry of child*) the windows of cottages, ever broke upon the utter silence. And all things contrived to throw back my thoughts upon the extraordinary person I had quitted . . . (*Fade, with cry of curlew.*)

*Miniature mechanical organ, property formerly of George III. "The Country Walk" from* Eight Songs for a Mad King.

One night, as often happened, during the Peninsular War, Wordsworth and I had walked from Grasmere, about midnight, in order to meet the carrier who brought the London newspapers by a circuitous course from Keswick . . . Wordsworth and I had walked out to a distance of about three miles. Upon one of those occasions, when some great crisis in Spain was daily apprehended, we had waited for an hour or more, sitting upon one of the many huge blocks of stone.

... At intervals, Wordsworth had stretched himself at length on the highroad, applying his ear to the ground, so as to catch any sound of wheels that might be groaning along in the distance ... (*Fade.*)

*Wind.*

NARRATOR: In those days it took six weeks—or was it six months?—for letters to arrive from China.

*Frog-pond. Frogs croaking. Rain begins. Rain on pond. Rain stronger, frog-croaking weaker.*

COBBETT: (*Surrey accent.*) Whence come the hurtleberries in some places, and the raspberries in others? (*Single frog croaks.*) Whence come fish in new-made places where no fish have ever been put before? (*Double frog-croak.*) What causes horsehair to become living things?

*Weaker single croak, more distant.*

What causes frogs to come in drops of rain, or those drops of rain to turn to frogs, the moment they are on the earth? What causes mosquitoes (*mosquito*) to come in rainwater, caught in a glass, covered over immediately with oil paper, tied down and so kept till full of those winged torments?

*High-pitched buzzing of insects.*

What causes flounders, brown on one side, white on the other, mouth sideways, with tail, fins, and all, leaping alive in the inside of a rotten sheep's (*demented buzzing of a bluebottle fly*), and of every rotten sheep's, LIVER? Answer these questions, prigs.

*Frog chorus in background.*

NARRATOR: Coleridge had powdered his hair and looked like Bacchus. Lamb made a short visit to Paris and developed a taste for frogs—nicer on the palate than rabbits. His sister was locked away for two months. Lamb was suffering from a bad eye, caused by another clerk, Wadd the "sad shuffler," throwing ink into it. And was supplying the chronically impecunious Coleridge with one hundred quills from the India House. Leigh Hunt had not long finished a two-year prison sentence for a libel on the Regent printed in his paper *The Examiner.* During a bad winter Lamb often visited him in prison. He had a furnished room in the infirmary of the Surrey Gaol, cultivated the garden and wrote, was visited by his family—quite in the manner of Cobbett.

VOICE: Leigh Hunt tells a story of Lamb drunk, as so often in the company of Hazlitt, running along the top of a high parapet wall in the Temple—so much to the terror of Hazlitt, that the latter cried out in a sort of rage.

HAZLITT: (*Wildly.*) Lamb, if you don't come down, I shall push you over!

*Big Ben.*

VOICE: Hazlitt and Crabb Robinson did not see eye to eye.

*Crabb Robinson's chambers. Grandfather clock, coal fire, Big Ben continuing to strike outside.*

CRABB ROBINSON: (*Ill-humoured.*) Hazlitt wrong as well as offensive in almost all he said. When pressed, he does not deny what is wrong in the character of Bonaparte. And yet he triumphs and rejoices in all the late events. Hazlitt and myself once felt alike on politics, and now our hopes and fears are directly opposed. Hazlitt retains all his hatred of kings and bad governments, and believing them to be incorrigible, he from a principle of revenge, rejoices that they are punished . . . (*Fade.*)

HAZLITT: (*Acidly.*) Let the enemy of old tyrannical governments triumph, I am glad, and do not much care how the new government turns out.

CRITIC: (*With some venom.*) Hazlitt talks pimply—a red-and-white corruption rising up in little imitation of mountains upon maps, but containing nothing, and discharging nothing, except their own humours . . . (*Fade.*)

DUTCH HISTORIAN: During the Napoleonic Wars the National Debt had more than tripled, and in the years after peace was formally won a third of England's total revenue was spent on interest to the fund-raisers, in addition to a considerable sum paid in pensions to half-pay officers and their relatives, and to others, including the Duke of Wellington. Cobbett considered the Iron Duke a parasite. Cobbett and Burke, critics of the new industrial society, saw the emerging class-structure, saw the consequences in class conflict.

Coleridge, for one, detested Cobbett's politics.

COLERIDGE: (*Choleric.*) I entertain towards the Cobbetts, and all those creatures, and the Foxites who had fostered the vipers, a feeling more like hatred than I ever bore to other flesh and blood . . . (*Fade.*)

*Military flogging.*

COBBETT: (*Speaking in the open air.*) All our properties, all our manners, all our minds changed. This, which I noticed, took place within forty, and, most of it, within ten years. The small gentry, to about the third rank upwards—considering there to be five ranks from the smallest gentry up to the greatest nobility—all went, nearly to a man, and the smallest farmers along with them.

DUTCH HISTORIAN: What were seen at the end of the seventeenth century as disparate interests, between which a man must choose and in the act of choice declare himself poet or sociologist, were, nominally, at the beginning of the nineteenth century, seen as interlocking interests: a conclusion about personal feelings became a conclusion about society, and an observation of natural beauty carried a necessary moral reference to the whole and unified life of man . . . (*Fade.*)

BYRON: (*Rather weary.*) All the discoveries which have yet been made have multiplied little but existence. An extirpated disease is succeeded by some new pestilence; and a discovered world has brought little to the old one, except the pox first and freedom afterwards . . . (*Fade.*)

NARRATOR: Lamb disliked Byron. Possibly he was jealous of him. To be Byron's friend, like the elegant voluptuary Moore, was, in Lamb's eyes, to be suspect. Shelley's squeaky voice irritated him. His comments on their deaths were very cold. Shelley had "gone down to the deep insolvent."

VOICE: Near Canterbury Cobbett was struck with the words written upon a board which was fastened upon a pole, standing in a garden near a little box of a house.

COBBETT: (*On echo.*) "Paradise Place. Spring guns and steel traps are set here."

*Rabbit in death throes; fainter and fainter into silence.*

DUTCH HISTORIAN: (*With relish.*) In the time Cobbett writes of, the wages of labourers in Hampshire had sunk to 6s. a week. It was even worse in Wiltshire. The tax-gatherers and dead-weights had moved in for the kill.

And because prices rose with the war, people believed that war was the cause. In reaction, the currency had been inflated by great issues of paper money.

To have plenty of everything that made life easy and pleasant was formerly one of the great characteristics of the English people. Good eating, good drinking, good clothing, good lodging; without these, people do not really live: it is mere staying upon the earth.

*Bonfire, up and under following:*

COBBETT: (*Speaking in open air.*) Good government is known from bad government by this infallible test: that, under the former the labouring people are well-fed and well-clothed, and under the latter, they are badly fed and badly clothed. A full belly to the labourer is, in my opinion, the foundation of public morals and the only source of public peace. (*Fade.*)

*Bagpipes playing dirge, up and under following:*

SCOTSMAN: Byron's funeral climbed Highgate Hill. Coleridge was being treated for opium-addiction by Dr. Gillman, close by. Forty-seven carriages followed—most of them empty—as an empty gesture from the nobility. His Lordship had died in someone else's war. Lady Caroline Lamb, recovering from an illness, asked whose funeral it was.

BYRON: (*On echo.*) The King-times are fast finishing;
　　　There will be blood shed like water,
　　　And tears like mist.

VOICE: (*Youth.*) Went into the Tump to see young Meredith who has had his jaw locked for six months, a legacy of mumps. He has been to Hereford Infirmary where they kept him two months, gave him chloroform and wrenched his jaws open gradually by a screw lever. (*Pause, gloomily*). But they could not do him any good.

NARRATOR: Lady Byron expired from a fit of uncontrollable rage upon opening a bill presented by her upholsterers. Her son in his time had run up a tailor's bill of £900. The Missolonghi medicos bled him white.

*Small spring breaking.*

CRABB ROBINSON: (*Scratching with quill.*) Wordsworth says that Bensen has informed him that from the particular friends of Byron he has learnt that Byron had an impression that he was the offspring of a demon . . . (*Fade.*)

NARRATOR: In 1823 the Lambs moved from Russell Street to Colebrook Row in Islington. It was the continuation of a number of moves: Islington, Enfield, Edmonton.

OLD MAN: (*Tentatively.*) Mr. Lamb was very fond of seeing the sun set from Cannonbury Tower.

*Street noises, Cannonbury.*

His occasional rambles rarely extended beyond Finchley, on the north. Dulwich College—for its pictures—on the south; and

TurnhamGreen, on the west. The east (*cackles*) . . . was unknown to him.

(*Pause.*) He was hand and glove with Goodman Symes, who was tenant of the Tower, and a brother antiquarian in a small way. (*Pause.*) He took pleasure in entertaining Mr. Lamb in the oak-panelled chamber where Goldsmith wrote his *Traveller* and supped on buttermilk. Islington he also visited, and drank ale at the old Queen's Head before it was pulled down.

*Bach, Toccata and Fugue in D Minor.*

FRENCH CRITIC: I was at James Valpy's one evening in June 1818, in his office where the candles must be lit at midday, and the fire in June, when a little dark old fellow came in. One could only distinguish a head, and then big shoulders, then a delicate body, and finally two *artistically* slender legs, which were almost imperceptible.

Under his arm was a green umbrella, and over his eyes a very old hat. There was neither health nor strength and scarcely sufficient reality in those poor spindles, clothed in stockings of Chinese silk, ending in impossible feet, encased in large shoes, which placed flatly on the ground advanced in the manner of a web-footed creature. But one did not notice these singularities. It seemed as if something purely intellectual was before you. Wit, sweetness, melancholy and gaiety gushed in torrents from this extraordinary physiognomy . . . (*Rapid fade.*)

NARRATOR: This curious apparition—"the little dark old fellow"—was Charles Lamb aged forty-three: a kind of web-footed La Bruyère, as described by the critic Philarète Chasles in the *Revue des Deux Mondes*, under the title "Le dernier Humoriste Anglais."

WASHINGTON ALLSTON: (*Forceful, American accent.*) Lamb was present when a naval officer was giving an account of an action which he had been in, and to illustrate the carelessness and disregard of life at such times, said that a sailor had both his legs shot off, and as his shipmates were carrying him below, another shot came and took off both his arms. They, thinking he was pretty much used up, though life was still in him, threw him out of a port. "Shame, damned shame," stuttered out Lamb, "he m-m-might have l-lived to have been an a-a-ornament to Society!"

VOICE: Wordsworth, the great poet, is coming to town! He is to have apartments in the Mansion House. He says he does not see much difficulty in writing like Shakespeare, if he had a mind to try it.

VOICE 2: (*Sceptical.*) It is clear that nothing is wanting but the mind.

*Mandolin strings plucked.*

VOICE 3: (*Resolute.*) A gentleman in London showed Mr. Ralph Waldo Emerson a watch that had once belonged to Milton, whose initials were engraved on its face. (*Pause.*) He had once shown this watch to Mr. Wordsworth, who—with the complacency which never deserts the true-born Englishman—took it in one hand, then drew out his own watch and held it up before the company. But, no one making the expected remark, he put back his own in silence.

*Mandolin strings plucked.*

EMERSON: (*Downright.*) There were torpid places in his mind.

NARRATOR: Charles Lamb was promised £30 for the *Essays of Elia* in volume form, but never received payment. He said he was his publisher's ruin. He was a kind-hearted man. Coleridge deferred to his critical taste. When he accompanied his sister on vacation he brought a straitjacket. The sea bothered him. The most social of men was to become unsocial. His friends had a habit of leaving him or dying. That troubled him. He was a kind-hearted man.

*Mandolin plucked.*

CRABB ROBINSON: June 19th, 1834. I had this morning at breakfast Charles and Mary Lamb, who came expressly to be seen by Willis the Yankee. I had had Willis before, and had seen him at Lady Blessington's . . . (*Rapid fade.*)

*Mandolin plucked.*

WILLIS THE YANKEE: (*Brashly.*) There was a rap at the door at last, and entered a gentleman in black small-clothes and gaiters, short and very slight in his person, his head set on his shoulders with a thoughtful, forward bent, his hair just sprinkled with grey, a beautiful deep-set eye and a very indescribable mouth. Whether it expressed most humour or feeling, good nature or a kind of whimsical peevishness, or twenty other things which passed over it by turns, I cannot in the least be certain. (*Pause.*) His sister is a small bent figure, evidently a victim to ill health, who hears with difficulty. Lamb was continually taking advantage of her deafness to mystify her. "Poor Mary," he said, "she hears all of an epigram but the point."

*Brief silence.*

MARY LAMB: (*Aged seventy, very frail ghost-voice.*) What are you saying of me, Charles?

WILLIS THE YANKEE: Lamb ate nothing and complained in a querulous tone of the veal pie. There was a kind of potted fish which he had expected our friend would procure for him. He inquired whether there was not a morsel left perhaps in the bottom of the last pot. Mr. Robinson was not sure ... (*Pause.*) Lamb left the table then and began to wander round the room with a broken, uncertain step, as if he almost forgot to put one leg before the other. His sister rose after a while, and commenced walking up and down much in the same manner on the opposite side of the table. (*Pause.*) And in the course of half an hour they took their leave.

VOICE: Willis, with letters of introduction from Walter Savage Landor, was passing himself off as an attaché to the American Legation. This he was not; but was serving up his London acquaintances in letters to the American press. In particular he wished to meet the Lambs.

NARRATOR: Towards the end of Lamb's own life, his unfortunate sister's bouts of insanity had increased from an annual six weeks to an annual twenty weeks; these fearful recurring bouts were to drain her brother of energy and life.

In July 1834 came a great sorrow for Charles Lamb: Coleridge died. Lamb began his own death, surviving his friend by only five months. Mary Lamb once again took refuge in insanity.

A couple of years previous to this, Lamb had met Carlyle. But Lamb did not like Scotsmen, and there was something about a plate of porridge placed before the Scots philosopher and, emanating from Lamb, jokes and remarks upon it insulting enough to lead to an open quarrel. Lamb was fifty-seven, and Carlyle within a month of his twenty-sixth birthday.

THOMAS CARLYLE: (*Sourly.*) Charles Lamb I sincerely believe to be in some considerable degree insane. (*Significant pause.*) A more pitiful, rickety, gasping, staggering, stammering tomfool I do not know. Besides, he is now a confirmed, shameless drunkard. Poor Lamb! Poor England!

*Water dripping.*

VOICE: (*Welsh, highly sceptical.*) Thomas Carlyle thinks that the only religious act which a man nowadays can securely perform is to wash himself well.

(*High.*) Edwin Chadwick proposes to supply every house in London with pure water, sixty gallons to every head, at a penny a week!

*Antiquated toilet flushing.*

NARRATOR: Years later, Turgenev met Carlyle in London.

*Doorbell.*

TURGENEV: (*Heavy.*) I spent an evening at Thomas Carlyle's house. He questioned me a great deal about the state of affairs in Russia. (*Pause.*) Carlyle is a man of great intelligence and originality, but he is getting old, and in the process has become impaled on paradox: the evils of freedom which he sees at close range appear intolerable to him, and he is now preaching obedience, obedience at all costs. (*Pause.*) He's very fond of the Russians because, according to him, they seem to possess the talent of obeying to a supreme degree. And he was not at all pleased to hear me say that this talent is not as complete as he imagines . . .

OLD MAN: (*Clare Islander.*) Did you know, a woman's brain has the same weight as a dog's—mebbe a sheepdog's. (*Wind, rain.*) And did you know whose the heaviest brain was, since brains were weighed?

*Pause, wind and sea.*

. . . (*triumphant*) Turg-a-niffs!

NARRATOR: Charles Lamb died after a short illness on December 27th, 1834. His sister lived on to be eighty-two, a kleptomaniac addicted to snuff.

*Purcell.*

In truth nothing matters. This dirty little world full of confusion, and the blue rag stretched overhead for a sky, so low that we could touch it with our hand.

VOICE: Wordsworth, old and cantankerous, disfigured by green goggles, his health good but broken by a fall, out walking with two lawyers, encountered Mr. Emerson.

(*Pause.*) And proceeded to abuse Goethe's *Wilhelm Meister*—though in fact he had never got beyond the first part.

OLD WORDSWORTH: (*Hoarse, choking voice.*) Full of all manner of fornication . . . like the crossing of flies in the air!

EMERSON: (*Sotto voce.*) A narrow and very English mind. A good Englishman shuts himself up in three-fourths of his mind, and confines himself to one-fourth.

NARRATOR: He died in 1850, twenty years after Hazlitt, fifteen after Cobbett had departed this world. Wordsworth survived Mary Lamb by a few years. Thomas De Quincey died in 1859, aged seventy-five. As was to be expected, Henry Crabb Robinson, the soundest man that ever stepped through the trammels of the Law, outlived them all—dying in 1867.

*Storm at sea, distant.*

EMERSON: (*Apocalyptic.*) The sea is masculine! The type of active strength. (*Sea and wind.*) Look, what eggshells are drifting all over it. Each, like ours, filled with men in ecstasies of terror (*sea closer*), alternating with Cockney conceit, as the sea is rough or smooth. (*Louder, above storm.*) Is this sad-coloured circle an eternal cemetery? In our graveyards we scoop a pit but this aggressive water (*howling wind*) opens mile-wide pits and chasms!

*Wind and storm.*
*Sudden silence.*
*Leak-in sheep-fold. Shearing. Baaing as before.*

NARRATOR: (*Slight echo; repeating text.*) "All the sheep stood under the trees to be sheared. (*Tumult of baaing.*) They were brought out of the field by Old Spot, the shepherd. I stood at the orchard-gate, and saw him drive them all in. Then they cropped off all their wool . . ." (*Fade.*)

*Wind lazily buffeting thick foliage. Breeze playing in leaves and groaning of wood to end.*

# Clouding Over

An unproduced monologue for radio. From the unpublished first
writings of Aidan Higgins.

Late one night, unable to sleep, I left my bed and began to wander about the draughty interior of the house, shining my bicycle lamp through a number of unwholesomely damp rooms bare of furniture with only the wind booming in them. Off the back stairs in the maids' quarters the boards were lined with lanes of apples, enough to last us the winter. Some of the fruit had rotted—I could tell as I came in. I took a hard one away in my pocket, and so down the back stairs again past the sagging curtain into the hall. I had begun this late rambling as a cure for insomnia, but of course the damp rooms did my rheumatism no good either. The cold is everywhere, it's dreadful. No escaping, it enters into your bones.

I opened a door and ventured into a long bare room. It had only a few odds and ends in it, like so many of the others. The bed remained, bereft of coverings; the laths had rusted off and the wire mesh showed through the ruined mattress. At one time she had lain snug in that same bed, discovered hot love there, too, perhaps with the horsebreeder Cooney. She read Nat Gould to him. With words, only with words would she lie down, the words which tear the tender labyrinth of a soft maid's ear. Well, thought I, you lie deep tonight and no mistake, with no Cooney for company. Nothing could survive that time in damp clay. Once she was, now is no more; as extinct today as the aurochs or Stellar's sea cow.

Dozens of matchboxes were strewn about the floor. I picked one up, pressed it open and fine dust and little white bones fell out onto my dress. Mouse bones. The smell was far from fresh. I lifted a book from the escritoire that had been forgotten, piled high with rubbish and old magazines. Among the *Picture Posts* and *Illustrated London News* I found one of her books with her name and a date on the flyleaf. Miss May Brett, September 5th, 1933. Mayer's *Diorama of Lucerne*. May rarely set foot outside her own county, much less her own country, though full of the most ambitious schemes for travel and self-advancement. She had spoken sometimes, a trifle wistfully, of joining the Countrywomen's Association; but on consideration she said she "could not abide all those gabby women," and had done nothing, unless you could call her dabbling with paints something. I laid the book down and passed into the second room.

It was an annex to the first, a narrow place that she had used as a studio and sewing-room, with a view of the orchard. I could see the apple trees, their knotty upper branches waving above the beech hedge. There was little space to move about. There stood her cane and wicker chairs, the footstools and cabinet with pier glass, the unknown shape draped in purple sash, all laid with dust and cobwebs, deterioration and decay. Lengths of cord hung from the picture rail and these—evidently once a novel form of decoration—draped themselves over the wallpaper bulging out from the mildewed walls. The muslin curtains hung on their last shreds. Many an evening she had sat there on the window seat, whiling away the hours gazing into the orchard, a bulky form in the gloom, lost in meditation; aye, there she sat and none dared approach her.

It was difficult to see the pictures on the walls, for the spiders had constructed their webs around individual frames until the whole resembled wrens' nests, only bigger, untidier. I poked among them until I had cleared one.

It was a press photograph of three aviators posed against the fuselage of a monoplane. They wore leather overcoats and carried goggles in their hands, standing in heroic attitudes. One was rotund, with little fat purposeful legs, and a monocle shining in his eye. The one in the middle was merely fat, and looked like a prosperous businessman or industrialist. The one beside him was lean and had the look of a hero. His leather coat was open so that you could admire his Free State Officer's uniform and highly polished leggings. The wind had made their hair stand up. It was Baron von Hünefeld, Captain Köhl and Major Fitzmaurice with the Junkers monoplane *Bremen* at Baldonnel Airport before their successful flight to America against the wind in April of 1928. They had landed on ice at Greenly Island, Labrador, and on their return to Europe were given the freedom of the cities of Hamburg and Dublin.

From the front bedrooms in the daytime it was possible to watch the Tiger Moths flying through the clouds, dropping down over the bends of the river and going in to land at Baldonnel. Once one of Papa's pilot friends had flown his machine through the telegraph wires suspended from the side of the house. That was Captain Shern.

Papa sometimes took us to see the planes at Baldonnel landing and departing, and it was a great excitement for me when I was young. The road runs lower than the airfield itself and around the perimeter the hedges had been cut low so that the buddleia and elder did not obstruct the view. We stayed in the Rover car behind Papa and looked out over the long field with its cinder path going away towards the hangars.

One day a soldier with a rifle was standing at the gate. He was dressed in a green uniform a shade lighter than the field against which he patrolled. To me he appeared a half-legendary being, scarcely physical, and so grand that I dared not look too hard at him lest I should encounter his eye and be transfixed.

The wind that was always blowing up at that altitude there between the TB Sanatorium and the Aerodrome blew along the runway and made the celluloid windows of our car vibrate; the canvas roof would suddenly tighten upwards, explode, then subside.

She came walking on high heels in the country on a summer evening between the low hedges, arrayed for her soldier lover. They met there by the gate, then began parading back and forth. They did not say much to each other, it wasn't necessary. It was evident they had an understanding, as the country people say. They seemed to be luring each other into something I did not understand, but which disturbed me greatly. Sometimes she sat on the low wall and watched him. He could not take his eyes off her. She would go with him a little then, seeing he could not stir beyond the small area he had to patrol, and each time they passed the gate the wind blew her thin dress tight against her, now before, now behind. She laughed at this, holding her skirt. She seemed sometimes on the point of touching his arm, but never did. As I looked at her standing against the soldier I knew I would never experience a love comparable to this.

When it was time for her to go finally she still could not drag herself away but kept coming back to him. At last she had to leave. I watched her go slowly along the road and on out of sight.

The fact of the matter is, one remembers people and things, as well as the feelings one ascribes to them, in fits and starts, imperfectly, then not at all. I may have seen those lovers as I have attempted to describe them, poised up against each other for the first wild foray into other ardours, seen against the long field where one of the ground crew was struggling to turn the propeller of a stranded plane, while the figure of the pilot sat bolt upright in his cockpit.

I cleared a glassless companion picture. Out of the dust came the faces of the two who were lost. Ill-fated Hinchliffe and the Hon. Elsie Mackay, failed in the England-America attempt of March 13, 1928. Lost in the cold Atlantic with Nungesser and Coli, with Minchin, Hamilton, and the Princess Lowenstein-Wertheim.

I pulled out a drawer onto the floor. In it I found a bulky folder of artwork barely held by a black ribbon. I opened this and began turning over a profusion of drawings, oil paintings and watercolours realised with painstaking fidelity to detail by May's nothing-if-not-methodical hand. I had before me a view of the house executed in oils, to all appearances sinking into the earth, backed by a livid sky into which the obelisk was rising. I shone my light over it. No. It wouldn't do. It would never do. They were all the same, tired simulacrums of nature, revealing nothing so much as their creator's boredom and indolence of spirit. Whereas if landscapes are terrible at all it is because they have no future, they exist only as the landscape, and not just any old hill; because they have history, because they remind us and yet have not gone with us, have separated themselves from us, have become different, no longer the old pal. I laid it down among the others. Letting myself out onto the landing again I made my way towards the main wing. The wind was surging through the almost empty house, booming away in the rooms where only a few sticks of furniture remained, the upended apple boxes doing service as bedside tables, the big brass bends headed into the walls.

My mother's room was lofty and damp, echoing like a church. I walked on shining linoleum, my shadow followed along the broken stucco mouldings. There in an alcove her light was burning.

On the makeshift table by her head lay the rinds and peels of oranges. Beyond the bed and the sweetish odour of oranges the lower panes of the window were blocked with brown paper and on the ledge below stood a small replica of the Infant of Prague with upraised arm. I stood close by her head and satisfied myself that she was sleeping. In these pauper surroundings her senses were leaving her one by one, her thoughts swept away like clouds. In her heyday she had been a beauty. Whenever she spoke of her former conquests the story of the riding-master from Oslo who had fallen for her charms was invariably remembered. He had made a regular show of himself, staring at

her in the most shameless way (this was in a public park) from behind naked statuary of a ferocious lewdness. "He made a dead set at
me," she confessed, "and I didn't know a word of the language."

"Oh if only your poor father knew half of the temptations I was
exposed to!"

The night-light would last until morning. There was a gateau cake
on the upper shelf of the bedside table. She had been helping herself.
She had a sweet tooth in her head, and would demand iced cakes, or
barley sugar from the chemist's.

Then she opened her eyes and looked up at me.

– Are you comfortable, Mother? I said. Can I get you anything?

She did not answer me. She said:

– Has that cross little article been back?

– Who, Mother? I said

– The horrid old one who used to come here with the hat.

It was me she meant. I was the horrible old one in the hat. My
lovely straw.

– Never, Mother! I cried.

– I don't want her back here, she said in a fretful way. She nags at
me. Keep her out.

– She won't be back, I said, don't worry.

– She thinks she's a beauty, my old mother said, but she's not half
as good-looking as I was.

– I know, Mother, I said.

She said:

– Lock the front door. Don't let her put her foot in.

– Very well I said. Very well.

She closed her eyes, then, satisfied, pretended to sleep.


In a little while I went to the door and looked back. The light shone
bravely in the alcove. I knew she was watching me through the chink,
feigning sleep, waiting for me to go so that she could get at the cake

again. Then I heard her fetch up a couple of heavy sighs, shift about in bed, and then fall silent again. I took the doorknob in my hand and let myself out onto the freezing stairs. As I went down, the weak and divided beam of the lamp with its weaker penumbra wobbled ahead.

I descended into the kitchen along the flagged corridor below the line of dusty bells that were connected with every room in the house. Nobody was there to ring them, nobody down there to answer them. I made myself a cup of hot cocoa on the Primus stove, climbed up to my room again with it, sank into bed again and drank the hot cocoa in the dark, warming my hands on the sides of the mug. Across the landing the cistern was roaring. It would roar all night; I had grown accustomed to it, hardly noticed it. When I had finished the drink I laid it aside and began to prepare myself for sleep. This is how I went about it: I laid my hands transversely across my chest, one crossed upon the other, the fingers in the salt cellars, the limbs straight down, the sole of one foot resting on the arch of its fellow, the eyes closed. Methodically, I began to forget my extremities, beginning with the uppermost foot as high as the knee. When nothing but the head remained I emptied it of thought and forgot it. Then I begin to fall asleep, deprived of limbs and memory. Good. The extremities and then the trunk and lastly the head. In this way I came to resemble the peaceful figure in the Kildare graveyard, the life-sized effigy in limestone four hundred years old, laid out on the open altar tomb on coarse grass and subjected to all the hazards of the climate. A big section of the left thigh was missing, the two feet were reduced to stumps that commence above the knee and the hands to remnants that begin and end six inches short of the shoulder blades. Most of the face is ground away. The poor trunk seems to be trying to recall with its neck the absent parts of itself that its nonexistent eyes can no longer see. At one time the feet, dreadfully pointed in chain mail, had rested on a dog (denoting fidelity) but of this animal only the end curl of the tail remained. The slab—the bed the effigy was laid upon—had split across in three places. The total effect was touching in the extreme. I made it my business to find out who it was, for in many ways it was myself in the toils of my insomnia.

Sleep, too, was dreadful in its way, for the limbs that sleep no longer belong to the sleeper, no bed can hold them, they are broken off, scattered, gone—like the human bones that time and earth expel out of the coffin and out of the grave.

So I forgot everything. In a short time I had arrived at the head. I emptied it of thought and tried to forget it. But it refused to be emptied. I could not forget it. The limbs that I had already laboriously forgotten came back to life, asserting themselves with their old claims on me. It was useless to go on; I was as wide-awake as when I had started. Only a couple of hours had passed since I had first risen up. A couple of hours of time, an eternity of something else. Birds were passing over the house at a great height in the dark, uttering their unearthly cries. Curlew and plover—they cried for rain.

Behind the Venetian blinds the sky is turning grey. In less than an hour it will be light. Quite soon. Frosty stars are shining over the grazing grounds, and the bundles of hay thrown out for the cattle lie steaming in the cold air; the ditches are full of slob-ice and the birds miserable and starving. Whips of snow lie on the Dublin hills. All is paling now. Soon the outline of the window will appear. How many times had I seen it come, an image out of this land and this house that will not let me go? Ditches and dykes; wet fields; low, common places; skies; a perimeter of flattened hills: the greasy road leads into the village. Here was I born; here I grew up.

The furnace-room is cold and deserted and all the radiators frozen. In the old days Feeney got it going in the morning before seven, feeding slag and coke into it in the dry heat, so that the fire was never permitted to go out and warmed all the rooms. But Feeney went long ago. I cannot stoke it on my own. I am resigned to the cold here. I let it be.

I must have dozed a little . . . I am going. I feel myself loosening. A ground mist has begun to disperse itself along the front field and into the road. They are driving through it on their way to early Mass, for I hear the sound of the tub traps passing and then the bicycle bells. It must be Sunday again. The poor are travelling in from the Council houses. I feel myself drifting away. Away from all this, away from me. One last grief. I am going now. Nervousness and tiredness, Saturday or Sunday.

# SELECTED DALKEY ARCHIVE PAPERBACKS

PETROS ABATZOGLOU, *What Does Mrs. Freeman Want?*
MICHAL AJVAZ, *The Other City.*
PIERRE ALBERT-BIROT, *Grabinoulor.*
YUZ ALESHKOVSKY, *Kangaroo.*
FELIPE ALFAU, *Chromos.*
  *Locos.*
IVAN ÂNGELO, *The Celebration.*
  *The Tower of Glass.*
DAVID ANTIN, *Talking.*
ANTÓNIO LOBO ANTUNES, *Knowledge of Hell.*
ALAIN ARIAS-MISSON, *Theatre of Incest.*
JOHN ASHBERY AND JAMES SCHUYLER, *A Nest of Ninnies.*
HEIMRAD BÄCKER, *transcript.*
DJUNA BARNES, *Ladies Almanack.*
  *Ryder.*
JOHN BARTH, *LETTERS.*
  *Sabbatical.*
DONALD BARTHELME, *The King.*
  *Paradise.*
SVETISLAV BASARA, *Chinese Letter.*
MARK BINELLI, *Sacco and Vanzetti Must Die!*
ANDREI BITOV, *Pushkin House.*
LOUIS PAUL BOON, *Chapel Road.*
  *My Little War.*
  *Summer in Termuren.*
ROGER BOYLAN, *Killoyle.*
IGNÁCIO DE LOYOLA BRANDÃO, *Anonymous Celebrity.*
  *Teeth under the Sun.*
  *Zero.*
BONNIE BREMSER, *Troia: Mexican Memoirs.*
CHRISTINE BROOKE-ROSE, *Amalgamemnon.*
BRIGID BROPHY, *In Transit.*
MEREDITH BROSNAN, *Mr. Dynamite.*
GERALD L. BRUNS, *Modern Poetry and
  the Idea of Language.*
EVGENY BUNIMOVICH AND J. KATES, EDS.,
  *Contemporary Russian Poetry: An Anthology.*
GABRIELLE BURTON, *Heartbreak Hotel.*
MICHEL BUTOR, *Degrees.*
  *Mobile.*
  *Portrait of the Artist as a Young Ape.*
G. CABRERA INFANTE, *Infante's Inferno.*
  *Three Trapped Tigers.*
JULIETA CAMPOS, *The Fear of Losing Eurydice.*
ANNE CARSON, *Eros the Bittersweet.*
CAMILO JOSÉ CELA, *Christ versus Arizona.*
  *The Family of Pascual Duarte.*
  *The Hive.*
LOUIS-FERDINAND CÉLINE, *Castle to Castle.*
  *Conversations with Professor Y.*
  *London Bridge.*
  *Normance.*
  *North.*
  *Rigadoon.*
HUGO CHARTERIS, *The Tide Is Right.*
JEROME CHARYN, *The Tar Baby.*
MARC CHOLODENKO, *Mordechai Schamz.*
EMILY HOLMES COLEMAN, *The Shutter of Snow.*
ROBERT COOVER, *A Night at the Movies.*
STANLEY CRAWFORD, *Log of the S.S. The Mrs Unguentine.*
  *Some Instructions to My Wife.*
ROBERT CREELEY, *Collected Prose.*
RENÉ CREVEL, *Putting My Foot in It.*
RALPH CUSACK, *Cadenza.*
SUSAN DAITCH, *L.C.*
  *Storytown.*
NICHOLAS DELBANCO, *The Count of Concord.*
NIGEL DENNIS, *Cards of Identity.*
PETER DIMOCK, *A Short Rhetoric for Leaving the Family.*
ARIEL DORFMAN, *Konfidenz.*
COLEMAN DOWELL, *The Houses of Children.*
  *Island People.*
  *Too Much Flesh and Jabez.*
ARKADII DRAGOMOSHCHENKO, *Dust.*
RIKKI DUCORNET, *The Complete Butcher's Tales.*
  *The Fountains of Neptune.*
  *The Jade Cabinet.*
  *The One Marvelous Thing.*
  *Phosphor in Dreamland.*
  *The Stain.*
  *The Word "Desire."*
WILLIAM EASTLAKE, *The Bamboo Bed.*
  *Castle Keep.*
  *Lyric of the Circle Heart.*
JEAN ECHENOZ, *Chopin's Move.*
STANLEY ELKIN, *A Bad Man.*
  *Boswell: A Modern Comedy.*
  *Criers and Kibitzers, Kibitzers and Criers.*
  *The Dick Gibson Show.*
  *The Franchiser.*
  *George Mills.*
  *The Living End.*
  *The MacGuffin.*
  *The Magic Kingdom.*
  *Mrs. Ted Bliss.*
  *The Rabbi of Lud.*
  *Van Gogh's Room at Arles.*
ANNIE ERNAUX, *Cleaned Out.*
LAUREN FAIRBANKS, *Muzzle Thyself.*
  *Sister Carrie.*
JUAN FILLOY, *Op Oloop.*
LESLIE A. FIEDLER, *Love and Death in the American Novel.*

GUSTAVE FLAUBERT, *Bouvard and Pécuchet.*
KASS FLEISHER, *Talking out of School.*
FORD MADOX FORD, *The March of Literature.*
JON FOSSE, *Melancholy.*
MAX FRISCH, *I'm Not Stiller.*
  *Man in the Holocene.*
CARLOS FUENTES, *Christopher Unborn.*
  *Distant Relations.*
  *Terra Nostra.*
  *Where the Air Is Clear.*
JANICE GALLOWAY, *Foreign Parts.*
  *The Trick Is to Keep Breathing.*
WILLIAM H. GASS, *Cartesian Sonata and Other Novellas.*
  *Finding a Form.*
  *A Temple of Texts.*
  *The Tunnel.*
  *Willie Masters' Lonesome Wife.*
GÉRARD GAVARRY, *Hoplla! 1 2 3.*
ETIENNE GILSON, *The Arts of the Beautiful.*
  *Forms and Substances in the Arts.*
C. S. GISCOMBE, *Giscome Road.*
  *Here.*
  *Prairie Style.*
DOUGLAS GLOVER, *Bad News of the Heart.*
  *The Enamoured Knight.*
WITOLD GOMBROWICZ, *A Kind of Testament.*
KAREN ELIZABETH GORDON, *The Red Shoes.*
GEORGI GOSPODINOV, *Natural Novel.*
JUAN GOYTISOLO, *Count Julian.*
  *Juan the Landless.*
  *Makbara.*
  *Marks of Identity.*
PATRICK GRAINVILLE, *The Cave of Heaven.*
HENRY GREEN, *Back.*
  *Blindness.*
  *Concluding.*
  *Doting.*
  *Nothing.*
JIŘÍ GRUŠA, *The Questionnaire.*
GABRIEL GUDDING, *Rhode Island Notebook.*
JOHN HAWKES, *Whistlejacket.*
ALEKSANDAR HEMON, ED., *Best European Fiction 2010.*
AIDAN HIGGINS, *A Bestiary.*
  *Balcony of Europe.*
  *Bornholm Night-Ferry.*
  *Darkling Plain: Texts for the Air.*
  *Flotsam and Jetsam.*
  *Langrishe, Go Down.*
  *Scenes from a Receding Past.*
  *Windy Arbours.*
ALDOUS HUXLEY, *Antic Hay.*
  *Crome Yellow.*
  *Point Counter Point.*
  *Those Barren Leaves.*
  *Time Must Have a Stop.*
MIKHAIL IOSSEL AND JEFF PARKER, EDS., *Amerika:
  Russian Writers View the United States.*
GERT JONKE, *Geometric Regional Novel.*
  *Homage to Czerny.*
  *The System of Vienna.*
JACQUES JOUET, *Mountain R.*
  *Savage.*
CHARLES JULIET, *Conversations with Samuel Beckett and
  Bram van Velde.*
MIEKO KANAI, *The Word Book.*
HUGH KENNER, *The Counterfeiters.*
  *Flaubert, Joyce and Beckett: The Stoic Comedians.*
  *Joyce's Voices.*
DANILO KIŠ, *Garden, Ashes.*
  *A Tomb for Boris Davidovich.*
ANITA KONKKA, *A Fool's Paradise.*
GEORGE KONRÁD, *The City Builder.*
TADEUSZ KONWICKI, *A Minor Apocalypse.*
  *The Polish Complex.*
MENIS KOUMANDAREAS, *Koula.*
ELAINE KRAF, *The Princess of 72nd Street.*
JIM KRUSOE, *Iceland.*
EWA KURYLUK, *Century 21.*
ERIC LAURRENT, *Do Not Touch.*
VIOLETTE LEDUC, *La Bâtarde.*
SUZANNE JILL LEVINE, *The Subversive Scribe:
  Translating Latin American Fiction.*
DEBORAH LEVY, *Billy and Girl.*
  *Pillow Talk in Europe and Other Places.*
JOSÉ LEZAMA LIMA, *Paradiso.*
ROSA LIKSOM, *Dark Paradise.*
OSMAN LINS, *Avalovara.*
  *The Queen of the Prisons of Greece.*
ALF MAC LOCHLAINN, *The Corpus in the Library.*
  *Out of Focus.*
RON LOEWINSOHN, *Magnetic Field(s).*
BRIAN LYNCH, *The Winner of Sorrow.*
D. KEITH MANO, *Take Five.*
MICHELINE AHARONIAN MARCOM, *The Mirror in the Well.*
BEN MARCUS, *The Age of Wire and String.*
WALLACE MARKFIELD, *Teitlebaum's Window.*
  *To an Early Grave.*
DAVID MARKSON, *Reader's Block.*
  *Springer's Progress.*
  *Wittgenstein's Mistress.*
CAROLE MASO, *AVA.*

## FOR A FULL LIST OF PUBLICATIONS, VISIT:
### www.dalkeyarchive.com

# SELECTED DALKEY ARCHIVE PAPERBACKS

**FOR A FULL LIST OF PUBLICATIONS, VISIT:**
www.dalkeyarchive.com